Activi

Activists Forever? explores the consequences of political involvemeni ...
an individual's life. While much of the research in this area has focused
on the motivations of entire protests groups, the editors of this volume
propose an approach that focuses on actors. This book examines political involvement's socio-biographical effects, or the ways in which
political commitment generates or modifies dispositions to act, think,
and perceive, in a way that is either consistent with or in contrast to the
results of previous socialization. The contents explore what political
involvement leads to rather than what causes involvement. Using a
variety of case studies, this collection of essays provides global coverage
with a focus on participation in major protests in the 1960s and
significantly broadens our understanding by looking outside the United
States. These essays look at the lasting effects of activists' knowledge,
connections, and symbolic capital on their future participation in politics, as well as their personal and professional lives.

OLIVIER FILLIEULE is a professor of political sociology at the Institute for Political, Historical and International Studies (IEPHI), research
director at the CNRS (Paris 1-Sorbonne), and a member of CRAPUL
(Research Center on Political Action, University of Lausanne). He has
extensively published on social movements and political commitments.
Among those are: *Demonstrations* (with D. Tartakowsky) and *Social
Movement Studies in Europe: A State of the Art* (with G. Accornero).

ERIK NEVEU is Professor of Political Science at Rennes University. He
co-authored *Introduction aux Cultural Studies* (with A. Mattelart,
2004), the first French textbook supplying a comprehensive presentation of Anglophone cultural studies; and *Bourdieu and the Journalistic
Field* (with R. Benson, 2004).

Activists Forever?

Long-Term Impacts of Political Activism

Edited by

OLIVIER FILLIEULE
University of Lausanne
Paris 1-Sorbonne

ERIK NEVEU
University of Rennes

CAMBRIDGE
UNIVERSITY PRESS

CAMBRIDGE
UNIVERSITY PRESS

University Printing House, Cambridge CB2 8BS, United Kingdom

One Liberty Plaza, 20th Floor, New York, NY 10006, USA

477 Williamstown Road, Port Melbourne, VIC 3207, Australia

314-321, 3rd Floor, Plot 3, Splendor Forum, Jasola District Centre, New Delhi - 110025, India

103 Penang Road, #05-06/07, Visioncrest Commercial, Singapore 238467

Cambridge University Press is part of the University of Cambridge.

It furthers the University's mission by disseminating knowledge in the pursuit of
education, learning and research at the highest international levels of excellence.

www.cambridge.org
Information on this title: www.cambridge.org/9781108450942
DOI: 10.1017/9781108690928

© Cambridge University Press 2019

First published 2019
First paperback edition 2022

A catalogue record for this publication is available from the British Library

Library of Congress Cataloging in Publication data
NAMES: Fillieule, Olivier, editor. | Neveu, Erik, 1952– editor.
TITLE: Activists forever? : long-term impacts of political activism /
edited by Erik Neveu, Olivier Fillieule.
DESCRIPTION: Cambridge, United Kingdom ; New York, NY : Cambridge University
Press, 2019. | Includes bibliographical references and index.
IDENTIFIERS: LCCN 2018030096 | ISBN 9781108428729 (hardback : alk. paper) |
ISBN 9781108450942 (pbk. : alk. paper)
SUBJECTS: LCSH: Protest movements–Case studies. | Political activists–Case studies. |
Political sociology–Case studies.
CLASSIFICATION: LCC HM883 .A28 2019 | DDC 303.48/4–dc23
LC record available at https://lccn.loc.gov/2018030096

ISBN 978-1-108-42872-9 Hardback
ISBN 978-1-108-45094-2 Paperback

D'Erik à Mia-Miou, d'Olivier au grand Babu,
Si Alberoni a raison de décrire l'amour
comme "un mouvement social à deux"
peut-être sommes nous des "Activists Forever !"

Contents

List of Tables   *page* ix

List of Figures   xi

List of Contributors   xiii

Acknowledgments   xix

Activists' Trajectories in Space and Time: An Introduction   1
Olivier Fillieule and Erik Neveu

I FROM SHADES OF RED (OR BLUE) TO SHADES OF GREY:
THE AGEING OF YESTERDAY'S ACTIVISTS

Introduction   37
Richard Flacks

1 The Diversity of Activist Outcomes: The Role of Ideology
in Shaping Trajectories of Participation   42
Catherine Corrigall-Brown

2 Biographical Impacts of Activism in the French "May '68"   62
Julie Pagis

3 Life Stories of Former French Activists of "68":
Using Biographies to Investigate the Outcomes of
Social Movements   84
Erik Neveu

4 Women in Political Activism: The Biographical Resonances
of the '68 Student Movement in a Latin American Context   108
Guadalupe Olivier and Sergio Tamayo

II   TERRORIST VIOLENCE, STATE REPRESSION, AND
ACTIVISTS' EXPERIENCES

Introduction   131
Jocelyn Viterna

5 Biographical Effects of Engagement: The "Activist
Generation" of the 1970s and Its Children in Morocco   135
Joseph Hivert and Frédéric Vairel

6 From Militancy to Activism? Life Trajectories of Sikh
Women Combatants   159
Laurent Gayer

7 "Married Forever," Activists Forever? What the Multi-Level
and Interactionist Approaches to the Study of "Exit" Reveal
about Disengagement from Radical Organizations in
Contemporary Turkey   181
Jordi Tejel

8 Contextualizing the Biographical Outcomes of Provisional
IRA Former Activists: A Structure-Agency Dynamic   202
Lorenzo Bosi

III   BIOGRAPHICAL TRAJECTORIES IN TIMES
OF TRANSITION: SOCIAL MOVEMENT ACTIVISTS
INTO POLITICIANS?

Introduction   221
Gilles Dorronsoro

9 When Prophecy Succeeds: The Political Failure of Dissidents
in the New Czech Democracy   224
Magdaléna Hadjiisky

10 From Grassroots Activism to the Cabinet. Round-Trip:
The Puzzling Political Career of a Peasant Leader in
Post-Communist Poland   251
Cédric Pellen

11 Red T-Shirt or Executive Suit: About Some Biographical
Consequences of Contentious Engagement in the Workers'
Party in Recife, Brazil   272
Camille Goirand

Addendum: Life History as a Tool for Sociological Inquiry   294
Olivier Fillieule

References   303
Index   331

Tables

1.1 Number of periods of engagement in groups and
protest over the life-course   *page* 48
1.2 The continuity of engagement in four groups   51
Appendix A Comparison of Total Sample and Participants in
Contentious Political Action   56
Appendix B Interview Sample Information   57
Appendix C Interview Sample Characteristics by Group   60

Figures

2.1 Exposure to the event and pursuit of activist activities *page* 66
2.2 Percentage of informants continuing activist activities
     after '68   67
2.3 Political impacts of activism in May '68   69
2.4 Importing activist dispositions into the occupational sphere   78

Contributors

Lorenzo Bosi is Assistant Professor at the Scuola Normale Superiore, Firenze. He is a political sociologist pursuing comparative analysis into the cross-disciplinary fields of social movements and political violence. He has directed and collaborated on a number of national and international research projects on topics relating to social movements, political violence, and political participation. Among his recent publications are *The Troubles: Northern Ireland and Theories of Social Movements*, coedited with G. DeFazio (2017) and *The Consequences of Social Movements: Policies, People and Institutions*, coedited with M. Giugni and K. Uba (2016).

Catherine Corrigall-Brown is an associate professor of sociology at the University of British Columbia in Vancouver, Canada. Her work focuses on social movement participation, particularly examining why some people sustain their engagement over time while others drop out or move in and out of activism over the life-course. Her research on this and related topics has appeared in journals such as *Social Forces*, *Mobilization*, and the *International Journal of Comparative Sociology* and in her book, *Patterns of Protest*.

Gilles Dorronsoro is a professor at Paris 1 Sorbonne University. He has developed an ethnographic approach to spaces of conflict and civil wars from Afghanistan to Turkish Kurd regions and now Syria. Investigating such a variety of conflict situations has allowed him to revisit and enrich major research questions (the role of social capital, conversion of capitals, territorialization of politics) and to formulate general and comparative hypotheses regarding civil wars. Among his publications are *Revolution Unending. Afghanistan, 1979 to the Present* (2005) and (with Olivier Grosjean) *Identity, Conflict and Politics in Turkey, Iran and Pakistan* (2015).

Olivier Fillieule is a professor of political sociology at the Institute for Political Historical and International Studies (IEPHI), a research director at the CNRS (Paris 1-Sorbonne), and a member of CRAPUL (Research Center on Political Action, University of Lausanne). Among his most recent books are *Demonstrations* (2010), *Social Movement Studies in Europe: A State of the Art*, coedited with G. Accornero (2016), *Marseille, années 68*, coedited with I. Sommier (2018), and *Changer le monde, changer sa vie. Enquête sur les militantes et les militants des années 68 en France*, coedited with S. Béroud, C. Masclet, and I. Sommier (2018). A list of his research interests and publications is available at: https://unil.academia.edu/OlivierFillieule.

Richard Flacks was one of the founders of the SDS and is one of its prominent members. He is Emeritus Professor of Sociology at the University of California, Santa Barbara. His contributions to social movement studies question the ageing of the activists of the sixties, the cultural dimensions of social movement (*Cultural Politics and Social Movements*, with M. Darnowsky and B. Epstein [1995]) and *Playing for Change: Music and Musicians in the Service of Social Movements*, with R. Rosenthal (2011).

Laurent Gayer is Senior Research Fellow at the Center for International Studies and Research (CERI) at Sciences Po, Paris. He specializes in the study of violent mobilizations and urban life in South Asia. He is the author of *Karachi: Ordered Disorder and the Struggle for the City* (2014) and has coedited (with Christophe Jaffrelot) *Muslims of Indian Cities: Trajectories of Marginalization* (2012) and *Armed Militias of South Asia: Fundamentalists, Maoists and Separatists* (2009).

Camille Goirand is a professor of political science at the Institute for Latin American Studies (Sorbonne University) and is a member of the Center for Research and Documentation on the Americas (CREDA). Her research work focuses on the political behavior of popular classes in Brazil, on associative and party engagement, as well as on the reshapings of mobilizations in Brazil since the street demonstrations of 2013 and 2015.

Magdaléna Hadjiisky is Senior Lecturer in Political Science at the Institut d'Etudes Politiques – Université de Strasbourg, Laboratoire SAGE

(Sociétés, Acteurs, Gouvernement en Europe), UMR CNRS 6373. Hadjiisky has published numerous articles and book chapters in French, English, and Czech on Central European politics and on the reform of the post-communist states, and has coedited a special issue of the review *Politix* on "businessmen in politics." More recently, her research has focused on the role of International Organizations in processes of policy transfer in the European space. She has coedited, with Leslie A. Pal and Christopher Walker, *Public Policy Transfer: Micro-Dynamics and Macro-Effects* (2017).

Joseph Hivert is a doctoral student at the Institute of Political, Historical and International Studies (IEPHI) of the University of Lausanne and a lecturer at the University of Mulhouse. He is preparing a thesis on the intergenerational transmission of activism within militant Moroccan families. He has published "Se désengager du mouvement du '20 février': le cas des étudiants du supérieur de la coordination de Rabat," *European Journal of Turkish Studies* (2013) and "Numériquement marginaux mais politiquement importants? La médiatisation internationale d'une association des Droits de l'homme au Maroc," *Journal des anthropologues* (2015 with Dominique Marchetti).

Erik Neveu is Professor of Political Science in the ARENES-CNRS Team in Rennes. His research are focused on journalism and the public sphere, public problems, and social movements. One of its aims is contributing to the international circulation of concepts, theories, and case studies (*Bourdieu and the Journalistic Field*, with R. Benson, 2004). His textbook "Sociologie des mouvements sociaux" has been translated into Greek, Italian, Korean, Russian, and Spanish. He recently coedited a collection of remembrances and narratives of May 68 by those who lived it (*Mai 68 par ceux et celles qui l'ont vécu*, with C. Rajnaraman and B. Gobille, 2018).

Guadalupe Olivier is a professor-researcher in the National Pedagogical University at Mexico City. She is a member of the research area in "Educational Policy, Institutional Processes and Management," and the Academic Group in "Sociology of Politics, Reform and Educational Change." Her main lines of research are Social Movements and Education, and Educational Privatization. She has several publications; among the most recent are "La démobilisation étudiante au Mexique: le double visage de la repression," in *European Journal of Turkish Studies* and "Challenge of Private Higher Education in Latin America: Between

Expansion and Resistance," in *IdeAs*, Idées dAmériques, France, Institut des Amériques, and the book *Faces of Higher Education. Public and Private Confluences.*

Julie Pagis is a researcher in political sociology at the French National Center for Scientific Research (CNRS) and a member of the Institute for Interdisciplinary Research on Social Issues (IRIS, EHESS). Her research on the biographical consequences of activism has recently been translated into English: *May '68, Shaping Political Generations* (2018). She devotes another part of her research to children perceptions of the social and political order, and recently published, with W. Lignier, *L'enfance de l'ordre. Comment les enfants perçoivent le monde social* (2017).

Cédric Pellen is Assistant Professor in Political Science at the University of Strasbourg and a fellow of the CNRS laboratory SAGE. He received his Ph.D. from Sciences Po Bordeaux (2010) and worked as a postdoctoral researcher at the Université de Montreal (2011–2012) and at the Université libre de Bruxelles (2012–2015). His research explores activism and political professionalization, with specific focus on post-communist Europe and diaspora politics. His work has appeared in numerous journals, including *Revue Française de Science Politique*, *Politix*, and *Critique Internationale*. He is also the coeditor, with Jérôme Heurtaux, of "1989 à l'Est de l'Europe: une mémoire controversée" (2009).

Sergio Tamayo is Head of the Research Area on Theory and Analysis of Politics, Department of Sociology, Autonomous Metropolitan University at Mexico City. He is General Manager of the Mexican Network of Studies on Social Movements and a member of the National System of Researchers. He works on collective identities and social movements; political culture citizenship and political appropriation of public space; and qualitative methodologies. He has recently published *Spaces and Repertoires of the Protest* (2016); *Silhouettes and Outlines of a Suffrage in Mexico 2012* (2015), published in Spanish with Kathrin Wildner and Nicolasa López-Saavedra; and "Think and Watch the Protest" (2015), published in Spanish with Hélène Combes and Michael Voegtli.

Jordi Tejel is a research professor in the History Department at the University of Neuchâtel (Switzerland). Between 2010 and 2016, Dr. Tejel led a research project on student mobilization in the Middle East from which his chapter is a direct result. Currently, he leads a research program funded by the European Research Council on Transborder Spaces, Circulations, and Frontier Effects in the Middle East. His most recent books include *Syria's Kurds: History, Politics and Society* (2009), *Writing the Modern History of Iraq: Historiographical and Political Challenges* (coedited with Sluglett, Bocco, and Bozarslan, 2012), and *La Question kurde: Passé et présent* (2014).

Frédéric Vairel is an associate professor of political science at the School of Political Studies, University of Ottawa. He has published *Politique et mouvements sociaux au Maroc. La révolution désamorcée?* (2014). He has also edited *Soulèvements et recompositions politiques dans le monde arabe* (with Michel Camau, 2014) and *Social Movements, Mobilization and Contestation in the Middle East* (with Joel Beinin, 2013), 2nd edition.

Jocelyn Viterna is Professor of Sociology and Director of Undergraduate Studies at Harvard University. She investigates how social mobilization shapes gender norms and gender practices in states, in warfare, in institutions, and in communities. She also evaluates how poor communities pursue their own development by recruiting "projects" from humanitarian organizations. Viterna is primarily a qualitative researcher who triangulates data from multiple sources – typically, in-depth interviews, ethnographic observations, and content analyses of legal and political documents – to answer theory-relevant sociological questions. Her current research investigates the recent reversal of abortion rights in Latin America. She is the author of *Women in War: The Micro-Processes of Mobilization in El Salvador* (2013).

Acknowledgments

The initial idea of this book emerged during the "Outcomes of Social Movements" conference organized at the WZB Berlin in June 2011 to celebrate Dieter Rucht. We wish to thank all participants for the inspiring discussions that took place there. The project took shape in synergy with a research project dedicated to the biographical consequences of activism for the French 68ers that started in 2013 under the direction of Olivier Fillieule and in which Erik Neveu initially participated.

Our gratitude goes of course to all the contributors to this book. This collective enterprise received new momentum during the research seminar that was hosted by Sciences Po Rennes in May 2014. These two days of brainstorming were possible thanks to the support of the Scientific Board of Sciences Po Rennes, of the Region of Britanny, and of Rennes Metropole. Special thanks go to Marylène Bercegeay, who, once more, was a first-class organizer. Finally, Agnès Aubry, a doctoral student at Lausanne University, collated the final bibliography and we thank her for that!

Activists' Trajectories in Space and Time

An Introduction

Olivier Fillieule and Erik Neveu

One can say that men go through a process as one says too that the wind is blowing, as if the wind were separate from its blowing, as if a wind could exist which did not blow.

N. Elias *Los Der Menschen*, 1987

No social study that does not come back to the problem of biography, of history and of their intersections within a society has completed its intellectual journey.

C. Wright Mills *The Sociological Imagination*, 1959

In 2011, *Time* magazine chose "The Protester" as its Person of the Year. And there is no doubt that the world is experiencing an unprecedented wave of dissent. In the course of 2012, "The Protester" voiced opposition to authoritarian leaders, first in Tunisia, and then in Egypt, Libya, Syria, Yemen, and Bahrain. "The Protester" in Greece and in Spain (the *Indignados*), but also the Occupy Wall Street protester in the United States, were struggling with a floundering economy. "The Protester" expressed anger over what were believed to be rigged elections in countries as diverse as Russia, Senegal, and the Democratic Republic of Congo. However, apart some notable exceptions to which we will come back later, individual actors are largely absent from social movements research, which has mainly looked at macro processes and social movement organizations in the framework of structural analysis. As Jasper states (1997:214):

Most protestors are compelled by a combination of motivations, compulsions, and desires, some of them conscious and others not. Simple models of human motivation, whether rationalist or crowd-based, miss the lion's share of reality. So do theories that look for the motivations of entire protest movements rather than those of the individuals who compose them. The biographical dimension of protest cries out for exploration.

There are at least five explanations for the failure of the literature to address this. First, activism has been less studied for itself than through the analysis of organizations that frame it. This leads naturally to reasoning in terms of stock rather than flow. Second, microsociological approaches to behavior, except for their economicist version of rational choice theory, have long been discarded in the name of the struggle against the paradigm of collective behavior which was considered – much beyond reasonable suspicions – as giving too much centrality to notions such as "frustration." Third, there is a scarcity of sources that can prove useful in understanding the activist flow. By definition, ex-activists are no longer present at the time of the investigation and, very often, organizations do not retain records of members that would allow researchers to track those no longer active or, if they do, they usually do not make them readily available to researchers. D. McAdam would not have produced his masterpiece without the availability of the long questionnaires filled by the Freedom summer's applicants. Fourth, there is the difficulty of moving from static approaches to a true processual perspective, which, in this particular case, is based on setting up longitudinal studies, whether prospective or retrospective (Fillieule, 2001). Finally, the overdominant structuralist framework of social movement research (Goodwin & Jasper, 1999) is largely responsible for the imbalance between research on recruitment by movements and that studying the effect of the institution on activists. Generally speaking, political behavior or participation in political organizations is usually conceived of as a dependent rather than an independent variable.

Notwithstanding, our book situates itself in the theoretical framework of social movement theory, as improved by the founding research of Tilly and Tarrow, with their strong historical attention to protest cycles and contentious performances. A major source of inspiration comes from McAdam's *Freedom Summer* (1988), a path-breaking case-study that highlights the lasting impact of high risk activism, and its effects on the matrimonial, political, and professional trajectories of ex-activists. It shows how such experiences predispose to remain politically committed, to behave as a social innovator. Two other strong landmarks are Della Porta's (1995) work on violent activism in Germany and Italy in the

1960s-1970s, and the work of the Italian historian Passerini (1996), who studied the Italian activists of the sixties with a qualitative and self-reflexive approach. The latter, with its attention to the role of emotions, affects, and beliefs, also invite us to borrow from research by Jasper (1997) and Polletta (1998a, b). The concepts of "micro-cohort" and "abeyance structure," respectively coined by Whittier (1995) and Taylor (1989), would be other sources of inspiration. The first showing how joining a movement two, four, or six years after its taking off often means experiencing different political socializations, facing different stakes, and living different experiences of the connection between the private and the political. The second allowing theorizing of the dynamics of mobilization, de-mobilization, and re-mobilization of activists networks along time.

More recently, promising perspectives have been opened up for future research by a less structuralist and movement-centric approach to political action: on one hand, the expansion of the analytical focus to actors other than social movement organizations in their relations to the state; and, on the other hand, renewed interest in the microfoundations of collective action. Here, the propositions recently advanced by some scholars, with a new conceptualization of the space of social movements (Fligstein & McAdam, 2012; McAdam & Schaffer-Boudet, 2012) and the effects of individual social engagement from a strategic perspective (Jasper, 2006; Jasper & Duyvendak, 2015), are particularly useful in offering the means to adopt a more sociological approach to protest mobilization, in particular, moving away from a restricted perspective confined to a narrow subdisciplinary field.

The present volume is consistent with this emerging return of sociological analysis in social movement theory in exploring the path-breaking direction of the personal and biographical consequences of protest activity, i.e. "effects on the life course of individuals who have participated in movement activities, effects that are at least in part due to involvement in those activities" (Fillieule, 2013).

We propose an approach of political unrest by focusing on actors. It examines political involvements' sociobiographical effects, that is, ways in which political commitment generates or modifies dispositions to act, think, and perceive, either consistent with or in contrast to the results of previous socialization. It is from the angle of how, in various contexts, trajectories are formed that we propose to broach this question and to determine what involvement leads to rather than, from a more conventional perspective, what produces involvement.

CHALLENGING THEORETICAL AND
DISCIPLINARY BOUNDARIES

Activists Forever situates itself at the intersection of a series of academic questions, foremost of which is the literature on movement outcomes (Giugni, 1998, 2008; Bosi, Giugni, & Uba 2016) and the biographical consequences of activism (McAdam, 1999; Giugni, 2007; Béchir-Ayari, 2009; Fillieule, 2009) but also political socialization along the life course and the question of political participation, which implies exploring the understudied links between social movements and parties (Kitschelt, 1993; Goldstone, 2003). Those questions are first and foremost dealt with in the context of Western democracies (see Viterna, 2013 for an exception), when in this book we also address them under nondemocratic regimes.[1] Let us expose briefly how three sub-fields of the literature interact here, before developing our objectives in this book.

Biographical Consequences of Activism

Literature on the consequences of social movements and protest activities addresses three types of consequences: political, biographical, and cultural (Bosi & Uba, 2009). To date, political consequences (that is mainly policy outcomes) have received the lion's share, the biographical consequences of activism remaining dramatically under developed, except for three empirical domains that have been quite well explored, paving the way for future research (seeMcAdam 1999; Fillieule 2005, 2009; Giugni 2007 for reviews).

---

[1] From that point of view, the book is also a contribution to the sociology of authoritarianism and transition to democracy. Literature on authoritarian regimes and democratization is characterized by a plurality of paradigms: deterministic, focused on cultural, social, and economic "prerequisites"; diffusionistic, focused on external/international factors (Torfason & Ingram, 2010) and transitological. This last paradigm, loosely embedded in a rational choice epistemology, analyzes democratization processes as a mode of conflict regulation and resource redistribution among elites (O'Donnel et al., 1986). Its pragmatism and its strategist character have widely inspired NGOs promoting democracy, but are not without scientific shortcomings (Carothers, 2004): Not all the transitions are moving toward democratization; the distinction between three successive sequences (opening, breakdown, consolidation) is not automatic; elections do not only help to deepen political participation and accountability; they can also contribute to an "autocratization" process (Lindberg, 2009). Following a new generation of research (Camau & Massardier, 2009), we propose to develop this approach through devoting greater attention to how individuals experience the processes of hybridization, social dynamics, and "concrete historical situations" (Jaffrelot, 2000).

A first flow of research deals with the study of black student activism in the civil rights and black power movements and of riot participants (Sears & McConahay, 1973; Gurin & Epps, 1975). It explores environmental influences as well as the impact of activism on political ideology and adult resocialization, suggesting that the riots themselves appeared to have resocialized not only the direct participants but those who only vicariously experienced them; a result that has recently been confirmed by studies on not-so-committed participants (Sherkat & Blocker, 1997; Van Dyke et al., 2000). But the value of this research lies primarily in analyzing how movements accomplish their socializing role, teaching young blacks to question the overall white system of domination through specific mechanisms and set ups like mass meeting, workshops, and citizen and freedom schools.

A second family of research, on the future of 1960s American activists, has addressed the question of the biographical consequences of social movement participation on the life course, based on a series of follow-up studies of former movement participants, suggesting that activism had a strong effect both on political attitudes and behaviors, as well as on personal lives of the subjects. Concerning the political life, former activists had continued to espouse leftist political attitudes; had continued to define themselves as "liberal" or "radical" in political orientation; and had remained active in contemporary movements or other forms of political activity. In terms of affective life-sphere, ex-activists had been concentrated in teaching or other "helping" professions; had lower incomes than their age peers; were more likely than their age peers to have divorced, married later, or remained single; and were more likely than their age peers to have experienced an episodic or nontraditional work history (Demerath et al., 1971; Jennings & Niemi, 1981; Marwell et al., 1987; Fendrich & Lovoy, 1988; McAdam, 1988; McAdam, 1989; Whalen & Flacks, 1989). These elements allow Fendrich to analyze the ex-activists as a "generational unit," in the Mannheimian sense, which McAdam confirms when he demonstrates that the risks associated with the Freedom Summer undoubtedly greatly contributed to making this experience "unforgettable" for participants. In other words, the eventual direction of trajectories must be related to the nature of the activist experience, the moral career of individuals very likely having been affected to some degree by the duration and intensity of their activism.

However, in addition to having a narrow focus on New Left highly committed activists of the 1960s, these studies suffer from methodological limitations (e.g. in the small number of subjects included, the lack of a control group of non-activists, and the lack of data collected before they participated in the movement) and are less interested in the very process by which movements act as socializing agents than by its long-term effects, as measured by statistical indicators (McAdam, 1988; Whalen & Flacks, 1989 for notable exceptions).

A third and prolific direction stems from feminist research and deals with the development of a gender consciousness through the women's movement (e.g. Sapiro, 1989; Whittier, 1995; Klawiter, 2008). The reason that this movement has served as an active agent of socialization is partly due to the fact that one of its central goals was to change women's self-understanding: that is, to provide a social space in which women can consider and negotiate their social identity as women and its relationship to politics. Moreover, beyond the specific case of the women's movement, feminist research suggests that all protest movements may operate like gender workplaces. As a matter of fact, activism can play a liberating role for women in permitting them to leave the domestic universe and acquire social skills previously inaccessible to them. This is the reason why, even in movements where women are kept in positions of subjugation, mere participation can foster emancipation (Blee, 2008). Finally, it is clear that activism can generate profound and widespread socialization effects on individuals by transforming their sense of identity and politicizing the resulting social identification (McAdam, 1999; Polletta & Jasper, 2001), especially in situations where activism is repressed or criminalized as we shall see in the following section.

Political Socialization

Political socialization is more and more frequently defined as the gradual development of the individual's own particular and idiosyncratic views of the political world, the process by which a given society's norms and behavior are internalized (Sigel, 1989). This has three main theoretical consequences: primary and secondary socializations are equally important in the socializing process; it is not only family and school that are central instances of socialization but also many other institutions active in the life spheres of work, affective ties, voluntary work, and political engagements; political dimension is at play in all socialization process and doesn't correspond to a specific domain of activity or designated institutions. However, scant attention has been paid to social movements. There are many reasons for this. As Sapiro (1989) states:

social movements are populated by adults, and only recently have socialization scholars turned their attention in any serious way to adult socialization. Moreover ... Socialization research has been aimed at understanding why individuals do or don't participate in politics not at revealing the effects of political activity. We have rarely studied the socialization effects of explicitly political organizations.

Four basic ideas about the ways political dispositions might vary with age or life stages could summarize most of the literature. The *persistence model* suggests that the residues of preadult learning persist through life, perhaps even hardening with time. Largely assumed rather than tested directly, this model faced strong critical reviews in the 1970s and 1980s, suggesting that "the primacy principle" had been overstated and that at best, the evidence for it, such as adult retrospective accounts of their own attitudes or longitudinal studies, had been quite indirect. Long-term longitudinal studies appeared, implying that partisan tendencies change more after the preadult years than the persistent view would allow (Jennings & Niemi, 1981). Those critics gave way to the *lifelong openness model*, which suggests that dispositions have an approximately uniform potential for change at all ages and at the end, that age is irrelevant for attitude change. Unfortunately, this model has been left largely unexplored so far. The first volume on adult socialization appeared only at the end of the 1980s (Sigel, 1989). This important series of studies examines the political effects of discontinuities within adulthood, such as entering the workplace, serving in the military, immigrating to a new country, participating in a social movement, getting married, or becoming a parent. Each of these cases incorporates three elements that potentially can affect political attitudes: crystallization of an individual's own unique identity; assumption of new roles; and dealing with the unanticipated demands of adulthood. This trend of research has been particularly convincing in stressing the fact that neither childhood nor adolescence adequately prepare mature adults for all the contingencies with which they have to cope over their lifetimes. Hence the necessity to adopt a lifespan perspective that takes into account the impact that individual-level events as well as macro-level ones have on the maintenance, modification, or abandonment of values and orientations to which the individual may have subscribed at an earlier point in his or her life. However, the authors agree that all these specific discontinuities also occur most often in late adolescence and early adulthood, which means that the model here is quite close to a third view, the *impressionable years model*. Three propositions are behind this model: Youth experience political life as a "fresh encounter," in Mannheim's words ([1928] 1952), that can seldom be replicated later; dispositions and attitudes that are subjected to strong information flows and, regularly practiced, should become stronger with age; the young may be especially open to influence because they are becoming more aware of the social and political world around them just at the life stage when they are seeking a sense of self and identity. Some important surveys support the formative years hypothesis, for example Jennings 2002, about the durability of protesters as a generation unit, but one should also think of Skocpol's *Reflections at Mid-Career by a Woman from the Sixties*, concerning her own experience of belonging to a critical and optimist "Uppity Generation" (Skocpol: 1988).

In this book, we contend that dispositions, attitudes, and behavior change throughout life, especially during formative years (i.e. between fifteen and twenty-five), and that some, possibly much, of early learning is of limited consequence for adult political behavior. As a consequence, not only does participation into social movements depend on political socialization, but also has to be considered as having potentially socializing effects, which means that social movement organizations and protest events have to be studied as explicit and implicit socializing agents. We argue that the almost exclusive analytic concern with the institutional consequences of political commitment and subsequent neglect of its "independent psychological effects" (Zeitlin 1967: 241) is certainly one of the blind spots of contemporary political socialization and social movement research.

That is why we propose a fresh analysis of activist socialization from a comparative perspective, seeing it as a process of individual transformation, directly or indirectly stemming from involvement, and with immediate or deferred repercussions in all domains of social existence (subsequent political commitment, of course, but also professional and affective life). Beyond the explicit learning dispensed by activist organizations, or the socializing effects of exposure to political events, it is a matter of studying the ways in which political commitment affects all individual behaviors and perceptions, in other words of considering that all participation, "however sustained or intense, has secondary socializing effects" (Fillieule, 2005: 39).

Political Participation, and Movement–Parties Interdependencies

People engage in politics in various ways, mainly by voting, signing petitions, forming political parties, joining unions, and participating in advocacy groups, social movements, and protests. So far, social scientists have conceptualized these forms of citizens' engagement as two distinct phenomena (conventional versus nonconventional participation) leading to a peculiar split between research on formal or institutional political participation and social movements. As a result, and among other dead angles, research on movement–parties connections has remained quite rare until the turn of the twenty-first century. R. Goldstone's edited book on *States, Parties and Social Movements* (2003) was among the first to attempt to mobilize comparative research "bridging institutionalized and noninstitutionalized politics."[2]

Party–movement relations can be explored as a complex game of strategic interactions (Schwartz, 2010). Coordination exists in alliances, even mergers. More often ambiguity prevails in the "invasive" strategies by which movements try to colonize party structures, or parties coopt movement leaders and troops. These relations are also made of conflict when parties are the target of mobilizations – e.g. the 1968 Democrat convention in Chicago – when mud-slinging campaigns try to weaken an organization perceived as a threat, or to purge party or movement members suspected of connivance with the "enemy."

The need for a relational approach, challenging the flaws of academic hyper-specialization is nicely illustrated in Raka Ray's (1998) study on Bombay and Calcutta. Analyzing the political spaces of these two huge Indian cities as fields, she shows how the presence (in Calcutta with the Communist Party) or absence (in Bombay) of hegemonic political forces on the left can inhibit or frame the expression of women's movements. In Calcutta they depend strongly on the economic support and ideological limitations of the Marxist hierarchy of legitimate social struggles, leaving themes such as the critique of patriarchy only to outsider social movement

---

[2] Many among the classics of political science on political parties suggest the continuities and influences between parties and movements. Rokkan's sociohistoric study of the genesis of party systems (2008) can be read as a map of the contribution of organized and mobilized interests (peasant, working-class, religious groups) to the birth of many European parties. Duverger (1951) coined the concept of "indirect party" to make sense of the peculiarities of (Catholic and social democrat) political organizations created by trade unions or voluntary associations. (see Luck & Dechezelles, 2011 for a review).

organizations, especially when they target local politicians. In Bombay, a more open field with a more balanced distribution of resources between political forces leaves more autonomy and space for critical expression to women's movements. The lesson is crystal clear. Beyond microspecializations (in party politics, social movements, and one may add interest groups), the understanding of political process needs a connecting approach, a global vision of the actors and repertoires of political action. Which brings us back again to one of the central statements of interactionist sociology, i.e. to always situate the phenomena under study in "interactional fields," which can be defined as a mix of temporal process and social contexts.[3]

Questioning the intricacies and dynamics of the movement–parties interdependencies has not only a theoretical dimension. The stake is also a better understanding of the current situation of democracies (Crouch, 2004; Hay, 2004; Mastropaolo, 2012). They may question the sociological closure of politicians' recruitment among narrower and narrower "fishponds," the trend toward earlier and earlier trajectories of investment of politics as a job market. The sociology of parties highlights how the age of cartel-parties is also a time of growing distancing between parties and civil society, replacing grassroots politics by monitoring devices (polls, surveys, focus groups), substituting the continuities between voluntary associations and parties with the "hydroponic" production of ideas and policy programs by think tanks and experts. A significant part of these changes and of their consequences could be explained by the dominant trend toward disconnection between social movements and ruling parties, in the structuration of contentious politics as an autonomous political space. The reasons as well as the strength of this divorce do vary from one country to another, according to institutional variables, party systems or resource allocation systems (for the US Case: Pacewicz, 2015). When parties are soft structures, when the bargaining opportunities are real, movements may keep a strategic interest in investing part of their resources, and in activists establishing something like a garrison inside party structures. Lisa Young's comparison of the women's movement's strategies (1996) in their interaction with parties in the United States and Canada is illuminating on this point. But the main trend is not dubious. The percentage of party members keeping a serious commitment

---

[3] On this notion of "interactional field," see Abbott, 1999: 193–222. See also Duyvendak and Fillieule, 2015 and Fillieule and Broqua, 2018.

in social movements and voluntary associations – those coined as "*the party in the street*" by Heaney and Rojas (2007) – is shrinking. This part of the party constituency, which was the seismograph transmitting to the party the moves and moods of the social world, is marginalized in the management of cartel-parties. The networks, skills, and legitimacy gained in protest politics and grassroots commitments are a resource of decreasing importance in party struggles. Hence, the potential for political innovation and imagination, the supply of grassroots leaders mirroring class diversity, and the legitimation and treatment of new social problems that were propelled by the conflictual cooperation between social movement and parties is often broken down. Exploring the birth of new parties and the renewal of political supply, Lucardie (2000) identified among the processes of party renewal two dynamics from without. "Prolocutors" (one can think of the Poujade movement in the France of the fifties) express unanswered claims in a pragmatic language; they plead for the representation of outsiders and neglected interests. "Prophets" push into the political field new issues and define new social problems (like the green movements of the seventies). Such sources of renewal have often come from the initial momentum of social movements, a situation less visible in most Western democracies today (the Spanish case, with Ciudadanos and Podemos expressing a rare counter-trend). The third and final part of our book contributes to this collection of case studies interested in understanding party–movement dynamics by focusing specifically on individual trajectories of people who circulate between different connected political arenas, which also function as various spaces offering at different moments in time opportunities and incentives, from the most symbolic to jobs and careers.

FOUR MAIN OBJECTIVES OF THE BOOK

Beyond the rich results aforementioned, much work is needed in order to build a comprehensive and solid theoretical model for the study of the multiple socializing effects of participation to social movements and activists' careers. And apart from a few exceptions, research has mainly dealt with committed activists, without exploring not-so-committed participants; little has been done in order to disentangle the respective effects of political organizations' molding and socialization due to the mere participation in protest events; in existing research, age seems not to be considered as playing a role in explaining individual outcomes. Indeed, age is considered as an important variable in explaining commitment propensity (see McAdam's notion of biographical availability). But when it comes to analysis of biographical consequences, age is not any more mobilized as a central variable; lastly, analysis of post-movement paths of individual development is less interested in the very process of subsequent life course than in understanding the sociohistorical structuring of activists' careers. Our book project aims at surpassing all these shortcomings by targeting four main objectives.

Studying Activism as a Process

While research is investigating and "following" the dynamics of events and mobilization, it pays less attention to following activists. Therefore, longitudinal studies focusing on the succession and variety of commitments to and disengagements from activism as a trajectory are highly stimulating. They suggest new puzzles, and produce data challenging both scientific common sense (e.g. how to explain that so many among the leaders of yesterday's "new social movements" could be identified twenty years after among the upper crust of social democratic and green parties ... a typically "old" structure) and journalistic common sense (e.g. all the activists and leaders of May '68 movement did not become wealthy, cynical, and politically conservative). We therefore aim at analyzing what have become the rank and file activists politically and socially in various countries. Did they follow trajectories that could be described as a slow or quick dissociation from their original radicalism? Did they shift from commitment to the quest of a successful career, of accomplishments in varied social spaces? Even for those of the activists who would have drifted far away from their youth's commitments, how is the reconversion process working? Were the skills, know-how, and networks built in the activist years reinvested in professions, social ambitions, or other civic commitments? How can we analyze the specific effects of repression and specific experiences like the loss of close mates, prison, and torture?

Here the literature that more or less directly broaches the question of disengagement is of great help (Klandermans, 1997; Fillieule, 2005, 2010). It emerges from social psychology, concerning the social functioning of small groups and sociability networks (e.g. Moss-Kanter, 1972; McPherson et al., 1992); the sociology of roles, in the Mertonian or interactionist tradition, especially in the literature on churches and cults, but also divorce and the professions (Vaughan, 1986; Fuchs Ebaugh, 1988); and from life course sociology, especially when inspired by symbolic interactionism.[4] As a matter of fact, interactionist approaches, especially in the version articulated by Strauss (1959) and Becker (1960 and 1963), offers a powerful tool for studying activism diachronically. In such a model, activism is conceived as a long-lasting social activity articulated by phases of joining, commitment, and defection. The notion of *career* initially developed by Hughes casts the stages of access to and exercise of a profession as a series of objective changes of position and an associated series of subjective upheavals. As Becker stresses, quoting Hughes, the concept of career comes back to two dimensions:

In its objective dimension, a career is a series of statuses and clearly defined offices ... typical sequences of position, achievement, responsibility, and even of adventure ... Subjectively, a career is the moving perspective in which the person sees his life as a whole and interprets the meaning of his various attributes, actions, and the things which happen to him. (1966:102)

This powerful concept allows us to focus on the process and permanent dialectic between individual history, social institutions, and, more generally, context. The outcome is less a case of predicting a state (activism, disengagement, and so on) than of rebuilding a sequence of steps, of changes in the individual's behavior and perspectives, in order to understand the phenomenon.

As a consequence, and again following Becker's recommendation, we argue that one must never reason exclusively in terms of "why" and shift to "how it happened," in other words, to the chain of facts that result from specific contemporary causes and are reconfigured as events unfold. In terms of methodology, a process model implies three elements: move away from reasoning in terms of "independent" and "dependent" variables, in favor of a "thick description" of individual trajectories, in order to concentrate on the process by which people join political organizations or participate in protest campaigns, remain involved, and/or disengage. This does not mean that we must renounce to any causal explanation. But that this can be achieved only after an analysis

---

[4] Coined by Blumer in 1937, "symbolic interactionism" is closely linked to the social behaviorism of Mead. Its subsequent usage belongs less to a school of thought than to a wide array of research sharing two standpoints: a common conception of the individual and their relation to society; and a way of doing research inherited from the Chicago School of Sociology (i.e. field work and qualitative methodologies). Symbolic interactionism can be defined as a microsociological and processual approach that *systematically* links the individual and the study of situations to broader contextual factors and social order rules and norms. In this perspective, not only are individuals and society interdependent but they also mutually construct each other.

of a series of mechanisms whose composition (in time and in space) produces observable effects; following this, move away from synchronic mechanisms toward diachronic variations with regard to context change, organizational transformations, and individual life course. In other words, move from *"analysis of* profiles *to* pathways, *and from* roots *(as in root causes) to* routes." (Horgan, 2009: XXIII); focus research on the individual level – i.e. one's life course and the justifications given for their actions – as a mean to investigate the complex interplay between micro, meso, and macro levels and to overcome the far too simplistic analytical distinction between instrumental, solidarity, or ideological motives.

Exposure to Political Events and Organizational Modeling

The interactionist framework offers a sociological conceptual toolkit to examine how activism can have a socializing effect on individuals. Two distinct main directions must be explored: exposure to political events and organizational modeling.

The study of the socializing effects of political events and communication about them is still underdeveloped (e.g. Neveu & Quéré, 1996; Sewell, 1996; Tackett, 2006, 2015; Kapferer, 2015; Latté, 2015; Pagis, 2018). Indeed, vivid political events should be important catalysts because they can have traumatic effects and stimulate heavy information flows. Events may have an impact at any age but, depending on one's position in his or her life-cycle, the socializing effects will differ, from strengthening and substantiation for older people to conversion and alternation for youngsters. Also, a distinction should be made here between the effects of direct participation and the impact of political events on "engaged observers" and even "bystander publics."

Secondary socialization within and by social movements has typically been neglected. The reasons for this blind spot are plural. One should mention again the structuralist orientation adopted by the sociology of social movements, even if, periodically, some authors underscored the imbalance between research on recruitment by movements and that studying the effect of the institution on militants (e.g. Keniston, 1968: 353–354; Killian, 1973: 36; McAdam, 1989:123). The growing hyperspecialization and editorial inflation of social sciences should also be blamed. When more and more academics are "specialists of their speciality" more than social scientists, when reading one's tribe's journals and books is almost a full-time job, bridging research fields and importing concepts and results become difficult. Yet the tradition of research on communities, religious structures, and "total" (Goffman, 1961) or "greedy" (Coser, 1974) institutions supplies a very rich legacy to make sense of the tools and institutional devices able to produce "patterns of undivided commitment" or at least a lasting influence on the membership (Moss-Kanter, 1972). It highlights also how and why organizations are able – or not – (Bennet, 1981) to safeguard critical cultures. Organizational socializations require close attention to make sense of how they can succeed (or not) engrossing social energies, channeling the human *libido* toward social goals and structuring dispositions that could have enduring expressions.

Actually, rare are the case studies perceiving social movements, as Goffman did with total institutions, as spaces of interaction having a substantial power of socialization (Flesher Fominaya, 2010; Beckwith, 2016 for notable exceptions). Nonetheless, movements do not simply produce repertoires and impacts on policies and politics. They also produce (or fail to produce) activists. Borrowing this phrase from the Eliasian sociology, they produce lasting changes in the "We-I balance" of part of their members, injecting in the social world activists with strong dispositions for collective action and the construction of claims and causes, entrepreneurs of social changes.

As a consequence, much work is needed in order to build a comprehensive and solid theoretical model for the study of the multiple socializing effects of social movement organizations. Within the interactionist framework, Gerth and Wright Mills (1954: 165–191) offer a strong sociological conceptual tool kit to examine the relationships between individuals and institutions. They define an institution as an organization with distinct hierarchical roles to which members must conform. The internalization of such roles occurs through secondary socialization, the strength of which needs to be studied – from conversion and alternation, in the sense used by Berger and Luckmann (1966), to strategic and limited adaptations – along with durability, from the viewpoint of biographical consequences in all spheres of life. This model places the Goffmanian notion of "moral career" at the center of the analysis of activism. It refers to *the selection of people* (to the incentives and barriers to joining, and the orientations of activities) and to *organizational modeling*, i.e. the multiple socializing effects of activism, themselves in part determined by organizational rules and modes of operation, understood as a set of constraints (status, proposed or reserved activities, leadership, and so on).

Organizations do a lot of work in socializing their members, understood as role taking, which allows individuals to identify the different roles they face and correctly fulfil their customary tasks. This secondary socialization can, at times, assume the form of explicit inculcations, the goal of which is to homogenize activists' categories of thought and their way of acting within and in the name of the organization. However, know-how and activist wisdom also frequently amount to a "practical sense," what Bourdieu refers to as "the anticipated adjustment to the requirements of a field, what the language of sports calls the 'sense of the game' (like 'sense of place', 'the art of anticipation', etc.), acquired over the course of a long dialectical process, often described as a 'vocation', by which 'we make ourselves' according to what is making us and we 'choose' that by which we are 'chosen'" (Bourdieu, 1980: 111–112). This process takes place outside of our conscious awareness.

If, then, an institution "leaves its mark" on social actors who are part of it "by modifying their external conduct as well as their private life" (Gerth & Wright Mills, 1954: 173), we need to examine both the content and the methods of the process of institutional socialization to understand activists' life course. Three dimensions may be distinguished: the acquisition of "know-how" and "wisdom" (resources); a vision of the world (ideology); and the restructuring of sociability networks in relation to the construction of individual and collective identities (social networks and identities) (Fillieule, 2010).[5]

Opening the black box of organizational modeling would help to better single out which organizational characteristics determine what outcomes – here *dispositions* – their duration and strength (which could lead to typologies of different kinds of groupings). It would give a real sociological density to the notion of "militant habitus" by specifying the variety of its social production, structures, and effects. On this, Corrigall-Brown's chapter offers to the reader very rich results and avenues for future research. The comparison of the differences of dispositions structured by the experience of the French '68 years and of the Moroccan years of struggle against the heavy-handed regime of Hassan II also supplies case studies inviting one to think of the variety of militant habitus.

---

[5] It is precisely these socializing mechanisms that Horgan attempts to capture by the notion of "community of practice" (2009:13) in order to take account of a learning process through repeated social and psychological interactions with an ideology and the related social and cultural practices.

Activism as a Tool for Change

Third, we also want to make sense of activism as a tool for social change, of micro-changes in culture, private lives, and work relations, which may be more important in the long term than the often imaginary promises of revolutions and insurrections. Many social movement studies are framed in a "heroic vision" (which probably also mirrors a male-gendered bias). Social movements sometimes look like medieval battles. Their analysts must be able to make sense of their strategic plans and tactical skills, to decipher the art and slyness of protesters in building networks and alliances, and tricking their opponents. If victory occurs, it is thus supposed to produce very visible outputs (budgets, policies, and new institutions or rights). Social movements may work like this. Yet, seeing only this dimension is, once more, forgetting that one of their major effects is to inject activists into most of the scenes and spaces of society,[6] and these activists are not simply mobilized during high-stakes battles. They have jobs, lifestyles, and low-key commitments to leisure or cultural activities. Bringing their critical dispositions, relational styles, and expertise acquired from past activism to these activities, they behave, in the silent logic of everyday lives, like micro-social change entrepreneurs as shown by Neveu in this volume. They inspire changes in organizational routines, and they shake hierarchical habits and redefine the functioning and goals of organizations, administrations, and even sometimes markets. This dimension has been studied at length by scholars working on "state feminism" and "inside agitators" (Eisenstein, 1996), for example by Katzenstein (1998) on the DACOWITS (Defense advisory board on women in the services) in America or by Banaznak (2010), who shows how by becoming "institutional activists" during the last forty years, feminist activists impulsed new political opportunities for policy changes in favor of women's rights.

However, one must add to that rather optimistic view of activists' lasting influence on social fabric the very fact that states are never unaware of those processes and may have a central role in coopting activists, as for example Bosi shows in his chapter on the effects of British counterterrorist policies and reintegration programs in Ireland.

---

[6] "Long haul" activists often trigger new kinds of movements, including subsequent movements, as literature on the spillover effect has shown. See Meyer et al. Whittier 2004; Whittier 1995.

Another crystal clear example refers to the role government played in the aftermath of May '68 in facilitating conversion of "activist habitus" into the profession. There is a good deal of indicators showing that May '68 certainly did play a role of "whistle blower" for the state authorities. Hence, the number of new job opportunities created in welfare and control of marginal and lower classes in order to better prevent social unrest, as well as in the research and teaching institutions, offering free spaces for critical researchers and the emergence of a counter-expertise movement that would fuel social movements in the 1970s (Pollack 1982: 165–185 on '68ers; Spanou, 1991 on environmental movement constituencies). This last remark opens up an interesting question: To what extent did the emergence of counter-expertise and hybrid forums in the wake of May '68 contribute to the development of a new relationship to the State, what Foucault in *La volonté de savoir* calls "governmentality," which we can define as a specific mode of association between power and knowledge (Foucault, 1976; 1994: 134–162)?[7]

Individuals In Context: Toward a Multi-Level Model of Analysis

Fourth, one of our central hypotheses is that one should not study individual trajectories without separating them from the contexts in which they take place. Following Wright Mills, we think that "Whatever else he may be, man is a social and historical actor who must be understood, if at all, in close an intricate interplay with social and historical structures" (Wright Mills, 1959: 158).

This may sound like a trivial argument and of course much social movement research contends that "individuals do not become mobilized out of a political void" (Marsh, 1977: 22). Calls for multi-level approaches are more and more frequent in the literature. However, scholars often content themselves to make an analytical distinction between three series of factors of commitment or withdrawal at the macro, meso, and micro levels, without offering a convincing explanation of their joint occurrence over time, therefore missing the very point of understanding how "the context in which human lives are lived is central

---

[7] For a general introduction to this notion see Gordon (1991) and, of course, for a conservative defense on the state side Crozier, Huntington, and Watanuki (1975).

to the core of meaning in those lives" (Andrews, 1991: 13). What we need is a model able to think of the commitment process diachronically, within the totality of individual life stories (Becker, 1970), and that can help to contextualize individual engagements and exits synchronically at both organizational and macro levels, rejecting the scholastic opposition between agency and structure.[8]

Activist trajectories are to be explained as well by idiosyncratic as by structural and contextual factors (i.e. the dialectic between dispositions and motives of the actors and their structural positions). Such an approach means that one should articulate micro (dispositions, primary socialization), meso (secondary socialization in protest groups and/or by exposure to political events), and macro (local and national economic, social and political contexts) levels of analysis. In other words, a multi-level approach to political commitment and disengagement. One can single out a certain number of characteristics that are at work in the complex web of interactions between individuals, organizations, and contexts. Let us summarize these characteristics.

At the macro level, there is the importance of specific contexts and the transformations in the structure of commitment and disengagement opportunities. The sociopolitical environment constrains organizational evolution at the meso level and shapes activists' expectations at the micro level. These elements are particularly visible in a diachronic perspective when one considers the observable differences between cohorts or generations of activists. A range of characteristics can be listed here, including the state of the commitment offer, the nature of state intervention (or the lack of it) in the public policy domain addressed by the mobilized network, and the public image of the cause.

By varying the national contexts studied, *Activists Forever* offers a means to study the weight of different interconnected dimensions: the timing and the extent of economic crises; the geopolitical context, i.e. the weight of international issues, such as the influence of France's May 1968

---

[8] We do not have space enough to discuss at length the reasons why we privilege such a theoretical approach of the link between agency and structure and why it seems more appropriate to us in this context than other conceptual tools like those elaborated by Bourdieu, Giddens, or Sahlins.

movement on Mexico,[9] Morocco,[10] and Turkey[11], of the Vietnam War or of decolonization's wars in Turkey and Morocco, and of regional conflicts such as the Israeli-Palestinian conflict. Also, while some countries studied share a common experience with authoritarian and semi-corporatist regimes, the dynamics of their democratic opening-up or closing vary, with three major patterns. In Poland and the Czech Republic, there was a transition and a process of democratic consolidation in the nineties. In Turkey, there was a period of democratic opening flanked by three coups marking an authoritarian closing up, and a slow normalization starting in the 1990s. In Mexico and Morocco, authoritarian and semi-corporatist regimes held on throughout the period despite numerous waves of protest. Finally, in the case of Morocco, there is the particular question of the role of the '68 generation in the revolutionary movement of 2011 (M20).

At the meso level of organizations, one must study at the national as well as the local level the extent of the development of the mobilized network (territorial spread and numerical growth, and therefore the extent of recruitment networks through people that know other people), the degree of homogeneity or heterogeneity of the group in terms of sociobiological and ideological characteristics (which also constrain the nature and range of acquaintance networks), and finally the degree of "openness" of the groupings studied (the voluntary recruitment policy, ways of integrating newcomers into the group, and so on). Here again,

---

[9] In 1968, Mexico witnessed a major wave of mobilization against the absence of democracy and the authoritarianism of a centralist and semi-corporatist political system (Combes, 2011). This phase preceded the end of the "Mexican miracle" in 1982, with several periods of economic crisis and inflation. Protest movements started with the student struggle of 1968 (Bolos, 1999; Tamayo, 1999) at the National Autonomous University of Mexico (UNAM) and at the National Polytechnic Institute (IPN). The regime responded harshly, occupying the university campus and the facilities of the IPN and opening fire on demonstrators, killing between 200 and 300 people (Tlatelolco, October 2, 1968). These events fed the protest, with an extension to other states (especially in Monterrey) and radicalization through guerilla actions leading to severe repression in 1974 (La Garza, Ejea, & Macías, 1986: 79–81).

[10] Actually, the Moroccan '68 starts earlier than in France with the events of March 1965, particularly in Casablanca and following high school reform. These revolts were violently crushed by the army and a state of emergency was declared. The year 1968 was experienced as a "revolutionary celebration" within the University of Rabat. It spread through direct and indirect connections with other movements abroad (Bennani-Chraïbi, 2003).

[11] The 1968 movement had a strong impact on Turkey. This movement was particularly characterized by its anti-American, nature (Uysal, 2009). Tension between students of the left and the right led to recurrent confrontations on campuses and many victims. On this, see Cormier 2016.

our book offers to compare different timing and extent of the repression of protest groups (harsh in Turkey and in Morocco[12]), with its repercussions for the paths to radicalization or deradicalization (the passage to terrorism of certain groups in Turkey notably), but also the existence of organized and powerful counter-movements (the nationalist extreme right in Turkey, and radical Islamic movements) or ethnic or religious cleavages (Turkey, Morocco). Consideration of all these organizational factors must be articulated to an analysis of the combination of the effects of protest events exposure and organizational modeling on the long-term commitment of individuals. This last point not only stresses the well-studied issue of collective incentives (be they positive or negative) that enhance or discourage individual participation, but also the great importance of institutional socialization and of its libidinal dimension.

At the micro level of the individual, we have the importance of 'institutionalized changes' and 'biographical ruptures' at different career stages. The pivotal nature of the plurality of life-spheres underlines that activist organizations are also comprised of individuals who are inserted in a variety of social space locations. Activists are thus permanently subject to the obligation to comply with different norms, rules, and logics which may potentially be in conflict. These different levels of experience may proceed simultaneously or successively; for the observer, the difficulty lies in studying the succession of events within each order of experience at the same time (the structure of each order) and the influence of each level on all the others. In such an approach, activist commitment is not a dependent variable to be explained but a variable co-varying with others.

STRUCTURE OF THE BOOK

The visible structure of a book is always the result of invisible processes that develop in the back stages of social research. The starting point of this book can be connected to a conference on *"The outcomes of social movements"* organized in June 2011 in Berlin, to celebrate Dieter Rucht.

---

[12] In Morocco, one speaks of the "years of lead," to point at the massive repression between 1965 and 1975 (Vairel 2005). In Turkey, the 1980 coup triggered harsh and widespread repression of the left, the closing off and banning of revolutionary groups, associations, parties and unions, and holding more than 650,000 people in custody. Two hundred and thirty thousand individuals were judged before tribunals, 98,404 for being members of a political party, union, or other form of association. Thirty thousand people were fired for political reasons, while another 30,000 left the country as political refugees (Cormier, 2016).

We were struck by the small number of papers that could be defined as actor-centered, or were focusing on the production of activists as precisely one of the significant outcomes of mobilizations. The idea of editing a book sprouted there. We mobilized two networks of colleagues whose research fitted with our theoretical orientations. A significant part of them were from French-speaking academic institutions. The causes of this situation had deeper reasons than our own institutional locations. Francophone political science is much more embedded in sociology and history than most of its foreign counterparts (Fillieule, 2016). The weak influence of the paradigm of Rational Action Theory has opened a space for what we consider as much more sophisticated and much more realistic visions of agency and human rationalities: from habitus theory to psychological approaches or a sociology of emotions. One of the strengths of Francophone social science (which may be the reverse of its frequent weakness in sophisticated quantitative data treatment) is also the strong use of qualitative methods (ethnographic approach, uses of interviews of life-stories). We mobilized simultaneously foreign colleagues able to join these dynamics or to bring stimulating variations. The story was from then on typical of any mobilization, passing through moments of enthusiasm – like the brainstorming weekend that we had together in Rennes in May 2014 – and episodes of disappointment when a participant, too busy or too bluesy, was stepping down. The final crop was made of eleven contributions.

Having shared many direct or mail discussions on these papers we easily agreed that the most logical organization of the book was to structure it around three major themes. One was the process of ageing of activists and especially those of the sixties. They had been a "vintage" generation, and focusing on a population of people that were then among the sixty and seventy-somethings was the optimum for a complete view of life courses. Reading and cross-commenting the chapters we agreed on the fact that experiences of activism for which one had serious chances of being thrown in jail, tortured, raped, or even killed were significantly different from demonstrating in Berkeley in 1964, Paris in 1968, or even Prague in 1988. The risks of commitment, its libidinal economy, its longterm impact on lives and self-esteem were too specific. Finally, other papers had a strong common denominator that could be labelled as their "liminal" dimension, the presence of multiple processes of bordercrossing. Borrowed from Turner's anthropology, the notion of liminality has been used by Yang (2000) to make sense of the Chinese Red Guards' experiences "As an antistructure, a liminal condition entails the suspension of normal structural constraints; in this sense liminality can be seen as in an inverse relationship to bureaucracy. ... A liminal situation is characterized by freedom, egalitarianism, communion and creativity" (383). Such was the experience of many activists in the final chapters of this book. Passing thresholds, going from social movements to politics, from "Red T-Shirt to executive suit," from prisons to official palaces, from an almost spiritual vision of commitment to the more cynical struggles of electoral politics, they faced exhilarating challenges, experienced new structures of interactions, and sometimes met – like yesterday's Red guards – bitter outcomes to their actions.

Opening with a short keynote introduction by prominent researchers, each of these three parts combines a strong focus and a fine weaving of the major themes that structure this book. They all pay attention to the dimensions of gender and generation; they invite one to think of political socialization as a life-long process, always able to be changed but also to oppose the hysteresis effects of solidified habitus when facing the border crossing process. Alongside these structuring questions, the reader will identify secondary questionings, as touches of color in a finely woven tweed. The book also deals with authoritarian regimes and post communism, with the questions of individual continuities and ruptures, of how can (or can't) activism be "forever."

Should we then, before going into the details of these three parts, claim as Voltaire's Doctor Pangloss that we built *"The best of the possible"* book structures? Readers could thus behave as the skeptical Candide and notice that considering the violence of repression in Mexico City in 1968 the Mexican chapter could have moved to Part II and that the "Moroccan" chapter of Part II also speaks of the role of the activists of the sixties generation that structures Part I. There is no doubt: themes overlap, and issues reappear. One would even argue, after reading some chapters, that gender could have been another structuring theme. Let's stick therefore with our three-fold structure. It comes from sound reflection and collective thinking. The existing echoes and overlapping between parts and chapters should be considered less as flaws in the structure than as the filigree, the patterns that give coherence and sense to an ambitious articulation or case studies.

From Shades of Red (or Blue) to Shades of Grey: The Ageing of Yesterday's Activists

The common denominator of the chapters in this first part is about questioning the ageing process of activists, mostly, but not only, those from the sixties generation. The puzzle here is firstly the question of the abilities/opportunities/probabilities to remain a long distance activist. Could the experience of strong commitment be forgotten? Could it be lived as a moment of madness in the life course that would be forgotten when facing the "serious" challenges of having a family and children, of managing a career, of showing a respectable social facade? What kind of socialization, of habitus shaping remains (or not) during the life course? Which experiences of activism have the more lasting effects? Can one identify the long-term influence of activism through generational transmissions, but also in specific styles of role-adjustment in work relations, in the reinvestment of activist skills or know-how in new styles of claim-making, new commitments? What became of the generation of activists from the 1960s in a variety of political contexts? Here, classically, the unifying element throughout the chapters is the identification of a single activist generation, in a range of circumstances and with differing opportunities for action, depending on how the various national political spaces evolved.

One of the main focusses here is to correlate activists' trajectories with a close attention to the effects of involvement in individuals' various spheres of life, among which affective life (i.e. romance, reciprocal affection, family life, and children, but also strong relational ties with friends). Literature on American sixties activists shows that they were more likely than their age peers to have divorced, married later, or remained single and were less likely to have children as Flacks reminds us. But those results are based on statistical analyses that are unable to understand and even less explain how and when various experiences in diverse life spheres interact and combine, producing a given result in the sphere of engagement. Sociologists have great difficulties accounting for phenomena that literature is often better placed to capture (Jasper, 1999: 215). Only a biographical approach (be it individual biographies of ordinary activists or collective biographies, i.e. prosopographies) can bring some convincing answers here, as Auyero masterly demonstrates in his *Contentious Lives* (2003).[13] In their chapter, Olivier and Tamayo illustrate that kind of approach by following the life course of two women whose commitment is rooted in different socialization processes, emerges at different points in time and space, but whose lives retrospectively appear as having followed a very similar life course along the years. Here,

---

[13] See also Passerini (1996) and Rupp and Taylor (1987).

as well as in the biography of Peter studied by Pagis, the successive bifurcations of the two Sikh women studied by Gayer, or the life course of a PKK activist couple analyzed by Tejel in Part II, romantic encounters and more generally the affective life sphere of the activists seem to play a dramatically important role in the way commitments evolve over time.

Understanding how the activist experience particularly affects the professional paths chosen and how occupation can in turn orient commitment is a tricky question.[14] Existing research has mainly taken two routes:

A first bias, shared by the literature on commitment and the research on social mobility, has been to focus on downward trajectories, forgetting the upward ones. These interpretations, hastily subsumed under a single "model of loss of social position," or more generally of "relative deprivation," are based on a problematic causal explanation according to which the malaise generated by the drop in social status and more generally frustration would almost automatically give rise to activism. Now, without denying the existence of this type of thinking (Johsua, 2016), most empirical sociological research on political involvement suggests a slightly different picture, that is, the tendency of actors who are rising socially to become involved. As a matter of fact, mobility may be prior to, concomitant with, or subsequent to activist experiences, these different patterns producing very distinct sociobiographical paths.

Second of all, research has explored the various forms of conversion and importation into the professional sphere of activists' know-how, aspirations, and self-images (e.g. McAdam, 1988; Whalen & Flacks 1989; Bennani-Chraïbi & Fillieule, 2003; Tissot et al., 2005; Neveu, 2008; Champy & Israël, 2009; Pagis & Leclercq, 2011). In her chapter, Pagis depicts a range of professional conversions post-68 that extends from professional activism to a rejection of salaried employment, and includes the subversion of professional practices and the invention of new professions. She shows that this importation of anti-establishment dispositions into the professional sphere varies as a function of social origin, gender, and type of political involvement engaged in immediately after May '68.

---

[14] It is very difficult to determine whether activism has produced a reorientation of trajectories or whether, on the contrary, it is by virtue of the same initial dispositions that the individuals studied participated, had a more distant relation with their families and to marriage, and finally chose one profession over another. The only certainty is that the choice of career that does not enter into contradiction with an activist disposition is probably related to their continued involvement.

Chapters in Part I also offer to study the effects of involvement in terms of social mobility, as well as the effects of social mobility in terms of involvement by pointing at three mechanisms that have recently been singled out by Leclercq and Pagis (2011):

First, study of how and when trajectories of upward mobility constitute favorable soil for involvement. "The upwardly mobile," in leaving their original social milieu, may find themselves confronted with contradictory injunctions leading to the double-bind phenomenon with regard to their class of origin, as well as their new milieu, resulting in serious tensions with respect to identity. Hence, "the upwardly mobile" are that much more disposed to believe in the possibility of social change since their trajectories "shake the foundations of the social order in weakening the borders between 'them' and 'us'" (Mauger, 2006: 31) and their positions as outsiders encourage a critical perspective on society.

Second, while aspirations to upward mobility may exist prior to political involvement, it is not uncommon for them to appear because activism often goes with meeting people from upper classes (Vigna & Zancarini-Fournel, 2009). The social heterogeneity of activist organizations, more or less strong, depending on the case and the contexts, combined with the social dimension of collective action, serves to decompartmentalize participants' social networks and, thus, facilitates social mobility. Crossing these usually watertight borders between social milieus and socializing with young activists from the upper classes, thus, may have contributed to changing the social destinies of young working-class activists. Even if in recent research on the personal consequences of commitment, one of us has shown the rareness of such durable encounters for '68ers (Fillieule et al., 2018).

Third, activism may in certain circumstances lead to a drop in class status. In some situations, the price of activism is a limit to professional promotion, especially in Autoritarian contexts, as Hivert and Vairel exemplify in Part II. Contrary to the depiction of a "Generation 68," unanimously opportunistic, moving upward, occupying socially recognized positions, an examination of an anonymous segment of this population reveals various points on their journeys where participants have descended the social class ladder because of their active participation in May '68 (Neveu, and Pagis, in this volume[15]). This reflection suggests that

---

[15] One of the striking results of Fillieule et al. 2018 is to have measured for the first time the downward mobility of French '68ers, which was 25.6 percent, while in the meantime it stood at 4 percent for the general population of the same age cohorts.

activism can generate frustration rather than result from it, when it produces aspirations not favored by actual objective conditions. Here, the opening up of theoretical possibilities does not coincide with real opportunities, and aspirations born of activist involvement remain unfulfilled.

Finally, by comparing the effect of various organizational contexts on subsequent experiences of participation, Corrigall-Brown demonstrates a cleavage between left-wing activists of the sixties who made career decisions on the basis of their ideological convictions and activists from the right whose career plans do not seem to have been changed for political reasons. A result all the more striking as the two groups show similar consistency in their ideological beliefs over time. What explains the different articulations between professional and activist life spheres is due to the changing forms of commitment by conservative activists over time, with a move from activism to what she calls "nominal activism," church-based networks being here the main cement of continuance commitment through close ties.

Terrorist Violence, State Responses, and Activists' Experiences

The four contributions of this second part are focused on case studies where activists had to face high levels of violence in the context of terrorism, armed struggle, and/or very strong repression from state authorities. How are these specific experiences of high-risk activism structuring specific trajectories and generational identities? How is it possible (or not) to move from armed struggle to "normal" politics and social life. What are the specific emotional dimensions – with their gendered variations – of these experiences of violence, death, and torture? How can state policies, political and military events but also private situations (pregnancies, immigration, deaths) work as turning points both in activists' careers and micro-group solidarities?

If activism can generate profound and widespread socialization effects on individuals by transforming the sense of identity and politicizing the resulting social identification, this is especially true in situations where activism is repressed or criminalized and takes the form of commitment to violent modes of action (Della Porta, 1995; Combes & Fillieule, 2011). In a variety of contexts, the chapters examine forms of involvement and types of trajectories that are physically violent and clandestine. The objective here, beyond everything that "extreme" cases allow us to see more readily in studying routine situations, is to more clearly explain the factors in the trajectories followed that are associated with the contexts and events, on one hand, and, on the other, with the very shape of the militant groups and their ways of functioning.

Another peculiarity of this part of the book is to give significant space to the question of the violent repertoire of collective action, and to the experience of armed struggle. Except for a few notable exceptions, case studies targeting participants in so-called terrorist or resistance organizations[16] have been rather uncommon (see Demetriou, Bosi, & Malthaner, 2014; Fillieule, 2016 for a review). The number and range of organizations using violence has significantly expanded since the nineties, with armed organizations in the Indian subcontinent, radical Islamic groups, and micro-nationalist groups within Europe. The scale of this repertoire of violent actions creates new theoretical challenges for researchers. Is it possible to develop a lasting commitment to terrorism and, if so, how? What could the idea of "career" mean here? What social logic can slow down the spiral of violence, and how can ex-terrorists manage the process of a return to normality? And what could "normality" mean after the "high" of their experience? Could such trajectories combine with a return to party politics or to peaceful contentious politics? If so, how can these new commitments work and with what degree of legitimacy, resources, or particular skills?

One of the most striking results of chapters in Part II stems from their focus on the micro level of the temporal development of the relationships between repression and protest.[17] As a matter of fact, scant research has examined the succession of "micro-cohorts" (Whittier, 1997) of militants who join and leave organizations at various stages of repressive policies. Research on the trajectories of radicalization of revolutionary movements in the 1970s under the effect of repression stresses that radicalization more readily affects those who did not experience the initial phase but joined the movement later, at the peak of the cycle of mobilization. This seems to be corroborated by a rise in the levels of violence with the second

---

[16] Radical forms of contentious politics may be called either terrorism or resistance, "depending on the circumstances and who is doing the naming" (Steinhoff & Zwerman, 2008: 213).

[17] Actually, the link between repression and protest has mainly been studied at both the macro and meso levels, especially with the notion of cycles of mobilization. See Tarrow (1989), Sommier (2010) and Zwerman and Steinhoff (2005) on leftist movements in the 1960s in France, the United States, and Japan; as well as Brockett (2005) on the cycles of repression in Guatemala and El Salvador.

or even third generation of militants (e.g. Della Porta, 1995; Steinhoff & Zwerman, 2005; Sommier, 2010).

Hivert and Vairel on Morocco, Tejel on the PKK, Gayer on Sikh militants, and Bosi on the IRA all show that, contrary to a homogenous vision of collectives, it is necessary to pay attention to two interconnected dimensions to understand the diversity of demobilizing effects of repression within a single movement: on one hand, the succession of militant generations in the center of the analysis of the internal dynamics of recruitment and selection, the transformations of collective identities, and the organizational and ideological changes that result; On the other hand, this ebb and flow of militants must be correlated with a historical period that includes a succession of repressive events. Traumatic episodes, such as the 1980s coup in Turkey or the massacre at Amritsar's Golden Temple during Operation Bluestar in June 1984, constitute properly speaking socializing events, the weight and individual consequences of which depend, in fact, on earlier socializing events and the particular generation of activists. Furthermore, the specific forms the repression takes for a given cohort translate into a whole series of socializing effects that lay the foundation for generational phenomena. So, analysts often consider the experience of prison and torture crucial, as incubators of militancy, serving as intense forms of socialization, and indeed a manner of redefining identities (see Hivert and Vairel). Finally, the importance of the succession of militant generations in understanding the individual effects of repression also raises questions about transmission of the memory of struggles, which could be disrupted and facilitate withdrawal when repression decimates an entire generation, as Bennani-Chraïbi (2003) shows in the case of Morocco, even if Hivert and Vairel also show how "activist schemes" were notwithstanding, and under certain circumstances, transmitted through family socialization from the parents to their siblings, nurturing the contemporary M20 movement.[18]

Biographical Trajectories in Times of Transition: Activists versus Politicians, Activists into Politicians?

Part III of the book explores three dimensions related to the conversion of activists from social movements to party politics.

---

[18] Studies on intergenerational transmission of activist schemes within the family have been developing only recently. See for example Pagis, 2009, 2018; Masclet, 2015; and Cormier, 2016.

The first dimension relates to the connecting spaces between social movements and party politics as being also venues for a complex collection of jobs and career opportunities, transforming activism into professions, recycling skills gained in activism into marketable abilities. The contributions of Gaxie (1977, 2005) on this question are illuminating. They show that commitment is the source of a wide range of gratifications, and how the value of these gratifications is also a social construction depending of the political context, of the life-cycle of activists. Activism produces social capital. It can open opportunities of transformation of commitment into semi- or fully paid jobs. It teaches skills and knowhow that could be reinvested in jobs and professions. Activism is also the cradle of a complex libidinal economy made up not only of friendships and loves, of feelings of self-esteem, exhilaration, and exaltation, but also of moments of despair and blues (Jasper, 1999). Activism creates interactions where rank and file members meet famous people and move under the spotlights of media visibility. Gaxie's approach also invites one to refrain from jumping to the analytical shortcut that reduces all these gratifications into comparable and convertible outputs. Which count unit should we use to translate the contribution of a love affair born in and from mobilization into something comparable with the proud feelings born from the dedication to something considered as a noble cause? And which count unit allows one to compare such emotional gratifications to the profits of an appointment as a paid employee of the SMO or member of the mayor's staff. On which time-scale should one develop the accounting of individual activism outcomes? Some are instantly visible when an activist is employed as a paid member of the organization's staff, or when she gains local celebrity in her city. But the cultural and social capital accumulated in the organization could produce its result 15 years later in the recruitment as project coordinator by an ex-comrade having developed a successful business; what is needed is a multi-scalar evaluation tool, a great wariness to reduce all the rewards of commitment into monetary equivalents.

What changes here with the possible bridging between SMOs and political parties? By the importance of their resources (money, patronage, policy developments) and their level of institutionalization, political parties, especially when they control power positions, expand and redefine the accessible gratifications of commitment. The very access to the space of political careers reorganizes the map of possible futures. This is clearly visible when yesterday activists or outlaws became important members of the government (the green Fisher in Germany, the ex-critical communist Kouchner in France, Lepper in Poland), or even heads of state (Havel in Hadjiisky's contribution, Lula in Goirand's). Accessing power positions also opens to yesterday's activists the novel power of appointing their ex-struggle companions to the jobs and positions under their control, depending on the peculiarities of the local spoil system or patronage habits. Such recruiting power also means gaining control or influence on yesterday's companions and peers. The development of connexions between social movements and parties also means, especially for activists coming from working-class backgrounds, opportunities of upward mobility that were unthinkable yesterday. Such situations are visible in the trajectories of the activists of the Brazilian PT, elected in local government or federal institutions, or in the topical story of the Polish peasant leader Lepper – studied by Pellen – round-tripping from agricultural unionism to parliament. But the limit of images such as "upward mobility" or "expansion" of the gratification system is its purely quantitative semantic. Bridging movements and parties, moving from street demonstrations or factory meetings to the parliament benches or the mayor's office cannot be reduced to comparative adjective such as "higher" or "bigger." One needs here a qualitative perception of what means changing activists into politicians. More than connecting two worlds of political participation, the process means a change in the rules of the game, the definition of (il)legitimate behaviors. Yesterday's activists enter into a new ecosystem, a new configuration of interdependencies with new actors. Gaining the big black car with chauffeur, lunching with business leaders, or being called Mr. President by deferent ushers may be the experience of a symbolic revolution. Yesterday's activists face new moral dilemmas, new challenges – among which is the Weberian opposition between an ethic of responsibility and the ethic of conviction. But they also enter in this new institutional and ethical space with dispositions, organizational styles (Cefaï, Carrel, Talpin, Eliasoph, & Lichterman, 2012).

A second track explored in Part III studies how the experience of such moves from activism toward politics or jobs sponsored by political godfathers is not always a happy one. Feelings and accusations of betrayal are usual, the practical reflexes and moral norms of the activist would not always fit with the rules of the political field.

What could appear to the academic gaze as an unexpected social escalator could be perceived by ex-activists as a threat, a challenge to their identity or integrity. As Neveu suggests in his contribution, the more protracted, the riskier, and the more able to shake one's initial common sense are activists' experiences, the longer they would remain active in habitus. Part of the answer to the puzzle of Tamayo and Olivier's notion of "resonance," of the long-term effect of movement socialization, could be found here. And "resonance" produces paradoxical effects – very visible in the case of Czech and Slovaks dissenters, but one could as well mention the soviet ones (Vaissié, 1999). Sometimes the qualities and skills that had allowed people to stay at the vanguard of movement activism could suddenly become detrimental or out of tune in party politics. At least two styles of such dispositions could be mentioned here. The Czechoslovak case suggests the impact of what could be coined an aristocratic vision of politics. This aristocratic style of commitment has several origins. It comes from the high level of cultural capital and the habits of theoretical discussion shared in a group whose members are often coming from intellectual professions. But also from the strong desire to preserve moral integrity as a way of managing the harsh experience of downward social mobility. This kind of commitment does not develop cultures of compromise or the group discipline of those "voting in battalions." If it prepares one for the management of a small group's dissensus, it does not prepare one to seduce large audiences. It is not a school of populist rhetoric. This aristocratic vision of politics will transform yesterday's heroes into misfits of the electoral competition.

Leaving the case of Eastern dissenters, a system of dispositions shared by a significant part of the Western generations of '68 was an "anti-institutional" mood (Bourdieu, 1979). This mood was made of reluctance toward the old disciplinarian institutions (army, school, churches, family), of the exhilarating feeling of freedom and boundless opportunities produced by the access to more material and cultural consumptions, to higher education and sexual freedom. Parties were one of the targets of this critical perception. The fact that not much more than 5–10 percent of the "soixante-huitards" from Neveu and Pagis case studies became members of political parties is an interesting indicator here.

A different dimension of the awkwardness of the newcomers in party politics comes from the suspicion, loudly or _sotto voce_ expressed, of their incompetence or illegitimacy. They are easily accused of not being serious or true politicians. In the best case they are perceived as amateurs or electoral accidents promising a quick disappearance. More often they are stigmatized as demagogues or barbarians spoiling the noble art of politics. The case of Lepper and his organization, _Samoobrona_, suggests how this criticisms can even be internalized and lead up to the suicidal tactic of recruiting more legitimate, more respectable candidates far from the initial rural constituency of the organization. No need to say that having both their own resources and no shared history or deep affective commitment with *Samoobrona*, those outsiders would rarely resist long the temptation of leaving the party who bought their social respectability with an MP seat, when another party overbids, offering them the position of junior minister.

If ex-movement activists can be accused of not being real "enough" politicians, the opposite criticism is even more common. Activists recycled into politicians – and the criticism could also be a self-criticism – are suspected of being traitors, selling out their cause for prebends or a good ranking on the election ballot. Moving into the official world of electoral politics, activists would forget their values and ideals. They would be entangled in the games and delights of the small world of politics whose very structure is made to disinhibit ambitions and ruthless careerism. The accusation of treason, of *"récupération"* to use the French phrase, is very powerful for at least three reasons. There is no shortage of empirical cases, in various countries, where ex-leaders of social movement became professional politicians, using the tricks and trades of the job, forgetting their initial commitments. The fear of betraying is also deeply present in the initial experience of the newcomers discovering the rules and habits of the new institutional world of party politics, the complexity of bargaining games often inevitable to progress in policy process. Such feelings of drift, of normative lag, are also endlessly reactivated by the simple process of cooptation among the movement ranks of new participants and partners in the political institutions under the control of the party born from a social movement. Goirand's analysis of the trajectories of ex-activists and trade unionists propelled into politics by the Brazilian PT is here illuminating. Newcomers among the newcomers, these outsiders are in the best position to identify the changes, the possible gentrification of yesterday's movement leadership. Expressing their surprise, gossiping on their leaders' changes, sometimes fascinated by the promises of upward mobility that they discover, these new recruits keep on the agenda the difficult questions of what are treason and loyalty to the movement's cause, to one's individual integrity.

The lesson is clear. Moving from movement logic to party or government logic are not easy processes, nor the simple invention of an art of combining repertoires or reinvesting skills. More exactly, such art feeds feelings of illegitimacy and clumsiness, and suggests the fear of treason, or the concern of homelessness.

How to react to the labeling process that suggests that a background of movement activism is a badge of illegitimacy or something that would not fit with the serious job of politics? The *Samoobrona* case suggests that giving pledges to the institution, over-investing in institutional conformism may not be the best solution. Transforming the stigma into a pride may be a better strategy, as long as it is more than purely cosmetic (wearing blue jeans in the lobbies of the parliament does not produce alternative policies). How to experiment with the paradox of anti-institutional outsiders becoming insiders of the institution (party, local government)? Their heretical dispositions, even their mistrust of officialdom, may work as powerful tools to produce innovations and question the invisible "taken for granted" of routines. How to manage the varied combination of guilt, anxiety, and exhilaration that is often the experience of movement activists entering into the new world of institutional politics ?

The question of the strains or ease of a move toward party politics should be questioned by combining at least four variables. The first one has already been developed: To which degree and under which circumstances acquired dispositions can be reinvested in party politics? Social movements are also a space where activists can learn arts of bargaining and rhetoric skills. They gain know-how to organize campaigns, sometimes to manage the SMO "machine." And such skills and dispositions could be transferred to party work. A second variable is the volume and structure of resources owned by individual activists: What is his/her level of education, social capital? To which degree are the resources linked to the activist moment open (or not) to individual appropriation? A third variable could be connected to the much-debated notion of political opportunity structures. The Moroccan case explored by Hivert and Vairel suggests how the relative opening of an authoritarian political system can redefine the costs, stigmas, and possible outputs opened by a move from movement activism to more partisan investment. Let's finally mention here the existence of moments or cycles of openness and closure in the relation between parties and movements. The seventies and early eighties have been in many European countries moments of proactive action from parties to open their programs and leadership to the claims of actors from the so-called new social movements. A comparable process was visible later in the United States, later again in France, with the regard expressed by the Republican party or the UMP toward Christian movements such as the "moral majority" or the "manif pour tous" (Carnac, 2014).

Finally, the variety of the situations explored in this book invites one to wonder if it would be possible to identify something like ideal-typical trajectories and modes of investment of these blurred spaces between politics and activism, activism as a way of life (Valocchi, 2013), and activism as a livelihood? A complete check-up of the variables ruling the experience of moves between social movement and partisan activism invites one to think in terms of trajectories (Kriesi, 1993). Trajectories should be studied considering the nature of the move in the space of political participation. Shifting from a highly disruptive or radical social movement toward a government party would in most cases trigger an embarrassing reflexive work, a rationalization of one's behavior, in the Weberian and Freudian meanings of this concept. Being coopted by a party to become a central actor of a policy program that applies a reform born from collective action is probably a smoother move.

Valochi (2012) also invites one to question trajectories as subjective experiences, whose nature depends on the social profile of their actors. The same intensity of commitment can be associated to very different structures of feelings and subjective perceptions. Among Vallochi's typologies, one must mention the opposition between several patterns of activism's perceptions and narrative expression. Middle-class activists often think of their experience as a "career" – thus a process of identity work, an exciting move through institutions and experiences. Such perceptions do not produce guilt or shame as the price of upward mobility linked to activism. They do not transform into moral dilemmas the shifts of militant energy from one cause or movement to another. Working-class activists experience more their stories as a "calling." They are the voices and defenders of their communities. Their very identity is rooted in the feeling of "we-ness." Such subjective perception would have a quite different connection to upward mobility, seen as the risk of selling out, of betraying one's social origins. The contradictory perceptions and experiences of the Brazilian PT activists offer a mirror of this difference. Some enjoy the "learning process" of the new experience of institutional politics. Others are unhappy when they see the growing distance between party MPs or members of local governments and the rank and file activists, when they the think of the heroic time of struggles as fading away.

Another way to use trajectories could be questioning the traffic directions. An implicit assumption in most of the research is that the usual movement goes from social movement to political organizations. It is worth questioning the simplicity of such a vision. If they are less usual, the opposite moves, from party to social movement, are worth mapping. Such moves can translate the "invasive" strategies described by Schwartz

(2010), when parties push some of their members to monitor or to take control of social movements. Such behavior has been common among European Communist or Leftist organizations. But Agrikoliansky's study of the French *"Ligue des droits de l'homme"* (2002) also suggests that some party–movement trajectories could express the disillusions and hangovers born from party commitment.

Mapping the directions and meanings of movement–party and party–movement trajectories brings us finally back to the starting point of this development. Using an oversimplified framework, whose aim is more to suggest questions than to supply a satisfying description of changes in political participation, we suggest the metaphor of three generations, at least in many West European countries. The middle of the twentieth century would have been the moment of an almost organic connection between social movements on the one hand (students and workers unions, youth movements structured by Catholic churches in Southern Europe) and parties on the other. The seventies would have given a new significant momentum to such interconnections, the "new social movements" acting also as brokers of new social problems, some of their leaders investing in party politics. One of the major scientific and political stakes of the present moment would then be to understand what looks like a third generation, a growing disconnection and mistrust between parties and social movement. No doubt an exciting research field exists here. What is the reality of such disconnection? How to make sense of its contrasting levels of expression, according to political systems, ideological locations, and class locations? Is this situation a moment of transition in the invention of a "post-democracy"? Should one move from a theory of party-cartel to a theory of post-party politics? Could it be sociologically reasonable to believe that social movements could fill the void created by the crisis of party politics?

FROM SHADES OF RED (OR BLUE) TO SHADES OF GREY

The Ageing of Yesterday's Activists

INTRODUCTION

Richard Flacks

I write this in February 2016, in the midst of the US campaign for president. The current Democratic Party candidates are Hillary Clinton and Bernie Sanders. It's sometimes noticed that both of these had their political starts as participants in the movements of the Sixties. Hillary gained national attention delivering the first student commencement address at Wellesley College in 1969, in which she claimed to speak for her generation's yearning for "human liberation." Bernie, in 1963, got media attention when he led protests at the University of Chicago against the university's complicity in housing segregation in that city. Their public and personal lives in the ensuing half-century were significantly shaped by their generational identity.

To study the "biographical consequences" of movement activism seems inherently valuable. Examining this question makes us aware of the fact that movements are vehicles of not only macro-social change but also of personal development and socialization. Accordingly, assessment of a movement's historical significance involves judgment, not only of its effects on social structures and rules, but of the individual lives that it fosters. As the work of Julie Pagis suggests, individual activists' political initiatives and choices, their efforts to remake professional roles, and their ideological shifts provide evidence at the micro level of the ongoing reverberations of episodes of mass mobilization.

These stories, in addition, provide empirical material for improving our understanding of citizens' capacities for sustained political engagement.

Political activism is, in principle, valued in a democracy – democratic theory assumes that citizen engagement is socially necessary and morally right. But few people are, in day-to-day life, motivated to be so engaged. Olson's "free rider" (Olson, 1974) provides a rationale for disengagement. More fundamental even than the free rider conundrum, I believe, is that the exigencies and demands of everyday life typically outweigh or compete with the demands and attractions of political involvement. Furthermore, on average, people feel themselves incompetent or inadequate for political roles even in formally democratic political cultures (Flacks, 1988).

In important ways, the sociology of social movements has produced a body of work that illuminates the circumstances under which ordinary people mobilize in spite of these sorts of constraints and contradictions. But the structural and situational focus of such social movement studies in recent years has left the social psychological matter of voluntary and sustained political commitment relatively unexamined. The studies offered here help overcome this neglect.

Conventional wisdom has had quite a bit to say about the matter. It regards sustained political commitment as relatively rare and sees those who are so committed as having peculiar psychological attributes. One view sees these attributes as pathological: "True believers" are fanatic, cut off from reality and from ordinary morality. An opposed standpoint sees commitment as rooted in qualities of courage, selflessness, and principle. Accordingly, conventional wisdom appears to doubt a core democratic value. Engagement, necessary for democracy, is, from the conventional point of view, not what most citizens are likely to display.

Studying engagement and its vicissitudes in the biographies of movement activists provides a crucial way to test conventional depictions of political commitment. Those depictions seem based on the notion that commitment is a matter of individual will. Systematic documentation and analysis of the historical, structural, situational, and personal conditions for political commitment provide us with the contexts for activity that conventionally gets labels like "fanatical" or "courageous." Work reported in this chapter provides clues about the conditions for commitment. For example:

- Activist commitment is more likely the more one is relatively free from conventional roles and their demands (e.g. household, family, work). A useful term for this generalization is "biographical availability" (McAdam, 1986). This is an important reason why "youth" is the stage in life when high-risk activism is most likely. Some of the stories told in the studies that follow suggest, however, that activists can organize their everyday lives to be available for activism, e.g. by working as organizers, by finding occupations that provide time and space, or by forms of collective living. "Availability," in short, is not just a situational happenstance or a moment in the life-cycle. It can be proactively enhanced.

- Movement activism and institutionally based activism are not contradictory. In the aftermath of movement upsurge, activists often seek roles in political parties and other political institutions. Such moves need not be seen as an abandonment of movement principles. For one thing, the movement may have fostered an opening of space within established parties and governmental structures – the "cooptation" of movement activists by established structures may be counted as movement success. Moreover, as the movement ebbs, the established political may be seen as a necessary arena for advancing movement goals. Perhaps most commonly, movement organizations, in the aftermath, establish themselves as vehicles for carrying the movement forward. These organizations, in their institutionalizing phase, provide livelihood and regularized leadership roles for movement activists – opportunities for sustaining everyday life in a relatively stable way while serving the movement.
- Established professional and vocational roles can provide a framework for continuing activist commitment. The "human service" professions inherently claim to be resources for ameliorating social dysfunction and advancing enlightenment. Movement activists, as they seek ways to continue commitment, are drawn to such professional roles, often working concertedly to insist that these professions live up to their claims. Such fields as social work, community planning, and all levels of education are examples. Indeed, in the United States, in the seventies, a host of projects aimed at "radicalizing" many professions were launched.
- Movement activism is rarely a momentary episode in a life story. First of all, many activists emerge from families and subcultures that fostered political commitment and particular ideological orientations conducive to it. The studies here didn't investigate the early socialization of activists, but a large literature about the social origins of sixties activists (and some work on other social movements) suggests that many activists, rather than being "converted" to a movement, regard their participation as a natural expression of their identities. The studies here provide strong evidence that, typically, members of the sixties generation were not disenchanted or disillusioned, did not

abandon their youthful ideals to join the "establishment," rediscover the virtues of conventional liberalism, or move from the new left to the new right. The conventional wisdom – that "bank burners grew up to become bankers" – is not a valid generalization (Whalen & Flacks, 1989). There are, to be sure, such life stories. But a virtue of detailed biographical study is to compel a much richer accounting of how ideology, interests, and identities intersect over the life-cycle.

The biographical outcomes of the sixties movements are particularly important for assessing the historical meanings of that period, since one of the central themes of the counterculture, and particularly of the student movement, was the rejection of conventional models of "adulthood." In their youth, sixties activists aspired to live lives that would challenge institutions, question authority, and redefine roles. The fact that the movement claimed to be the crucible for new ways of living and being leads us inescapably to want to know how it all turned out. The "sixty-eighters" are now 68 years old; they have now lived through the life-courses they had vowed to make over. It's, accordingly, rather strange that little research examining those life-courses has been done.

The work reported here helps overcome this deficiency by providing some fairly rich empirical material relevant to the question. But that material is not, for the most part, presented by these authors as reflections on the sixties. Instead, understandably, they situate their work in the wider context of social movement studies in general – and my effort here to draw out some generalizations from their work does the same.

Still, these studies can have the particular value of contributing to understanding of the historical meanings of the "sixties." The subjects of these studies may in their youth have believed they were making revolution – and all, quite soon, had to confront the fact that their revolutionary hopes were quite overblown. One consequence of youthful belief in imminent revolution is that it seems to erase the need to plan one's personal future – imminent revolution would mean that one's personal future will be determined by history. Revolutionism was replaced in the early seventies with a wide range of experiments in countercultural living – undertaken deliberately outside of established occupational structures. We can see in some of the life stories reported here that many such experiments bore fruit in the work and the styles of life that have taken root since.

But I think we can also learn from these studies a rather remarkable thing about the fate of the sixties generation: Many of its members found their life work in the front lines of societal crisis – *doing the jobs necessary to sustain social life and repair the social fabric in the midst of social decay and breakdown.* As schoolteachers, social workers, health professionals, environmental scientists, public administrators, etc. members of the sixties generation made their livelihoods by helping to hold the social order together.

Collectively, sixties activists went on to help lead what sociologists came to call "new social movements." These new movements embodied the generation's youthful hopes – for a just society, but not for "revolution" (as the sixties youth revolt imagined it).

Work such as the research reported here helps illuminate the individual and collective experience of that generation – but one hopes much fuller documentation and reflection on that experience can be done before its members pass from the scene.

I

The Diversity of Activist Outcomes

The Role of Ideology in Shaping Trajectories of Participation

Catherine Corrigall-Brown

Scholars have consistently found that social movement participation can have long-term transformative effects for activists, shaping their careers, families, and ideological commitments for the rest of their lives (Downton and Wehr, 1997; Giugni, 2007; Klatch, 1999). However, previous studies have largely focused on high-risk, high-cost movements on the political left. While this research has been critical for highlighting the potential effects of engagement on individual biographies, it may not be representative of all types of activism. Given that high-risk, high-cost leftist activism constitutes only a small proportion of all social movement organizations and activities, we can question the extent to which these findings generalize to participation as a whole. While there has been considerable focus on the leftist activists of this period, individuals at this time engaged in a diversity of groups on the political left and right. In this chapter, I argue that we must compare individuals across movements in order to assess how the ideological context of engagement shapes the biographical consequences of activism and the trajectory of individual participation over time.

When individuals engage in social movements, they do so within a specific movement and organizational context that shapes their experience of participation. This chapter examines the effect of this organizational context on the later engagement of individuals. In particular, I examine participation in groups on the political left and the political right and assess how these group contexts and the ideologies of the activists themselves shape their later participation. By comparing individuals engaged in social movements in these differing ideological contexts, we can assess the extent to which our understanding of the biographical consequences of activism is related to the leftist context in which it is usually examined.

This chapter will examine three major research questions. First, is an activist's political ideology related to their propensity to later engage in a social movement organization or activity of protest? Second, how is the nature of political engagement different over the life-course for individuals on the political left and political right? Third, what are the implications of these different amounts and forms of engagement among rightists and leftists for social movement causes and campaigns generally?

Two major data sources provide the basis for these analyses. First, I examine the effect of ideology on later participation through the use of a large longitudinal survey of high school seniors in the United States from 1965 until 1997 (N = 1,669). These data allow us to focus on the subset of young people who were active in the movements of the late 1960s and early 1970s (by protesting or engaging in a social movement group in the 1965–1972 period of the survey) and to assess the extent to which their political ideology shaped their participation over the course of their lives. These data help to answer the first research question and understand, at a general level, how ideology is connected to social movement participation over the life-course.

I use qualitative interview data to answer the second research question. I interviewed activists in four groups in the United States who were active in the late 1960s and early 1970s (N = 60): Catholic Workers, United Farm Workers, Concerned Women for America, and a Homeowners Association. Two of these groups are on the political left and two are on the political right. By comparing the individuals involved in these groups, and their participation over time, we can better understand *how* the participation of leftists and rightists might differ over the life-course. This work highlights the important biographical consequences of activism while also emphasizing that the differing modes and contexts of engagement can affect biographical outcomes for individual activists. I conclude with a discussion of the implications of these findings for both individuals and movements for social change.

THE BIOGRAPHICAL CONSEQUENCES OF ACTIVISM

Social movements ebb and flow over time in cycles of protest. The late 1960s and early 1970s was a time of high levels of protests across Europe and North America. The individuals who engaged in these events are the focus of this chapter. Examining their trajectories of participation over time is critical not only for helping us to assess the biographical consequences of activism but also for understanding the social and political impacts of this wave of contention.

Research on the biographical consequences of participating in social movements consistently finds that engagement in social movements can have important, long-term implications for individuals. Much of this literature is based on follow-up studies of the New Left activists of the 1960s. These studies follow individual participants over time periods of up to 20 years after their engagement and assess the biographical and personal consequences of participation (see e.g. Fendrich, 1993; McAdam, 1989; Whalen and Flacks, 1989). All of these studies point to the powerful and enduring impact of engagement on the biographies of participants, both politically and personally.

The political consequences of engagement are two-fold. First, follow-up studies find that activists tend to continue to hold leftist beliefs and continue to define themselves as liberal or radical in political orientation. Second, individuals who join social movements are likely to continue to engage in political organizations and remain active in contemporary movements and other forms of political activity (Klatch, 1999; McAdam, 1988).

There are also important personal consequences of activism. Former activists are concentrated in the teaching and other helping professions at a higher rate than non-activists. They tend to have lower incomes than their age peers, in part because they often have episodic or nontraditional labor force participation. In their personal lives, they are more likely than their age peers to have remained single, married later, or divorced (see Giugni, 2007 for a summary of this work). This research highlights the potential long-term and enduring implications of social movement engagement.

The significant body of work on the biographical consequences of activism focuses on leftist movements of the 1960s and 1970s. While these movements were the bulk of the mobilizations occurring in this period, there was also a significant wave of rightist social movement activity at the time. The long-term consequences of engagement in these rightist movements have not been the focus of extensive study. As a result, we cannot know if the widespread implications of engagement in social movements are generalizable or are a result of the leftist context in which they have been studied.

THE ROLE OF IDEOLOGY

The role of ideology in political participation, including social movement engagement, has been the focus of a wide body of literature. Political ideology has long been understood to be an important element of how people come to participate in social movements. Protest is often seen as a tool for liberals who want to change the political establishment and who feel a need to go beyond the traditional political arena to get their views heard. Research in the United States supports this argument, showing that leftists are more likely than others to report participating in protest (Dalton, 2008; Dalton, Van Sickle, and Weldon, 2010; Hirsch, 1990).

However, later work argues that it may not simply be that those on the left are more likely to engage in social movements and protest. Instead, individuals with stronger ideological commitments on either the left or right are more likely than others to engage in political activity, including protest (Corrigall-Brown, 2011; see also Andersen and Jennings, 2010; Lee, 1997; Muller and Jukam, 1977). It is clear that political ideology is an important precursor of engagement in social movements. However, much less is known about how political ideology shapes participation over time for individual activists.

Despite this general gap, Braungart and Braungart (1991) compare the effects of engagement in 1960s activism for individuals on the political left and right. This research compares leaders of Students for a Democratic Society (SDS, on the political left) and Young Americans for Freedom (YAF, on the political right) in the United States and examines the biographical consequences of activism for these two different groups of participants (Braungart & Braungart, 1991). Braungart and Braungart find that both the leftist SDS and rightist YAF leaders tend to maintain their ideological commitments over time and stay involved in political issues. However, the *ways* that they continued to engage differed. The leftist SDS leaders remained active in a variety of groups over time, ranging from the "Democratic party and local community politics, to public interest groups, to organizing, writing and demonstrating for specific causes such as the environment, women's rights, Jewish revivalism, peace, and an anti-interventionist policy in Central America" (1991, p. 306). The rightist YAF leaders tended to select jobs related to their political beliefs and engage in volunteer work with political groups (such as the Republican party and other conservative groups). In essence, while both the right and left activists maintained their ideological commitments over time, their later engagement differed, in part, because of their different political orientations.

In *Patterns of Protest* (2011), I also find that ideology is not a strong predictor of continued participation – those on the left and right both tend to maintain their ideological commitments and be engaged, in some way, in movements and causes over the life-course (Corrigall-Brown, 2011, 2012). However, my work shows that the nature of these long-term biographical effects of activism is quite different for activists on the left and right. This chapter will further develop this insight and test the role of ideology in the amount and form of later engagement.

The analyses in this chapter are based on two types of data. First, I examine the effect of ideology on later participation through the use of a large longitudinal survey of high school seniors in the United States from 1965 until 1997. This data allow us to understand, at a general level, how ideology and later participation are connected.

Second, I examine the relationship between individual ideology and later engagement through the use of interview data. I interviewed activists in four groups (Catholic Workers, United Farm Workers, Concerned Women for America, and a Homeowners Association) in the United States. Two of these groups are on the political left and two on the political right. By comparing the individuals involved in these groups, and their participation over time, we can better understand *how* the later participation of leftists and rightists differ. We begin with the macro-level survey data.

THE BIG PICTURE: A QUANTITATIVE ANALYSIS OF IDEOLOGY AND ENGAGEMENT

The quantitative data come from a nationally representative longitudinal probability[1] sample of American high school seniors (N = 1,669) with subsequent surveys of the same individuals conducted in 1973, 1982, and

---

[1] To achieve this sample of 1965 high school seniors, a selection of American schools was first made with probability proportionate to size. About nine in ten of the schools selected agreed to take part in the study. Within schools, systematic random samples were taken. In total, 1,669 students were interviewed in 1965, an average of 17 seniors per school. Of those seniors selected, the response rate was over 99 percent. As a result of this sampling procedure, the youth panel is a probability sample of the American high school senior class of 1965.

1997 (N = 934, 56 percent of original sample) (Jennings et al., 2004).[2] I selected only individuals who were active in a social movement group or activity of protest in the period between 1966 and 1972 in order to capture, at a general level, activists of the 1960s and early 1970s.

There are two dependent variables. First, the survey asks about engagement in a social movement or civic group in each period (prior to 1965, 1966–1972, 1973–1982, and 1983–1997). Second, the survey has questions about contentious political activity in each time period with the following questions: have you engaged in a protest, demonstration, march, or rally (prior to 1965, 1966–1972, 1973–1982, and 1983–1997).

The main independent variable of interest is political ideology. It is measured on a scale of 1–7, with 1 indicating politically left. I control for race, gender, and SES. Race was coded as a dummy variable, comparing whites with all other races. Because of the very small number of respondents indicating that they are a race other than white, I could not further differentiate the "other races" category. Gender is coded with males treated as the reference category. Socioeconomic status is coded as working (0), middle (1), and upper class (2) based on the respondent's self-categorization. I also control for two major biographical constraints that might hinder later activism (marriage and having children) (Corrigall-Brown, 2011). Marital status is a dummy variable, with 0 indicating that the respondent has never been married. Having children is also a dummy variable, with those who do not have children as the reference category of 0.

The models presented in Table 1.1 examine only individuals who were active in groups or activities of protest in the 1965–1972 period in order to capture the 1960s and 1970s cohort of activists. Model 1 examines the effects of ideology and the control variables on later participation in social movement groups. Model 2 examines the effects of ideology and the control variables on later participation in acts of protest.

The group engagement model (Model 1) shows that ideology is not related to later engagement. Among individuals active in the 1965–1972 period, those on the political left and right are equally likely to engage in periods of group membership later in life. Women and non-Whites who were active in the 1965–1972 period are more likely than men and Whites to later engage in

[2] The M. Kent Jennings et al. data (2004) are available through the Inter-university Consortium for Political and Social Research through the following catalogue numbers: 1965 (ICPSR07286-v3), 1973 (ICPSR07779), 1982 (ICPSR09553), and 1997(ICPSR04023-v2). I am grateful to Jennings and his colleagues for making these unique data sets publicly available

TABLE 1.1 *Number of periods of engagement in groups and protest over the life-course**

	Model 1 GROUP ENGAGEMENT (Number of periods active)		Model 2 PROTEST ENGAGEMENT (Number of periods active)
Sex 0 = men 1 = women	0.279 (0.111)	*	0.004 (0.106)
Race 0 = white 1 = all other	0.853 (0.193)	***	0.661 (0.181)
SES 0 = working 1 = middle 2 = upper	0.022 (0.070)		0.254 (0.069)
Married 0 = no 1 = yes	0.243 (0.215)		0.416 (0.204)
Children 0 = no 1 = yes	−0.010 (0.170)		−0.268 (0.146)
Ideology 1 = Left 7 = Right	−0.003 (0.055)		−0.159 (0.048)
Constant	1.618 (0.299)	***	2.578 (0.275)
R²	0.129 0.103		0.128 0.112

* Sub-sample for the analysis is individuals active in groups or protest in 1966–1972 period.

social movement groups. Social class and biographical factors (marriage and children) are not related to later group engagement in this model.

In Model 2, ideology is a significant predictor of later participation in acts of protest for those active in the 1965–1972 period. Individuals who are one point to the political right on the ideological spectrum participate in 0.159 fewer periods of protest, on average. This means that an individual who is a 7 on the left-right scale will, on average, participate in one fewer period of protest than a person who is a 1 on the left-right scale. In addition, in this model, non-Whites are more likely to later participate in activities of protest as are those with higher SES. Individuals who are married are also more likely to engage in acts of protest, although having children suppresses engagement.

These models highlight the different long-term effect that activism can have for individuals on the left and right. Leftists and rightists are both engaging in groups with the same frequency; however, those on the political left are much more likely to participate in protest activities over the life-course.

These results lead us to wonder if the types of group memberships leftists and rightists have may differ. Perhaps these activists are engaging in the same *number* of groups, but those on the political right are participating in a more passive way. They are, therefore, still reporting the same number of engagements in groups, but this engagement is not leading to protesting or other movement activities. Leftists are equally likely as rightists to remain part of groups, but are much more likely to participate in protest events. Does this mean that the civic engagement of the late 1960s "activated" leftists more than rightists? *How* are the biographical consequences of activism different for these two groups?

THE MICRO-CONTEXT OF PARTICIPATION: IDEOLOGY AND ENGAGEMENT

In order to examine, in more detail, *how* individuals on the left and right participate in social movements over time, I analyze in-depth interviews with individuals in four social movement groups. First, the United Farm Workers (UFW) is an organization that seeks to organize and promote the rights of farm laborers. Second, I examine a small Catholic Workers (CW) community in a Midwestern city that is involved in both anti-war mobilization and programs for the homeless. Third, Concerned Women for America (CWA) is a women's group that engages in a variety of issues on the religious right. Finally, the Homeowners Association (HA) attempts to limit the number of homeless in their city and promote homeowner rights. The first two groups are politically left (UFW and CW) and the second two are politically right (CWA and HA).

I selected fifteen individuals who participated in each of these groups in 1970 (for the UFW and CW) or 1980 (for the CWA or HA) for a total of sixty interviews.[3] The interview was composed of questions about initial

---

[3] I created the sample of Catholic Workers by interviewing all but one of the individuals who were actively involved in the community in 1970–1971 (my sample time frame). I had two methods of contacting past participants in Concerned Women for America. I randomly selected ten women who were listed as prayer action chapter leaders in the

engagement, participation, and disengagement (if this occurred) from this social movement organization. I also traced the individual's participation in other social movement organizations and activities, as well as other personal and professional changes, over their life-course.[4] The interviews lasted from 45 minutes to 4 hours and were tape recorded and transcribed in their entirety. They were initially coded with Atlas.ti software for major theoretical themes and then were hand coded for further refinement.

Comparing the survey and interview samples

In order to assess the representativeness of my interview sample, I compare it with the national sample I analyzed in the first portion of this chapter (Jennings and Stoker, 2004). This large panel sample follows individuals from 1965, when they were high school seniors, to 1997. As a result, the Jennings sample is approximately the same age as my interview sample. In general, my sample of social movement participants closely mirrors the random national sample both demographically and biographically. In particular, the national sample is very similar to my sample in terms of marital status and childbearing. My sample, however, slightly over-represents Catholics (as one of my groups was Catholic) but has similar levels of religiosity. My sample is also slightly more educated. In general, the participation of my sample over time is very similar to that of the national population, although the national sample is marginally more likely to disengage. This is partly because of my selection of two groups that required relatively high levels of commitment initially, the Catholic Workers and the United Farm Workers. For sociodemographic information about my respondents, and a comparison of my sample with the census sample at the time, see Appendix C.

---

group newsletter. I also contacted a state chapter leader and snowball sampled from this woman to four others. The UFW interviewees were all volunteers who lived for a time at La Paz in 1970–1971. I snowball sampled 15 individuals from the 175 to 200 people who lived at La Paz at the time. For the Homeowners Association, I interviewed members of the original board of directors, which was composed of all interested individuals who attended the first meeting of the group in 1980. I interviewed fifteen of these nineteen individuals.

4 Biographical reconstruction and memory failure are always a problem in retrospective interviewing. A number of techniques were employed to protect against these biases. To address the accuracy of recall, I structured my questions around past events rather than past attitudes because memories of events are more reliable (Markus, 1986; Schacter, 1996). In addition, research shows that more salient, less repetitive events are remembered with more accuracy (Beckett et al., 2000; Scott and Alwin, 1998: 114). Therefore, I asked respondents about memorable life events, such as the birth of a child or marriage, and then asked if this event had occurred before or after pivotal participation events. This made it possible to assess more clearly the temporal order of events.

TABLE 1.2 *The continuity of engagement in four groups*

	Average Years in "Activism"	Engaged in a group or activity after 1980 (%)
Leftist Ideology	13.8	72
Rightist Ideology	6.5	23

* Based on interview data (N = 60)

All of my interview respondents remained consistent in their political ideology over time. This was equally true of respondents on the left and right. As Patricia, a leftist in the Catholic Workers, explains "I remain interested in all the things that I was interested in 35 year ago. More than ever I think that they are important, critical issues. I continue to believe that environmentalism as a movement is bankrupt if it does not consider issues of justice and equity. So my own politics are not too different from where they were before, I have just refined what I think. And where I want to put my energy." Activists on the political right were equally likely to have a consistent ideology over time, generally being raised by parents with rightist ideologies and maintaining these beliefs over the course of their lives.

Despite the fact that both leftists and rightists had similar continuity in their ideology over time, the *form* of their engagement differed notably by political ideology. Looking at the interview data at a general level, in Table 1.2, we can compare the average number of years that the participants on the left and right engaged in social movements and protests over the life-course. On average, those who were involved in leftist groups and/ or who defined themselves as leftists were involved in the social movement of study for 13.8 years, while those on the political right were active for only 6.5 years. Leftists were involved more than twice as long, on average, than rightists. In addition, while only 23 percent of those on the right later engaged in another social movement group, a full 72 percent of those on the left did so.

In addition to the length and continuity of participation, activists on the left and right also engaged in very different profiles of participation. Those on the political left were much more likely to select jobs based on their ideological commitments. For example, Cynthia works as a lawyer and describes her work as "labour, education, housing, landlord-tenant- ... I would say about a third on my practice is pro-bono dealing with the working poor – farmworkers and others" (UFW, left). Mark, another lawyer who had been involved with the United Farm Workers, also dedicated half of his working hours to the farmworker movement on a pro-bono basis for 10 years after he left full-time work for the union. James and Sylvia, a couple who had joined the UFW together but had to leave when Sylvia became ill, started a series of Cesar Chavez service clubs. These clubs worked to educate the public about the farm worker movement and the problems associated with migrant farm labor. These employment trajectories were clearly tied to their leftist ideologies.

The Catholic Workers, also on the left, were equally likely to make career decisions based on their activism. Jeremy explicitly stated that "my occupational choices were shaped by my engagement with the CW." CW volunteers became social workers, teachers, housing specialists, and priests in order to further their leftist ideological commitments.

The significance of these later jobs, tied to their leftist ideology, was in the connections these jobs facilitated for activists. These jobs kept the leftist activists of the 1960s and 1970s in this sample in touch with others and facilitated their reengagement in later protest. Almost three quarters of the leftist activists I interviewed were involved in later protest and this was, often, a direct result of their workplace ties.

Current protest engagement was widespread among the leftist activists in the sample and these individuals protested for a wide range of causes. Phil engaged in seven or eight protests a year for issues ranging from resisting the Iraq war to supporting same-sex marriage (CW, left). Arnold had been at a protest event the day before our interview focusing on US policy in Latin America (CW, left). Margaret attended yearly Summit of the Americas protests and stood vigil outside of the prison each time there was an execution (CW, left). Chris and Neal (CW) were both active in anti-war protests and John rallied against Coors beer for their anti-union stands (UFW, left). The leftist activists did engage in groups; however, a much larger percentage of them participated in protest activities.

This picture of later activism differed notably from the later engagement of those on the political right. Those on the political right were much more likely than those on the left to be members of social movement groups. Often this membership came as the result of loose coalitions between their original group and other groups on the political right or through connections made in religious institutions. However, this engagement tended to be mostly symbolic – while they were members and often paid dues to these groups, they did not participate actively in meetings, protest events, or campaigns. This sort of "checkbook" or nominal activism is quite different in nature from the later participation of those on the political left, who were not as likely to be in groups, but actively engaged in protests and other contentious political activities.

This engagement pattern is illustrated by Joanne, a member of CWA (right), when she says "I am a member of other public policy organizations ... I get mail from and we support in a small way groups like Family Research Council and the American Family Association and Focus on the Family, and other organizations like that that also deal in public policy." Christine has a similar pattern of engagement in a variety of groups at a low level of involvement. She describes her involvement in other groups as "at a very low level of commitment. One of the things that I do as the state director is work with other pro-family groups in the state. I have joined the state chapter of the Eagle Forum and I have joined the state Society for Human Life and the Family Foundation. Because we all kind of work together and it is just a way of acknowledging the importance of the things that they do and getting on their mailing list and email list so I know what they are doing. So it is kind of solidarity" (CW, right).

Penny explains that "we often work together with other groups. As far as supporting and joining, I do support some of the pro-life groups and we work in kind of loose coalitions. This year we had the marriage amendment that we were trying to get passed and we had quite a diversity of groups, home-schoolers, the Catholic conference, campus for life, some of the economic groups, conservative economic groups that are working with us ... We do that a lot" (CWA, right).

In essence, those on the political right had a higher number of more casual memberships later in life. While employment tied those on the left to causes over time, church participation worked as the mechanism that informed those on the right about later social movement engagement. Sally illustrates the role of the church in connecting her activism: "I joined an Association for Life organization, a professional women's fellowship and other groups that I learned about through my church." However, for Sally and others on the political right, the nature of this engagement was very group focused and tended to involve little contentious political activity.

DISCUSSION AND CONCLUSION

The end of the 1960s and early 1970s was a period of active and dramatic protests across Europe and North America. Examining what happened to the activists engaged in these events is critical to our understanding of both the biographical consequences of activism and the larger ebb and

flow of movements and causes over time. This chapter examines the
different trajectories individuals on the left and right took after engagement in the 1960s and 1970s. Through the use of quantitative survey data
following activists from 1965 until 1997 and qualitative interview data
with individuals in four social movement groups, we can come to better
understand the impact of ideology on engagement over the life-course.

The first main finding is that ideology is not related to one's propensity
to later engage in social movement groups. The survey data show that
those who were active in the late 1960s and early 1970s in social movements on both the left and right were equally likely to participate in a
social movement organization later in life. However, individuals on the
political left were much more likely to later engage in acts of protest, such
as demonstrating, marching, and other contentious political activities.
This macro-level analysis demonstrates that, while those on both the left
and right may be continuing to engage in social movements, the format of
this engagement differs over time.

The qualitative interview data allow us to examine these differences in
more detail. Through comparing individuals on the left and right who
were active in the late 1960s and early 1970s, we can see that the
character of their engagement differed. Individuals on the political left
(in the Catholic Workers or United Farm Workers, in this analysis) were
much more likely to select their jobs based on their ideology. They tended
to choose to work as teachers, social workers, lawyers working with the
poor or on housing issues, and in other professions that are connected to
their leftist activism. These jobs then became an avenue through which
they were later remobilized to social movements. In addition, the character of their later engagement was very activity focused. Many of them,
even if no longer active in groups, were engaged and consistent protesters.
They tended to attend and participate in far more protest events that those
on the political right.

The individuals interviewed who had engaged on the political right
(the Concerned Women for America and the Homeowners Association, in
this analysis) tended to develop (or maintain) close ties with their
churches over time. These religious organizations were often the route
through which they were remobilized to later social movement engagement. While the nature of their engagement later in life was very group
focused, their ties to groups tended to be loose. They were listed on
membership rosters and even sometimes paid dues, but rarely attended
events with these groups.

All of the individuals I interviewed maintained their ideological commitments over the life-course and many remained active in movements. However, the form of that engagement was very different for those on the left and the right, with the leftists being active in protest and those on the right maintaining loose affiliations with groups. These different profiles of engagement have implications for both the individuals and for social movement causes and campaigns.

At the macro-level, these different patterns of engagement can help to account for the differing forms of later activism on the left and right. The political right has tended to be more active in institutional politics and lobbying. This is easy to understand based on the character of the involvement of the rightists in this study – they are apt to sign up for groups and give money, but unlikely to attend protest events on the street. As a result, lobbying and electoral politics make sense for this constituency. Those on the political left are much less likely to join groups, but will show up for dramatic events. This has been the general shape of political leftist politics, particularly mobilizations like Occupy. Occupy was clearly not group focused (perhaps even anti-group) but required active engagement in protest events.

By comparing the participation of activists over time with differing ideologies, we can come to a better understanding of the biographical consequences of activism. This analysis also helps us to assess the extent to which our understanding of these consequences is related to the leftist context in which they are usually studied. These relationships can help us to make sense of the nature of politically left and right politics over time.

Appendix A Comparison of Total Sample and Participants in Contentious Political Action*

		Nonparticipants		Participants only**	
		Mean	Percent	Mean	Percent
Ideology					
Political Ideology	1=Left; 7=Right	3.897		3.766	
		(0.987)		(1.484)	
Resources					
Income	1997 dollars	32492.56		47970.65	
		(20524.9)		(22321.9)	
Postsecondary education	(0 – 7+ years)	0.938		1.398	
		(1.683)		(2.013)	
		(2.674)		(1.170)	
Biographical availability					
Marital status	Never married		6.3		10.4
	Has been married		93.8		89.6
Children	Never had children		16.8		28.4
	Had children		83.2		71.6
Demographic					
Gender	Female		41.9	52.3	
	Male		58.1	47.7	
Race	White		96.6	91.2	
	Black		2.4	7.6	
	Other		1.0	1.2	

* Data Source: Jennings Survey Data
** Individuals who participated in an act of protest or social movement organization in one or more periods.
Numbers in parentheses are standard deviations.

Appendix B Interview Sample Information

	Pseudonym	Gender	Age	Occupation	Years in focal group
Catholic Workers					
1	Brenda	Female	66	Nun	4
2	Patricia	Female	55	Lab technician	14
3	Phil	Male	55	Social worker	4
4	Nancy	Female	70	Nurse	36
5	Daniel	Male	67	Priest	22
6	Jeremy	Male	62	Shop owner	14
7	Arnold	Male	57	Librarian	3
8	Janet	Female	68	ESL teacher	20
9	Sean	Male	81	Judge	15
10	Margaret	Female	63	Nurse	16
11	John	Male	53	Carpenter	2
12	Dennis	Male	68	Social worker	2
13	Chris	Male	53	Social worker	15
14	Harriet	Female	57	Editor	5
15	Neal	Male	53	Nonprofit	10
Concerned Women for America					
1	Joanne	Female	57	Stay at home	23
2	Christine	Female	55	Consultant	20
3	Sally	Female	51	Stay at home	20
4	Penny	Female	63	Stay at home	18
5	Judy	Female	51	Stay at home	10
6	Helen	Female	80	Social work	1
7	Rebecca	Female	68	Stay at home	6 mo.
8	Shirley	Female	50	Stay at home	3 mo.

(*continued*)

(*continued*)

	Pseudonym	Gender	Age	Occupation	Years in focal group
9	Betty	Female	61	Teacher	2
10	Lisa	Female	76	Stay at home	6 mo.
11	Ellen	Female	62	Teacher	6 mo.
12	Irene	Female	81	Manager	1
13	Connie	Female	70	Stay at home	2
14	Ann	Female	65	Stay at home	3
15	Virginia	Female	60	Stay at home	1

United Farm Workers

1	Joan	Female	73	Farm worker
2	David	Male	56	Media consultant
3	Anthony	Male	59	Union organizer
4	Tom	Male	63	Lawyer
5	Charlie	Male	72	Nonprofit
6	Andrew	Male	58	Consultant
7	Valerie	Female	64	Social worker
8	Kevin	Male	61	Union organizer
9	Karen	Female	52	Social worker
10	Cynthia	Female	57	Lawyer
11	Mark	Male	53	Lawyer
12	Teresa	Female	48	At UFW
13	Bert	Male	70	Priest
14	James	Male	65	Education
15	Sylvia	Female	64	Real estate

Homeowners Association

1	Amy	Female	59	Stay at home
2	Diana	Female	70	Manager
3	Polly	Female	69	Manager
4	Robert	Male	62	Lawyer
5	Jimmy	Male	65	Doctor
6	Lynn	Female	51	Stay at home
7	Peggy	Female	75	Stay at home
8	Vicki	Female	71	Entrepreneur
9	Sherry	Female	77	Stay at home
10	Charlotte	Female	55	Teacher
11	Ruth	Female	61	Lawyer
12	Anna	Female	46	Teacher
13	Darlene	Female	80	Sales
14	Henry	Male	75	Architect
15	Kenneth	Male	47	Engineer

Appendix C Interview Sample Characteristics by Group

	Catholic Workers	Concerned Women for America	United Farm Workers	Homeowners Association	Total (four groups)
Gender					
Female	40% (6)	100% (15)	40% (6)	73% (11)	65% (38)
Education					
Less than high school	7% (1)	–	–	–	2% (1)
High school graduate	7% (1)	27% (4)	7% (1)	20% (3)	15% (9)
Some college	–	20% (3)	13% (2)	–	8% (5)
College degree	33% (5)	33% (5)	40% (6)	40% (6)	37% (22)
Advanced degree	53% (8)	20% (3)	40% (6)	40% (6)	38% (23)
Occupation					
Homemaker	–	66% (10)	–	27% (4)	23% (14)
Manual labor	7% (1)	–	7% (1)	–	3% (2)
Service	7% (1)	–	–	7% (1)	3% (2)
Professional	87% (13)	33% (5)	93% (14)	66% (10)	70% (42)
Marital status					
Single	30% (3)	–	13% (2)	7% (1)	10% (6)
Married	53% (8)	73% (11)	73% (11)	80% (12)	70% (42)
Divorced/ separated	27% (4)	–	13% (2)	13% (2)	13% (8)
Widowed	–	27% (4)	–	–	7% (4)
Has children	66% (10)	100% (15)	87% (13)	60% (9)	78% (47)
Religion					
None	33% (5)	–	–	33% (5)	17% (10)

	Catholic Workers	Concerned Women for America	United Farm Workers	Homeowners Association	Total (four groups)
Catholic	60% (9)	–	80% (12)	7% (1)	37% (22)
Mainline Protestant	7% (1)	27% (4)	7% (1)	40% (6)	20% (12)
Evangelical Protestant	–	73% (11)	13% (2)	7% (1)	23% (14)
Jewish	–	–	–	13% (2)	3% (2)
Other	–	–	–	–	–
Mean Age					
At time of interview[b]	61.87	63.33	61.00	64.20	62.60
Range	(53–81)	(50–81)	(48–73)	(46–80)	(46–81)
In 1970 or 1980[c]	25.87	37.33	25.00	38.20	31.60

[a] Mainline and evangelical Protestants are not distinguishable in the national sample.

[b] Interviews were conducted in 2005.

2

Biographical Impacts of Activism in the French "May '68"

Julie Pagis[1]

Conducting research on biographical impacts of participation in the events of May–June 1968 in France means delving into the events' role in processes of political socialization (Tackett, 2006) and renewing study of the formation of intellectual and political generations. For Karl Mannheim, the driving interconnection of a "generational ensemble" lies in its members' exposure to the social and intellectual symptoms of a *dynamic destabilization* (Mannheim, 1952). But to what extent were the diverse participants in the events of May-June '68 destabilized, and how to account for their possible influence on their trajectories? Do they still carry, 35 years later, traces of their past engagements? And if so, how to objectify them?

If these interrogations as yet have but a few responses in France, they are nonetheless in line with Anglophone literature on the biographical consequences of participation in social movements (Andrews, 1991; Valocchi, 2013). They join work begun in the late 1970s questioning what came of student protesters in the United States (Fendrich, 1977; DeMartini, 1983; Marwell, Aiken & Demerath, 1987; Whalen & Flacks 1989 see McAdam, 1999 for reviews). Most are quantitative studies that agree on the persistence of political behaviors particular to the studied former-activist population in comparison to nonengaged populations: "former activists [are] more likely than non-activists to define themselves as politically 'radical,' espouse leftist political attitudes, eschew traditional

[1] I would like to thank Juliette Rogers for the translation of this chapter.

career and family commitments, and remain active in movement politics."
(McAdam, 1988, p. 213). Yet save for a few exceptions (McAdam, 1988;
Whalen & Flacks, 1989; Jennings, 2002), these works are "less interested
in the very process by which movements act as socializing agents than by
its long term effects" (Fillieule, 2013, p. 971). In addition, as "little effort
has been made to examine the possibility that the personal consequences
of activism may vary for different groups of activists" (Van Dyke, McA-
dam, & Wilhelm, 2000, p. 161), these works do not discern intragenera-
tional differences. Such differences appear, however, as soon as one
changes the scale of analysis and starts being attentive to the different
socializing effects of the event. I aim to analyze the oft-overlooked relationships between activists' social backgrounds, the forms taken by their
activism, and its impacts on their biographies after the activist moment,
based on my doctoral research on the biographical impacts of activism in
May '68 (presented in Box 2.1).

Box 2.1 The study's corpus and materials

The materials employed in this chapter come from a study conducted with
170 families in which at least one parent participated in the events of May '68
in France (Pagis, 2018). The corpus was constructed based on the second
generation. Using student records, I found the "children of '68ers" educated in
two experimental primary schools over the period 1973–1985. These schools
participated in a widespread post-May '68 movement critiquing social
relations of domination by subverting pedagogical relationships. This unique
point of entry into the field selected for '68ers (*soixante-huitards*) who had
transferred anti-institutional and activist dispositions to the familial and
academic spheres, putting them into practice.

  If this sampling method doubtlessly over-selected for certain kinds of
'68ers, it did allow working around various methodological problems
common to studies on biographical consequences of activism (Giugni, 2007,
pp. 499–502). Other than allowing a relatively significant sample size
(170 families), approaching the subject through their children, more than
35 years after the events, allows access to a great diversity of '68er
trajectories (in terms of age, social background, pre-1968 forms of
politicization, etc.) and is especially appropriate for tracking down those
who disengaged in the intervening years.

  Two questionnaires, one sent to former pupils and the other to their ex-'68er
parents, comprise the quantitative part of the study. Of the 666 questionnaires
sent, 350 were returned, 182 from "parents" (those mobilized in this article)

and 168 from "students." This is a return rate of 53 percent, which is relatively high in light of the length of the questionnaire (nearly 250 questions).[2]

A parallel study was conducted in a portion of these families diversifying parental activist profiles, social backgrounds, ages, post-'68 professional and personal life changes, and other variations as much as possible. I conducted eighty-nine interviews – fifty-one with former '68ers and thirty-eight with children of '68ers – between 2004 and 2008.

Collecting narratives of practices and recollections of May–June 1968 more than thirty years after the fact confronts the investigator with the limits of memory and the challenge of biographical reconstruction. Various means were put in place to deal with, work around, or analyze this assemblage of interpretive layers and allow controlled use of life stories. First of all, these *ex-post facto* reconstructions partly reflect the meaning and place informants retrospectively give to May '68 in their trajectories. Next, crossing different points of view in the same family proved to be effective: comparing interview data with questionnaire responses by the same people – or by their (ex-) partners or children – thus allowed statistical re-enforcement of the observations.

In line with work studying the political futures of activist cohorts compared to their nonengaged contemporaries (Fendrich & Lovoy, 1988; McAdam, 1988, 1989) and questioning the persistence of a "collective identity" in radical feminists (Whittier, 1997), this chapter aims to show the repercussions of May '68 activism on interviewees' political and professional trajectories.

To highlight the plurality of the types of trajectory touched by the events of '68, I will articulate quantitative and qualitative approaches in the two parts of the article, devoted respectively to political and professional impacts of participation in May '68. The statistical approach will be used in both phases to deconstruct the commonly used but misleadingly homogenizing category of "the '68 generation" by putting types of biographical impact in relation with informants' traits. I show that if the event destabilizes participants, its effects are not mechanical and are dependent on trajectories anterior to the event as well as the repertoires

---

[2] In comparison, in Doug McAdam's Freedom Summer (FS) study (1988), 556 questionnaires were sent by mail and 348 replies were returned, of which 212 were former FS participants and 118 were FS "no-shows" (that is, subjects who had asked to participate in FS but who ended up not doing it).

of action (Tilly, 1986) invested in during May '68. The analysis of life stories will allow us to better see the processes through which activism produces effects on individual trajectories. More than a simple complementarity of two approaches – which relate to scales of analysis, registers of demonstration, and different viewpoints – the articulation that I propose is the confrontation of different kinds of sociological objectification (statistical and life history) in the same corpus of informants. This avoids using life stories merely as illustrations or examples, allowing a greater insistence on crossed analysis's contributions to the reciprocal enhancement, or even correction, of the two approaches. In so doing the article engages with and contributes to the discussion on "measuring mechanisms of contention" (McAdam, Tarrow, & Tilly, 2008).

POLITICAL TRAJECTORIES SHAPED BY PARTICIPATION IN MAY '68

Before analyzing its effects I would like to define what I mean by "participation in May '68." In order to select actors having participated to various degrees in events of the time, from the casual protestor to the most engaged, I opted for a wide definition of the concept of participation.[3] This avoids imposing *a priori* an arbitrary definition of "'68ers" and the exclusion of less audible or visible registers of participation (feminine in particular), while favoring the after-the-fact development of a typology of ways of participating in the events. Lastly, this choice also allowed me to compare biographical impacts according to the intensity of participation, as we shall see.

The Political Event at the Origin of Collective Entries into Activism

Only 44 percent of informants (N = 182) had activist precedents prior to the events of May '68, while nearly 70 percent say they continued activist activities in the years after: this difference is an initial, rudimentary way of highlighting the political crisis' role as catalyst for entry into activism.

But these numbers hide differences, especially in activist pasts: 83 percent of those who made their entry into the activist field before May '68 would continue activist activities in the following years, as opposed to

---

[3] Participation in demonstrations in favor of the movement at the time and/or in political meetings over the months of May–June 1968 were the minimal criteria for inclusion in the corpus.

54 percent of those who hadn't been activists before. The simple cross-tabulation reveals distinct forms of political socialization from the event, according to previously accumulated activist resources. But a process of dynamic destabilization also relies on the terms of participation in the event, so let's cross the intensity of participation[4] with whether or not they continued activist activities in the months following the events (Figure 2.1).

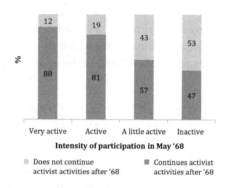

FIGURE 2.1 Exposure to the event and pursuit of activist activities

These results confirm the hypothesis, but behind their apparent obviousness they hide a double reality. Indeed, the intensity of participation in events is very clearly correlated to the probability of continuing activist activity in the following months or years for the first-time activists, while it is much less so for the others (Figure 2.2).

This seems logical, but objectifying it prevents us from falling into mechanical and overly general interpretations of the role of events in the political socialization process. Put another way, we cannot understand what activism produces without a joint analysis of what produced it. And to do so, factor analysis is particularly appropriate because it allows putting types of impact of activism into relation with a variety of variables characterizing informants.

---

[4] To account for the intensity of engagement, I built a variable based on questions addressing the frequency of participation: in demonstrations and general assemblies in May '68, as well as ten other activities (writing tracts, postering, attending clashes with the forces of order, occupying universities or factories, attending political meetings, etc.). A number of points were then attributed to each modality of the concerned questions to obtain a numeric variable, which was then recoded in four modalities.

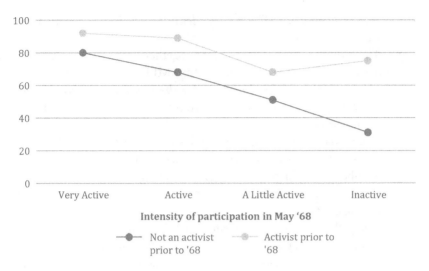

FIGURE 2.2 Percentage of informants continuing activist activities after '68

What Kinds of Activism in the Post-1968 Years?

In which forms of engagement would first-time activists invest in the years after the May'68 movement? Do they spark new struggles, or do they invest in preexisting organizations? What do their elders do, who in some cases had already been active for nearly a decade? To characterize the forms of activism in which informants invested between 1968 and 1974, I recoded the replies to the open question addressing their activist activities subsequent to May '68, as seen later in the chapter. Among those who continued activist activities after the events, I distinguished five modalities corresponding to primary activist activities:

1. The modality "extreme left and anarchist" concerns activists engaged in Anarchist, Trotskyist, and Maoist organizations (categories bundled together because each was too small for quantitative analysis[5]).
2. The modality "unionism" brings together informants whose main activist involvement is in union engagement, in the CFDT (*The*

---

[5] This category bundles activists who in 1968 were to the left of the PCF, which accused them of being "leftists."

French Democratic Work Confederation) or CGT (*General Work Confederation*).

3. The modality "feminism" groups together women whose primary activism is centered on feminism: MLF (*Women's Liberation Movement*), MLAC (*Movement for the Freedom of Abortion and Contraception*), etc. Another variable more widely includes all "feminist sympathizers."

4. The modality "non-organizational activism" assembles informants declaring numerous activist activities 1968–1974, but without membership in a political organization (participation in feminist or anti-nuclear demonstrations, participation in the Larzac mobilizations,[6] etc.)

5. Lastly the modality "activism in a left-leaning political party" is composed of activists in the PCF (*French Communist Party*) and PSU *(Unified Socialist Party)* who, though not sharing the same ideology, exhibit a left-wing partisan activism.

To account for these different engagements, I conducted a factor analysis integrating the variables that might have been influential on this phase of the activist trajectory. After having tested the significance of different factors (by cross-tabulation and Chi-square calculations), the following active variables were retained: sex, age, social background, having been an activist prior to May '68 or not, status in '68 (employee or student), the intensity of participation in events, political position in May '68,[7] having had a "back to land" experience, having lived in a commune, having participated in the Larzac mobilization, and the dominant form of activism between 1968 and 1974.[8]

First let's look at how the two axes composing the factor diagram[9] are composed (*cf.* Figure 2.3). Sex, age, employment status in '68, and the

---

[6] A mobilization starting in 1971 opposing the commandeering of a large portion of the Larzac plateau for the extension of a military training camp that took on a "back-to-the-land" dimension.

[7] Variable recoded in five modalities: "leftist" (including Trotskyists and Maoists), "PCF," "PSU," "UNEF-High school" (grouping UNEF (*Union Nationale des Etudiants de France*) and high-school activism), and "autogestion-feminist."

[8] Informants are distributed among the six modalities in the following proportions: "not activist" (33 percent), "unionism" (17 percent), "extreme left" (16 percent), "feminism/feminist" (7 percent), "non-institutional activism" (18 percent), "PC/PSU" (9 percent).

[9] The first axis represents 14 percent of the total inertia of the cloud of points, and the second 12.5 percent. The number of active modalities retained in the factor analysis being high, the cumulative percentage of the first two axes is highly satisfactory.

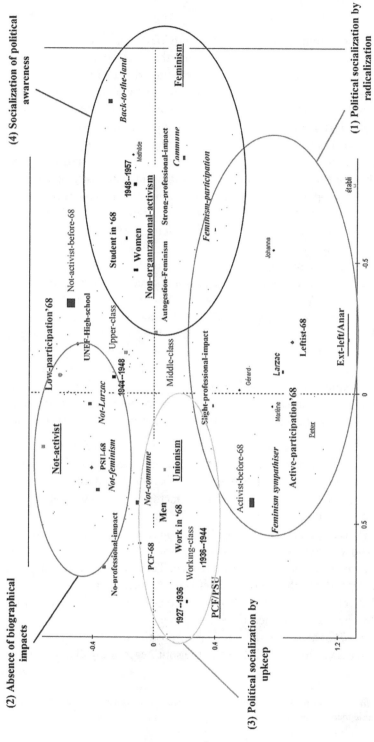

FIGURE 2.3 Political impacts of activism in May '68

69

degree of institutionalization of activist activities prior to '68 are the main variables contributing to the x-axis. This then puts the corpus's older men, who were working in 1968 and active in structured political organizations on the eve of the events of May–June '68 (west in the diagram), in opposition to the younger women in the corpus, students in May '68, investing in less-institutionalized forms of activism afterward (east).

The y-axis is structured by variables relating to activist experience and intensity (the two variables that contribute the most to this axis being the fact of having been an activist prior to 1968 and the intensity of activism in '68). It thus opposes informants who had never been activists prior to 1968 and whose participation in the events was not very intense (north in the diagram) to those having had prior activist experience who were active participants in the events.

To recap (and simplify): Each informant has one position on the factor diagram, on which the x-axis indicates *the degree of institutionalization of activism* in the years after May '68, and the y-axis indicates *the intensity of activism in May '68*. This factor diagram can be considered to represent a protest space in the first half of the 1970s. Next, the focus must be shifted to the subpopulations of informants occupying spatially close locations in the diagram to explain their similarities and to account for the variations in their politicization consequent to their activism in May '68. Four main subpopulations emerge, corresponding to the four main types of political socialization brought about by this participation.

(1) The first, in the south of the diagram, is characterized by significant political impacts caused by what I called a *political socialization by radicalization*: activism in extreme left organizations in the early 1970s, becoming an *établi* in a factory,[10] participation in the Larzac movement, etc. It includes informants of both sexes, between 20 and 24 years old in 1968, predominantly students, who participated quite actively in the events of May '68 (most having had prior activist experience). These activists are thus characterized by their political leftism. Among them, I distinguish between those with pre-1968 experience and first-time activists. Indeed, for the former, the events provoked a *political socialization by reinforcement* of their activist dispositions. This is, for example, the case of Johanna, located in the south-east of the diagram. Born

---

[10] "*Établis*" are students who got jobs as factory workers in order to prepare revolution alongside the working class.

in the United States in 1948, she is the daughter of a university instructor and an actor, both of them Jewish and Communist. She grew up in the United States, protested against the Vietnam War, and upon arrival in Paris in 1966 joined the CVN (*National Vietnam Committee*, Trotskyist). She signed up with the JCR *(Revolutionary Communist Youth)* at its creation (1967), where she was very active in May–June 1968, then became a permanent member of the newspaper *Rouge*[11] in 1970, active in the OCI *(Internationalist Communist Organization)* in the late 1970s, all the while being an activist in the MLF. On the other hand, for those who have had nearly no activist experience prior to May '68, the events will prompt a *political socialization by conversion* to activism. This was the case for Gérard (in the south of the diagram, slightly east of the y-axis), born in 1948, son of two leftist engineers (protestant, in the Resistance during the war), who on the eve of the events became a permanent member of the LCR (where he would remain for over 15 years) despite only just having begun studies at *l'Ecole Centrale de Paris*, one of France's most prestigious engineering schools. For this group, politicized but up to this point not activists (due mostly to their young age), May '68 is the occasion to activate latent dispositions for protest (mainly inherited from parents politicized to the left: Percheron & Jennings, 1981; Roth, 2007; Pagis, 2010).

(2) In contrast, the second subpopulation, located in the northwest of the diagram, is characterized by the absence of activist activity in the years after May '68. It is primarily composed of informants who were not activists before 1968, many from higher social strata, and whose participation in the events was not very intense. This population serves as a sort of control group: Their very low exposure to the event corresponds with an *absence of biographical impacts*.

(3) For the third collective profile, in the west of the diagram, the events of May '68 serve as *political socialization by upkeep* of preexisting activist tendencies: a predominantly male population, relatively older, from working-class backgrounds, employed in 1968. These informants had begun their activism well before 1968, so their way of interpreting the world had become well

---

[11] The *Communist Revolutionary League*'s newspaper.

stabilized by the time their trajectories crossed the May 1968 political crisis. Afterward, they continued to be active in institutionalized political organizations (cf. "unionism" and "PCF/PSU"). Guy, born in 1937, sums up the main characteristic of this group in these terms: "What's important, in my case, is found *before*."

(4) The fourth subpopulation, in the east of the diagram, contains informants for whom the events of May '68 would bring about *a socialization of political awareness*. In contrast with the preceding group, this one is for the most part female, from middle- and upper-class backgrounds, the youngest informants of the corpus, students in 1968, who invest themselves in forms of activism that are very weakly institutionalized in the following years. Mathilde is in this group (identified in the diagram), born in 1948, daughter of Catholic royalist artisans, educated in a religious boarding school, with broken family relations, who marries very young (1967). Pregnant with her first child in 1968 and enrolled in the Humanities at the Sorbonne, she enters fully into the activist space the following year via alternative nursery schools and various forms of private sphere politicization. An "anti-authoritarian activist," she lambasted familial and scholastic institutions, lived in various communes in the 1970s, refused salaried employment (as we will see later), was active in the MLAC and anti-nuclear movements – so many engagements characteristic of the *counter-cultural leftism* of this population. For these first-time activists, May '68 played a role of *biographical destabilization*, influencing their political as well as professional and private trajectories to different degrees. Young, mainly female, activists experiencing this destabilization had much less affinity with existing political organizations than the preceding group, largely because they had not inherited a political vision of the social world. They would seek to pursue the opening of possibilities represented by May '68 by other means: In the 1970s they participated in the politicization of causes previously outside of the political sphere (especially the family, the situation of women, the environment, and education).

A quantitative approach thus allows us to discern different group profiles, each characterized by distinct forms of political impacts of activism in May '68, and to situate them in terms of age, gender, social background, accumulated activist resources, and register of participation in the events.

However, as heuristic as they may be, quantitative approaches do not allow us to understand *how* a collective event could leave various footprints and influences on biographies. I will analyze the trajectory of Peter (found in the south of the factor diagram), a borderline case in that, from 1968–1974, he went from activism in the PCF (typical of the third population, located in the west of the diagram) to a biographical phase marked by political leftism (*cf.* first group, south of Figure 2.3) to then convert himself back to counter-cultural leftism (*cf.* fourth group, to the east). Thus, while Peter's position holds steady in the multiple correspondence analysis (MCA), further case analysis lets us integrate statistical observation into his trajectory's temporal and dynamic depth, allowing us to consider the play that is still possible between determinations and encounters (especially romantic ones) and to conceive of ways in which life spheres – activist, professional, and private – may interlock.

Contrary to the examples of Gérard, Johanna, or Mathilde, which were representative examples of statistically objectified group profiles, the borderline case of Peter serves another purpose. Like an ideal-type, his trajectory alone concentrates the characteristics and phases of post-'68 transitions found among the various trajectories studied but rarely in that of a single person. His story is richly illustrative for its passage through such a variety of biographical phases.

Peter: Biographical Impacts of the Breakdown of Social Barriers

Peter was born in 1943 in a working-class suburb of Paris, where his father was a street market vendor and his mother was a textile factory worker become secretary. His parents divorced when he was three years old and he was raised by his mother and stepfather (Armenian, an invalid since catching tuberculosis while in captivity). Peter grew up in the south of France in a poor family, his mother providing for all the family's material needs alone because his stepfather would not receive a handicap pension until 1958, that did not talk about politics but which read (especially the satirical political weekly *Le Canard Enchaîné*). He developed an early taste for reading. At school, Peter repeated his final year of middle school to take the entrance examination for the national teachers' college, but he failed: at 15 he got a worker position at the PTT (Postal, Telephone, and Telegraph service). Shortly thereafter he joined the CGT union and became a member of the PCF in 1960, his political conscience affirming itself during the war in Algeria.

In 1962 Peter passed an internal examination at the PTT and was hired as a telephone operator at the *Inter-archives* central office in Paris. He was 19, living in a PTT dormitory, and an active member of the PCF when he met his future wife, Marlène.[12] During this period Peter attended PCF schools, institutions serving as substitute schools that would re-enforce his scholastic inclinations (Pudal, 1989). He got married in 1963, and his daughter Nathalie was born the following year. Up to that point, Peter had all the characteristics of the subpopulation located in the west of the factor diagram (male, from a working class background, born in 1943, activist in the PCF prior to '68, salaried worker), but upon meeting Josiane in 1967, he would start a social and political shift. Peter had an affair with the young student, daughter of a worker, in social ascension, a Maoist activist in the UJCml (*The Marxist-Leninist Communist Youth Union*). Yet he continued living with his wife and being active in the PCF, with an increasingly distant relationship:

Josiane, it's the discovery of another form of love enriched by the intellectual stimulation that she brings me. [*The university of*] Nanterre, political radicalism, brilliant friends. It's the first time I'm in contact with this kind of people and that I participate in discussions among students, among politicized intellectuals ... I'd started to disagree with certain things well before: de-Khrushchev-ization was a problem for me, and I said so ... [13]

Peter accompanied Josiane to the Nanterre campus on March 22, 1968. He went on strike in May and participated in general meetings at his workplace (shy, he fainted the first time he stood up to speak), but he was quickly requisitioned to assure emergencies at the *Inter-archives* central office. He worked nights, went home to care for his daughter in the morning, and then joined Josiane in Paris' Latin Quarter. "The tremendous happiness" that this suspended time of May–June '68 represents for him is inextricably linked to his love affair – May '68 is also an opening to sexual possibilities – and to the lowering of social barriers put to the test daily in the Latin Quarter:

[12] Marlène (located in the south of the factor diagram) was born in 1942, the daughter of communist workers; at the time she was employed at the PTT, and an activist in the PCF. Peter and Marlène's proximity on the diagram shows the homogamy of his first union (to the contrary of those to follow).

[13] After having conducted an initial interview by telephone with Peter (7/8/2008), we took up a sustained electronic correspondence. From July to December 2008, Peter sent me over thirty emails, to which he attached a file containing replies to my follow-up questions.

May '68!!! Josiane and I are so in love, we're participating in something that deeply shakes up society!!! ... What's the most striking is the freedom of speech ... You've got to remember the cloak that covered French society at the time to be able to appreciate this liberation, even if it's just the power to speak. ... It's just regular people who come, discuss, give their ideas, not just students ... I remember some rather young workers, not that used to speaking in public but wanting to express themselves.[14]

And although his salary, like his wife's, went from roughly 800 to 1300 francs in this period, Peter is among those young workers who try to delay the return to work and feel betrayed by the PCF's attitude (Vigna, 2007):

The Grenelle agreements [*between union leaders and the government*] didn't make the activists I knew jump for joy (or me either). Just the opposite, since for us it represented the end of a movement that dreamed of going a lot farther ... We'd experimented with a power to act. There would still be a few of us to think it would be possible to make things move again.

Shortly after, he was unexpectedly transferred to another telephone central where the PCF activists' attitude toward him – "they passed it around that I was gay" – was the last straw, breaking his relationship with the party.

At the start of the 1968 academic year, Josiane returned to university and encouraged Peter to sign up. His aspirations for social mobility, re-enforced by the socially improbable activist encounters made before and during the events of 1968, became possible when the university in Vin-cennes opened its doors to students who had not passed the demanding *Baccalauréat* examination, a necessary prerequisite for university access. Peter enrolled in law before taking part in the creation of an entry-level degree (*licence*) in Political Science, and was an engaged activist in the *Gauche Prolétarienne* (GP; Proletarian Maoist Left) in Vincennes, while continuing to work at the PTT.

The events of May–June '68 thus brought about a triple shift: social (by resuming studies and obtaining a *licence* degree, in sociology), polit-ical (break from the PCF and shift to the extreme left), and familial. Peter left his family permanently in 1972, when he meets Nicole, who had "a great access to the Tunisian protest milieu in Vincennes, which I would discover thanks to her." Romantic encounters would play a central role in his trajectory: prompting, accompanying, or updating his social and political movement according to each case. After his first homogamous relationship, hypergamy characterizes his subsequent encounters.

---

[14] Excerpt from an email received August 17, 2008.

For the 1969–1972 period, Peter thus joined the "leftist" subpopulation in the factor diagram's south (the first one in Figure 2.3). But what statistical analysis cannot show is his movement toward the subpopulation in the east (the fourth one, *counter-cultural leftism*) in the following years:

Around 1972–73, Maoism starts losing ground, the GP declines … and me, I changed sweethearts so my interests shift, too … At that time a more anarchist [*libertaire*] and environmental movement emerges and I find myself more in it, it seems to me closer to my ideas: with the MLF also, which I'm very close to …

With his new partner – feminist, anarchist, and environmentalist – Peter converted his inclination to protest into counter-cultural leftism, aspired to go "back to the land" for a while (he got a CAP vocational degree in farm machinery repair) and to "denounce alienation by work and consumption by changing [*his*] life." These aspirations must be put in relation to the increasingly intolerable discrepancy between his work at the PTT and his extra-professional activities (activist, academic, romantic), as well as to the state of political options in the activist space of the mid-1970s.

Using life histories – and I will resume Peter's in the following part of the paper – thus allows us to reintroduce the dynamic and temporal aspects of trajectories and comprehend how events may "act" on individual trajectories. Accounting for processes of transfer, importation, reconversion, "fatigue," or back-burnering of activist dispositions in different spheres of life, during changes in the sociopolitical context, allows us to relativize in getting past the oft-reified dichotomy between political leftism and counter-cultural leftism – reinforced here by factor analysis – by showing multiple passageways between these activist networks (Sommier, 2008, p. 296).

Conversions of Activists' Dispositions in the Professional Sphere

Limiting the study of biographical impacts of participation in the events of May–June 1968 to the political sphere would be tantamount to forgetting the nesting of politics into professional and family spheres.[15] These spheres are the privileged frameworks for converting activist dispositions (Fendrich, 1977; McAdam, 1989), especially when the devaluation of extreme-left organizations in the space of activism makes it extremely costly to maintain revolutionary engagements and when the need for social reintegration is increasingly weighty. After briefly presenting the

---

[15] The familial and private impacts of activism in May '68 are not raised in the context of the article, but they have been analyzed elsewhere (Pagis, 2018).

social space of the professional impacts of activism in May '68 (constructed using factor analysis), I will compare it with the analysis of Peter's trajectory.

PROFESSIONAL TRAJECTORIES IMPACTED BY PARTICIPATION IN MAY '68

In response to a question on the possible impacts of the events of May '68 on their professional trajectory,[16] 42 percent of informants gave a positive response, 20 percent opting for the modality "a slight impact," and 38 percent gave a negative response. The following section only concerns informants having declared that May '68 had direct or indirect repercussions on their professional trajectories, and I will limit analysis of their responses to the open question "If yes, what is the impact?"

An initial presentation of the material presents informants' reactions when facing the need to reclass themselves while staying faithful to past engagements: disaffection with work, quitting higher studies to become a professional activist, inventing or redefining professions according to their activist aspirations, resuming studies, or, finally, critically renovating professions (especially through union engagement). The appeal of a statistical analysis of textual data is being able to relate these effects and their expression to the categories of actors who use them. This allows us to draw up a social space of May '68 professional impacts, and identify possible correlations between political and professional consequences.

Without going into the detail of the textual factor analysis, the following diagram sums up its results (Figure 2.4).

The x-axis differentiates the individuals according to the form and volume of their accumulated *activist resources*, counterposing the relatively older respondents, who were activists before 1968 and took an active part in May 1968 (to the west of the diagram) to those who are younger, were not activists before 1968, and who took a less active part in the events (in the east of the diagram).

The y-axis is structured by variables relating to social status: The respondents of working-class origin and who were employees in 1968 are in the north of the plane, whereas those who were students in 1968 occupy the south.

Several subpopulations stand out in the factor diagram for the distinctive forms their reconversion of activist capital took in the professional sphere, reconversions that are socially and politically situated.

---

[16] The question is formulated as follows: "Did the events of '68 have an impact on your professional trajectory? (1) Yes, (2) a slight impact, (3) No; If yes, what is the impact?"

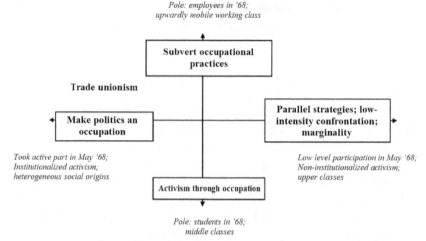

FIGURE 2.4 Importing activist dispositions into the occupational sphere

At the institutionalized pole of activism (in the west of the factor diagram), one finds collective forms of critique of the social organization of production, whether in trade-union activism or through *making activism itself one's occupation*, for those who became *établis* or political cadres like Gérard or Johanna, who, as has been seen, became LCR cadres. In opposition to these strategies, in the east of the diagram we find individual strategies for the perpetuation of activism, which take the form of radical professional changes and socially marginal trajectories (the informants then speak of "refusing to work," "breaking away," or "choosing their own lives"). To understand this first defining opposition, one must take account of the volume and distribution of the interviewees' various resources following the events of May–June 1968.

Indeed, the great majority of the respondents who took the route of becoming *établis* or of occupational commitment in politics or trade unionism are men, relatively older (born before 1944), having had activist experience before 1968, and having taken an active part in the events of that year (west of the plane). They had thus internalized dispositions toward activism and political schemes of perception of the social world that enabled them to perpetuate the opening up of possibilities that was experienced in 1968 in a collective and political mode.

Across the diagram, we find a population that is younger, more feminine, coming from middle and upper-class backgrounds – consequently not possessing the same resources to combat the re-sectorization of society. This zone is not composed of workplace activists trying to transform modes of production, but of people (individually) refusing to be subjected to the salaried workforce through various exit and parallel strategies (Bennani-Chraïbi & Fillieule, 2003: 71), as in Mathilde's case. In this pole, one finds a range of strategies for rejecting work and biographical ruptures character-ized by the existentialist injunction to change *one's own* life to "change life *itself*," with the hope of diffusing the model through the logic of exemplarity. Their conviction to be free to "choose their own lives" should be put in relation with their higher social background and to the resources that allow them to break with the future toward which their primary socialization oriented them. The radical change in professional paths and the transgres-sive social trajectory are here the principal tools of "activism."

Let's now turn to the y-axis. The respondents in the south of the diagram seek to be *activists through their occupation*. This other way of perpetuating the social weightlessness experienced in May 1968 consists in reorienting oneself into the social sector and sociocultural education – or journalism and social science research – to work with and on the side of the dominated (young people in working-class neighborhoods, offend-ers, the handicapped, the mentally ill, etc.). These middle-class inform-ants' investments in relatively uncertain professional sectors, where the relationships between titles and jobs were still little codified, allowed the reconciliation of activist loyalty with parental mandates for social ascen-sion. François's answer about the impact of May '68 on his professional trajectory is revealing of such strategies inventing new social positions (Bourdieu, 1978) that were simultaneously adapted to their skills and political aspirations: "Define my job, my occupation: revolution through popular education." So François becomes a sociocultural activities coord-inator, and gradually professionalizes his activism, like many former activists who convert themselves to "helping professions." The profession here is a tool of activism: One works (in the professional sense of the term) to change the social world.

A final form of reconversion of activist resources in the professional sphere concerns employees who, instead of reorienting their activities, critically renovate their profession (to the diagram's north). Older than the last group, employees in 1968, from more working-class backgrounds (but for the most part in social ascension), this subpopulation includes a lot of teachers who relate the transformations they put in place in their ways of exercising their profession. Here the activist dimension is found in the subversion of social-professional relationships (rejection of arbitrary authority, refusal of hierarchy, collegial administration, auto-gestion, etc.).

Thus on the y-axis, strategies of (re)definition of "new" professions, adapted to activist aspirations (to the south) are in opposition to strategies of importing activist resources into the professional sphere, which goes through the redefinition of professional practices (to the north).

The statistical approach thus allows the diversity of biographical impacts of May–June '68 activism to be highlighted, and puts them in relation with interviewees' sociological characteristics. But objectifying the biographical effects of engagement after the fact does not permit us to understand how the informants comprehend the renegotiation of their identities and the necessary "grieving work" that comes with it. This is where the need to articulate statistics with life histories becomes clear. The next steps in Peter's trajectory, which concentrates several different "post-'68" phases, will allow us to analyze the conditions of possibility for passing (or not) from one phase to the next and the forms taken by overlapping activist, professional, and private spheres.

From Telephone Operator to Social Sciences Instructor: Political, Professional, and Conjugal Reconversions

After 17 years in the PTT, and by now feeling the maladjustment with his position too keenly, Peter quit in 1977. Once again, it was a romantic encounter that triggered the reconversion, and Peter became an *éducateur*, a kind of social worker for young people that was typically redefined over the 1970s by the importation of activist dispositions (Muel-Dreyfus, 1983). But he stopped after a year and experimented with a wide range of activities, some of which he has trouble admitting retroactively, taking several exchanges of email to open up:

> After a period of unemployment, I decide to take advantage of the facilities offered to the unemployed to sign up in the commerce register as an itinerant vendor. I'll sell oysters, then jewelry, I'll run a *crêperie* the summer of 1981. We are in this period dripping in "liberal" ideology ... and I think it's because I'm isolated (that's the only excuse I find for myself) that I kind of got pulled into it.[17]

Faced with the alternative movement's loss of steam in the late 1970s and cut off from his old social networks, Peter was tempted by the quest

---

[17] We see here the value of being able to return to speak with (or have continued exchanges with) an informant: without the exchange of emails that followed our initial interview I wouldn't have been able to deconstruct the apparent coherence of the trajectory of a salaried worker without a Baccalaureat who, after having taken up his studies, would become a teacher.

for individual salvation and withdrawal into himself (in one of his last emails – April 2009 – he confided that he "drank quite a bit" at this time). In agreeing to open up about the dabbling that marked his trajectory between 1977 and 1981, Peter turned over a highly rich material revealing the hesitations, inconsistencies, adjustments, and adaptations that characterize the process of identity renegotiation that accompany the critical moment of political disinvestment and social reintegration that runs through the '68ers' various collective trajectories.

The political context was once again determinant in the next step along Peter's trajectory: He benefitted from the wave of recruitment of auxiliary instructors following François Mitterrand's election as president, and became a middle school French teacher in December 1981. He once again enrolled in university, this time in sociology, and formed a couple with Nanou, a teacher in a vocational high school. Obtaining a *maîtrise* (roughly equivalent to a Masters) in 1983, he joined a union and was tenured as Teaching Assistant in Economic and Social Sciences in 1985. His son Julien was born the following year. In the mid-1990s Peter earned his CAPES (an examination allowing teaching at Middle- and High-school levels), had new relationship problems, asked for a transfer to Brittany in 1996, and shortly after met his current partner, a librarian.

A union activist since he joined the national education system, Peter has continued to vote for extreme left parties in the first rounds of elections and regularly participate in demonstrations, and he does not seem to have lost hope for radical change:

After '68, for a long time I expressed the idea that we had planted a seed that would germinate some day, I'm beginning to find the latency period to be rather long, but I still think that capitalism is the worst way for humans and the planet to function.

If the conditions of possibility for Peter's exceptional social mobility are found prior to May '68 (early taste for reading, frustrated professional plans to become a schoolteacher, activism and PCF schools, meeting Josiane), May '68 had a legitimating effect on his cultural aspirations that had up to that point been experienced as stigmatizing – his work colleagues considering him unusual because he didn't share their musical, athletic, and literary tastes. May '68 widens the field of possibilities, at least subjectively ("it gave some hope that it was possible"), and the opening of Vincennes to students without the *Baccalauréat* creates objective conditions of possibility. The next phase of Peter's trajectory of upward mobility held him in an awkward position that was propitious to maintaining activist dispositions, activated in different forms according to the political choices available as well as his professional and familial engagements. It bears pointing out that the recurrence of separations and formation of romantic relationships is hardly just anecdotic in Peter's trajectory: his romantic encounters, concomitant to the main professional and political bifurcations, could be analyzed as the reflection, even the actualization, of his social displacement. But this would be to underestimate their role: indeed, Peter's successive partners reveal biographical horizons hitherto unimaginable to him (or that had previously been limited to simple, more or less conscious, aspirations), and these hypergamous unions make his ascendant social mobility possible, accompanying it along the way.

In conclusion, I will sum up a few of the great collective postures implemented in the 1970s in the face of the double necessity of social reintegration and carrying on past political engagements.

First of all, there are cases in which the liberation of aspirations brought about by participation in May–June '68 is accompanied by a real opening of possibilities, but they remain unusual. One can observe some exceptional trajectories of ascendant social mobility (like that of Peter), marked by continued engagement. The activism of these actors coming from the working classes engenders social, political, professional, and conjugal displacement, and hypergamy is a fundamental element in these trajectories, accompanying and prompting the progressive conversion of ways of perceiving the social world.

A second collective form of reaction to the disjunction between political aspirations and the professional means to satisfy them is found among informants who imported their critical dispositions into the professional sphere. Over the 1970s, they would participate in the redefinition of a certain number of professions, invested at first in a hybrid way in the grey area between activism and employment. The conversion of activist interests in politics into a professional interest in politics and the reconversion of activist skills (of investigation, of speaking with working-class activists, of social critique, etc.) in the professional sphere drove many activists to go into journalism, social science research, or into sociocultural organizing. Here, "happy" renegotiations were made possible by the existence of transitional spaces between the activist and professional spheres, as in the daily newspaper *Libération* or the University of Vincennes, which allowed the progressive remodeling of activist dispositions into professional dispositions, thus assuring the conditions for maintaining self-esteem.

While those in this last group try to modify their environment to make it conform better to their aspirations, in the opposite pole we find those who will adapt themselves, readjust themselves, to respond to the pressures of the environment. Here, professional investment is accompanied by a rather early political disengagement due to contradictions between representations and resistance of daily reality (Neveu, 2008: 312).

Lastly, among those for whom the discord between aspirations to live another way and the means to put them into practice find no socially recognized form of resolution, we see the production of utopian aspirations that lead to various forms of counter-societal conversion (Lacroix, 1981). Contestation of the dominant order can then happen via a withdrawal into marginality and the development of parallel strategies that may take the form of individual exit (depression, escape through drug use, distant travel, etc.), anti-institutional moods (refusal of work, rejection of family and scholastic institutions) or communal utopias, as we saw with Mathilde.

By associating a political event with a "socializing effect" that would come to similarly destabilize the trajectories of all who participate in it, generation-based conceptualizations eliminate what happened before, during (situational variables), and after the event, preventing us from understanding how the political event acts on individual trajectories. If the notion of *dynamic destabilization* (Mannheim, 1952) remains heuristic for characterizing the encounter between individual trajectory and collective event, this study shows that all participants are not destabilized in the same way. The statistical approach allows reconnecting types of biographical impacts to forms of politicization that preceded the event, as well as to sex, social background, age, and forms of participation in the event. It seems thus more judicious to speak of and determine *generational micro-units* of people who are marked by similar "imprints of the times," that is, comparable forms of political, professional, and private destabilization. These destabilizations are not just the simple fruit of participation in May '68. They are the product of a form of activism in May '68, which was itself generated by prior histories, both collective and individual. Put another way, there are no more "spontaneous generations" in social sciences than there are in animal biology.

3

Life Stories of Former French Activists of "68"

Using Biographies to Investigate the Outcomes of Social Movements

Erik Neveu

The question of social movement outcomes is a classic and extremely challenging one in this research field (Tilly & Tarrow, 2006, Chapters 4 & 5). Gamson's path-breaking research (1975) has provided strong evidence of the connection between a significant level of movements' organization and the importance of practical results. Kitschelt (1986) has highlighted the mediating effect of political systems supplying a useful typology of outcomes – do they have a direct impact on the political system, or on political coalitions? Do they satisfy substantial demands? Do they give rise to new tools and regulations for the treatment of demands? Other approaches have broadened the analysis to include the impact of social movements on public opinions, beliefs, and cultural representations (Giugni 1998; Chabanet & Giugni in Fillieule, Agrikoliansky, & Sommier, 2010).

This contribution will track the footprints of a sample of fifty-eight activists who belonged, in the '68 *years*, to the network of leftist organizations active in Brittany. As strongly suggested by Taylor (1989) and Rupp (1986), one of the outcomes of social movement is also the production of "long haul activists." The sociology of social movements needs a category of "embodied" outcomes: habitus and dispositions, biographical pathways and lifestyles. This chapter also focuses on the micro-politics of social change. Thousands of '68 activists have channeled their energies, together with the skills and beliefs they gained in social movement, into jobs and institutions. This process cannot be reduced to a surrender to "business as usual." They have invented new jobs, they have challenged established professions, and they have shown a flair for identifying "soft" institutions and positions (Bourdieu, 2015: 301) – in other words, those that leave room for creative practice. They have played a major role in many kinds of social movements. How significant are the social changes that they have thus helped bring about, and what are their limitations?

Answers to these questions will come from a "processual" (Elias, 1984) approach, paying close attention to the interactionist notion of "activist careers." Such an analytical framework arises out of three sources. The first of these is McAdam's "Freedom Summer" (1988), which, while still a landmark in explaining how commitment changes activists, also highlights the continuities and ruptures in their lives (see also Whalen & Flacks, 1989). A second influence comes from research questioning abeyance structures and processes (Taylor, 1989). A recent illustration of such an approach can be seen in Johsua's 2015 study, which covers 40 years of the sociology and history of the French Trotskyite organization *Ligue Communiste Révolutionnaire*. Despite several crises, it has, since the 1970s, functioned as a support and coordination structure for many social movements. Lastly, inspiration comes from francophone research that is indebted to the sociological tradition of Chicago's symbolic interactionism. Questioning processes of disengagement, these researchers provide a sociological account of activists' careers, following long-term involvement, abeyance, and reenlistment processes (Gottraux, 1997; Revue française de science politique, 2001; Fillieule, 2005).

To help make sense of this chapter, two points demand an initial "tune-in."

The first of these is linked to the intellectual status of *Mai '68* in France. The production of books, fiction, and articles on *Mai '68* extends well beyond the reach of a cottage industry. Hundreds of books, articles, and memoirs have been published. And the editorial tide reaches excessive heights each time another decennial commemoration comes around (Rioux, 2008). Such a level of interest should have resulted in in-depth understanding, and stimulating interpretations, of the movement and its consequences. Unfortunately, most of this enormous interpretative flow has shared two flaws. The first was an astonishingly casual approach to the mobilization of empirical data: fieldwork and original investigations have been rare. The cherry-picking of events, characters, and data in support of *a priori* interpretations has been the unwritten rule. A naïve teleology – the fallacy *post ergo, ergo propter hoc* – has explained the aims and beliefs of the activists through social changes that are visible 10 or 20 years later. Institutionalized in the 1980s, the doxa-memory (Sommier, 1994; Neveu, 2014) relied on two pillars. *Mai '68* shrinks, to become a student, leftist, and Parisian event. More than merely the most recent revolutionary crisis in French history, *Mai* expressed the cunning of modernist reason: The revolutionary students were unconscious agents of a modernization of lifestyles and institutions, culture and governance, in a backward capitalism. The character of the ugly 68er *(soixante-huitard)* – cynically jettisoning his youthful ideals in favor of behaving like a frantic and successful social climber, always ready to contemptuously lecture younger generations on the mirages of revolution and the beauties of democracy – appeared only in the 1990s (Neveu, 2015), becoming the third pillar to this grand *Mai* narrative. Needless to say, certain embarrassing details – such as the greatest working-class strike in history, or the mosaic of mobilizations even in rural areas – and *Mai*'s anticapitalistic discourse had to be brushed under the carpet to fortify this interpretation. One had to wait until the nineties to see the take-off of serious social scientific research on "May, and its afterlives" (Ross, 2004). A fresh flow of empirical research tracked the activists and investigated the strikes, opening up police archives and mapping the sheer variety of mobilizations among social groups and in local spaces (Sommier, 1998; Dressen, 2000; Gruel, 2004; Vigna, 2007; Artières & Zancarini-Fournel, 2008; Dammame, Gobille, Matonti, & Pudal, 2008; Porhel & Sainclivier, 2008). The result of these investigations was – within academic circles at least – a challenge to the established doxa and the unveiling of its meaning: a normative narrative the result (and sometimes the aim) of which was to highlight the unattainable nature of radical social change.

Taking this background into account, the scientific logic of the sample used here should become clearer. The choice was to focus on a population of activists whose commitments had, for the most part, been developed in Brittany. The fifty-eight members of this sample had a deep and hands-on commitment to the radical and leftist movements that developed between the end of the Algerian war (1962) and the crumbling of organized leftism (1978–1981). The sample is open: it includes activists from a variety of organizations (the left-leaning student trade union UNEF, Trotskyites, Maoists, and anarchist organizations – as well as activists supporting the cultural and political demands of the Breton[1] movement. There are two cohorts of activists (Whittier, 1995): the elder group, which had been

---

[1] Brittany – home of the Breton people – is a region in western France having distinctive peculiarities: strong influence of the Catholic church, level of education higher than the French average, late industrialization, and significant mobilizations in support of local culture and the Celtic language.

directly involved in *Mai '68* and trained in UNEF[2] after the Algerian war – these activists were often Communist youth movement dissenters or from Catholic movements – and the younger group, which arrived at university during or after *Mai '68* and joined the booming expansion of leftist organizations. Building a provincial (and this is a pejorative adjective in French) sample has also meant investigating hitherto-unexplored *Mai '68* territory, and focusing on other characters than media-savvy Parisian leaders.

Some facts and figures on the 'Breton' sample

All fifty-eight activists had in-depth involvement in radical organizations, whether in student politics, left-leaning peasant/trade unions and/or other leftist organizations, between 1963 and 1980.

The sample is composed of twenty-one women and thirty-seven men.

With the exception of one peasant born in 1934, all participants were born between 1943 and 1956.

Many of these activists moved from one organization to another, especially those from the older cohort. However, some moves had very weak chances of happening (from Trotskyite to Maoist organizations, and vice-versa). The sample mainly comprises ex-Maoists (n = 37) and ex-Trotskyites (n = 12). Other activists were members of the *Parti Socialist Unifié* created in the 1960s, or the leftist fringes of the Breton nationalist movement.

Paternal occupation:

Civil servants (n = 14 – 24.1 percent – including seven teachers)
Farmers (n = 13. 22.4 percent),
Industrial workers (n = 9. 16.5 percent),
Shopkeepers and craftsmen (n = 9. 16.5 percent),
Professionals (n = 5. 8 percent),
Managers of private companies (n = 4. 7 percent),
Employees (n = 2. 3.4 percent),
Businessmen (n = 1).

---

[2] *Union Nationale des Etudiants de France*, the main students' union. The UNEF was very active in the mobilization against the war in Algeria, and had to reinvest in more academic, bread and butter issues after 1962. Almost all the left activists at the university were or had been members of UNEF.

Depending on whether or not junior civil servants, primary school-teachers, and small shopkeepers and craftsmen are included, the percentage of activists coming from the "working classes" is between 42 percent and 64 percent.

Ex-Activists' Employment Status in 2010

Public sector (n = 40, 67.2 percent) vs. Private sector (n = 18, 32.8 percent)
Teaching and Research (n = 25. 43.1 percent)
Detail: 1 Primary School Teacher, 11 Secondary School Teachers, 6 University Academics, 1 Full-Time Researcher, 2 Librarians, 5 Administrative Staff).
Civil Servant (n = 13, 22.4 percent)
Detail: Local Authorities n = 6, Finance and Public health n = 4, Post Office, Telecommunications n = 3
Culture (n = 5. 8. 6 percent).
Detail: 1 Poet, 2 Video-Makers, 1 TV-Archive Manager, 1 Curator.
Professionals (n = 4, 1 Physician, 1 Engineer, 2 Barristers)
News and Journalism (n = 3)
Businessmen (n = 3)
Farmers (n = 2)
Social Workers (n = 2).

Nothing could be more illuminating than comparing this sample to *Génération*'s name-index (Hamon & Rotman, 1987, 1988). This double volume of excellent investigative journalism became the best-selling official narrative of the *Mai* generation and the matrix of official memory. Here, the most oft-cited names – those promoted as the figureheads of *Mai*'s activism – are leaders of the dissenters within the Communist student organization (UEC) in the 1960s, students of the prestigious *Ecole Normale Supérieur Ulm*, or those who had already reached a significant level of social recognition in the early 1980s. It goes without saying that all are Parisian, and almost all are male. A provincial sample brings rank and file activists back in, so that the analysis ceases to focus on activists' worth in terms of how often they are invited onto chat shows or whether they are self-appointed *ad vitam aeternam* interpreters of the event.

This chapter is structured by a threefold analysis. It sets out from a paradox: If great social movements are made by activists, one of their major outcomes could be the production … of activists who have lasting "careers" in social and political struggles. The surprising frequency of such cases calls into question the dispositions that support them. What might a militant *habitus* be? What experiences might structure it, which situations might put it in abeyance, unmake, or reboot it? Challenging the commonplace cliché of the activist as a warrior (or *guerillero*) of social struggles, the second section invites you to also think of activists as "entrepreneurs." They bring causes and social problems into the public sphere. They develop practical experiments and social innovations. They redefine and subvert roles and social functions in their jobs and daily life. Mobilizing cases of such behaviors and skills invites us to pay attention to the micro-dimensions of social change, its silent and ordinary "simmering" in experiments and resistances. A shorter section will conclude, drawing attention to certain paradoxes and contradictions in the management of *soixante-huitards'* commitments and lives. The activist element of this generation may have had its champions of social climbing – yet more often it was a reluctance to attain positions of power and a mistrust in social symbols of recognition that was expressed.[3] But should this be identified as a sign of virtue? Or a cause of powerlessness? What if, in the end, those who targeted political change and resource redistribution had truly been no more than the defenders of a slow, century-old, process of informalization (Wouters, 2007)?

SOCIAL MOVEMENT AS LONG-HAUL ACTIVIST FACTORIES

Continuities and Re-Commitments

The lasting legacy of the *soixante-huitards'* commitments is visible, first and foremost, in their membership figures and involvement in trade unions. Half of the sample participants (n = 28) are still union members (or were, prior to retirement.) And let's not forget that the percentage of the workforce belonging to a union in France is a mere 5 percent within the private sector, and 15 percent in the public sector. Although half of these union members were not heavily involved in their organizations, the other half has (or has had) a significant level of commitment, such as being in charge of a local union federation or head of the union within their administration or company. Four sample members had even been

---

[3] The old French tradition of "anarcho-unionism" from the nineteenth century had among its mottoes and moral values *Le refus de parvenir*. The French verb *parvenir* means both to reach and to succeed; it has given the pejorative word *parvenu*, which exists in English too. The *refus de parvenir* is not the will to fail, but the refusal of becoming one of "them," of betraying one's group and class by social climbing.

appointed *"permanents"* – that is, full-time activists paid by the union. Several activists became de facto spokespersons for their unions in official meetings or during collective bargaining sessions – despite never having agreed to become official representatives, in order to protect their independence.

The CFDT union – which is historically dominant in Brittany and less repressive to activists from the radical left – attracts two thirds of all those who join a union. With its more radical positioning, the young SUD union (founded 1981) has recruited a significant number of longstanding activists, especially at a time when the CFDT was fiercely criticized for its lack of fighting spirit against a national reform of pension funding in 2003. Members of our sample can also be found in the CGT – the biggest French trade union – as well as in teachers' unions (FSU), and *Confédération Paysanne* – the only left-oriented farmer organization. It is worth noticing how several former leftists reinvested in trade unionist skills and know-how, the better to mobilize. As a CGT representative, Paol had led a powerful strike in one of the region's big public hospitals. Fed up with seeing his hospital union stigmatized by the communist majority of the local CGT, he decided to join the new and radical union SUD: within 5 years, SUD was the most powerful union in the hospital. Patern, a peasant activist of longstanding, was able (at the age of sixty and in a region to which he has retired, far from his Breton roots), to organize hundreds of retired farmers to stand up for better pensions for themselves. Morgane, who worked for a formerly state-owned telecoms company, helped lead industrial action by writing and publishing a leaflet explaining to her fellow workers what a Leverage Buy Out (LBO) was, and how it would ruin the company.

Union membership is not, however, the only indicator of ongoing activism. Listening to activists' life stories is like reading a "Lonely Planet Guide" to the contentious French between the late 1970s and early nineties. Stories of soldiers rebelling in the barracks, of the fight for "free radio," of feminist struggles and experiments in the alternative economy (*économie solidaire*), environmental protection and nuclear energy protests – to name but a few. The work of activist hands can also be discerned in solidarity movements with Bosnia, in organizations promoting the language and culture of Brittany, or the ATTAC movement against financial capitalism. And it is important not to overlook the founding of institutions, teaching and education forums providing for the working class, the organization of *café-débats* as local public spheres, the countless associations promoting solidarity between the northern and southern hemispheres, and fair trade. The nature and style of renewed commitment varies greatly by decade, by local environment and by resources available to activists. In the biggest of the region's cities, one academic strongly connected to local industrial workers' unions created a European network of all trade unions at European shipbuilding companies. In one small village, an unemployed former activist decided to give back to the community by offering services and support to the village's least fortunate children: "I set up a library at X to help children who had homework to do and were under-achieving at school. I launched a cyber-service. I even played host to teenagers in difficult situations every Wednesday and Saturday. I threw myself into these things and I kept at it for years ..."

Totaling the figures for trade unionists and those who maintained their commitment to various social causes (n = 30), more than two-thirds of the sample members have kept – either permanently or during periods of reengagement – a lasting commitment, connected to their youthful values.

Militant Habitus?

If we are to describe activism using the interactionist lifelong "career" frame, then the famous interactionist *How is Why* may be challenged. *How* does not always provide all the *Why* answers. Sometimes the *Why* can illuminate the *How*. Using Bourdieu's concept of *habitus* (1979), the notion of activist *habitus/habitus militant* can explain the dispositions that support this long-haul activism and its genesis. Militant *habitus* can be described as a lasting input of social energies to involvement in collective action and struggles, shaping a set of skills, interpretative schemes, and ways of behaving that support this orientation. Four explanatory considerations will render this notion more precise.

At the core of this habitus, we find the appreciation of commitments to causes and groups that Durkheim (1974 [1902]) mentions as one of two possible bases for moral behavior, defined as acting in the interest of the community. Where do such dispositions come from? Primary socialization weighs heavily in the making of altruistic dispositions. Religious influences are highly visible – especially from the "left" and "social" segments of the Catholic universe, with their values of devotion to the common good, care and service for those who are weak or suffering. Most of the activists (n = 32) in our sample had parents who were active Catholics, attending mass each week, or who were (n = 13) involved in parochial organizations or Catholic movements. Forty percent of the sample spent all or most of their primary and secondary years attending

Catholic schools.[4] Twenty percent of sample participants had strong attachments to Catholic youth organizations – which were also closely tied to critical and radical thinking in the 1960s. The fact that four members of the sample had begun training as priests in seminaries is far more than an anecdotal detail. If one adds to these figures the eleven families in which the parents were either communists, active in the world of left-oriented organizations, or had been members of the armed *Résistance* against Nazi occupation, the percentage of activists socialized in normative patterns that strongly stressed the value of commitment to groups, or solidarity with the less well-off, is almost 75 percent (n = 44). However, it is also worth emphasizing the impact of organizational socialization among leftist groups, and its combination with extraordinary expectations of social change. Mannheim invites us to think of the impact of such experiences during the "impressionable years" of youth: an impact multiplied by students' unfettered availability for high levels of commitment. Channeling dispositions built in by primary socialization (a majority of Maoist activists came from strong Catholic backgrounds), many "revolutionary" groups demanded unquestioning and rigid devotion to the cause, its servants, and organizations (*"remise de soi"*). Their members embodied high levels of self-discipline, held in place by the ever-present threat of the guilt-trip. These were "greedy institutions" (Coser, 1974), consuming high volumes of time, energy, and emotional investment. They celebrated we-ness, valuing the self-restraint of individual desire as a major achievement ... a long way from the retrospective invention of *Mai '68* as the cradle of "narcissistic hedonism."

A second major element of militant habitus was strong self-esteem. This refers to the confidence expressed by many activists with regard to their legitimate right to address audiences, challenge authorities, support struggles, and make sense of situations. Although the concept of "self-esteem" has been borrowed from the psychological lexicon, it does have a sociological basis. Most of the activists we interviewed were over-achievers at school. Their performances can be evaluated using a comparative logic: many interviewees (especially those whose parents were farmers or industrial workers) recall being the only pupil in the whole school or village to reach the holy grail of the *baccalauréat*, and to discover university. Comparative performance should also be used to

---

[4] A high percentage but, however, a bit under the average in Brittany, the only French region where private Catholic schools have nearly 50 percent of "market-share" in schools from kindergarten to *baccalauréat*.

make sense of the paradoxical success at university of students who dedicated most of their time to activism, rarely attending courses or lectures. Activists' academic achievement levels can also be evaluated in a more absolute way: a significant minority (n = 11) of the sample obtained top marks in their school or faculty, achieving highly selective diplomas (Agrégations, or PhD's). Such cognitive resources, which back up this self-esteem, also arise out of the appropriation of various versions of Marxism and its hybridizations with the social sciences of the 1960s.[5] These provided analytical tools, as well as a belief in their almighty power of explanation. Forty years on, such resources may seem weak – even pathetic. As Mauger (1994) suggests, the arrogant "Cahiers Marxistes-Léninistes"[6] motto "Marxist theory is almighty because it is true" was not so ridiculous in its historical context, when working class strikes and social movements were on the rise; when many French intellectuals were expressing their admiration for Marxist theory; and when national liberation movements were destroying the last remnants of colonial empires, and defeating the US Army in Vietnam. Moreover, political theories and formalized learning should not be considered as completely distinct. The socialization provided by Catholic youth organizations (JEC, JAC, JOC), as well as within many small revolutionary organizations, supplied a parallel intellectual curriculum, offering tools for thinking, teaching the arts of expression and Marxist thought. Social relationships between activists included group preparation for exams. Knowledge of critical theories and of political history that was gained in activism has been used to write essays and pass exams more than once, and some young academics were open to fashionable and *"progressiste"* critical thinking. An example of the bridging between academic and activist knowledge is

---

[5] The existence (or not) of a "68 thinking" is hotly discussed among French historians of ideas. If a *"Pensée 68"* ever existed, it is not what is described by the eponymous book (Ferry & Renault, 1985) making of Bourdieu, Lacan, Derrida, and Foucault the four horsemen of an apocalypse of the free subject. The most evident objection is that, but for Bourdieu and Passeron's first book (1964) on changes among the student world, a few percent of the activists ever read any of these authors' difficult (and expensive) books. The intellectual menu of these years was much more a mix of second-hand sociologized and highbrow Marxism (L. Althusser, Ch. Betheleim, A. Gramsci), of "counter-cultural" thinking (Illitch, Palo-Alto, W. Reich), of keywords borrowed to critical social sciences and fashionable theories (structuralism, semiology). On these questions: Audier (2008).

[6] The journal of the Maoist *Union des Jeunesses Communistes Marxistes Léninistes* (UJC-ML). Lindendberg (1975), a political scientist and former member of this group, highlights how its leaders had the feeling of reinventing a living Marxism, making sense of the present, and giving them a fantastic strength for action.

offered by Patern – a trade unionist peasant who farmed cattle. He emphasized the help he received from student "comrades" in economics and agronomy: This was what allowed him, as a union leader, to develop an analysis of agro-industrial company strategies. The activist habitus of the *68ers* thus includes forms of *libido sciendi*: ambition and a claim to understand the world, to develop on-the-spot investigations, and to learn and produce knowledge about anything – from industrial relations law, to ecology, to analyses of company strategies. Here, Bourdieu (1979: 404–431) supplies a stimulating analogy. Mapping the changing class landscape of the French 1960s, he contrasts the shy, deferential and docile "cultural good will" of the traditional petty-bourgeoisie (in its search for intellectual salvation and social elevation through submission to the academic institutions), with the self-confident, ambitious, and glib *"prétention armée"* (*prétention* meaning both pretentiousness and a sense of entitlement) of the new petty bourgeoisie, richer in cultural capital. Here, the combined experience of university plus activism creates a bridging process that shifts dispositions from "cultural good will" to "armed *pretention."*

This bridging dimension invites us to pay close attention to a third element of these militant habitus: their ambivalences. Beyond the differences between activists, each one embodied surprising combinations of contradictory beliefs and dispositions. A fascination for knowledge was capable of joining forces with a coarse anti-intellectualism that targeted the institutions and productions of both academia and press. A taste for theory was often combined with highly "practical" skills (such as investigating, or building connection with manual workers). Near-religious dispositions to sacrifice the self to the Cause could be combined with resources and dispositions for entrepreneurship or individual achievements. The vocation of heterodoxy mixed with surprising obedience to organizations' political orthodoxies. The enchanted perception of an "oceanic" space of change and mobility combined with the fear of betraying one's origins, of becoming a cog in the "System." Such contradictory, unstable polarities of militant habitus are key to understanding the variations – and sometimes surrenders and U-turns – featuring in the careers of yesterday's activists.

A last element of this militant habitus of the 1960s has been termed the "vocation of heterodoxy" by Gobille (in Dammame, Gobille et al., 2008). This suggests the strength and breadth of critical, anti-institutional thinking that challenges established forms of social division between manual and intellectual activities, the specialist and the layperson, the city and the countryside. As Gitlin (1987) emphasized for the US case, such a disposition cannot be understood without reference to the experiences of the baby boomer generation as it faced a world in which material restrictions were loosening and opportunities of upward mobility increasing, while cultural and moral patterns were being shaken. A vision of boundless horizons developed – especially among those accessing the social escalator provided by university – the "oceanic" (Freud) feeling that the whole world was ripe for change. Since there is no habitus without *illusio* (a mobilizing belief that channels one's energies into a social game) the sociological profiling of the activists should be made complete by emphasizing the strength of their belief in imminent and radical change. Rather than a clear political program, "Revolution" was the keyword expressing this promise. This faith in the opportunity of a historical turning point is visible in the initial – almost universal – contempt for "making it" in terms of social recognition and career achievements. Beyond answers provided to interviewers, this reluctance is clearly visible in biographical data: Eleven members of our sample (often bright students) dropped out of university to start work at factories or dockyards so as to gain more influence among workers, while others chose jobs for which they were overqualified, since they refused to be "bosses."

Habitus change. As they were restructured by new experiences, how could militant *habitus* endure the test of time? It is more difficult to believe in Revolution in 2015 than it was in 1970, harder to remain indifferent to wealth at the age of 40, with a family to support, than it was as a student barely past the age of 20. Although variations are visible in activists' commitments, continuities prevail. Two explanatory logics should be brought into play: the first refers to the past, questioning the myth of aging *soixante-huitards* being transformed into liberal yuppies. Our sample confirms McAdam's analysis of "Freedom Summer" participants (1988; see also Fendrich & Lovoy, 1988; Braungart & Braungart, 1991). The more such commitment carries practical (rather than purely intellectual) dimensions, the more it means taking risks and facing repression, the more it threatens professional careers and social success, and the more it entails experiencing the feeling of "otherness" brought about by direct contact and interaction with subordinate and working-class social groups ... and the more it finally produces powerful and lasting militant *habitus*. It is no surprise here to see that those who became "établis" at factories, those who were sentenced to jail or faced serious threats (such as a woman who struggled under the Pinochet regime) are among the most persistent of activists.

A second explanatory dimension must be researched, following activist life stories, in the relationship between their resources and the opportunities they face. What is the nature, structure, and volume of each activist resource? What is the balance between individually owned resources (a family inheritance, a PhD) and those arising out of activism (a job as a journalist for the newspaper *Rouge*, a good network among trade unionists)? Is it possible to transfer activist skills to new activities, or to reinterpret existing jobs ... or not? The ability to devote oneself to institutions can find a continuation in a new style of managerial skills, channeling a low-key militant brand of commitment into institutions and jobs, in a way that is less formal yet efficient, capable of mobilizing peers and colleagues. These are precisely the types of know-how valued by modern capitalism's new management, transforming activist know-how into marketable resources (Boltanski & Chiapello, 1999). Following life-stories also means mapping the "ecology" of (ex)activist lives. In a nutshell, the more activists remain in a social space in which their ex-comrades are both present and socially significant, the more unlikely complete abandonment of any commitment becomes. This is a form of social control, of soft pressure that renders certain career decisions costly, since they are labelled as betrayal. More often, however, high-risk and lasting commitments to activism create strong ties, which in turn give rise to displays of solidarity and faith (as well as aversion and disappointment). A striking fact about our sample is that almost all its members (n = 55) still live and work in Brittany. This choice – and it often is a carefully considered choice – of a low level of spatial mobility also means remaining within a social ecology in which the potential of abeyance, the links with the activist milieu, survive.

Lastly, the development of a close follow-up of the changing combinations of resources and opportunities would help make sense of the variety of trajectories also arising out of the unstable habitus dimensions already mentioned. Sometimes the simple fact of moving to a new city and job just a few hundred kilometers from the location of one's initial activist life is enough to break with routine and trigger the process of habitus reformation. The militant super-ego, made up of fear of being judged by one's peers and the desire to retain the trust and warmth of the militant cocoon vanishes; social energies can be channeled toward individual success. Over-investing in activism and then facing the turning point of the organization's disbanding, of the micro-event that raises the question " is it worth such effort?" can trigger feelings of bitterness, of having been fooled, detracting from new commitments. An academic in the sample still remembers the day in 1974 (which was also the turning point at which he had to channel more time into his PhD to maintain any hope of tenure) on which he left his organization: "What I felt that day – it's what a prisoner who sees the prison doors opening would feel." He is also one of the few who never again became engaged in social movements. Conversely, other trajectories almost require continuity in commitment. How could Yvon, our sample's poet, who is well known for performing during strikes and industrial action, manage a continuity of image and identity if he were to repudiate his past?

ACTIVISTS AS SOCIAL CHANGE ENTREPRENEURS

The study of activism in social movements and political parties has often been held prisoner to conflict-focused indigenous representations. Here, the activist is portrayed as a soldier, a fighter – a vision that is also androcentric. Mobilization resource theory (McCarthy & Zald, 1977), which raised the profile of the character of the "entrepreneur," has highlighted another aspect of the skills and logic involved in collective action – even though it may initially have narrowed how entrepreneurs were perceived, reducing them to an impoverished economicism. Jasper (1997), who thought of social movements as spaces of creativity and innovation, offers a more satisfying vision of this entrepreneurial dimension and its power of invention. It may be worth quoting the reflections of two French researchers, Rosanvallon and Viveret (1977: 124–126), who invited us to think of activists as "new entrepreneurs," responding – in French society of the 1970s – to

a deep aspiration to enterprise ... as an alternative to the crisis of activism. ... The longing for self-government (*autogestion*) cannot be disconnected from rehabilitation, an extension and a socialization of the function of the entrepreneur in society. ... It's in the realm of social life that one should now undertake and develop innovations. The real enterprise becomes the one which changes social relations – that is, the relationship of people to institutions.

Inventing Causes and Redefining Styles of Commitment

The importance of continuities and re-commitment has already been stressed. Considering the involvement of the *soixante-huitards* from the 1980s onward, twenty-eight of the sample were members of trade unions, half of whom held leadership positions. Ten were active in environmental movements (against nuclear power plants, the pollution of water through intensive farming, and oil spills by tanker wrecks). Nine were involved in fair trade, north–south, and solidarity movements. Eight were active in developing alternative media and public debate spaces. Six were involved in feminist movements, and the same number in the galaxy of cultural and political movement that supports Breton culture and identity. Two-thirds (n = 39) of the sample were involved in one or several of these causes. It would be ridiculous to suggest that the *soixante-huitards* were the soul of most activism in France over the past 30 years, but it is reasonable to suggest that they have reinvested their skills and energy in a broad variety of social movements.

Their style of action is worthy of three remarks. First, the nature of the *soixante-huitards'* commitments invites us to reconsider the link between '68 and the supposed triumph of so-called new social movements. There is no doubt that several of the struggles that mobilized members of our sample could be labelled as "post-materialist." However, the weight of investment in trade unionism, ATTAC's criticism of financial capitalism, and the lasting links forged between activist groups campaigning for justice for countries of the southern hemisphere and the legacy of anti-imperialism show the ongoing importance of an anticapitalistic dimension, of materialist claims – as already ascertained by Fillieule's study (1997) of the French demonstrations of the 1980s and 1990s. Second, the ex-*soixante-huitards'* style of activism uses the classical repertoire of demands and actions "against." Yet it goes beyond this, revealing that the idea of the activist as social innovator is more than just a theoretical vision. While still in his thirties, Malo, a peasant activist, was one of the founders of a cooperative – CUMA[7] – and was elected chair by the membership. Through networking, Arzela, a feminist activist, ultimately won the support of local authorities to create a *"Maison des femmes,"* a space for care, debates, and women's rights activism. Ex-Trotskyite Lenaïg became the main regional organizer of ATTAC, organizing public debates in Rennes, the regional capital, promoting research groups on issues such as the environment or global companies' use of tax havens. Gurwan's action is also typical. Strongly committed to Breton culture and heritage, he created one of the first environmental reserves, collecting a whole range of regional trees and flora, prior to setting up a national network of such institutions. A third of sample members have had this type of entrepreneurial-style commitment. Another particularity of the

---

[7] *Coopérative d'Utilisation du Materiel Agricole*: self-organized cooperatives used by farmers to buy and share machines like combine harvesters and round-ball bundlers.

career choices made by the '68 activists is their lasting mistrust of party politics. Just eight members of the sample have ever run for election, and always at local government level. Only three were elected. The only one who reached a significant position of power, within the inner circle of a big city executive body, was also one of very few activists to have actually joined the Socialist Party (n = 4). All the other ex-activists' electoral experiments shared a specific set of features. They began, long before campaign time, with the construction of an association, networking processes, and the production of a small journal used as a forum for debate on local affairs. The result of this process was a campaign based on practical proposals for action. And though ex-activists usually had partnerships with traditional left-wing parties, they always kept a certain distance – a long spoon tactic, critical, often bordering on conflict – from local leaders of the Socialist and Communist parties.

Reinterpreting Jobs and Roles

It would be a mistake to think that a militant *habitus* could only be activated by the presence and promise of action. It can also find expression in the invention of new ways of occupying posts, or of being in charge of institutions. Some *soixante-huitard* trajectories can also be seen as the challenge of turning activism into a career, of inventing roles and activities that would allow some continuity between the militant and the professional spheres.

The massive upward mobility experienced by the student generation of '68 (and not just the activists) is a well-documented fact, a "social elevator" effect of the morphological changes in the structure of jobs and education during the 1960s (Chauvel, 2002). But the reality of this social mobility should not stop us asking sociological questions. Were jobs, career and occupation structures unchanging between 1955 and 1985? What happens when people coming from dominated groups gain access to dominant jobs and roles? Have they no choices, no wishes other than occupying these roles using the norms, behaviors, and social relations previously established? A reflection on social change, based on activist biographies, should take into account the social logics that allow micro social changes.

A first set of situations exemplifies strategies (rarely thought of as such) in which militants "professionalize" skills gained in activism, transferring their militant mindsets to their jobs. The case of Gurwan – the "Breton communist" and ecologist who created and organized a network of flora

botanical reserves – has already been mentioned. Yvon offers a remarkable example of inventing a new job profile. By making many sacrifices,
he was able to earn a living (just about) as a poet, a constant presence
alongside social struggles. He remembers having suffered from the cold
every winter until he was in his forties, due to not having enough money
to pay the heating bills. He may be far from wealthy, yet he earns a
living – insecurely – as a cultural producer who commands respect within
the small community of poets, and maintains a permanent connection to
social struggles and international solidarity movements. The sample also
includes two documentary film producers who have transferred in this
activity their militant habitus and skills: taste for social investigation,
desire to discover unknown and ordinary social groups and determination to support those who engaged in a struggle for justice.

In a second set of scenarios, some former activists have had the social
flair to invest in emerging and weakly institutionalized occupations, seiz-
ing them as spaces of innovation and social change. Here is a partial
explanation for the significant number of academics in the sample. The
former leader of a Maoist organization explains,

In our university, if you have an idea, and the determination and conviction to
push it, if you belong to a group of insiders, you can achieve all you want, it's
quite open. So all the adventures: creation of the Cooperative College, the Institute
of Social Sciences of Work Relations, and other areas in which I was less proactive, cultural policies, innovations in adult education, Applied Foreign
Languages ... it's a privilege of academia. I felt that there were few institutions
with such scope for freedom. It's an uncommon space, with its ability to accommodate forms of energy, inventiveness, and creativity ... And then our R & D in
urban planning structure was created. I almost stopped teaching law then; I leapt
into this field of study, making surveys and fieldwork in the urban space in crisis,
the inner core of small towns. I started with this stuff ... and it gave me a
completely new motivation for my teaching tasks.

Such freedom to act and experiment may explain the significant presence
of former activists in areas such as local authorities, urban development,
or social welfare, in a context where these sectors are growing or undergoing deep reorganization. It is interesting to compare these "soft" situations to those in which activists have gained access to more organized,
structured professions. There, they have managed to occupy specific
niches. Neither of the barristers in our sample pleads in court for business
interests – because both have, after more than 30 years of practice,
retained a strong belief in causes such as women's and workers' rights,
and the defense of activists. Another former Maoist leader managed to

transform his job as "socio-cultural instructor" at an agricultural college into a "mission" of promoting sustainable development across a network of these colleges, gaining enormous freedom of action and adding a dash of activism to his job.

In a final set of situations, another style of subversion (or transgression) is visible. Activists work to break the disciplinary dimension of social relations, to shake the division of hierarchical work or to legitimize practices long considered heretical. As a revolutionary organization was shrinking, its printing department – including several full time activist-workers – had to find contracts and resources elsewhere in the market. The team of activists was forced to behave like businessmen employing a workforce. Yet this was not "business as usual." When the small company faced a crisis, the bosses were the first to take a reduction in wages. They opened an art gallery in the company building to host exhibitions; they offered financial support to the Afghanis struggling against soviet occupation in the 1980s. Artus, a social worker employed at a children's home, explains: "When we arrived there were uniforms. All the kids had the same pajamas; they were crammed into the canteen, 50 kids. We put a stop to all that, we made groups. It was reorganized. All the bloody cloaks and stuff from the uniforms went in the bin. We individualized relationships, reorganized. We were starting over with very fresh ideas. Yeah, at that moment I really had the feeling that the job... I believed a hell of a lot in what I was doing'! So we changed things, we changed mindsets. Social work, we saw it as different from charity." In a harbor that was once a major French port for slave traffic, a museum curator had tried (unsuccessfully) to organize an exhibition questioning the role the city had played in this ugly business. Two former activists with significant administrative responsibilities in city governments claim to have developed a different style of work relations. "I do believe ... and I have feedback which makes me think that I was not hallucinating dreaming when I felt I had a style of using responsibilities that had ... that had value. Many people now tell me: 'We've never had this before, nor since, nor anywhere else'." And the "general secretary" of a mid-sized town explains:

I've got a policy based on the idea that competition is the number One enemy, that we shall promote cooperation everywhere. So in the organization I favour peer collaboration, creating two person teams. Two people work on each task, and not necessarily in a relationship of subordination. I favour cooperation. I wanted to enrich everyone's job, so that no-one had to do the same task, day in, day out. But it was not that easy to do. If there were a theoretical reference to mention, I would say Gorz, his reflection on the organization of work.

Soft and hard social worlds

During one of his lectures at the Collège de France in 1982, Bourdieu sketched some remarks on how *Mai 68* changed the behavior and styles in many activities. He noticed how, among the Parisian bus and metro controllers who were often the symbols of petty bourgeois respectability – clean, stern, and serious – were appearing new styles with long hair and beards, cool and less stand-offish. Comparing the primary school teacher and the social worker, he suggests hard versus soft positions, "Those who will import improper dispositions into a hard position will thus have strong chances of being defeated by this position, of being weaker than it is whilst those who are importing improper or unfitting dispositions into soft positions have strong chances to re-shape the position according to their dispositions" (Bourdieu 2015: 301).

The notions of hardness and softness can be objectified by three parameters: Some professions and activities are highly institutionalized and leave reduced margins for improvisation and redefinition. Others are in the process of being invented like many social workers' tasks in the sixties (Muel-Dreyfus, 1983) or are restructured by morphological changes (when the number of tenured academics is multiplied in France by two between 1963 and 1973, and again by four between 1973 and 2003 are they still doing the same job?). The nature of the recruitment process suggests another opposition in the level of required "conformity." Are specific diplomas required? Is there something like long training by a school under the control of the profession? Is the process including interviews or individual investigations allowing checking of ideological or ethical correctness? A third parameter could be given by the opportunity (or not) to express opinions, to take stands in the very practice of the job: a behavior prohibited or risky for the tax-collector, or the judge, allowed to the academic, almost compulsory in some cultural activities (such was the case of the small community of the novelists writing "*néo-polars*," a popular style of detective novels with a strong dimension of social criticism. Having been an activist of the '68, or at least a fellow-traveler, was there a badge of authenticity and legitimacy: Collovald & Neveu, 2001)

Beyond the small population studied in this chapter, several research projects suggest that many among the '68 activists has a flair for identifying the soft positions and institutions; Spanou (1991) explores how activists or ex-activists quickly invested the new "militant" ministries created in the seventies and eighties (women's rights, environment, consumers' rights). Salles (2005) supplies many examples of how the small Trotskyite newspaper "*Rouge*" worked as a kind of extra-curricular journalism school, boosting some of its ex-staff members in major professional positions, as in Plenel's deputy editor-ship of "*Le Monde*," where he developed an aggressive investigative reporting.

Tissot, Gaubert, and Lechien's (2005) edited book maps some of these soft social spaces of the post '68 years. The networks of public administrations, consulting companies, and nonprofit organizations working on urban policies, academia, and social work. But this archipelago of softness includes many cultural activities like publishing and libraries, the press and media, later – and more ambiguously – the growing business of evaluation of companies' fairness in job management. Conversely, hard institutions (the army, justice and police, or central administrations on the public side, the major industrial and financial companies on the private one) were rarely colonized or challenged by ex-activists: And when such challenges existed (soldiers' committees of conscripts between 1973 and 1978, the "Red judges" movement in the sixties) they rarely had a lasting influence.

SOME '68ERS PARADOXES: COMMITMENT, HABITUS, AND OUTCOMES

Reluctant Social Climbers

The memory and mythology of *Mai '68* often depicts the *soixante-huitards* as being cynical and frantic social climbers. Some of the trajectories of '68's figureheads may explain such judgments. The philosopher A. Glucksmann, leader of one of the most radical and vocal Maoist groups, soon became a champion of the *"nouvelle philosophie"* that linked any idea of strong social change to a totalitarian fascination; he ended his political life campaigning with and for N. Sarkozy. B. Kouchner, a leading dissenter within the communist youth organization, created the "French doctors." He also served as a minister under both F. Mitterrand and N. Sarkozy, and created a highly profitable consultancy firm. S. July, another Maoist leader, became a famous press-editor and neoliberal columnist. Focusing on such profiles, however, suggests at least two analytical short-cuts. The first is the classical *pars pro toto* fallacy, which depicts a whole generation out of the stories of its forty most media-savvy members. The second is the risk of replacing sociology with ethical or political judgment. The most surprising U-turns and career changes that are visible in certain life stories are often linked to individuals having very specific and significant individual resources (degrees from *grandes écoles*, or strong social capital among cultural producers) – and cannot be understood without attention to the above-mentioned contradictions (read: instability) of the '68 militant habitus.

Most of our sample members have experienced upward mobility. Yet
their trajectories were not exceptional, when compared to those that are
typical of the educated baby boomer population. It is even more important to highlight, from our data, that most have managed something akin
to self-limited mobility. The number of ex-activists having tried, in their
jobs and professions, to avoid positions of authority, to leave room for
cooperation and deliberation, and to promote social innovation, is close
to 50 percent – a figure which means that in fact almost 80 percent of
those having enough responsibility or autonomy to make such experiences a reality did so. Further investigation would be required to check
how real these changes and innovations were, and to call into question a
dimension of self-legitimation. Some hard facts remain: The percentage of
those moving to Paris (often an indicator of social status in Jacobin
France), of those earning more than €2,500 per month at the time of the
interviews, or the number reaching high levels of responsibilities or
social visibility never gets above 15 percent. These cautious or self-limited
relationships to social mobility often express the lasting effects of a
militant *habitus*. This acceptance of certain limitations is coherent with
the priority given to parameters of social usefulness and quality of life
ahead of income and power, in defining an interesting job. It also fits with
anti-institutional orientations and mistrust of most forms of organized
authority. This *refus de parvenir* is neither masochism nor civil martyrdom but rather a malaise or discomfort with the potential for abuse that
exists in any symbolic or hierarchical power. This is expressed in the
workplace by the equivalent of Freudian slips. Finding a balance between
being efficient colleagues, deeply invested in institutions or workplaces as
well as heretical insiders producing (sometimes unconsciously) signs of
critical or mocking feelings and attitudes about the pompousness and
myths of one's social world is a risky tightrope-walk. This style of
professional commitment, at once serious and distant, intense and reflexive, produces innovations and performing management. It also opens up
the risk of the inside-outsider being "punished" by the promotion of
colleagues, who are less skeptical, more deferential, and a better fit with
the institution's own myths.

Micro-Social Change and Its Limitations

Such reluctance to ruthlessly climb the social ladder has another ambiva-
lence. It could challenge the routine of micro-power relationships. Yet
simultaneously, as in the "sour grapes" fable, it prevents the ex-activists

gaining access to higher levels of authority, and thus from implementing changes top-down. Revolutions or major changes from inside institutions are rarely made by the wretched of the earth – but by actors rich in capital. Speaking of two combined traps would make sense here. The first arises out of the activists' own double-bind logic, often consciously playing the strategy of promoting micro-social change, yet reluctant to compromise by occupying the power positions that would boost it. The second arises out of the concentration of yesterday's activists in the institutions of the state's so-called "left hand" (culture and education, social care). The arrival of so many leftists in academia's social science departments fits with their *libido sciendi* and the opportunities opened up in such institutions. It could also mean channeling many of their critical energies into endless departmental meetings or the writing of research papers. As Bourdieu suggests, "social mechanics are often cleverer than the cleverest of dominants" in preventing radical change.

One of *Mai*'s central interpretative tools in the dominant memory narrative is the "cunning of liberal reason." The *soixante-huitards* believed that they were actors in a replay of 1917, whereas the real result and meaning of their action was the modernization of archaic French capitalism, the consecration of hedonism and individualism. Where, then, is the paradox? It lies in the fact that even the ex-activists themselves, who are reclaiming the anti-capitalist, "materialist" dimensions of their struggles, agree that the measurable effects of their activism are more evident in the field of culture and lifestyles. When asked, *"All this activism – was it like a drawing in the sand or did it leave lasting results?"* the most common response is to discuss changes in gender relations – but not a redistribution of material resources or power between social groups. One could argue here that the *soixante-huitards* were more efficient as agents of "informalization" than they were as revolutionaries. But one should also add – against the retrodictive reading of *Mai* – that even if such has been the result, this informalization was never the movement's main goal, nor the imaginary space of the movement.

Explaining the limited results of the soixante-huitards' commitment is beyond the scope of this contribution. Doing so would call into question the very possibility of a "Revolution" in contemporary Western societies. The ambivalences of over-investment in the institutions of the state's "left hand" have already been mentioned. The reluctant relation to engagement with political parties is also worthy of some attention. Our interviews show that almost 90 percent of sample members voted for the Socialist candidate in the second round of presidential elections between

1988 and 2002, and a small majority even voted Socialist in the first round. At the same time, just four members of the sample are (or have ever been) Socialist Party members. Other party commitments exist: Four sample members are still active in leftist organizations, and nine are or have been members of the French *"Verts"* (Greens) . . . a figure that rightly suggests the connections between this party and the *soixante-huitards*. The political culture of the *"Verts"* has remained a repository of habits: mistrusting any power – including party leadership; of an almost baroque celebration of democratic rituals;[8] and a space of fierce conflicts between cliques as well. This anti-institutional culture inside the party organization is one of the reasons for the poor political impact made by the French Greens. It invites us back to a major question addressed by Hadjiisky in this book about the Czechoslovakian dissenters: How and why do some systems of dispositions, *habitus*, and visions of political action produce energetic, strong-willed, and effective activists, yet prevent them from adopting the style and behavior that will fit in with the rules of the established political field?

Beyond the mosaic of yesterday's activists' trajectories, this contribution invites, following a path opened by McAdam, paying more attention to one of the most important but unseen outcomes of social movement: the production of activists able to reinvest their energies in a great variety of movements during many years. No need to say that these activists are not unflagging fighters and that they are constantly facing the challenges of the contradictory calls and gratifications of commitment, professional careers, and private passions. A dispositional analysis, the use of the concept of habitus, can precisely allow to escape two normative traps. The first is the complacent celebration of the activists' virtues and unflinching commitment; the second is the cynical quest of the signs of possible treason or *embourgeoisement*. Going beyond these normative approaches, making sense of the variety and ruptures between and among trajectories needs a sound theoretical frame: What are the social conditions of production of dispositions – and precisely which ones – by different kinds of activism? To which extent are such dispositions deeply embodied, able to last, or, conversely, superficially rooted or flawed by contradictory polarities? What are the psychic dispositions, skills, and resources accumulated and restructured by the experience of collective

---

[8] Until the early nineties, a real and strong commitment to the organization was not even requested to apply in the *"Assemblée Générale"* for being selected as a candidate running for the Greens at local or parliamentary elections.

action? To which degree could they be reinvested for other aims than collective mobilization? Which kinds of social fields and locations, and which opportunities or threats would activate or inhibit the potentialities of militant habitus? No doubt that developing this research program on other social movements would reveal the peculiarities and limits of the *soixante-huitards*' experience; no doubt that it would also improve our understanding of the dialectics between the collective and the individual in social movements.

4

Women in Political Activism

The Biographical Resonances of the '68 Student Movement in a Latin American Context

Guadalupe Olivier and Sergio Tamayo

INTRODUCTION

The life histories of two activists of the civil and social movements in Mexico, Mariluz and Juliana, highlight the consequences of the 1968 student movement. Their histories explain the relentless struggle of women and the transcendental changes in the exercise of citizenship over the course of half a century. Their histories do not only casually respond to the question: "Why do they mobilize?" but, overall, to inquiries on the biographical and historical consequences of activism, such as: "How did they participate in and impact the large-scale scene of political contention? What were the forms of opportunity that maintained their activism in the long run? What were the political and social resonances of their participation?

The student movement in Mexico was the social response to the violent retaliation of local authorities. The government acted in this way as an instigator, attributing responsibility to the rebel groups. It falsely accused the students of planning agitation and subversion. The symbolic date that commemorates the movement is October 2, the day in 1968 on which the armed forces and the police massacred dozens of students at a peaceful meeting. That was the day the movement ended (Olivier-Téllez, Tamayo, & Voegtli, 2013).

The student struggle in Mexico was part of the wave of protests that took place throughout the world in 1968. The May Revolt of that year in France supplied an example of a radical, intellectual, and politicized youth to Mexican students. The student revolt in Germany, the Prague Spring, the protests against the war in Vietnam, the hippie movement, liberation theology, were all contemporary examples of struggles for liberation. Mexico, on the other hand, brought the economic development model that had previously surged as the dominant project to culmination: industrialization by import substitution and the strong participation of the national business sector under the auspices of the Welfare State. The year 1968 is considered the turning point that slowly gave way to a new horizon of modernity that would shape the main changes in the political, social, and cultural spheres in the country (Tamayo, 1999). Mariluz and Juliana were profoundly impacted by this movement. During their lives, as in other regions of Latin America, large waves of expanding protest expressed the claims of wide sectors of the rural and urban population (Gunder Frank & Fuentes, 1995). Struggles reinforced alternative projects on citizenship and shaped stages of political (Tamayo, 1999; McAdam, Tarrow, & Tilly, 2003) and democratic transition (Przeworski, 1996; Inglehart, 2008). For almost half a century, the social contract was restructured between distinct civil society actors and the State under which political stability was maintained (Camou, 2001). Likewise, the economic and political model shifted from one based on social welfare promoted by populist governments, to one sustained on free trade and underwritten by neoliberal governments (Roberts, 1995); the policy outputs of the fifties and sixties that reinforced social citizenship were challenged by privatization of large sectors of production and services (Olivier, 2007).

The analysis of the political trajectories of women activists that is proposed in this work uses three theoretical keys. A **first** focus explores the *Historical and Biographical Resonance of Activism*. Social sciences have used categories such as social resonance, biographical consequences of collective action, generational effects (McAdam, 1988, 1999; Giugni, 2007; Juhem, 2009; Chabanet & Giugni, 2010), and effects of socialization (Persell, 1990; Bargel, 2009) to define the diffusion and social and personal impact of a historical event. For us, historical resonance should be thought of as the multidimensional presence of events, reverberating in other events, constructed by social and historical processes. Just as the meaning of resonance in the context of sound and music means the prolonged articulation of sound through time, social resonance is understood as the prolonged articulation of social and historical events through time. At certain phases, the resonance gradually diminishes, but can sustain itself at different magnitudes. These levels of resonance can be explained by inflections that are acquired at specific historical moments: by curvatures, redirections, weaknesses, and strengths that are achieved or lost with the passing of time. Resonance here is neither considered linear nor univocal. We would have to consider the existence of one or more events that may be more relevant than others, and subsequently those events dialectically provide either more or less emphasis on their resonance. Even if the strength of the resonance diminishes over time, the moment of inflection allows it to diversify, articulating itself with other processes and new resonances, keeping it from disappearing.

In order to explore these tracks, our **second** choice has been a qualitative approach: *Comparing the life histories of two women with a gender perspective.* We chose Mariluz and Juliana for the potential meaning of their lives in politics from a feminist standpoint (Serret, 2001). Our aim is to highlight the gender inequalities that Mariluz and Juliana had to face in activism and outside of it, in order to assume and maintain a permanent commitment to social change. We reconstituted their life histories through their militant experiences, in a longitudinal study that covers four periods. Each is identified by the course and cycles of actions taken by the activists, and their commitments to and investments in organizations. Each is associated to the component and historical resonances of the local, social, cultural, and political context.

Box 4.1 Life histories

Using the life histories method to further explore the biographical resonances of activism was the key to studies that have attempted to measure the cause–effect relationships of activism. In qualitative terms, the life history joins fragments of a person's life. Memory is developed into one of the essential instruments of the method by conversational interaction. Narration was carried out without adjusting to a static or pre-established format. In this manner, the biographical discourse was elaborated based on memory.

A network of argumentations for situations and meanings was built that possibly neither of them have stopped to think about. At the end of the day, the important part of our conversation is not the reliability of the facts, but rather the genuine interpretation of the facts. As Goodwin and Jasper (2003) suggest, the point of view of the interviewees was the decisive factor: What did they want to achieve with their participation? What were their demands, with or against the movements? What type of feelings were stirred or brought out from protesting? What ran through their minds at those moments? Are lifelong activists highly peculiar profiles? So we delved into the hearts and minds of Mariluz and Juliana; their narrations revealed their imaginaries and were interwoven into networks of nodes of meaning (Vila, 1997).

There were approximately fifteen interview hours for each of our informants. Their story ran on a chronological format that was followed at each of the sessions. The subjective responses, just as in other cases (Lipsitz, 1988), constituted the "facts" in and of themselves. In this work we chronologically reconstituted the biographical resonances in their discourse. Biographies are never complete and all inclusive. There are situations that were consciously or subconsciously ignored and others that were forgotten. Exploring and expressing emotions was, for instance, a sensitive dimension. By reconstructing their biographies we are searching for a theoretical explanation of activism and its lasting effects.

We consider that social movements and the environment of political organizations clearly define peculiar militant profiles (Combes, 2012). Spaces of interaction, effects of socialization, social networks, and political alliances produce specialized activists with specific worldviews (Luker, 2003). Social movements then not only outline activists' characteristics, but also bring into society activists that are constantly – and not only in times of collective effervescence – working to transform society. The categories that we use are a synthesis of the approaches taken by various studies of the biographical consequences of activism. Even if our own analysis is more "qualitative," such a conceptual tool kit remains fruitful to make sense of life stories and the concept of resonance can facilitate analysis. We examined three dimensions: (a) the activists' political experience through their various forms of recruitment and commitment, and their levels of involvement in social and political organizations; (b) the value placed on the political impact of the activists' personal participation (biographical resonances). We observe not only the footprints left by Mariluz and Juliana's participation, but also the marks left by the activists along the trajectory of the movements, through personal innovation, the change in the militant life course and worldview, and moments of radicalization and/or demobilization and (c) the activists' life course through their academic and professional training, changes in employment, personal and familial relationships, and lifestyles, as well as obstacles and opportunities for female participation in politics.

Box 4.2 The biographical resonance of lasting activism

Just as in the case of Black activist Ivory Perry in the United States (cf. Lipsitz, 1988), Mariluz and Juliana have a long trajectory as activists and union and community organizers. They grew as activists into a discourse of dissidence and, therefore, at times "encapsulated" their narrations with ideological schematics of complex social processes. Definitely, Mariluz and Juliana were formed as radical activists, but that does not imply that they are impulsive or lacking organizational discipline. They are firm and steady in their anti-neoliberal and anti-capitalist convictions and confident in their actions. But they are not the type to appeal to provocation, or prone to the use of social violence.

The local and national events and situations that were referenced by Mariluz and Juliana in their interviews were corroborated using archives, chronologies, and secondary sources on social movements, political conflicts, and social change. At some sessions, we used these sources in the interaction with the interviewees, even to provoke reactions from them that provided more information about certain public events. As Lipsitz (1988:8) suggests, the goal is not portraying heroines, but rather about presenting activists that have successes and failures, with complexities and contradictions, as leaders made of flesh and bone.

The in-depth interview, as opposed to the so-called follow-up surveys that longitudinal statistic methods use (Giugni, 2007), allowed us to better understand the influence of individuals, institutions, movements, ideologies, and organizations that were fundamental to the development of values and beliefs in Mariluz and Juliana's actions (cf. Lipsitz, 1988). Biographical reconstruction allows, even when the nodes of particular meaning interweave, leaving out of multiple and varied personal experiences, it is possible to reevaluate a coherent discourse that makes memories emerge and shed light on resonances and personal effects of social change. Different from other biographies, where the sacrifice of personal life is prioritized over commitment, in Mariluz's and Juliana's histories having a personal life and participating in activism did not mean extraordinary negation of any kind, except in the economic sense. Yet, even job instability was not presented as a symptom of sacrifice. On the other hand, emotional stability in romantic relationships at any given moment gave way to further dedication, merit, and commitment in social struggle. Their lives have been, over the course of their experience, very enjoyable and exciting.

Our **third** analytical choice has been analyzing *Biographical availability as a biographical resonance of activism*. No one, as McAdam (1988) states, is automatically available for activism, even when he or she is a sympathizer of the cause. Interpreting biographical availability requires identifying family, personal, educational, and professional backgrounds. When associated with the unique experience of activists, and only then, can the cultural typologies of social and political activism be clearly spelled out. Who are they and what socioeconomic particularities can identify Mariluz and Juliana? What family, educational, and professional background characteristics helped to persuade or dissuade them from becoming a part of specific social movements? McAdam (1988) admits that people attempt to manage or change social tensions if particularly motivated for protest. In other words, people sometimes make themselves biographically available for protest, regardless of their socioeconomic status. In all, individuals may become dissuaded due to responsibilities they have in their daily life, with family or work. Consequently, biographical availability has more to do with personal will and values than with material conditions. Mariluz and Juliana were not biographically available to substantially modify their own life expectations; the moment they decided to participate in social movements changed their lives forever. It was a combination of environmental and cognitive mechanisms (McAdam, Tarrow, & Tilly, 2003): The processes of modernization of Mexico City and those of urbanization and proletarianization of the mid-range city of Cuernavaca, linked to their own socioeconomic backgrounds, explain their involvement and future commitment.

Box 4.3 Mariluz and Juliana

Mariluz was born in 1951, in the bosom of a working class family of Mexico City. Her father was a day laborer in the production industry stimulated by the protectionist policies of the internal market that were promoted by the populist governments of the time. The working and living conditions of workers of that time were much better both in terms of salary and social benefits, which were based on a growing attention to social rights. Participation in unions, despite being corporatized by State leaders and employees, generated a strong class identity among unionized workers at a time when the social contract considered the participation of the working class in national development inevitable. Belonging to the working class was a point of pride that transcended the walls of the factory. Even though he was never a part of the union elite, his experience as a worker representative inserted him into other spaces of social experience with his neighborhood and family. In this way, Mariluz experienced the strong charismatic leadership of her father in community activities of the working-class neighborhood where they lived, through the organizing of soccer matches and religious holidays. She was moved by the afternoon talks with her father, reinforced by generous and daily follow up by her mother. The idea of solidarity among workers in an environment in which social justice was above individual interest definitely marked her.

Juliana was born of a poor family, migrants from the rural areas of the state of Morelos in south-central Mexico. She grew up in a situation of economic hardship. With an alcoholic and irresponsible father, it was her mother who was the moral pillar and breadwinner of the family. With difficulty, she sustained herself working as a fruit vendor near the city market. Life expectations were centered on work and the struggle for survival, nothing more. Her mother was hardly ever home. It was in the streets where Juliana established a personal, family, and work life, socializing daily with informal day laborers and vendors, with whom she weaved solid networks of solidarity. Her mother was quite generous with those in need, to whom she frequently offered up her home and the few resources she had, without payment for expenses (Quintanilla, 2014). Juliana did not go to school, but a sense of independence was generated, even when she had yet to become conscious of her age, and, given the example set by her mother, the need of having to work for herself resonated when she was still a small girl.

Just as with Mariluz, Juliana internalized the idea of social justice. However, Juliana's definition was based on solidarity and equality, stemming from poverty and a gendered attitudinal affinity. Mariluz's definition resulted from a class-conscious exercise of social citizenship.

Consequently, the objective of this chapter is to reconstruct the life histories of two activists who participated in the main social struggles of the country and were trained as leaders. They lived a complete life – emotional and familial, political and professional – strongly tied to their life partners. The biographical resonances of their activism allowed them to recruit other participants, influence their worldviews, inspire new strategies for the struggles and become part of the impact made by other activists on their society. The narration of their histories explores their trajectories and resonances through four stages. We begin with the joining of the movement, attitudinal affinities, and the initial handling of emotions during a time period beginning with the 1968 student movement through to the labor movement of the mid-size cities in 1972.

Next, we differentiate recruitment by political organizations from commitment in social movements, in order to highlight processes of radicalization over a span of ten years, between 1973 and 1983. Following this, we focus on the development of gendered leadership, in a case more clearly feminist, during the 1980s, a decade of the great economic crisis. Finally, we explain the paradoxes of the "diasporisation" of the left-wing that occurred between 1987 and 1989, which had fundamental historical resonances on Mariluz and Juliana and whose consequences were reverted after personal resonances of sorts toward the social movements at the end of the twentieth century. Mariluz's and Juliana's stories genuinely converge with the political moment in which they unfolded, in such a way that in each section the social and historical contexts are revealed.

STAGE ONE (1968–1973): INSERTION INTO THE MOVEMENT. BIOGRAPHICAL AFFINITIES, FAMILY INTEGRATION AND MANAGING AFFECTIVITY

The bonanza period of Mariluz and Juliana's generation, the "economic miracle" of the 1950s, came to an end in 1968. This year was the core of a global and national political crisis, at the very moment when the government aimed to project to the world the image of a modern country, hosting the XIXth Olympics. The student movement had social consequences of at least three orders. The resonances of the first order are biographical and directly impacted the central leaders of the movement, who then had decisive political influence in long-term national politics. By second order consequences, we refer to the biographical impact on mid-level activists, who were directly or indirectly influenced by the student movement, as in the cases of Mariluz and Juliana. Finally, by impact of the third order we mean the long-term effects that the student movement has had over time on other social movements and the political life of the country (Tamayo, 1999).

After the strong repression suffered by the student movement in 1968, a decade of collective effervescence emerged. It was characterized by the inclusion of many young university activists in various social movements: of the guerrilla struggle, movements for land for *campesinos*, for democracy in the factory unions and at universities, for urban space and housing in the cities, feminist movements, movements against repression, justice for the forced disappearances and freedom for political prisoners. Mariluz and Juliana participated from this moment onward. Their militant lives crossed, unbeknown to them, across professorial activism, unionized democracy, and the feminist struggle.

In all, Mariluz and Juliana are activists and leaders with different characteristics. At a young age, the movements of '68 marked the political life of Mariluz with a profound sense of social justice. The case of Juliana was relatively different. The 1968 movement had an indirect impact in her initial involvement. Two years after the '68 events, students from the Universidad Nacional would constantly step in at the factory where she worked in the small city of Cuernavaca, 80 kilometers from Mexico City. From then on, they recruited her for organizing and political work. Juliana had lived within a difficult environment of a poor rural migrant family. Her mother was the head of the household. She worked a stand at the Municipal Market. Juliana never had access to formal education, given the need to work from a very young age. It was political activism, rather, that provided her with professional training and the capacity to study the great revolutionary texts. She took courses and seminars on History and International Politics, which gave her abilities for writing manifestos, reviews, and, later, books on issues mainly associated with the women's worker movement and human rights. Regardless of these differences, the two women have similar trajectories in terms of the positions they have taken within their social and political organizations. They became leaders with organizers' abilities: initiative and creativity to reflect on and to plan collective actions. Both benefited from the extraordinary dynamics of the sixties, "amplifying participants feelings of efficacity through the creation of new emotional framings and collective identities conducive to protest" (Taylor, 2010). And this empowering trend was specifically visible for women, in a cultural context where machismo was expressed without restraint. Mariluz and Juliana recruited and inspired others to act for social change (Morris & Staggenborg, 2007). Yet, the clearest difference can partly be found in their biographical backgrounds, in their biographical availability (McAdam, 1999).

Mariluz's access to studies and academic training provided her with opportunities in the medium term. Juliana's need to work from a young age made her a worker in the large textile factories, in the great industrial corridor of the city of Cuernavaca. The circumstances that led Mariluz to associate herself with a small revolutionary group around the journal "Punto Crítico" (Critical Point), as a result of her activism in the '68 movement, are different from Juliana's experience: she met a group of young students who then recruited her to start her political career in the Internationalist Communist Group, which would later become the Revolutionary Workers' Party (PRT for its acronym in Spanish). The analysis and reflection both women had within their respective organizations instilled in them a particular vision and set of ideologies, Mariluz's being initially Guevara-ist, revolutionary and anti-voting, while Juliana's was Trotskyist, feminist, and pro-voting.

Between 1968 and 1973, Mariluz and Juliana participated for the first time in social movements. They directly participated due to their attitudinal affinity, a result of the work and personal development environments to which they belonged. Their insertion via their socialization within organizational networks generated in them a strong sense of social belonging, both to the movement in which they participated and the specific historical trend, barely perceivable at that moment, of class and social struggle. At this stage, the skills for handling emotions that they had to develop were just budding in the face of the visible risks of State-sponsored repression mechanisms, and of their own political inexperience as fledgling activists.

Attitudinal Affinity

The participation of Mariluz was rooted in an attitudinal affinity that developed from her childhood and adolescence. Attitudes and values based on social justice edged her and motivated her into participating in the 1968 student movement. Mariluz studied in the mornings at a primary education teachers' school. In the afternoons, she took high school courses at a branch of the Universidad Nacional. The two schools separately joined the general strike. Without any precedent of social participation, Mariluz decided to participate, enthused by the political effervescence:

Not all of my schoolmates entered as activists. I was just one more participant without any political consciousness. It was the idea of justice that called to me. The dilemma was clear: what the students demanded was just. What was unjust was what the government was doing. It could be said that two currents were formed: the students were the good guys, the bad guys were the government and the police.

(Interview with Mariluz, January 2014[1])

Two important factors explain Mariluz's attitudinal affinity (McAdam, 1988). The first refers to the principles and values that she learned from her family. The second, which we consider as significant, stems from the content of her curriculum and the lessons taught to her at the National School for Teachers, which reinforced the nationalist-revolutionary spirit and the predominance of the worker and farmer struggles in the history of the country. We must include another important element of historical resonance: the socioeconomic origins of the student population that came from places with a long tradition of *campesino* or peasant farmer struggles. It was from this attitudinal position that the 1968 student movement took on meaning for her. Such resonances, more than previous political training or recruitment, allowed Mariluz's, yet undefined, ideas of social justice to take on precise meaning.

[1] All interviews' translations are made by the authors.

Juliana's case is similar in terms of her attitudinal affinity toward the collective effervescence of the labor movement in Cuernavaca, although experienced under different conditions. In 1969, set on "keeping busy with something," she began working at one of the textile factories that was part of the growing push for industrialization in the city, changing the demographics of the local population toward a process of proletarianization. This process had a gendered dimension too: the automotive industry mainly hired men, while the textile factories' workforce included 80 percent women. Juliana began working without any qualifications. She decided to study at school, where she graduated as a textile production teacher, which helped her to become a qualified worker with better income. Two years later, in 1971, unexpectedly and for the first time, Juliana was faced with a union movement when the managers decided to wrongfully terminate 110 temporary workers. The women that were still employed came together in solidarity with those who had been fired and a large movement for their reinstatement began. It was a sense of justice, as in Mariluz's case, that led Juliana to participate in the factory strike. But in this case, a male union leader played an important role. If he motivated the mobilization of women workers, he also touched a nerve regarding Juliana's questioning of gender differences. This leader of the most important workers' federation in Mexico, the CTM,[2] was both a charismatic personality for women and a mysoginistic organizer, keeping total control over the management and direction of the union in which – even though the union membership was mostly women – men dominated power structures.

Managing Emotions

The participation of individuals in the movement is charged with emotional resources, and, even though they have hardly been considered determinants of action (Goodwin, Jasper, & Polletta, 2007; Jasper, 2008), include three types of emotions that make processes of political debate dynamic: reflective emotions, affective ties, and long-term or moral emotions. Frequently, emotions converge and act in conjunction with one another. This occurred in the case of Mariluz and Juliana throughout their trajectory, in which reflective emotions, affective ties, and virtuous feelings came together. One situation that serves as an example is Juliana's union participation in 1972, the struggle for the reinstatement of the

[2] CTM = Acronym in Spanish for the Federation of Mexican Workers (Confederación de Trabajadores de México).

fired workers. The textile union decided to leave the CTM to rally a new Independent Workers Union. Alliances between unions were important for the women textile workers union and auto-industry union at Nissan, which was predominantly male. It gave way to a process of solidarity among workers from both unions, but also to base-level affective ties that strengthened their union commitment:

The alliances were strengthened because the NISSAN men, very happily, would come to the factory to see and hang out with the [textile] production women. And the women, also happy with the attractive men from over there. In that environment there was a lot of solidarity, a lot of support.

(Interview with Juliana, February 2014)

The labor strike took place amid a series of mobilizations that included marches and sit-ins in the city square. In the process, many new couples were formed and many women became pregnant during the time that the strike lasted: "sarcastically, it was said: what do we gain from the strike? Many children! They would exclaim in chorus ..." The participation of women was not easy, despite the new affective commitments that were made. Women constantly faced sexual harassment; they had to control their fear in order to stand watch at night and deal with their husbands' or boyfriends' jealousy and anger at their participation. In an environment deeply rooted in machismo, Juliana developed, in contrast, an independent view on gender. Her participation allowed her to control her feelings of sadness and anxiety, substituting them for audacity and strength. She learned that many of those who intended to flatter women were in reality offensive and that cooperation and class solidarity could not be bought by allowing sexual harassment. As time went on, there was a sense of discomfort because the leaders considered the women "foolish" and justified the fact that it was the men that led and watched over the women at protests. The major lesson learned at this stage was: "fear cannot paralyze me: us women have to show strength in order to gain spaces [for ourselves]." If any involvement in social movement includes a dimension of "emotion work," the balance of power between movements and their opponents, the cultural peculiarities, should be carefully considered. When Cheryl Hercus (1999) describes the action of Australian feminists as a "mobilisation of anger" against patriarchal relations, the practical and symbolic weight of patriarchy suggests more in Mexico of a "mobilization against one's own fear."

Affective ties such as love, hate, respect, or trust persist through time, in contrast to reflective emotions that are basically immediate reactions in light of specific events. As Goodwin, Jasper, and Polletta (2003:418) note, as opposed to reflective emotions, affective emotions can originate during the course of a conflict as well as instigate a conflict. Such is the case of the textile strike in Cuernavaca. The trajectory of the strike generated a multitude of contradictory affective emotions with distinct personal results that broke or redirected the life course of many women activists. These emotions caused a first-order biographical resonance in Juliana. They opened a new stage that was both a turning point and a moment a crystallization of a gendered consciousness, which would from now on structure her commitments (Einwohner, Hollander, & Olson, 2000).

STAGE TWO (1972–1983): POLITICAL RECRUITMENT

Mariluz and Juliana participated in the 1968 student movement and the labor movement of 1972, respectively. But they would soon be absorbed into political activism. How, why, and by whom were they channeled into such commitments (McAdam, 1999)? What we notice here is an inflection in the construction of a collective identity, initially emerging from the social movement and reinforced or transformed through political action. It is a way of biographically explaining the basic question noted by Charles Tilly (2008) on the shift from the social to the political and a way of radicalizing social commitment.

Inspiring Leadership

The labor movement in the state of Morelos was linked to many organizations of many kinds. Initially, Juliana experienced the process of union democratization through the union's shift from being a central corporatized State union to a union of larger openness and political independence. At the same time, the historical resonances derived from a Christian-based movement justified by liberation theology and promoted by the progressive bishop Sergio Méndez Arceo established roots in the city of Cuernavaca. Many churches supported the creation of social networks (Martínez, Quintanilla, Hernández, & Melchor, 2002). Juliana then began her growth as a conscious activist; her role as woman, mother, wife, and worker stood out, qualitatively defining her in her social participation. It was precisely at this state that diverse political groups emerged, such as the Mexican Communist Party and the Trotskyist GCI. Many different militant groups of youth – known as "the students" – which had reorganized into small leftist revolutionary groups, arrived in Morelos after the repression of the 1968 student movement. Some enlisted in the guerrilla struggle of those years and others set out to work with the social movements in the country. Such connection pushed forward the collective effervescence of the seventies known as the "popular, peasant, and worker insurgency." Juliana then found herself courted by many political groups. Her recruitment was not a linear external process, but rather a result of a personal decision based on her own reflection of her experience within the union and the philosophy derived from such groups. She decided to join the Trotskyist group because of the strength of its feminist discourse and the charisma of its leaders.

After the student movement of 1968, Mariluz began working as a teacher and continued studying economics at the university. Despite the demobilization of the students after the 1968 repression, she found herself in a local surrounding of extraordinary politicization at the university and she participated in the students union struggles. With other teacher colleagues, she formed study groups on social issues. Her ideals of becoming a "missionary" teacher led her to organize literacy campaigns for neighborhood residents. Mariluz's growth as an activist inspired the organization and social consciousness of the people and also contributed to her academic training. All together, these activities placed her in a pedagogical militancy of sorts within her academic and work experience. During these years, Mariluz was influenced by various groups – Maoist, Trotskyist, and Guevara-ist – but due to her inclusion into the Economics Department at UNAM, she became part of the Punto Crítico group, inspired by her teacher Alejandro Álvarez, who was one of its founders. She became involved via Marxist workshops and study groups at the political junction with the social revolutions in Latin America.

From Love to Politics, the Shift in Life Course

It was at the borderline between social movements and political participation that Mariluz and Juliana finally found the love that led them emotionally and politically throughout their entire life journey. Historical and biographical resonances came together at a specific point. The lesson here is that a renewed vision of leadership is needed (Morris & Staggenborg, 2007). Research on gender and social movements has strongly emphasized the peculiarities of women's positions, their frequent exclusion from leadership, as the importance of their contribution as "bridging leaders," structuring an "intermediate layer of leadership, whose primary tasks are bridging potential constituents and adherents as well as potential formal leaders of the movement" (Robnett, 1996: 1688). If this dimension can make sense of a part of Mariluz's and Juliana's commitment, both in their organization and in the coordination of different networks for Mariluz, this case study invites us to focus on another dimension: how leadership inspires and takes on the form of moral authority, touches people's consciousness, and motivates participation. Mariluz and Juliana found themselves with another type of leadership, one that is collectively built in the everyday life of the group. Several feelings bloomed all together. For both women, love was one of the focal points of their political participation. This love was not only love toward their significant others, but also toward their professional and activist activities: a sense of love for justice, liberty, and social change. In a patriarchal culture, it is notable that their respective life partners were also companions in the struggle and, far from establishing a relationship of subordination to a patriarchal authority, they were able to generate egalitarian relationships that helped propel their political participation. The feeling of finding themselves in situations of equality within their emotional relationships instilled strength in them in the political and professional sense. They admired the work of their partners, but at the same time felt supported and admired by them.

This is how Mariluz met Antonio, a militant of Punto Crítico, healthcare movement activist, and member of the healthcare union. Juliana met José, a Trotskyist linked to political activism and efforts in solidarity with the labor movement. Through their political organizing, Mariluz and Antonio worked within the professorial and labor movement in Morelos, while Juliana and José were political activists in other unions and groups within the same movement. Their lives almost met; they ran into each other without knowing one another. They identified themselves within the same processes and assemblies and with the same leaders. José would become Juliana's life partner from this point onward, and since 1985 Antonio would be Mariluz's life partner. With them they lived through social struggles. Together they discussed politics and defined plans of action. They also built their own families. Mariluz and Antonio had two daughters who are now university students and Juliana and José had a son. José and Antonio have provided emotional and ideological support that was fundamental for the women's lives. They have built a space of tolerance and respect that is matchless. Mariluz and Juliana left behind their past lives and took on new obstacles. In the midst of falling in love, they radicalized their action within union struggles in a context of politicization and learning. They brought their personal and politically active lives together. Their life partners represented a biographical resonance that defined their future in activism.

STAGE THREE (1983–1989): LEADERSHIP COMMITMENT AND THE STRUGGLE FOR HEGEMONY

The time when Mariluz and Juliana began to play a fundamental role in collective leadership within their respective organizations paradoxically coincides with the moment in which the socialist perspective disappeared in national and local contexts, thus dissolving the apparatus that gave them political identity. The eighties survived one of the worst economic crises in Mexican history. The great labor mobilizations and the organization of national civic strikes added to the growing mobilization of 1985's earthquake victims. By 1986, 18 years after the student movement of 1968, a huge mobilization of students at the country's main university was organized in favor of free public education. This crisis and collective effervescence caused a schism in the hegemonic institutional political party (PRI), opening two different paths: a nationalist democratic route perpetuating the Welfare State, and on the other hand the neoliberal route, seeking to embed greater globalization tendencies. These alternatives confronted each other in the 1988 presidential elections and have since marked the main fronts dividing the nation. The creation of the social-democratic and nationalist party, the Democratic Revolutionary Party (PRD for its acronym in Spanish), in 1989 caused the coming together of large sectors of the political and social left-wing into one party. It was confirmed by the nationalist revolutionary left-wing of the PRI, as well as the social leftist democratic and nationalist group, and the, now extinct, Socialist Mexican Party, along with various small groups of the leftism and social movements. But such changes also transformed the left-wing, which could not rally the new party into a loose diaspora, leaving many activists – including Mariluz and Juliana – without organizations with which they could identify. Many abandoned political activism, or their organizations fragmented (Klandermans, 2003). Others reinvested the civil association sphere, which in the nineties launched the momentum for environmental issues, gender equality, human rights, and the transition to democracy.

Leadership Training

Social historical resonance helped to mature the political conditions for building large networks and alliances among diverse social sectors. National councils of field workers, unions, and the poor population of some cities were formed to reclaim the expansion of social citizenship. Feminists and gay-lesbian groups formed movements, which side by side with the *Frente Nacional contra la Represión* became the pillars of the struggle for citizenship in Mexico. The political reforms of the previous decade had allowed more participants from parties and left-wing groups into the federal and local elections, pushing political and civil rights to expansion.

The economy and feminism seemed to be the issues chosen by Mariluz and Juliana, respectively. The experience Mariluz had gained in the union allowed her to develop organizational and discourse abilities, linked to the ideology of *Punto Crítico*. Soon she became a member of the Economics Commission of the organization, whose influence was at a national level. Juliana came from an important labor experience with an increasingly rooted feminist perspective, which was fundamental for the Trotskyist party to which she belonged. She soon became part of the Central Committee and part of the State Political Committee of the party. They had gained significant political and symbolic capital, in Bourdieu's (1981) terms, as well as dispositions and abilities that allowed them to have more biographical availability as political directors. Both learned the hegemonic discourse. They internalized a methodology to think problems through. They developed an ability to associate those problems with the political program and started to take part in the collective production of interpretative frameworks and discursive activism (Snow, 2001). Their leadership combines the resources gained from long experience and new opportunities. For example, Juliana's charisma enhances her, in spite of her small height; she represents the experience of a laborer with feminist awareness, symbolizing a subject in transformation by excellence – something every revolutionary spirit aspires to. Mariluz's spirit represents and inspires a latent commitment, articulated with her political capacity, reinforced by her academic education. Although, neither of the two became, at this stage, a central leader inside their organizations, they were recognized – and self-recognized – as having a strong perception of political opportunities and a sense of collective action. The resources accumulated by their activisms create biographical resonance and in turn influence the history of social protest.

From Hegemonic Discourse to the Battle for Hegemony of Discourse

With the support of their partisan environment (Combes, 2011), Mariluz and Juliana gradually became able to develop the hegemonic discourse of the revolutionary left. But they had to face the peculiar situation when an inside battle is unleashed. Should the political discourse remain unchanged or be reframed (Laclau, 2003)? How to structure a discourse that is coherent with the mobilization of the masses (Bourdieu, 1981)? How to add to a leader's charisma the strength of a discourse constructed upon sound theoretical capacities and historical analysis? Bourdieu suggests that leaderships are based on the relationship between political, social, and symbolic capitals. Some activists are more culturally deprived, and therefore tend be more centered on loyalty to a certain hierarchical leader or trend; others can rely on long pragmatic experience of struggles, and others are rich in symbolic or cultural capital. Mariluz and Juliana do not coincide with any of the specific profiles because they identify with all of them.

They were part of a specific trend to which they had to be faithful, whether because of the sum of experience due to socialization, or because of the loyalty given to a certain discursive constellation. But at the same time, they were part of a specific militant experience, Mariluz in the teacher's movement and Juliana as a feminist in the labor movement. Their militancy and leadership were built within a dynamic of intimacies and distanced relationships. Mariluz lived through several ruptures in the Punto Crítico organization. But Mariluz's loyalty to a particular trend, which had been the fundamental base for her recruitment and her subsequent political growth, positioned her as part of the group that resisted to keep the group's internal cohesion. In contrast, Juliana experienced an internal conflict based on identity differences, similar to what Goodwin, Jasper, and Polletta (2007: 421) call states of mind. For these authors, movement leaders frequently try to instill feelings of hope and optimism in the participants, a sense of action that can have a positive, transforming effect. But sometimes leaders, instead of looking to instill positive states of mind, instill negative states of mind in order to persuade participation. This occurs when identity groups are created inside organizations, emphasizing competition more than cooperation between activists with different structures of resources. Juliana's authority directing the organization at a national level and her own vision that articulated labor struggle and feminist work was challenged in the mid-eighties, with the emergence of the earthquake victims' and seamstresses' movements. Juliana was suddenly displaced by a feminist current, a painful challenge for someone who had always combined trade-unionism and feminism. She did not break away from the party then, but she retreated to her local work in Cuernavaca and left her position as national director.

STAGE FOUR (1990–2000): WITHDRAWAL FROM THE PARTY
AND COMMITMENT TO THE MOVEMENT

In spite of the particularities of Mariluz's and Juliana's biographies, they share a common and extraordinary trajectory in their activist lives. They have built a process of coming to awareness, of collective empowerment, of ideological polarization, and of left-wing political identity. Therefore, it is important to define the stages in the construction of activism and to rebuild the form and intensity of commitment (Cf. Hirsch, 2003). Some of the aspects in which they differ are in the roles they played regarding feminism, in the course of their personal lives as much as in leadership. Another significant contrast is the possibility of having access to academic institutional training. Mariluz was able to obtain a doctorate in Latin American Studies, and she was employed by the most prestigious institution of higher education in the country. She also belonged to a family with a strong maternal presence that, though tolerant and traditional, was without gender equality awareness. This is contrary to Juliana, who was only able to finish elementary school and acquired her entire theoretical and applied training through activism and partisan political work. Nevertheless, her clarity in her feminist practices is a result of the combination of her family, labor, and ideological backgrounds. However, their processes of experience and participation in social movements, the time periods and specific moments in which they inserted themselves in social activism and political leadership, are extraordinarily similar. Another biographical match can be seen at the moment of rupture with their political organizations. They sustained a commitment, outside of the party, but always within the movement and social struggle. This activism based on commitment, solidarity, and social awareness became a way of life. These women provide a clear example of historical resonance on personal biographies. They are also an example of personal biographical resonance on the history of social movements in the country.

"I Retreat from the Party, but Not from the Movement"

The student movement of 1968 was a political turning point for Mexico, as was the year 1988. In the midst of a cumbersome political shift that tried to impose an economic model based on free trade, the privatization of public goods, and the disintegration of the social pact and unions, the presidential elections in Mexico could have been the first changeover to a left-wing nationalistic government. The main political forces of this confrontation were not the existing social movements, but instead the political trends of the hegemonic party of the country, which divided without reconciliation: the nationalistic and revolutionary trend led by Cuauhtémoc Cárdenas, and the neoliberal trend lead by Carlos Salinas de Gortari. When Cárdenas separated from his party he beckoned all forces, including the most radical ones, to form a coalition for the 1988 elections. As we have seen, many accepted and created an electoral front and the PRD, a new political party. A majority of associations responded to the beckoning call. But it implied dissolving the old organizations and committing to the formation of a new political party of an electoral type sometimes totally different to the ones these groups had strategically planned to build. Critical Point, Mariluz's organization, decided to participate individually in the new party, after their formal dissolution. Juliana's organization, the Workers' Revolutionary Party, split from a small group of intellectuals who decided to follow the new organization. Although in quantitative terms it did not mean a great loss, such diasporization of the left-wing affected the party, whose influence collapsed, before dividing in two.

Like many left-wing activists from that time, Mariluz and Juliana lived with feelings of uncertainty and dismay. In contrast with 1968, radicalization was not a significant path for activists (Klandermans, 2003) after 1988, and just one year before the fall of the Berlin Wall they disbanded, losing ideological and organizational direction. Following the PRD was a total change of the utopias that had been strongly internalized during the more than twenty years of struggle. What type of retreat, if any, would define the one Mariluz and Juliana experienced? In Klandermans' (2003) typology, retreat from a movement is partly due to the very existence of the movement. But when movements were crumbling into diasporas, what type of reflection and emotions ran through the minds of important radical left-wing activists in Mexico? It was not necessarily a personal abandonment because it was the organizations that practically abandoned them. They did not have the strength to persist like those Klandermans refers to as those who stay behind as a prophetic minority keeping up expectations. It was not like that for Mariluz. It could have been like that in Juliana's case, connected to a group that vigorously kept-up the foundational principals of their party. How are we to regard those unwilling to shift in their principles? Are we to classify them as Messiahs, who "were left behind," because they did not accept the change that was offered?

Even if in Juliana's case it meant a type of abandonment from the small group that remained, in Mariluz's case it meant staying as an activist for the change in the leftist social movement, in spite of the fact that Antonio accepted going with the PRD. Juliana and Mariluz define themselves as political. They still consider it important to build a revolutionary political party that does not yet exist. They left behind political activism and they became active in other movements. Mariluz continued to be in the teachers' union and even founded a tri-national organization in defense of public education with unions from Canada, United States, and Mexico. Juliana founded the Independent Commission for Human Rights of the State of Morelos. Now, without political affiliation, the two women have become intellectual leaders who inspire and influence new dynamics in social movements. Lipsitz (1988), referring to Gramsci, considers organic intellectuals to be an influence on organization and theory, and an inspiration for new visions of life for everyday people. Mariluz and Juliana contributed, for twenty years during their training and experience as activists, to the configuration of a collective organic intellectual, represented in the organization and political party. After 1989 Mariluz and Juliana became organic intellectuals by means of biographical resonances, which reconfigured a culture of opposition and political activism. This has been, perhaps as a result of the sum of political capital, the most productive and creative period of their activism forever.

ACTIVISTS . . . FOREVER?

Since the nineties, Mariluz's and Juliana's activism has had different orientations. Each one, within her area of participation, built a project of her own that was as much a result of each of their paths as that of their commitment to social struggle. They supported mobilizations by civil society backing the Zapatista National Liberation Army (EZLN) in 1994 and the transition to democracy. The political shift that had long been awaited by a majority of Mexicans came in the year 2000 when the conservative right, represented by the National Action Party (PAN), won presidential elections, in the face of the evident impotence of the electoral left-wing. Yet, for most Mexicans the democratic expectations were not reached with the change in political regime. During the first decade of the twenty-first century, social struggles were polarized by two big contention models, one that transgresses institutions through social movements, and another that stays within institutional frameworks. Mariluz and Juliana adhered to the transgressive model that was reinforced with the emergence of movements that had great national impact, such as the struggles led by the National Front for the Defence of Land (*Frente Nacional en*

Defensa de la Tierra), the Assembly of the People of Oaxaca, which brought together the teachers' union struggle with demands from the indigenous communities, the EZLN in the Chiapas, the resistance movement of the Mexican Electricians Union in the center of the country, and the struggle against State violence and femicide, particularly in northern cities. The other contention model (the containing type), demonstrated tirelessness in the face of fraud and inequality in electoral processes, both of which were vigorously articulated with the mobilization of large groups of people, like the massive mobilization led by Andrés Manuel López Obrador and his party, the National Regeneration Movement (MORENA for its acronym in Spanish), from 2006 onward. In all of these great mobilizations Mariluz and Juliana were direct or indirect participants from the trenches of their own social activism. After almost 50 years of continuous participation, the experiences that began during the '68 movement or had been incited by their student leaders reached a climax. Globalization and the neo-Zapatista influence on global movements allowed Mariluz to take a significant part in the formation of the tri-national association in favor of unions and public education. Juliana, on her end, emerged as one of the leaders of the human rights movement in the Morelos region.

So, what theoretical implications can one identify in the lasting activism of two women who were recruited for the '68 student movement and continued for the rest of their lives? What political historical and biographical resonances explain – or can't explain – the dynamic of social change? The objective of this chapter was to rethink the biographical consequences of activism as resonances. The cultural repercussions are marked by the presence of historical impacts in concrete situations. Those experiences are remembered by many activists. A multidimensional plot is developed, paying attention to the mechanisms, paths, and social and historical processes that in time influence or cross each other, or are articulated by one other. Resonance is a prolonged articulation of social events through time. Mariluz's and Juliana's lives were transcended by these historical resonances as larger social processes that irrevocably touched them in their own personal experiences. At the same time, their role had an impact, whether conscious or subconscious, on imperceptible or large fragments of other trajectories, without which they would not have occurred in the way that they did.

Their first insertion in the social movement was during the student movement of '68, which guided their future activism. A plot of historical arguments has developed around the meanings of the student movement and its symbolic effects on democracy and social justice. Such a plot has varied and had strong impacts on other movements and on political strategies. Each in their own way, Juliana and Mariluz were as much influential to as they were influenced by the boom of union insurgency in the seventies. Both were recruited by the revolutionary left-wing at the end of that decade and then both deployed leadership qualities during the next decade, in the eighties. They broke free of the hegemonic tendencies of the time, which were to align with reformist alternatives, to fall in the whirlpool of the institutionalization of social protest. They then decided to break away from their political parties, but not from the autonomous social movements into which they placed all their efforts. We highlighted four decisive stages, defined by the political context and the militant's particular forms of activism. The first is the insertion into a social movement, which resulted from the unfolding of the student movement of '68, and which was articulated to significant aspects of biographical affinity, such as family integration characteristics and the emotional management of fear and risk perception. Political recruitment occurred later, at stage two, it was a result of their initial activism, combining the rise of a politically inspiring leader, and intense feelings of love that happened just then, thus invigorating their political commitment forever. Stage three expresses the radicalization process in political activism, the appropriation of an ideology based on class struggle and feminism, and the learning of exceptional collective leadership abilities. This stage also brought along the challenge of the inevitable internal struggle for hegemony in the direction of their organizations. The final stage combines ruptures and continuities. The withdrawal from participating in the political organization does not mean isolation or the dogmatic resistance of small groups, but the preservation of political commitment within the social movement, and the persisting ideology of union politics and human rights. Our two activists personify a major trend of contentious politics in twenty-first-century Mexican life: a non-partisan but not-apolitical trend.

II

TERRORIST VIOLENCE, STATE REPRESSION, AND ACTIVISTS' EXPERIENCES

INTRODUCTION

Jocelyn Viterna

In the 1980s, the question of whether "high-risk" social movement activism could transform the life course of the activists themselves took center stage in the US media. Several high profile stories suggested that the progressive leftist activists of the 1960s and 1970s had by the 1980s transformed into capitalism-loving conservatives. Such stories insinuated that the powerful and often life-threatening activism of the earlier era was generated by nothing more than the whimsical idealism of youth, and that such idealism would regularly disappear over the life course as youth grew into rational, calculating adults.

Sociologist Doug McAdam provided a powerful challenge to these popular assertions. In a rare stroke of academic luck, McAdam uncovered the records of all students who applied to be, and were accepted as, participants in "Freedom Summer," a 1964 civil rights campaign that sent, mostly, white college students from northern US states to the US South to register black voters and teach black Americans in "Freedom Schools." Some of the applicants accepted into the campaign did indeed participate in Freedom Summer, but others did not. By tracking down these same applicants 20 years later, McAdam was able to demonstrate the powerful impact that Freedom Summer had on participants' future "biographies." Specifically, he found that individuals who participated in Freedom Summer were more likely than their nonparticipating counterparts to maintain political activism throughout their lifetime (McAdam, 1988). They were also more likely to adopt nontraditional family structures, and to work in jobs that were aimed at helping others. McAdam's findings have since been supported by others' research (Fendrich, 1993; Sherkat & Blocker, 1997), and a relative consensus has emerged: High-risk activism transforms participants' biographies such that they will live the rest of their lives as politically engaged citizens.

The articles in the second segment of this volume show the importance of this line of social movement research as well as its limitations. Like McAdam, these scholars overwhelmingly suggest that, once an individual adopts an activist identity in a high-risk, militant movement, then that identity will continue to structure his or her life course long after formal movement participation has ended. Indeed, it seems that the particular sacrifices required of, especially militant, activism is a key factor in developing this politicized trajectory. However, moving beyond earlier studies, the scholars in this section reject the tendency to make sweeping claims about high-risk activism's impact on "activists" more generally, and instead seek to uncover the interactive processes that might account for both variation and continuity across activist trajectories. They ask, how do activists choose what mobilization path to take? How are these individual-level decisions constrained by the resources, networks, and the cultural and political context in which activists operate? How might different individuals understand and interpret the same activist experiences differently given their unique social and cultural positions in society? And how might strikingly different mobilization experiences nevertheless result in strikingly similar post-militant engagement with society? In answering these questions, our scholars help us understand not just whether high-risk activism has biographical consequences, but also the complex social, political, and cultural processes through which these consequences unfold.

The readings in this section also move forward existing analyses of activist trajectories by bringing a diversity of movements, from a diversity of societies, into a conversation too long dominated by studies of the US Civil Rights movement. The activists from the four cases in this section all experienced mobilization in contexts with high levels of violence and strong repression from state authorities. Hivert and Vairel use the case of Morocco to investigate a relatively unexplored dimension of an activist trajectory: the question of how activist socialization may transform biographies by transmitting new opportunities and experiences to activists' children. In his study of Sikh female fighters in the Indian state of Punjab, Gayer demonstrates how activist trajectories are deeply gendered. The women activist he studies are similar to those highlighted elsewhere in that they worked hard to forge a postrevolutionary lifestyle that allowed them to continue identifying as militants even after giving up militant lifestyles. Yet, as women, their activist trajectories were also intimately and unavoidably tied to their personal trajectories, as each activism decision in turn shaped intimate decisions about whom to marry, when to divorce, or how to parent. Tejel's review of the life course of a married couple participating as militant student activists in Turkey finds that disengagement from a militant organization can be long and complex. Feelings of loyalty, cultivated through militant socialization, can make leaving an organization difficult, even in the face of resource shortages and state coercion. Yet emotional ties to an organization can be a double-edged sword. When activists feel betrayed by the organization that previously inspired life-altering loyalty, the rejection of that organization can be powerful and complete. And finally, in his study of former activists from the Provisional IRA in Northern Ireland, Lorenzo Bosi argues that individuals' postrevolutionary, anti-state activism is dramatically shaped by the state itself; first through prison; then through the demilitarization, demobilization, and reintegration strategies designed by the state; and eventually, through the state's financial support of the very community organizations in which ex-PIRA participants profess to maintain their political activism. Provocatively, Bosi contrasts the diversity of activist trajectories prior to and during militant mobilization to the relative similarity of post-activist experiences, and suggests that it is the overarching effects of the state that account for this reduction in the variation of activist experiences. Indeed, the state interventions he dissects in his study of the IRA seem to be deeply implicated in the activist trajectories highlighted in the other chapters as well.

At a most fundamental level, revolutionary movements would not exist without the willingness of individuals to participate despite heavy personal costs. Understanding individual-level trajectories – that is, understanding how individuals come to interpret a particular context as worthy of great self-sacrifice, and how individuals reintegrate as politicized actors into society after leaving militant activism behind – is therefore a crucial step to understanding both social continuity and social change in social movement research. The articles in this segment provide an important step forward in this research. Although being able to study a complete population of activists, as McAdam did, is likely impossible in such high-risk, clandestine movements, the studies in this collection nonetheless suggest that there may be some factors, like gender, state repression and reintegration processes, organizational commitments, and the resources associated with social class, that may regularly interact with particular political contexts to shape individual trajectories across movements. Future research would do well to continue to examine these factors across those who remain politically active, as well as to seek out those who have exited activism – either purposefully, or due to a lack of opportunity for continued mobilization – to see how their experiences differ.

5

Biographical Effects of Engagement

The "Activist Generation" of the 1970s and Its Children in Morocco

Joseph Hivert and Frédéric Vairel

Dealing with the "generation of the 1970s" *(Jîl al-Sab'înât)* and their children in Morocco, this chapter revisits the biographical consequences of activism in an authoritarian situation. In the last 15 years, the fate of the "years of lead" activists and this period of harsh repression that Morocco underwent, especially the biographical consequences of activist involvement, have been getting more and more attention in academic studies. These studies, unlike previously, are now less focused on reducing Moroccan politics either to the relationship between the Palace and the country's political parties or to limiting political protest dynamics to Islamist organizations. Above all, this literature criticizes openly the normative bias of literature about "civil society." This latter was considered the mother of all virtues as the last step on the road to democracy and the antidote to Islamism.

On the Moroccan case, research follows two directions related to activists' long-term fate. On the one hand, several studies contemplate how repression influenced the activists' careers – disengagement, transformation of their relationship to activism, their horizons of meaning, and their courses of action – and these studies highlight the effects of political constraints (Burgat, 1988; Vairel, 2008). They demonstrate the variability of repression's effects on activists' careers depending on the actors' political positioning and affiliations, but also on their own resources and social position. In addition, the literature studies the activists' aptitudes and skill sets in different professional spheres, especially after being released from prison. Sometimes, these reconversions are a condition for activists to preserve their political involvement in a new form. They have some effects on both the way activism and collective action are considered (managerial references' introduction, NGOs' proliferation, and continuous internationalization of Moroccan activists' spheres) and their relationships to public policy (Vairel, 2014). While the relation between the sphere of involvement and the professional sphere in activists' trajectories has been the subject of several studies (Cheynis, 2013), this relation has rarely been thought as linked to activists' social mobility (Cheynis, 2008; Bennani-Chraïbi, 2013). However, understanding how involvement affects activists' social mobility and vice-versa seems all the more necessary when activists' trajectories are characterized by their upward social mobility. As a result, we aim to analyze how the years of lead "high-risk activism" (Loveman, 1998; Nepstad & Smith, 1999; Parkinson, 2013) played a role in the activists' socialization and transformed their biographical trajectories by transmitting to their children certain ways of perceiving and relating to the world in general, beyond the political realm.

The analysis of activism's biographical impact is enriched by taking into account the actors' resources (mainly access to education, diplomas, economic resources, and also political skills) and their ability to enter and position themselves within social networks. It is also useful to link the individual and organizational trajectories with the constraint imposed by the regime to gain a more comprehensive perspective.

The word "generation" disguises diverse situations: belonging to a same age class or to a "generational unit" (Mannheim, 1952: 302–312) does not imply an ideological or organizational loyalty to activist origins. Despite its uncertainty, the "1970s generation" has an analytical interest: It incites us to think about the heterogeneity of trajectories, which include continued involvement, professional reconversions, and political disengagement.

As in Western Europe and North America, in Morocco the 1960s and the 1970s were "a particular period characterized by strong social movement mobilization" (Giugni, 2013: 143). This case displays three key differences with the literature. First, "among the range of dynamic processes that strengthen, weaken, or transform the settings within which groups tend to mobilize" (Goldstone & McAdam, 2001: 221) one needs to take into account the authoritarian situation. In other words, in Morocco activism cannot be "the realm of the many" (Corrigall-Brown, 2011: 4). While social characteristics, "ties and identities affect the length and continuity of an individual's participation," we find it necessary to look beyond the "relational and organizational context" (Corrigall-Brown, 2011: 59) and to take into account the effects of repression on individuals. At least until the 1990s, prison was one of the potential outcomes of activism in Morocco. Second, movements have taken ground in universities in a country with a very low literacy rate. During this period, not only did leftists think of themselves as a "political vanguard," but they were also part of the intellectual elite of society.[1] This advantage on the job market was reduced but not cancelled by state violence and biographical disruptions. There is a link between the social conditions of activism, latter involvements, and upward social trajectories. Third, while it may seem an obvious outcome of intense activism, transmission to children is rarely taken into account in the literature on the biographical consequences of activism (Pagis, 2014; Masclet, 2016). Political beliefs pervaded parenting and were consequently passed on to the children.

In this chapter, we consider the fate of activists by analyzing the constitution of protest organizations in a context where the regime's stabilization is achieved by oppressing its opposition, whether it was the parties' opposition or the (leftist, then Islamist) "movements'" opposition. Then, we examine how the political and physical defeat of the far-left organizations had an impact on both the activists' political involvement and on their professional careers during the 1970s and the 1980s. Because of the 1990s authoritarian decompression, the barriers between professional and activist spheres could be removed, which allowed activists to reconcile work and political involvement. It became possible to consider oneself an activist, including during one's professional activity, and a parent. The attention given to intergenerational legacy emphasizes the effort made to align the familial universe with the political one, but also emphasizes the logics of allegiance to past affiliations that occur through the political legacy handed down to children: more than a socializing event, the 20th February Movement (M20F), the Moroccan equivalent of the 2011 Arab uprisings, has worked as a "developing bath" for political skills, resources, and schemes of perception acquired during primary socialization. At the same time, the 20th February moment confirmed these activist skills and young activists "self-understandings and self-identifications" (Brubaker and Cooper, 2000: 2).

AUTHORITARIAN STABILIZATION AND THE CREATION OF POLITICAL ORGANIZATIONS

Despite its possible structuralist formulations, it is possible to bring "near-experience" (Geertz, 1974: 58) the notion of generation for all that

---

[1] In 1956, the year of independence, the country had 2,500 students. There were 4,847 by 1962, 11,700 in 1964, 12,770 in 1970, and 16,547 in 1975 (Figures from Adam and Granai, 1962; Adam, 1969, 1971, 1976). At that time, a university degree meant a job.

one bears in mind that actors of a "generational unity" (Mannheim, 1952) do not consciously belong to it in the moment. Individuals belong to a generation "afterwards," when they reconstruct the past while looking back at it. In the actors' narratives,[2] three elements embody the "1970s generation" of Morocco.

First, the expression is meaningful in regard to actors' experience inside organizations. Founded in 1956, the National Union of Moroccan Students (UNEM) works as a password in Moroccan political scenes: The three biggest activist groups that made Moroccan political history since Independence bore, at one moment or another, this political name. Leftists, socialists, and then Islamists have been politically socialized through the UNEM. Despite their diverse, and sometimes opposed, political positions, the actors who were UNEM members acquired a shared repertoire of action that mixed students' "awareness-raising" – mainly through "*jalsât*," sessions during which an activist student lectured his fellows seated around him or her – and service offers on a corporatist basis (course notes, hand-outs, second-hand book sales) (Geisser, Karam, & Vairel, 2006).

Second, the "1970s generation" expression takes its full meaning in regard to a national and international context. Between 1963 and 1976 – that is to say between the beginnings of "the Moroccan parliamentary experience" (Chambergeat, 1965) and the annexation of the Western Sahara by Morocco with the Green March (1975) – the regime's control system was being set up: This period was distinguished by its acute political instability. Violence was both the background and one of the resources of the power struggle between actors – monarchy, opposition political parties, and putschists – whose relationships were based on profound hostility. During this time, the country's opposition groups suffered harsh repression and the regime was undecided about its own form: popular republic, military regime, or conservative monarchy. Generational belonging cannot indeed be dissociated from the contentious experiences that were affected by repression: law enforcement violent

---

[2] In this article, we are drawing on two fieldwork investigations. The first was led between 1999 and 2003, and completed during multiple research trips, about the functioning of social movements in Morocco, using direct observation of contentious practices and biographical interviews with NGO activists as well as political parties and trade union activists. The other one is carried out for a PhD dissertation started in 2011. It aims at understanding which practices and worldviews 1970s activists have transmitted to their children. We use a survey combining matched interviews (parents and siblings) with observations of "children" involved in collective action such as the 20th February Movement (20FM). More than twenty activist families have been interviewed.

practices, arbitrary arrests and detentions, disappearances and extrajudi-
cial executions, unfair trials. During these years, activism meant "crime"
and implied a very direct relationship to political constraint; in fact, after
weakening the main opposition party, the National Union of Popular
Forces (UNFP), the regime directed its attention and the repression
toward UNEM, which was demanding "the land for the peasants, the
factories for the workers and education for everybody." After the annexation of the Western Sahara by Morocco, a unanimous construction of
the polity took place. Political parties endorsed the monarchy's nationalist
rhetoric. The first victims were Sahrawi people and their Marxist-Leninist
supporters.

Beginning in January 1972, when leaders A. Serfaty and A. Laâbi[3]
were arrested, protests broke out in many universities and high schools
and were met with a brutal crackdown. Repression and compulsory
military service aimed to stop the protest movement. The 1973 and
1977 Casablanca trials broke these organizations and attempted to gain
control of this political wave by permanently keeping its leaders away.

At this time, Morocco was taking part in an international cycle of
protests against "imperialism and its running dogs," nourished by
Marxist-Leninist, Maoist, and Trotskyist influences. In the Arab world,
with the Nasserist experience and the Palestinian cause, nationalism had
become a mainstream political idiom. Only the Arab defeat of 1967[4]
relativized nationalist domination, or, to be more precise, the ways this
nationalist domination was expressed. Thereafter, Islamists became the
standard-bearers of Arab nationalism. For this reason and because of
their mobilization capabilities, they were the first targets of repression.
In 1974, the year of the UNEM ban, Abdelslam Yacine was committed to
a psychiatric hospital, and then placed under house arrest after admon-
ishing Hassan II and telling him to choose between *Islam or the Flood.*

THE TRANSFORMATION OF POLITICAL ACTIVISM:
RELEASE FROM PRISON, DEMOBILIZATION
AND RE-INVOLVEMENT

At the end of the 1980s and during the 1990s, the diversity of activists' life
courses reminds us how important it is to view the "1970s generation" in

---

[3] One of the group's leaders. His arrest, the torture he suffered, and his experience in jail are
briefly related in Laâbi, 2001.
[4] About the importance of the 1967 defeat in activists' trajectories, especially about nationalism's handover from leftists to Islamists, see Burgat, 1988.

its plurality. This diversification varied depending on individual resources (social, economic, and political capitals), preserved relations with activists, and their perception of the political context. First of all, prison experience did not play an unequivocal role, although it was meant to crush activists and their families. The activists survived this ordeal in diverse ways: Prison is not a black box from which you get out either defeated or radicalized. Social and political situations combine to produce a series of variations that influence post-prison itineraries. Consequently, activists' re-involvement does not operate as an existential alternative between preserving one's revolutionary position and choosing demobilization. Indeed, belonging to the same political organization at a given time does not imply that later engagements will be similar as well.

The Role of Networks and Activist Ties

Activists who were endowed with more political and social capital were certainly more able to face prison's constraints. *Ilal Amâm*'s leaders, A. Serfaty and A. Laâbi, had stable professional positions when they were incarcerated in Kenitra after the 1974 trial. While others had to focus on their studies, they could devote themselves to activism while in jail, organizing protests and hunger strikes to obtain newspapers, books, and, above all, the status of political detainee. This was not the case for the Bnou Hachem group detainees who were arrested in their last year of high school or first year of university for their Marxist-Leninist sympathies, after the movement was disbanded as a result of repression. After 10 years of torture and penal colony, they had to return to university or look for employment. The Islamists judged and condemned in 1984 for conspiracy against national security fought for political detainee status in their first struggle in prison. Many of them were freed by royal grace, without a diploma. The 1970s Marxist-Leninist detainees were more fortunate, as the regime allowed them to study in jail to keep them busy and avoid further mobilizations. The political and judicial situation of the activists played a crucial role in what they would become after prison.

The penitentiary world does not foster the communion of souls, and more so in an authoritarian context. Struggles, disagreements, interpersonal disputes, or political debates continue and are exacerbated in prison. These struggles may lead to personal resignation or continued political involvement. Here, the issue of activists' social ties preservation is fundamental. Activist disaffiliation begins in prison either because of their isolation (for example, Abdelaziz Mouride[5]), or because of their weak political and social capital that make it more difficult to reestablish social and political ties. Sometimes both processes coexist and reinforce each other.

As activists are released from prison, social support systems and networks play a decisive role in the continuation of their career: This moment is a key indicator of an activist's re-involvement or disengagement mechanisms. Some Marxist-Leninists, who were freed in 1976 after short prison terms, waited ten years before resuming activism, this time from within human rights associations. At their liberation, the political situation had seemed unchanged with continued police controls, repression, and demobilization. In contrast, detainees released in 1984 took advantage of the networks founded by victims' families or the Moroccan Association for Human Rights (AMDH).[6] Political context transformations and biographical availability both result in more diverse possibilities for re-affiliation and renewed engagement.

Activists with less social and cultural capital, such as post-secondary diplomas for example, reengage only if they are part of activist networks. In fact, continued relationships with other activists compensate the lack of resources and economic challenges upon release from prison or secret detention center, allowing them to remain an activist more easily. For example, Abdallah Zaâzaâ, in spite of being a mere industry worker, founded a magazine, *Al-Muwâtin* (*The Citizen*), with other activists and launched a series of critical political debates about Tazmamart, the Amazigh identity as well as the constitutional question and the king's powers in the regime. Zaâzaâ focused on the neighborhood where he grew up and where he has lived since 1953. With his wife, he became an advocate of women rights. He worked afterward with the neighborhood's youth, who asked him to run in the municipal elections of 1993. The community association that he founded in his neighborhood became a model for the whole country. The association promotes citizenship values based on self-supported community efforts in their claims to the State.

A. Bnou Hachem, a Marxist-Leninist supporter, kidnapped in his last high-school year, found a job after his BA in Law thanks to one of the

---

[5] Sometimes described as the "father of Moroccan graphic novels," his first comic narrates the Casablanca trial, torture at the Derb Moulay Chérif secret detention center in Casablanca, and his time in prison (Mouride, 2001).

[6] The AMDH was established in 1979 by the Socialist Union of Popular Forces (USFP) members, but was taken over by leftists starting from the end of the 1980s. It has now more than ninety branches in Morocco.

Moroccan Organization for Human Rights (OMDH) founders, who was an editor of a "right-wing" newspaper. Although he continues to be in contact with other activists since his liberation, he refused to resume activism until the beginning of the 1990s because he mistrusted those who approached him and was scared of informers and undercover police officers. Support from other activists is crucial to preserve consistency between the many worlds these individuals belong to, if economic needs have been met.

Generally, disaffiliation appears after conflicts between activists' different social spheres. The tension resulting from belonging to different social realms (activism, family, profession) is intensified after having been in prison. After prison, activists enter into adulthood and its corresponding roles (worker, spouse, parent). Family ties and professional careers require dedicated time that is all the more significant as they were deprived from it for many years. Biographical availability for activism (McAdam, 1988) is reduced by competing pressures from the need to fulfill other requirements in the activists' social life (Cress, Miller, McPherson, & Rotolo, 1997). For many activists, it seems hard to sacrifice their professional career and their family life after what they have already sacrificed for the sake of activism (torture, prison, etc.). Actors prioritize other forms of social activity in their new lives. The strict surveillance that they were still under at the beginning of the 1990s in the form of intimidation, threats, shadowing, etc. impeded them from reconnecting with activist involvement, which undoubtedly seemed all the riskier because of the changes in their personal and family life. Family life and paternity dissuaded many of them from taking political risks.

After their liberation, activists with fewer resources, who could rely neither on their family nor on skills gained before their time in jail, preferred to dedicate their time to the pursuit of personal happiness. At his release, Abdelaziz Mouride, a former member of the 23-March movement, "distances himself to see things more clearly." He devoted himself to his family, his work, and his drawings. As a journalist, he "gives a hand" from time to time, "keeps himself informed," and "does activism through his drawings."

Jamal is an ex-member of the Islamic Youth. Arrested in 1984 for having held a banner criticizing the regime with some comrades, he was sentenced to death. He was first tortured and then imprisoned after an unfair trial. Saved from death row thanks to Amnesty International and human rights international organizations, he was granted pardon in

1994. Afterward, he experienced a long period of unemployment and disengagement. Only after the establishment of the Truth and Justice Forum (FVJ) in 1999 – an organization aiming to mobilize all victims of gross violations of human rights – he considered that changes in the political context would allow him to resume political activities. Jamal got actively involved in committees supporting the Palestinian and the Iraqi cause, and in an Islamist group not permitted by the authorities, *Al-Badîl al-Hadarî* (Civilizational alternative). This collective is distinguished by its bold positions about the translation of political concepts as secularism and democracy in an Islamic framework. In both Mouride's and Jamal's lives, the other universes of meaning take precedence over activism upon their release. Their social status and economic situation do not allow them to go beyond this tension to reconcile a continuous insertion in the contentious space with the other universes they belong to.

In contrast, activists with strong political capital were able to commit their skills and resources to new collectives, which they often helped found. Frequently, this is operated by their ability to professionalize political know-how. Driss Benzékri, a leader of *Ilal Amâm*, studied human rights issues and linguistics in prison (he obtained his MA while in jail). After serving a seventeen-year prison term, he became a journalist and soon after joined the OMDH, becoming executive director. He also took part in the organization of group therapy for victims and in A. Serfaty's rehabilitation support group. He was one of the kingpins of the FVJ's strategy outline, and was its first president in 1999. Here, political and professional resources as well as preserved activist ties produced a coherent identity. Activist involvement is always perceived as obvious. Reading Eastern European dissident literature helped Moroccan activists to abandon Marxism, either Maoist or Trotskyist, as their reference and horizon of practices in order to adopt a lexicon based on human rights. These individuals never experienced the period of confusion experienced by activists with less capital and connections.

"Join Up, They Said! It's a Man's Life, They Said!" but Where?

We can distinguish four forms of remaining active in politics after having been at UNEM, which are not always aligned with the experiences of the first activists.

To use an economic metaphor, the first form of involvement can be compared to the concept of profitability. It sometimes overlaps with the figure of the "traitor," denounced repeatedly by activists who consider themselves guarantors and loyal guardians of the initial revolutionary ideals. Some former members of UNEM eventually joined the regime's institutions. These status changes affected both their political positioning – from fierce opposition against the regime to participation in its institutions – and their professional career, as they accessed highly paid jobs.

Latifa Jbabdi, an ex-member of 23-March, served a prison sentence from 1977 to 1980, and, after her release, helped establish the Organization of Democratic and Popular Action (OADP), the political party heir to the 23-March movement, allowed by the authorities in 1983. She distinguished herself by starting the first feminist publication in Morocco, 8-Mars, and was the founding president of the first Moroccan feminine association, the Feminine Action Union (UAF). In 1993, she was one of the lead campaigners to obtain a million signatures in favor of the Personal Status Code reform. In 1996, she participated in the OADP's scission, and followed the branch that voted "for" the constitutional referendum. She also linked the UAF to the new party, the Social-Democratic Party (PSD). Taking advantage of her skills as an activist, by the end of the 1990s she had aligned herself more closely with Princess Lalla Meryem's cabinet, which allowed her to enter the princess-presided Organization for Children's Rights. In 2002, she was appointed by the king to the Consultative Council for Human Rights (CCDH). She was the only female commissioner of the Equity and Reconciliation Instance (IER), the Moroccan Truth and Justice Commission. After the PSD merged with the USFP in 2005, she was elected as a Member of Parliament from 2007 to 2011 on USFP's National List for Women.[7]

The second form of engagement is chosen by activists who, after their prison term, invested their expertise in institutional political parties. The OADP is a clear example of this participation. To reinvest their political capital, former members of 23-March needed to modify their practices. They were able to enter the legal political field because of their position on the Western Sahara. Furthermore, this participation was facilitated by the presence of one of their leaders who was an important figure of resistance against French colonial occupation, Mohammed Bensaïd Aït Idder. These activists faced a great challenge during the 1980s and the 1990s: "to participate without losing [their] soul" or "accept compromises but no

---

[7] The National List is an ad hoc mechanism created to improve female representation in Parliament (Vairel, 2009). In 2002, thirty seats were reserved for women on the basis of an informal commitment by political parties. This quota was maintained in 2007 and 2011.

compromise of principles."[8] The PSD scission from OADP of 1996 illustrated this challenge. The new party was created by the supporters of the new constitution, which was rejected by the OADP, to show their rallying to the monarchy and to secure positions in the future "alternate government." This rallying reveals the sociological transformation of activists who experience upward mobility, and their attempt to complete it by obtaining positions of power. These actors used their organizational skills, ideological training, and ability to produce political discourse to serve other engagements, far removed from Marxism-Leninism.

Some former members of UNEM chose a third type of political reconversion: between associative and political worlds. These trajectories are the result of several processes' intertwining. First, "civil society" has a definite power of attraction over multiple actors whose motivations are extremely diverse: the Moroccan regime, development agencies and international donors, and activists. Assimilated here into nongovernmental organizations, civil society is ironically seen as the most righteous way to do politics precisely when it has become, in Morocco, on the contrary, a practice of depoliticized politics (Catusse, 2002). This is how many professional politicians "get involved in civil society" or activists "enter in party politics" because of their supposed altruistic efficiency and their sound "on-the-ground" knowledge.

Finally, other activists deliberately stayed away from party politics when they chose to reengage after prison, without refusing, however, public involvement for others and activism, or testing their conceptions of the political community. Their relationship to politics has changed. Involvement in political parties is considered corrupt or inefficient. The regime is still negatively perceived by these activists, who were its fierce adversaries in the 1970s and 1980s. As a result, these actors were more motivated by committing to their "close community" or to the country's socioeconomic development. From the 1960s to the 1980s, participating in UNEM activities was directed against a capitalist mode of production because of its unjust implications. To them, working in development today by promoting micro-finance, literacy and girls' education in rural areas, income-generating activities, and fighting corruption, is a way to continue the struggle on the ground, without risking being repressed.

---

[8] Expression used by a 23-March ex-member, who became an OADP leader and played a significant role in the Unified Socialist Left or GSU's constitution (Catusse, Vairel, Interview, Casablanca, December 4, 2001).

The above-mentioned Abdallah Zaâzaâ's trajectory is a clear example of this type of re-involvement.

THE 1970S AND 1980S: PROFESSIONAL CONSEQUENCES OF POLITICAL INVOLVEMENT

The professional careers of activists are influenced by activism on many levels (McAdam, 1989; Fillieule, 2013). Activists' school curricula are more disrupted than the average, and occupations are concentrated in the middle and upper intellectual professions (Fillieule, 2016). Beyond identifying the impact of activism on professional careers, the stake is to think together the sphere of professional activities and the sphere of commitment on long-run careers (Dauvin & Siméant, 2002). This means paying attention to the "social, practical, intellectual forms of hybridization that are formed in action, particularly between activist practices and professional activities" (Champy & Israël, 2009: 8). Having gained access to university during the 1970s, when higher education was made accessible to the masses, this "generation" more easily climbed the social ladder.

Coming from working-class backgrounds, their time at the university raised for these actors an aspiration for upward social mobility and made it possible. At the end of their studies, many activists practice an intellectual profession (teacher in high school or university teacher, senior public service, engineer, lawyer, etc.).

However, this general trend of intergenerational upward social mobility should not lead one to underestimate the effects of commitment on activists' professional careers and moreover the costs of activism on school curricula and professional trajectories.[9] To the contrary, it is all the more acute as the professional destiny to which this more educated generation could then claim was characterized by its upward mobility. This is demonstrated by the trajectories presented in this section.

Born in 1955 in Casablanca in a working-class family (his father is a policeman and his mother a housewife), Ahmed attended high school in Rabat in 1970. He entered politics at the National Union of High School Students, at that time closely linked to UNEM, which was controlled by the Marxist-Leninist movement. After graduating from high school, he

---

[9] In this respect, Abdeslam Yassine's trajectory, a former high school inspector, is typical. His entry into politics coincided with the interruption of his career, based on the decision of the authorities. The only possibilities for activism and employment available to his children remained within the organization he heads: Justice and Beneficence.

chose with his friends to enter the Mohammadia School of Engineers (EMI) for political reasons: Abraham Serfaty, a leftist leader, was the School Academic director. Joining EMI in 1973, Ahmed graduated in 1980, two years late. Giving priority to activism, he had repeated his first year. In 1977, he repeated another year because he was arrested and imprisoned due to his involvement with *Ilal Amâm*, then an underground movement. At the end of their studies, Ahmed and his EMI comrades found their professional way guided by militant and ideological consi-derations. They aimed to join sectors that would put them in touch with the "working classes" in order to try to mobilize them. Heavy industry (mining, oil, electricity, etc.) was a prime target for their professional investments. Affiliated with UNEM, the National Union of Engineers (UNI) eased the spread of Marxist-Leninist engineers in labor-intensive industries, including the National Office of Drinking Water (ONEP) and the oil company Société Anonyme Marocaine de l'Industrie du Raffinage (SAMIR).

If entering university permitted upward mobility, particularly visible in the case of engineers, political activism has generated downward mobility as well. Amina's trajectory shows the weight of activism on academic progression as much as the professional costs of activism.

Born in 1957 in Oujda (in the Oriental region, in the north-east of the country) to a blacksmith father and an illiterate housewife mother, Amina completed high school in 1977. She continued her graduate studies at the École Normale Supérieure (ENS) in Rabat, which trains high school teachers. During the first year of her studies, she participated with friends in a cultural week organized within the EMI, where she met her future husband. He played a decisive role in her entry to the world of activism. Initially a supporter of the student union, she started to frequent more regularly the activist circles that her future husband belonged to, and she subsequently agreed to join the UNEM section at ENS in 1979. At the time, UNEM was born again on campuses under the leadership of the Socialist Union of Popular Forces (USFP) youth. In 1980, Amina and her UNEM friends were excluded from the ENS as their activities were considered too subversive. Forced to stop training early, she obtained a school teacher position in lieu of the high school post she would have obtained had she completed her training.

This trajectory shows how activism can direct school curricula as well as shorten or lengthen them. This trajectory also demonstrates how average or above average upward mobility can be slowed or interrupted by an arrest, imprisonment, or school exclusion for political reasons.

Political commitment deflects the trajectories of their likely professional destiny and thwarts individuals' aspirations. The professional cost of political commitment is neither measured by the number of years spent in prison nor assessed by the sole criterion of political risk. As evidenced by the case of Amina, one does not need to serve time or be an activist in a revolutionary organization to suffer professional downgrading.

In interviews, consequences of activism on professional careers are formulated in terms of costs and downward social mobility. A few activists are able to link political and professional activities. The repressive context of the 1970s and 1980s prevented the conversion and importation of activist skills and aspirations into the professional sphere. It aimed rather to divide the political and the professional. Accessing the labor market meant leaving UNEM and engaging in other political structures since opportunities of engagement are reduced because of repression. The Teachers National Union (SNE-SUP), the National Union of Labour (UMT),[10] and the Democratic Confederation of Labour (CDT)[11] were subjected to continuous police surveillance, which was intensified following the 1981 "bread riots." In this context, activist public servants had few opportunities to reconcile their job and their activism. The constraints that repression exerted on Marxist-Leninists activists – compelled to go underground – also affected their professional activities. From this point of view, clandestinity works as an obstacle to the politicization of the professional sphere and contributes to the divide between political and professional work.

Author of one of the first books on political detention (Bouissef Rekab, 1989), Driss Bouissef Rekab is now a professor at Rabat's Faculty of Literature. As a member of *Ilal Amâm*, his experience is comparable to many others. Between May 1975 and January 1976, he led a "double life," teaching at the Faculty of Literature during the day and participating in discussions about the best way to "mobilize masses" at night. The impermeability between professional and activist spheres became a condition for maintaining a revolutionary commitment driven into clandestinity resulting in increased isolation from the working classes it intended to mobilize. The repressive climate of the 1970s reduced the possibility of living as an activist in one's professional practice.

---

[10] Created in 1955, the UMT was constituted of unionists affiliated with the UNFP, the National Union of Popular Forces.

[11] The CDT was created in 1978 by the Socialist Union of Popular Forces (USFP).

THE 1990S: A RELATIVE OPENING UP OF PROFESSIONAL AND ACTIVIST SPHERES

If the 1990s are a particularly suitable period to observe changes in political involvements, they are also indicative of how activism affects the professional sphere. Upon release from prison, political prisoners faced the need to resume careers that were interrupted when they were imprisoned. Removed from public service since their trials, it was not until the 1994 amnesty declaration that opponents "to his majesty" have officially been allowed to return to work. The context, marked by the relaxing of repression and the emergence of new opportunities of involvement, created opportunities for converting activist skills and relations in the professional sphere. Different professional worlds became spaces for re-commitments to activism. There, activists could reconcile their professional activity and activism without systematically suffering the costs of downward social mobility while career changes offered the possibility of continued commitments. Professional skills, valued by the associative sector, are invested in the activist world. In connection with this circulation of activist resources and professional skills through different social universes, three profiles of "committed professionals" were identified in our sample study. These profiles revealed hybridization between professional practices and activism and also the importation of activist expertise in the field of paid activities.

First, a number of activists became journalists, specifically in the "independent" press. Abderrahim, A. Zaâzaâ's colleague, belonged to the group that publishes *Al-Muwâtin* in 1991. He became editor-in-chief until the newspaper ban in 1992. Abderrahim's career is exemplary both for activist re-commitments, which operate in the professional sphere, and for professional resources and skill reconversion, in part derived from the activist universe. A philosophy student at the University of Rabat and a member of *Ila al Amâm*, he was arrested in 1984. Five years later, he was released without work. While his teacher wife supported them, Abderrahim taught a few philosophy classes in high schools, but the revenue he collected was insufficient and unreliable. In prison, he began writing and discovered his calling as a journalist. So, he logically founded *Al-Muwâtin* newspaper with his comrades. In 1994, with another group of activists, he participated in the creation of the first independent Arabic daily, *Al-Maghrib Al-Yawm*, as editor-in-chief. His career led him from various daily "independent" newspapers (*Le Journal, Assahifa)* or newspapers linked to political parties (*Al Bayane*) to the public channel 2M in 2004.

His professional journey was marked by a career change that allowed him both to maintain his activist identity, redeploy, and even to climb the social ladder. Starting in the 1990s, his political re-commitments (OADP, Unified Socialist Left, Unified Socialist Party)[12] fed and guided his professional practice. Thanks to the integration of his political and professional social networks, his work could become an extension of his activist practice. Constraints on him and his comrades (prohibition of newspapers, court appearances, accusations) fed the perception that they had dangerous occupations compared to their political commitments of the 1970s and 1980s.

Another profile of a "committed professional" emerged in the early 1990s: that of "expert activist" (Cheynis, 2008). Connected with the proliferation of NGOs, the new emerging practices value expertise and promote the conversion of professional skills. They also prompt activist reengagement, valuing professional skills that can be invested in the field of activism.

A former executive at *Ilal Amâm*, Samir Bensaid, was a student at EMI in the 1970s. He went into exile in France until the 1994 amnesty. In exile, he devoted himself to his family and his job. After more than ten years without political commitment, he decided to reengage upon his return to Morocco in 1999. Occasionally and on technical issues, he offered to the AMDH his professional skills. The AMDH solicited him as a water and sanitation engineer related to advocacy for the right to water and against the marketization of drinking water. Samir considered these actions "more concrete, more down-to-earth but with significant scope." The promotion of activist expertise in the associative sector eased the reengagement of activists who broke with political commitment but had skills and technical know-how. At the crossroads of professional and activist worlds, such "concrete" and "localized" micro-investments clearly indicate the permeability of these social worlds.

The politicization of professional spheres favored by authoritarian decompression in the 1990s corresponds with a third profile. By investing in the trade unions (mainly the UMT and CDT), long-term activists can still perceive themselves as "committed" in the sphere of their professional activities but also resolve, at least in part, identity-related tensions resulting from their upward social mobility and their positions as

---

[12] This political party was created in 2002 after the gathering around the OADP of various small leftist groups whose members decided to participate in elections. Many activists behind these dynamics of gathering were also engaged at the AMDH and the FVJ.

"class defectors." Facing double bind phenomena that arise from a relative discordance between their social class of origin and their achieved social class (Leclercq & Pagis, 2011), involvement with workers can be a way for activists to reduce the contradictions they face. For many socially displaced activists (Memmi, 1996), involvement in trade unions cannot be separated from the problem of upward social mobility.

A former AMDH president and a member of the Democratic Path, Khadija Ryadi was born in 1960 to a worker unionist in the steel industry and an illiterate housewife. She became an engineer in statistics and two years later married an activist she had met at UNEM. She gave birth to her first child in 1987. During the late 1980s, despite domestic and family responsibilities, she campaigned intensively with UMT in favor of the unionization of female workers. This engineer's involvement with workers made sense in view of the "imperative of activism" she felt and the need of proximity to the popular classes to which her own parents belonged. Activism requires making sacrifices in the name of loyalty to one's own values, and the quest for "inner harmony" was repeatedly mentioned in her interview.

This explains why these actors maintain high levels of commitment despite the changes that operate in their biographical trajectories (marriage, work, and birth and education of children). Ultimately, the opening up of professional and activist circles in the early 1990s favored the integration of activist and professional activities, giving rise to hybrid activist practices, differentiated based on professional spheres and the nature of commitments.

Professional consequences of activism underscore the importance of taking into account the relationship between involvement and social mobility in understanding activist trajectories. The attention to long-time careers offers the possibility to comprehend in a diachronic and synchronic perspective both how commitments affect social mobility and, in turn, what social mobility does to commitments. During the "years of lead," activism has mainly produced downward social mobility but two decades later it has sometimes facilitated career changes: paths toward upward mobility generate and even require commitment.

ACTIVISM'S IMPACT ON THE SECOND GENERATION: THE HEIRS AND THE 20TH FEBRUARY

The analysis of professional and activist careers helps to explain processes of the transmission of activist legacies. Influenced by professional and political reconversions, parents' activism is echoed in their children's generation and, therefore, biographical consequences of activism on the second generation deserve special attention (Pagis, 2014; Masclet, 2016). Our inquiries allow us to explore socialization processes in families of activists, the content of parent-children transmission, and the appropriation work performed by heirs along with modalities of its activation in given contexts.

Surnames given to children are the first – and probably the most meaningful – way to transmit a political family memory and, through it, a collective history. Many individuals in the survey population bear a name directly borrowed from a Moroccan or Arab activist or linked to a political event that was so significant to their parents that they named their child after it.[13] They bear traces of the contentious space of history and the struggles that took place in it.[14] Beyond surnames, the legacy of family activism is transmitted through cultural preferences (protest songs, political literature, and autobiographical books sometimes written by the parents). Through these references, children acquire the codes and values of their social milieu. Children of activists also share various social characteristics and experiences.

First, in the interviews, they recalled political debates during family meals, bustling and sometimes heated arguments between their parents about political themes. A means of transmitting the appetite for political debate (Percheron, 1974), this precocious exposure to political discussions helps shape children's linguistic universe. However, they are not only exposed to the language of adults; they are also, early on in life, integrated into the social world to which this language refers. Places like political parties, trade unions, organizations, objects and symbols such as flags, songs, slogans, etc., events (marches, sit-ins, etc.), and activists constitute this social universe. This is why the party and the trade union are organizations that children relate to themselves, their families, and their milieu. If this social world is so familiar, it is because it used to be a

---

[13] One can find Jamal, a recall of Gamal 'Abd al-Nassîr; Naji in tribute to Naji al-'Ali, Palestinian cartoonist assassinated in London in 1987 because of his cartoons against Israeli occupation; Abdelkrim, surname chosen in homage to Abdelkrim al-Khattabî, a Rifi and main figure of the struggle against French and Spanish occupation during the Rif war; Tahani or Amin in honor of martyr Tahani Amin, a *Ilal Amâm* militant tortured to death in 1984; or Sabra in remembrance of the Sabra and Shatila massacre.

[14] This bears implications: surnames are symbolic and social markers that contribute to shape individuals' social identity (Bozon, 1987).

space for games and family gatherings: parties and trade unions organize activities for children while their parents attend meetings.

Second, children of activists share similar universes of household norms, revealing the importation of activist behaviors at home. Most parents assert their atheism and explain not to fast during Ramadan. They celebrate neither *'Aïd al-Kabîr* (the Festival of the Sacrifice) nor any other religious festivals. They have acted in order to secularize their domestic universe, refusing to allow religion to interfere with family relations. Logics that underpin the secularization of family universes are based upon the transposition of "activist schemes" in the family milieu (Pagis, 2014). This lack of religion in the family is a form of "deviance" compared to the prevailing religious norms and the role of families in their transmission (El Ayadi, Rachik, & Tozy, 2013). This is why children experience very early a "conflict of standards" generated by dissonant sources of socialization (primary/secondary) (Lahire, 2007). These conflicts appear sharply when children of activists go to school and face a religious and apologetic discourse in religion classes (El Ayadi, 2004) that contradicts what they hear at home. Exposed to school apocalyptic religious discourse, in which their parents are miscreants (*kâfir billah*) and atheists (*mulhid*), children discover the influence of stigma in some social spaces (like school), where they experience mocking, sanction, and sidelining. Activists' children go through a religious period during which they express conformity and reject their family positions: They fast during Ramadan, want to learn how to pray, and criticize their parents' atheism. This religious period closes during the last years of high school.

Third, activists' children share various social experiences, notably summer camps. Because they belong to activist families, these children participate in the Moroccan Association for Human Rights[15] summer camps or those organized by the Moroccan Association for Youth Education.[16] These are places where children learn how to be an activist:

---

[15] For teenagers 15–18 years old, the AMDH organizes summer camps aimed at encouraging "civic consciousness." It also delivers a card, called "Friends of AMDH," for those under 18 who are too young to be full members of the association.

[16] The AMEJ was created in 1956 in the heart of the Istiqlal Party, the Independence Party. In 1959, the association joined the UNFP then the USFP, two left parties. Popular Childhood (*Al-Tufûla Al-Sha'biyya*), another youth organization, experienced the same trajectory. Beyond the management of summer camps and voluntary work camps, which they traditionally organize, youth organizations formed during the years of repression were places of refuge for political activities and political socialization spaces, which then served as recruiting grounds for political parties. Although they do not host illegal political activities, they are still places of significant political socialization.

Young apprentices experiment through political debate, developing their political knowledge with workshops on human rights, gender equality, and secularism. Summer camps are not only places where people talk about activism; they are also places where one can learn and experiment with political practices and collective action. For example, young activists organized a sit-in during summer camp in 2007, demanding coeducation in dormitories and a later bedtime. These political learnings are particular, since they function as learning through play: Children play while they invent slogans, make banners, and defy established rules. At the same time, summer camps allow for the acquisition of knowledge and activist know-how, which may be used in contentious situations. Summer camps enable children to meet other children who have similar social dispositions and to discover their specificity and their similitudes as children of activists. In view of stigmatizing experiences suffered at primary school or high school, summer camps work as "back places where persons of the individual's kind stand exposed and find they need not try to conceal their stigma, nor be overly concerned with cooperatively trying to disattend it" (Goffman, 1991: 81). It is as if these "back places" offered the opportunity to exhume and accentuate what was repressed in the past: Young activists claim their atheism, and distinguish themselves by their practices (not to fast during Ramadan, drinking alcohol) and their discourses (atheism). In short, they "return the stigma."

Finally, because summer camps are places where people share meals and parties, where one interacts with children of other activists during political learning and free time and where one first flirts,[17] the repeated experience produces attachment to an organization and a political collective. Producers of affiliation, summer camps also encourage involvement, as demonstrated by the time apprentice activists dedicate to the AMDH after attending its summer camps.

Despite their shared social and familial properties and their common social experiences since childhood, children of activists do not constitute one homogenous category. Children's profiles are as diverse as their parents' trajectories. If many children of our research sample are "perfect heirs," since they continue the family political belongings, others are at odds or maintain an ambivalent relationship with the familial legacy. The plurality of the profiles of activists' children is linked, at least in part, to

---

[17] Some respondents explained having repeated the experience of summer camps not only because "the atmosphere was good," but also because they were allowed to meet girls and were provided with opportunities for flirting.

varied family configurations and transmission processes differentiated by multiple factors and often interwoven: class and gender, the child's place in the family, academic position, and expectations that parents have for their social destiny (Bessière, 2004), but also his extra-family experiences, his idiosyncrasies, and his parents' political trajectory in relation to their social mobility.

To remain focused on "heir" activists, it is essential to mention the importance of the 20th February Movement (20FM), the Moroccan equivalent of the 2011 Arab uprisings,[18] in the trajectories of these activists' children. To them, the 20FM was a moment when they could put to work dispositions to activism and sociabilities developed during summer camps and their childhood. The analysis of individual trajectories shows how, beyond the diversity of life courses, activists' children converge at a given point in time, in the same protest movement as a result of shared habitus and the acquaintance networks in which they are enrolled (Hivert, 2013: 26). The trajectory of Muntasser, Khadija Ryadi's son, the former AMDH President, is typical of this phenomenon.

Muntasser's story

Born in 1991 in Rabat, Muntasser grew up in a group of militant families belonging to the social and activist Moroccan elite. His parents, one an engineer and the other a teacher, joined the Democratic Path, a Marxist-Leninist movement formed by former leaders of *Ilal Amâm*. They are also committed to the UMT and to the AMDH. Most of Muntasser's friends are also children of party activists. They participated in many of the actions and demonstrations conducted by the UMT and the AMDH, advocating for the rights of children and minors. At the age of 15, Muntasser participated in his first AMDH summer camp. He socialized with older and more politicized teenagers. He then became the AMDH youth club coordinator.

[18] The 20FM is a protest movement that emerged in February 2011 following the December-January protests in Tunisia. Organized in coordination in more than ninety towns in the country, the 20FM gathers young activists from AMDH, Attac-Maroc, or the Alternative Movement for Individual Liberties (MALI), youth organizations from the nongovernmental left (The Democratic Path, the Unified Socialist Party, the Democratic and Socialist Action Party), and some dissidents from the Socialist Union of Popular Forces and the Justice and Development Party youth organizations. Activists from tolerated but illegal organizations like al-'Adl wal-Ihsân (Justice and Beneficence) and Al-Badîl al-Hadarî (Civilisational Alternative) also joined the coalition. See Bennani-Chraïbi & Jeghllaly, 2012; Vairel, 2012; Smaoui & Wazif, 2013.

He participated in two other summer camps in 2009 and 2010, the summer before February 2011. His earliest independent political engagement was in high school. There, he protested against the War in Iraq, and supported the Palestinian cause, joining the school's "Human Rights Club." Like his friends, he distanced himself from Marxist-Leninist ideology and from the Democratic Path his parents adhered to, deeming it "too strict, too removed from the mainstream and too inward-looking." He saw himself more as an anarchist or a libertarian than a communist. In 2010, he passed his Baccalauréat exam and studied for the *Selectividad* (the entrance exam for Spanish universities) with plans to matriculate at a design school. The social unrest during the 2011 Arab uprisings led to travel restrictions that disrupted his plans. Meanwhile, he and some other young activists produced the AMDH clip putting out on YouTube a nationwide call for a demonstration to be held on February 20th. A few weeks after the February 20th demonstrations, he abandoned his study plan and committed himself to full-time political activism. His parents were members of the National Council in Support of the 20th February Movement (NCS20FM).[19] They were demonstrating night and day themselves. This is why they approved of their son's decision. His mother explained: "The fact that his studies have been interrupted isn't that bad. After all, it's for a good cause – starting a revolution (laughter)." His parents' support (moral, emotional, and financial) enabled Muntasser to stay involved. Without their support, financial and educational constraints would have surely hampered his activism or forced him to abandon it altogether.

The above raised the question of intergenerational political socialization in the course of protest. By gathering many activists' children and their parents, protests intensify moments devoted to family exchanges about activism. Parents put their skills and expertise at the service of youth; they provide advice concerning tactics to be adopted in the organization of protest events and the strategies to be followed toward *al-'Adl wal-Ihsân* Islamists who participated in the 20FM, bringing to the movement its numerous activists.

The mobilization results in intergenerational discussions and exchanges within families. This is why the 20FM can be considered a key moment in the formation of activist replacement. However, if the increase of

[19] Many activists from the 1970s and 1980s support the protests and participate in marches or joined the NCS20FM set up on February 23, 2011 by various political and activist groups who share the youth demands. The NCS20FM provides logistical and political support to the 20FM.

these exchanges during the protest sequence offered young activists socialization opportunities, it also provided opportunities to distinguish themselves from their activist heritage. Ultimately, this emphasizes the influence of sociopolitical context on family transmissions and more widely on the intergenerational effects of political socialization.

CONCLUSION

Belonging to UNEM – including its leftist configuration – does not guarantee participation in a shared activist destiny. Nonetheless, UNEM cannot be reduced to nostalgic activist memories or to an isolated moment. To the contrary, we have shown how, because of the various cohorts who facilitated it, the organization resembles a "locality" of the social and political space. Until recently, it has been a central training place for Moroccan political elites.

This absence of unity in activist destinies underlines the effects of the regime's constraints at the organizational level, with the dismantlement of Marxist-Leninist organizations and the ban on UNEM in the 1970s, and at the individual level. The effects of repression and time served in prison by actors are as diverse as their social and political characteristics vary. Nevertheless, effects of regime constraint are far from limited to physical harm through torture, disappearance in some cases, or imprisonment. On the medium and long-term, activism works as a stigma whose effects, depending on the individuals concerned, are more or less discreet but persistent, so much so as to structure marital and educative strategies.

Second, professional careers are also marked by political involvement. The authoritarian decompression of the 1990s does not invalidate this analysis. While changing spaces of mobilization, authoritarian decompression fosters reenlistment of activists who sometimes disengaged upon their release. This transformation of the regime's constraint also allows the mobilization, in a professional setting, of activist resources (e.g. expertise and relations).

Third, political engagement is also reflected at the household level and in the transmission of activist legacies to children through family political socialization. Summer camps root children in activist milieus and transform family calls to perpetuate involvement into dispositions willing to continue it. These sociabilities relay the activist culture of the families and social environment. Nevertheless, political legacies never work as a "carbon copy" (Jennings & Niemi, 1968, 184): transmission varies depending on relations to the activist past, family organization, and professional situations. It also varies depending on the diverse ways parents maintain their political positioning as much as how their children appropriate these legacies. By paying attention to the transmission of political legacies, we have been able to combine an analysis of the political effects of social resources and dispositions (activists' different capacities to reengage after prison, their individual economic condition) and an analysis of the impacts of activism. During the 20th February Movement, these legacies were transformed into political resources: from one cycle of mobilization to another, two generations meet despite their differences and the distance of years.

6

From Militancy to Activism? Life Trajectories of Sikh Women Combatants

Laurent Gayer

I can't say I returned to the mainstream, but can't even say I have given up
the movement ... that is in my blood by now. It is another matter that
I have decided not to lift a gun, but will fight politically.
                    Jasmeet Kaur (quoted in Pushkarna, 1998b)

Between 1984 and 1995, the Indian state of Punjab was the theatre of an
uprising known as the movement for Khalistan, which pitted Sikh separatists and fundamentalists against Indian security forces. Most of the
recruits of this movement were male, but a handful of women also took
part in the armed struggle for an independent Sikh state during this
period. By retrieving the role played by women in this uprising, and more
generally by paying attention to the relations between men and women
within the movement for Khalistan, the following pages aim to contribute
to the emerging literature on the sexual politics of insurgency. To date,
this literature remains primarily concerned with the sexual division
of work within insurgent movements (Falquet, 2003; Horgan, 2009;
Kampwirth, 2002; Lanzona, 2009) and, from my point of view, suffers
from two serious weaknesses: a lack of longitudinal depth resulting
from an excessive focus on insurgent careers to the detriment of post-
conflict trajectories; a neglect of reproductive issues, both within armed
groups and in the aftermath of the conflict. The contribution of active
sexuality and of the politics of care to the fashioning of (post-)militant
selves, in particular, remains largely unaddressed in this literature, except
for a few exceptions (Gayer, 2013; Havryshko, 2016; Shahnazarian,
2016; Viterna, 2013).

By looking in detail at the process of decommissioning of Sikh women militants, this chapter also aims to examine the differentiated socio-biographical effects of this high-risk activism. Thus, to what extent did women's participation in this armed uprising alter their life course, their worldviews and their aspirations? More specifically, how did it affect their capabilities for action, both in their private and public lives?

In order to address these questions, this study relies upon a series of individual and collective interviews conducted between 2001 and 2009 with ten former Sikh female fighters. These interviews were supplemented by a published autobiographical account (Kaur, 2004) and focused on the family antecedents of these women combatants, their socialisation and politicisation process, as well as their concrete experience of the armed struggle and later on of decommissioning. The life stories uncovered through these narratives have been extensively reviewed elsewhere (Gayer, 2012), and instead of providing a panoramic view of Sikh female militancy, the present contribution offers a close-up on two individual trajectories – a methodological choice that allows thicker descriptions of individual trajectories and of moral and practical dilemmas associated with successive turning points (on the merits of this approach for the study of biographical dimensions of activism, see Auyero, 2003 and the Introduction to this volume). After a brief overview of the norms and lived realities of gender relations in the rural regions of Punjab that became the cradle of the Sikh insurgency in the mid-1980s, I examine the journeys of Ravinder Kaur and Amandeep Kaur (not their real names) in and out of militancy. These two women's trajectories were relatively atypical, especially as they tried to prolong their former engagements through non-violent forms of social and legal activism, while coping with additional challenges in their domestic lives. In their very exception-ality, these two trajectories – whose coherence was challenged by these women's return to civilian life – are an invitation to consider the uneven distribution of bifurcative resources among women veterans of the Khali-stan movement. While some of these women seem to have been endowed with greater resources to negotiate this turning point, such resources can never be taken for granted, however. Their effects are unpredictable and prone to significant variations over time. Be they material, social or symbolic, both resources *for* action (dispositions, habits) and resources generated *through* action (which endow actors with various forms of capital) do not exist independently from their implementation and their confrontation to a specific, dynamic context (Soulet, 2010). And while bifurcative resources demand an active involvement on the part of individual actors to become effective, they remain fragile and always face the risk of exhausting themselves. As the context of their actualisation undergoes swift transformations – a process exemplified by the changing perceptions of Khalistani guerrillas by their society, from the early 1990s onwards – what could initially pass for resources may even turn into liabilities, setting more constraints than opportunities.

TEARING DOWN THE CURTAIN: WOMEN IN THE MOVEMENT FOR KHALISTAN

By the mid-1980s, and despite the socio-economic changes brought by the Green Revolution of the preceding decades, Punjabi society remained essentially agrarian and continued to enforce a strict form of sexual segregation – a system locally known as *purdah* (lit. a curtain) or *chardewari* (lit. the four walls of the house). To this day, this system remains in force among rural Sikhs, and in particular among the Jats – the dominant agrarian caste that provided Sikh insurgent groups with the largest number of recruits.

Besides veiling in the presence of strangers and elder male relatives, *purdah* involves behavioural norms limiting the movements of women outside their household while regulating their behaviour within it, such as the prohibition to leave the house unescorted, to speak in front of elder male relatives and to enter the *baithak* (reception room) (Sandhu, 2009).

This system of sexual segregation and the social norms informing it go a long way to explain why women played such a limited role in the Khalistan insurgency – not only did their families and Sikh insurgents themselves discourage them from breaking away from conventional behavioural norms to leave the household in the company of male strangers, but their confinement within the courtyard of their natal home prevented most potential recruits (young, unmarried women) from engaging in face-to-face interactions with insurgents. Women's participation in the insurgency, especially when it involved joining a moving band of armed fighters, was considered a serious breach of custom (*riwaj*) and highly deviant behaviour, compromising these women's honour (*laaj*) as well as that of their family (*izzat*). As a result of these structural constraints, only a few dozen women (as compared to thousands of male recruits) took an active role in the militancy throughout the Khalistan insurgency (1984–1995).

While most of these women followed their militant husbands underground, out of compulsion, a minority among them chose to enrol in the militancy, no matter how costly this entry proved to be. These volunteers often drew inspiration from historical figures of Sikh female warriors. As they were confronted with strict norms of sexual segregation and female modesty, they found inspiration and legitimation in women fighters and rulers of the past, whose feats have been eulogised in the Punjabi folklore.[1] These women also found comfort in the precepts of the Sikh religion, which in principle at least emphasises gender equality. Thus, in her autobiography, Sandeep Kaur (who would later on join one of the most dreaded Sikh armed groups, the Babbar Khalsa) emphasises how, as a pre-teenager, her attempt to follow rigorously the tenets of Sikhism in a fast-secularising environment became a terrain to test and strengthen her character. It also helped her gain respect within her family and larger entourage, where the relative liberalism of her father was counterbalanced by the stiffness of her brother, who inspired so much fear to the young women of the family that 'many of them gave up their dreams' (Kaur, 2004: 2).

Although the few 'princesses' (Kaur), a title used by Sikh women as a last name or middle name,[2] who enrolled in the militancy rarely participated in military operations along with their 'lions' (Singh, the male equivalent of the title Kaur), they all underwent some military training and took part in 'encounters' with the security forces – armed clashes with law and order forces, to be distinguished from pre-planned attacks against security forces (policemen, paramilitaries) or civilians (informers, political rivals, Hindu villagers). This involvement in the militancy did not necessarily, and in fact rarely did, involve a conscious act of resistance against local gender norms. In the opposite direction it could even operate as a 'declaration of dependence' – that is, an aspiration to social relationality through voluntary subordination (Ferguson, 2013) – towards new forms of male domination. Thus, aspiring women recruits were required to marry a cadre of the movement and place themselves under his protection and authority. Paradoxically, at least from the point of view of an emancipatory liberalism, this movement of subjection could be empowering.[3] It opened a new world of possibilities, including for women who

---

[1] The most popular among these Sikh women warriors is Mai Bagho, who led Sikh armies against the Mughals in the early eighteenth century.

[2] The title Kaur literally means 'prince' and by making it mandatory for female members of the Khalsa (the community of full-fledged, initiated Sikhs), Guru Gobind Singh (the last in line of ten Gurus who founded the Sikh religion) made a strong argument in favour of gender equality within the Sikh community.

[3] For a similar reflection on 'empowering subjection' see Audrain, 2004.

went 'underground' by accident or under duress, such as those wives of guerrilla commanders who were constrained to follow their husbands to escape police repression. For all these women, even the least politicised and the least motivated to join the movement, life in the 'underground' turned out to be a challenging but exhilarating experience. While all my interviewees insisted on the hardships inherent to this clandestine and highly mobile way of life – especially during their pregnancies – they also claimed to have derived an intense pleasure from it (*khushi*). Without entirely denying this possibility – the sudden expansion of their sociability and their access to firearms, in particular, seem to have been perceived across the board as a particularly thrilling experience – one should factor in the social context of these recollections, which tend to be tainted by nostalgia for a seemingly exalting past.

MILITANCY AND ITS AFTERLIFE: THE TRAJECTORIES OF TWO SIKH WOMEN FIGHTERS

The two life-stories presented in this section do not merely aim to put some 'flesh' on Sikh female fighters. More importantly, they allow us to observe at close range the effects of correlation between social structures reflecting upon processes of socialisation, violent mobilisations leading to the formation of insurgent organisations, and idiosyncratic attempts to navigate simultaneously through 'social' and 'biographical' time.[4] In the process, these two life-stories lay stress on the self-generative and self-transformative effects of a particular form of high-risk activism. As the life-worlds of these women successively expanded (through their participation to an armed uprising) and retracted (following their return to civilian life), their forms of engagement also experienced significant changes, from armed militancy to non-violent activism. Thus, to what extent were these personal adjustments and political repositionings the outcome of past engagements and to what extent can one talk of an activist habitus providing these veterans of the Khalistan movement with specific resources to act upon their life-course and, more specifically, to negotiate 'successfully' – that is, with minimal social, economic and psychological side-effects – the successive turning points in their lives?

---

[4] This distinction between social and biographical time is borrowed from Fillieule, 2005.

From Militancy to Social Work: The Trajectory
of Ravinder Kaur

Ravinder Kaur was born in 1961 in the Jullunder district of Punjab. Her parents belonged to the dominant agrarian Jat caste and were middle landowners who supported the Shiromani Akali Dal (SAD), a moderate Sikh regionalist party that has been at the forefront of religious and political struggles involving the Sikh community of Punjab since its creation in the 1920s. However, Ravinder's folks also lent an ear to the revivalist discourse of Sant Jarnal Singh Bhindranwale, the radical preacher who was initially supported by Indira Gandhi's government against the more moderate SAD and who ended up fortifying himself with his men in the Sikhs' holiest shrine, Amritsar's Golden Temple, before being killed there during Operation Bluestar in June 1984 – a military operation which outraged Sikhs across the world and inspired thousands of them to pick up the gun against the Indian state.

At the age of seventeen, while studying at the Government College of Hoshiarpur, Ravinder attended a lecture given by Bhindranwale and was deeply impressed by the *sant* (holy man, in the Sikh tradition). The same year (1978), thirteen supporters of Bhindranwale were killed by the rival sect of Sant Nirankaris.[5] Ravinder and her family were, in her own words, 'deeply disturbed' by this incident. Thus, the family household was the first site of radicalisation of the young woman. In the evening, male members of the household and their occasional visitors engaged into heated discussions on Sikh political and religious matters. These discussions sensitised Ravinder to the revivalist and martial discourse of Bhindranwale. Through her elder brother, a close confident of Bhindranwale, she gradually inserted herself into the social networks of Sikh religious radicalism. Ravinder's brother was a close friend of Bhindranwale's right arm, Surinder Singh Sodhi,[6] who stayed at Ravinder's house each time he visited their area. And if Sodhi was one of the best friends of Bhindranwale, he was also his hitman, in charge of the elimination of his rivals, particularly of Sant Nirankaris. In this context, Ravinder's radicalisation was an incremental, almost unconscious process: she was required to

---

[5] The Sant Nirankaris challenged one of the basic tenets of Sikhism by claiming that their religious leader was a 'Guru' (whereas the Sikhs consider that the line of living Gurus terminated with the death of the tenth master Guru Gobind Singh in the eighteenth century).

[6] Surinder Singh Sodhi, the right handman of Bhindranwale, was supervising the assassinations of deviant Sikhs and Hindu opponents of the Sant. He was murdered in April 1984.

provide some 'services' in the preparation of these assassinations, by resorting to surveillance activities or by providing logistical support. These responsibilities provided her with an opportunity to transcend daily routines as well as traditional gender constraints: 'when I returned from school, I always had something to do, it was great!'

In the early days of June 1984, as the Indian army prepared to launch its assault on the Golden Temple, she joined her sister and her brother-in-law (himself a member of Bhindranwale's first circle) in the precincts of the temple. Shortly before the final assault, Ravinder and her relatives managed to slip away and go into hiding. Ten days later, Ravinder's brother-in-law announced his decision to go underground and commit himself to the armed struggle that was being launched across the province by the survivors of Operation Bluestar and likeminded Sikhs, eager to extol revenge against the sacrilegious Indian state. Ravinder's sister was pregnant and refused to go underground with her husband. Ravinder did not face the same constraints, however, and she offered to take the place of her sister – by joining her brother-in-law in clandestinity and eventually by marrying him. According to her, her sister did not resent her decision, as she considered that Ravinder would provide protection to her husband by projecting him as a respectable family man.

A month later, Ravinder and her brother-in-law crossed over to Pakistan, like hundreds of other aspiring militants, by swimming across the river that demarcates the border between the two countries. Once in Pakistan, they were taken in charge by intelligence agencies. Her brother-in-law was offered protection by the Pakistanis, but Ravinder faced the threat of being sent to jail. In order to avoid that fate, she married her brother-in-law. Although she gave birth to a boy a year later, motherhood did not distract her from her militant activities. During the six years that she spent in Pakistan, she claims that she made several clandestine trips to India in order to 'coordinate action between various armed groups'. Far from being a liability, being a mother with an infant provided her with a tactical advantage: during her 'missions' to India, she often brought her child along and posed as a banal housewife. Thus, according to her, 'the baby protected us'. One may find here a first indication of the 'martial feminism' (Schalk, 1997: 69) of this former fighter, eager to question gender stereotypes denying to Sikh women the martial valour attributed to their fathers, brothers and husbands. Indeed, Ravinder Kaur is convinced that 'women make better fighters than men. Their determination makes the difference, even if they are weaker physically'. Moreover, through her participation to the armed struggle, she claims that she aimed to 'become a role model for other women, so that we are better recognised'. Beyond the defence of her faith and nation, she thus claims to have fought 'for women's rights'.

Despite their self-professed arch commitment to the cause of Sikh independence, Ravinder and her husband seem to have experienced a precocious burn out. In 1991, they left Pakistan and returned to India clandestinely to rebuild their lives. Ravinder's husband opened a clothes boutique in a Delhi suburb, before the family shifted to Guwahati, in Assam, where they briefly ran a car shop. However, after a few months, they had to shift again, out of fear of being identified by Indian security forces. They resettled in Ahmedabad (Gujarat), where Ravinder's husband joined the transport company of a distant relative. But in 1993, his cover was blown and he was arrested and deported to Punjab. Ravinder was arrested two days later in Himachal Pradesh and transferred to a secret detention centre in Punjab. A year later, her conditions of detention slightly improved after she was transferred to Patiala jail. But she fell ill (a result of the extensive torture to which she was subjected) and obtained permission to reunite with her husband.

Ravinder and her husband were set free in 1998, after some understanding with the authorities. With the financial support of diaspora Sikhs, the couple opened an orphanage for the sons and daughters of the 'martyrs' of the armed struggle. But the return to civilian life took its toll on the couple and, after a few years, Ravinder took the bold decision to separate and to manage the girl pensioners of the orphanage on her own. The way she justifies this decision is exemplary of her sense of independence and self-confidence, which predated her participation in militancy but was certainly strengthened by it:

Family life was working just fine but we had serious disagreements on professional matters. He didn't listen to me. I didn't agree with him on the localisation of the school. He did not have any experience in the field of education since he had been working in a bank [before joining the militancy]. So it could not work. For four years, we quarrelled a lot. He was saying that he would do this, and that, but he never did. And for me, when you commit to something, you do it. After we were separated, both of us met with success. When we bumped into each other at the Golden Temple after some time, he asked me how many children I was in charge of [as of 2004, the orphanage had 105 residents], and he was quite surprised! [laughs].

This testimony emphasises how personal, even intimate developments came to overlap with political engagement throughout the life-course of

Sikh women fighters. Like most female recruits of the movement for Khalistan, Ravinder Kaur was constrained to seek the protection of a male cadre – in her case, these pressures were reinforced by her decision to stay in Pakistan, where the military patrons of Sikh insurgents were wary of individual recruits roaming freely in their country and attempted to 'fix' them in various ways (through marriage in the case of women, through their assignment to prison quarters in the case of rank and file male recruits or through what amounted to house arrest in the case of 'commanders'). For most women recruits, marriage was the rite of passage that formalised their enrolment into the Khalistani counter-society. And while some women were married by accident to Khalistani fighters (through arranged marriages to young men whose political affiliation remained unknown to the bridal party), others used this opportunity to overcome the social barriers to their enrolment into the militancy. Most of these Khalistani brides lost their husbands during the armed struggle and Ravinder's case is truly exceptional in this regard – among the ten women veterans of the movement I interviewed, eight were married into the movement and she is the only one who was not widowed during the uprising. Widowhood was a source of intense social suffering for these women veterans, as they were pressurised by their families to relocate with their in-laws, where they often faced the acrimony of their mothers-in-law, who were constantly reminded of the premature death of their sons by the presence of their widows. Ravinder's case was different in this regard, since she had to deal with a husband who, from her point of view, had become a liability, as he prevented her from reinserting into civilian life on her own terms. It is obviously difficult to establish whether Ravinder derived this strength of character from her militant experience or from previous socialisation – indeed, her precocious involvement in militant activities and the conditions of her enrolment into the movement for Khalistan tend to suggest that she developed an anti-conformist attitude early on. Her participation to the uprising certainly reinforced her sense of autonomy, however, and her aspiration to realise herself through social and political work. This is particularly obvious in her claim that women make 'better fighters than men', because of their greater mental resolve – a moral virtue which she considers herself particularly endowed with, unlike her allegedly more versatile husband.

Her separation from her husband was not an attempt to break away from a controversial past. On the contrary, it seems to have been the precondition for maintaining continuity with it. First of all, social work was a way to honour the memory of her fallen comrades. Thus, she claims that the idea of the orphanage was born after the young son of one of her jail mates, who was repeatedly tortured in front of her before being executed by the police in 1993, was rejected by his grandparents. During our conversations over the years (we met twice, within a spite of two years), she also emphasised that the vocation of the Trust was not merely to impart vocational training to destitute children, but also to form religiously and politically the next generation of fighters for Khalistan. Ravinder never really admitted that the struggle was over; it merely went through a temporary setback. While providing her with an opportunity to prove herself in the eyes of a society that rejected her for her militant past, the orphanage was also a way to maintain continuity in her engagement and convince herself that the battle was going on. In turn, her relatively high profile in the movement – she has been eulogised by various pro-Khalistan websites as a heroine of the uprising – provided her with some resources to pursue a 'philanthropic' career autonomously. While government authorities and Sikh politicians were reluctant to support this former militant, Sikhs from the diaspora (where the demand for Khalistan retains some support, especially in Canada) contributed financially. So did the religious institution in charge of the management of Sikh shrines in the Punjab, the Shiromani Prabandhak Gurdwara Committee (SGPC). The support of the latter was, however, terminated after another veteran of the movement accused Ravinder of misappropriating the funds. To defend herself against these allegations, Ravinder filed a defamation suit against her rival, who supported the orphanage of another former woman militant. Whatever the truth behind these allegations, these struggles over the meagre funds allocated to these orphanages point at another continuity between the militancy and the social activism of its veterans, both of which were marred by factionalism and mutual accusations of moral turpitude. This time, however, Ravinder chose to defend herself in court, thus acknowledging the sovereignty of a state she had been combating for almost a decade.

A Reluctant Warrior Turned Legal Activist: The Trajectory of Amandeep Kaur

Amandeep Kaur was born in Delhi in 1969, in a middle class Jat Sikh family (her father was in the army and opened a taxi stand after his retirement). She grew up in a highly religious atmosphere, under the tutelage of a devout mother and benevolent father, who supported his daughter's education and ambitions. Both her parents were members of the Akand Kirtani Jatha (AKJ)[7] and her father was close to the leadership of the Damdami Taksal,[8] being familiar with its two successive principals, Sant Kartar Singh and Sant Jarnail Singh Bhindranwale. The family residence in Delhi was regularly attended by some leading personalities of the AKJ, such as Sukhdev Singh Babbar, who would later on become a prominent insurgent commander. Therefore, Amandeep grew up in a radicalised environment, where she learnt early on to detest the Sant Nirankaris. Notwithstanding these predispositions towards militancy, she would probably have followed the medical career she was destining herself to had it not been for the 1984 anti-Sikh pogrom that followed Indira Gandhi's murder by her Sikh bodyguards.[9] On 2 November 1984, her father was lynched in front of her and she claims that she was herself the target of a murder attempt after she testified in front of some public figures who had been visiting the army camp where she had been taking shelter with her mother and brothers following her father's murder. Despite her intense desire for revenge, she initially tried to get on with her life. A few weeks after the riots, she left for Punjab in order to complete her studies in a more serene atmosphere than the one prevailing in Delhi. In Jullunder, where she joined the Lyallpur Khalsa College, she stayed with an uncle of hers, who was tightly connected to some prominent figures of the emerging Khalistan movement, such as Manbir Singh Chaheru, the founder and first commander of the Khalistan Commando Force (KCF),[10] who was a frequent visitor at her uncle's residence. Her college was also a hotbed of Sikh militancy and she became an activist and soon a local leader of the Sikh Students Federation. Amandeep's political trajectory thus followed a different route than that of Ravinder and, as such, offers a different observation post to scrutinise the 'meeting point between biography and contention'. As Javier Auyero suggests in his study of two Argentinian women protesters, the dominant trend, in the

---

[7] The Akand Kirtani Jatha is a fundamentalist Sikh sect, advocating a strict adhesion to the tenets of Sikhism. It provided the Babbar Khalsa, one of the most fearsome Sikh insurgent groups, with the bulk of its militants.

[8] The Damdami Taksal is the largest and most prestigious Sikh religious seminary. Under the leadership of Bhindranwale, it became the primary recruitment network of Sikh militants.

[9] Following Indira Gandhi's assassination by her Sikh bodyguards (as revenge for Operation Bluestar), thousands of Sikhs were brutally murdered in North India, particularly in Delhi.

[10] The Khalistan Commando Force (KCF) was the first insurgent Sikh group and the largest component of the 'first Panthic committee', launched in 1986 in Amritsar.

literature on the gendered dynamics of engagement, is to focus on long-term activists who join political protests intentionally and self-consciously. This methodological bias leads to under-problematizing of other dynamics of engagement, such as those involving women with no history of activism, who are less attracted to social movements than they are 'sucked up' into them, through interactions shaped by their biographies (Auyero, 2003: 67).

This is precisely what happened to Amandeep during her stay in Jullunder. As she struggled to turn the page and lead an ordinary life, her family background as well as her new social relations on campus inexorably pushed her towards the movement for Khalistan, which was taking shape at the time. It is in this context of personal and collective radicalisation that she resorted to take revenge for her father's death, by eliminating those responsible for the Delhi pogrom. But she was single and she feared that if she took part in a military operation with a group of married men, her detractors would accuse her of having an affair with her comrades. Therefore, she decided to marry the man who would accompany her through her lethal mission. Following the advice of Manbir Singh Chaheru and Bimal Kaur Khalsa (the widow of Beant Singh, Indira Gandhi's assassin), she set her eyes on a militant of the KCF, Arun Singh (not his real name), who had already proved his worth by taking part in the assassination of an influential Hindu press editor in 1981. The wedding was celebrated in October 1985 and, a few days later, she and her husband travelled to Delhi to murder the four Congressmen who had been playing a leading role in the pogrom. But the plan did not go as expected. The night before the attack, the third member of the commando had a fight with Arun Singh. During a short absence of the latter, he had been entertaining prostitutes in their common flat, spending a great deal of the money that was meant for the mission. Following this altercation, the young man went to reveal the whole plan to the police, who arrested Arun Singh and later on Amandeep. She only saved her life with the support of a Sikh policeman who handed her a turban while she was going to the washroom, which she used as a rope to escape from the police station. In the following days, she returned to Punjab and after a few months of hiding, during which she gave birth to her first child, she joined a group of fighters, with whom she fought Indian security forces until her arrest in 1988 and again, following her release, between 1990 and 1993.

None of the female recruits of the movement for Khalistan whom I interviewed over the years ever complained in front of me about being discriminated against by their male counterparts. On the contrary, these women insist that they were treated as 'sisters', or even as 'brothers'. These women have not come to reconsider these gender relations in the light of their post-combat experience, which sets them apart from other female fighters such as those of Central America (Kampwirth, 2002). True, none of these women has ever been part of feminist networks, but one could have expected them to become more critical with the passage of time. Actually, it is the opposite that happened: since their return to civilian life, these women have idealised their underground past as an unmitigated moment of liberation and gender equality. Therefore, these testimonies may be more revealing of the challenges faced by these ex-combatants after their return to civilian life than of actual gender relations within the Khalistan insurgency.

Indeed, Amandeep Kaur's return to civilian life has been a true ordeal. Rearrested in 1993, she was freed after committing to remarry and reconstruct her life (which suggests that, for the Indian judiciary, the crime of these women fighters was not only to have waged war against the state but also, and maybe more importantly, to have evaded their domestic responsibilities; reassigning them to conventional gender roles as caring wives and mothers was therefore perceived as a major requisite for their rehabilitation). But this second marriage soon went sour. Her husband, a former sympathiser of the Babbar Khalsa, eloped with a relative and, during the next few years, extorted money from Amandeep, before kidnapping and torturing her. Her predicament only came to an end after her second husband's death – according to Amandeep, he was poisoned by his mistress. Since then, Amandeep has been trying to fall back on her feet and she has set up a small business of textile and jewellery import-export. Unlike most veterans of the insurgency, she is extremely bitter about her past commitment and considers that she has 'ruined [her] life' by becoming a militant.

The context of her recruitment into the movement for Khalistan must here be recalled to account for this disillusion. Having been socialised into a devout Jat Sikh family with links to some prominent figures of the movement for Khalistan, Amandeep showed significant predispositions to join the uprising. In this regard, her trajectory shows striking affinities with that of Ravinder Kaur. Unlike the latter, however, Amandeep was a reluctant warrior: she joined the insurgency under duress, and was less attracted by its ideology and by promises of epic adventures than by a compulsion to avenge her father's death. Despite paying a heavy price for her participation in the armed struggle (she spent more than eight years in jail, while her mother was imprisoned for three years for 'sheltering a terrorist') she failed to obtain retribution. Much like Ravinder, however, she did not disengage from politics altogether following her return to civilian life. She became actively involved in the movement demanding justice for the victims of the anti-Sikh riots of 1984, and in 2009 she was one of the eleven witnesses who testified before the Central Bureau of Investigation (CBI) against Congress leader Sajjan Kumar, one of the leading instigators of the riots. She does not hold illusions about the outcome of this fight for justice but, much like Ravinder, she seems to have found in this non-violent form of activism a way to honour the memory of the 'martyrs' and to pursue her struggle by other means.

In 2013, Sajjan Kumar was acquitted by a Delhi district court, despite the fact that the CBI had acquired the conviction that he was directly involved in this anti-Sikh pogrom. This decision outraged Amandeep, who then went on a hunger strike as a sign of protest against the judgment. The location for this protest was significant: she chose a public ground in front of the Jantar Mantar (Delhi's astronomical observatory), which has become the most popular centre for non-violent public protests in the Indian capital. By choosing this location and endorsing a mode of protest popularised in India by Gandhi – and thus associated with the doctrine of *ahimsa* (non-violence) – Amandeep seemed to have completed her mutation, from dreaded terrorist to non-violent activist. On the sixth day of her strike, the *jathedar* (caretaker) of the Akal Takht (a shrine located within the Golden Temple complex in Amritsar and symbolising the temporal power of the Sikh community), Giani Gurbachan Singh, intervened and assured Amandeep that her demands would be met. Showing some concern for her deteriorating health, he added that this form of protest was against the tenets of Sikhism and he ordered her to break her fast. Amandeep complied with this request but, shortly there- after, declared publicly that she had been fooled and that she had betrayed the Sikh community. While this episode suggested that she was still somewhat insecure in her new identity of civic protestor, the letter of protest that she wrote to Giani Gurbachan Singh in the following weeks also showed that she had somewhat managed to fuse the political cultures of religious militancy and non-violent, secular activism. Thus, to counter the argument that fasting was against the Sikh *maryada* (code of con- duct), she invoked the figure of Bhai Randir Singh (1878–1961), the founder of the AKJ, who occasionally resorted to hunger strikes as a form of protest but who also took part in an armed uprising (the Ghadr movement of 1915) against the British government and who, as a result, was sentenced to life imprisonment for 'waging war against the state'. Once again, one should refrain from assuming that the apparent shift from militancy to activism among some veterans of the Khalistan movement was a clear turning point in their lives, at least in their own eyes. Even as they shifted to non-violent forms of mobilisation or social work, these former combatants continued to draw inspiration from militant role models, and they remained dedicated to the ideals that had led them to pick up the gun in the first place (social justice, religious freedom, national sovereignty). The sense of continuity that this conferred to these veterans was not available to all of them, however. Here, one should return to other, more banal experiences of reinsertion into civilian life, on the part of women fighters who faced (even) greater challenges after being decommissioned.

TURNING POINTS AND THE UNEVEN DISTRIBUTION OF BIFURCATIVE RESOURCES

As already emphasised, many women veterans of the movement for Khalistan did *not* shift from militancy to non-violent forms of activism after their return to civilian life. All the women I interviewed emphasised that Sikh politicians boycotted them. Even Simranjit Singh Mann – a former police officer known for his proximity with Khalistanis, who spent five years in jail after being accused of complicity in Indira Gandhi's murder and was elected twice to Parliament (1989 and 1999) – seems to have maintained some distance with the women veterans of Khalistan. In 1989, the SAD (Mann) got the widow of Beant Singh, Indira Gandhi's assassin, elected to Parliament. However, Bimal Kaur Khalsa (who did not take part in the uprising, although she was imprisoned for two years after an incendiary speech) died in 1990 in mysterious circumstances and she remains the only pro-Khalistan woman to have embraced a professional political career, however briefly. In any case, the SAD (Mann) was nowhere to be seen during the 2004, 2009 and 2013 elections, a confirmation that the Sikh electorate was determined to bring closure to the conflict that had torn apart the province from the early 1980s to the mid-1990s.

As they were being denied an entry into party politics, some women veterans turned to social work. Out of the ten former Sikh women fighters I interviewed over the years, four opened orphanages for the children of Khalistani 'martyrs', which seems to have been the easiest way for them to preserve a sense of continuity between their past engagement and their current life as a 'civilian'. All these women came from relatively well-off families and retained the support of their kin, had been married to prominent guerrilla commanders and were more educated than average (Ravinder Kaur, for instance, studied up to college level; Sandeep Kaur, who runs the Mata Gujri Trust, near Amritsar, for her part completed her studies in jail, up to the BA level). Many others did not have the social and financial resources necessary to launch themselves into such ventures, however. At this point, I must emphasise that my sample of interviewees presents a strong bias: I only had access to women who, somehow, remained in touch with their former comrades, which enabled me to 'snowball' from one interviewee to another. Other women veterans, however, broke away with their former comrades, sometimes under pressure from their families. Some had to remarry under duress and their new in-laws generally tried to hide their militant past, which was perceived as a source of dishonour for the family, while exposing it to police harassment. While most Sikhs looked at former Khalistani militants at large with hostility, women veterans were the targets of even greater animosity. Thus, according to Jasmeet Kaur, the widow of a commander of the Bhindranwale Tigers Force of Khalistan (BTFK):

People started looking at us with suspicion and hatred. They blamed the terrorists and their families for their harassment by the police. They felt we women could have corrected our husbands. The behaviour of the in-laws was the worst. My parents cooperated with me. So I didn't have many problems. Yes, I had financial difficulties, and worked for the Shiromani Gurdwara Prabandhak Committee. I did feel orphaned, worried and insecure. (quoted in Pushkarna, 1998b)

Rather than providing women with skills and social resources that they could have used to reinsert themselves into society, their militant past was generally a liability. While Jasmeet Kaur was relatively lucky in this regard – besides her parents and the SGPC, she received some support from sympathisers of the movement for Khalistan, who helped her set up her own orphanage – other women faced greater difficulties. This was particularly true of those widows who were rejected by their in-laws and had to take shelter, with their children, in *gurdwaras* (Sikh shrines). This dependence upon charity was all the more painful that it compromised the sentiments of self-esteem that these women's association with the armed struggle had nurtured. This experience of marginalisation also points at the fragility of the resources generated through social proximity with the militants. As the attitudes of the larger society evolved along the course of the conflict, in relation to state repression but also to the exactions perpetrated by the militants themselves, Khalistani fighters and their relatives were gradually deprived of the aura that they had initially been endowed with. What could initially pass for a form of social capital fast devaluated and as the conflict came to an end, veterans of the armed struggle and their families became increasingly ostracised. The sense of hurt related by many women veterans thus underlines their estrangement from a collective transition towards a post-conflict society, which compromised their own attempts at social reinsertion.

This was not only true of former women militants but also of widows of combatants who had remained 'overground' during the conflict. In a 1998 interview with an Indian weekly, one of these widows (Maninder Kaur, whose husband, Sarbjit Singh, was with the Khalistan Liberation Army and was killed in 1992) explained that in the early years of the insurgency, 'People used to come to me for help in all sorts of things ... land disputes, petty fights, family disputes and problems in marriage. ...They knew we had clout and would use it wisely'. However, following the death of her husband and the decline of the movement, she claims that '[People] abandoned us. Neither the militant outfit nor the public cared. I worked hard, sewing clothes, doing dishes and the like. I sent off my daughters to Anandpur Sahib [an important place of Sikh pilgrimage] because I wanted to spare them the agony' (quoted in Pushkarna, 1998a). This sense of self-esteem – of pride, even – conferred by these women's association with the 'Singhs' was well identified by their male interlocutors. And even among their well-wishers, it evoked mixed feelings. Thus, according to Jaspal Singh Dhillon, a human rights activist and a supporter of the movement for Khalistan, who helped Jasmeet Kaur set up her orphanage, 'These are women who had stood up and done what they wanted to. Many of them had huge egos too' (quoted in Pushkarna, 1998a).

Women who were readmitted into their former homes or re-married into new families, for their part, faced the risk of being reassigned to traditional gender roles as mothers, wives or – even more precariously – as widows. Most of these women were also confronted to harassment from the police, to bureaucratic red tape (obtaining birth certificates for their children was often a true ordeal as these women generally gave birth after being admitted in local hospitals under a fake identity) and economic hardship. The widows of former civil servants (policemen, railway employees, etc.) were denied pensions and provident funds by their husband's former employer, who usually claimed that they were not aware of their death. Like Maninder Kaur, many widows of Khalistani commander had to take menial jobs to make ends meet, which made them vulnerable to stigmatisation and sexual harassment from their neighbours and relatives. Moreover, for those women who came from relatively well-off families, taking a job was seen as a form of declassification. Far from being lived as a tool of emancipation, these forms of employment were perceived as a downgrading and alienating experience (Kumar et al., 1999). In this context, re-marriage appeared as the best of the worst options for some of these women, providing them with some form of social and economic protection. At this point, their past experience in the militancy did provide them with some resources. After resigning themselves to remarry, three of my interviewees chose to do so with sympathisers of the movement, who had been loosely associated with it. While these ideological and religious affinities (these men were always deeply religious and several of them earned a living by singing religious hymns in Sikh shrines) spared these women the burden of justifying their acts or hiding their past altogether, they also seem to have empowered them, as their militant past reinforced their authority within their new household. This was made particularly clear during my interview sessions. Although their husbands sometimes attended them, they did not utter a word until I solicited their opinion on their wife's trajectory or more generally on the participation of women to the insurgency – a restraint that was clearly at odds with conventional gender relations.

CONCLUSION

Even more than their male counterparts, the women recruits of the movement for Khalistan had to cope simultaneously with tremendous challenges in their public and private lives. Their 'life moments' (Le Goff, 1996: 19) were more clearly delimitated because of the greater interpenetration of biographical and social time among them. Personal and political developments were systematically intermeshed among Sikh female fighters: they were married into the movement and became at risk of being estranged from it during and after their pregnancies; finally, unlike for men, their demilitarisation threatened them with being reassigned to a primary if not exclusively domestic role. Each new sequence of their political career was precipitated by a turning point in their private lives. These women dealt differently with the personal and political challenges induced by such turning points, however, which reveals significant variations in the allocation of adjustment resources among them, a key issue for the study of biographical bifurcations

(Hélardot, 2010: 167). At each turning point, moral and material support from their families proved determinant. Other resources (their education level, their access to politico-religious institutions and diasporic funding) played a more specific role, when these women had to face the multiple challenges induced by their decommissioning. While these women's past militant credentials did generate some resources (especially as far as the attention of the SGPC and Canadian Sikhs was concerned), these proved to be contested and transient ones. Thus, while some of these women tried to capitalise on their status of widows of 'martyred' guerrilla commanders to attain some degree of social and political recognition or to generate funds for their post-militancy ventures, they soon realised that this status was fast devaluating, in a society determined to move forward by resolutely turning its back on a controversial past.

Besides their emphasis on the uneven distribution of bifurcative resources, these two life trajectories are an invitation to reconsider the role of the state and that of the politics of care in the gendered politics of activism. If the personal and the political are so enmeshed in the political trajectories of women activists, it is not merely because of spill-over effects from their sexual careers – which would suggest that, because of their reproductive role, women's political involvement would be 'naturally' over-determined by their life (if not biological) cycle. Instead, the activist careers examined here emphasise the structural contribution of state power to this personalisation. Thus, when Amandeep's legal counsel advised her to remarry in order to get out of jail quicker, he did not only hint at the sexually conservative streak of the post-colonial Indian judiciary. Instead, he advocated a tactical use of a much larger phenomenon, characteristic of the judicial treatment of women by the modern state, that is, its 'sexually differential management of illegalisms' (Cardi and Pruvost, 2012: 20–21). Even in supposedly more sexually liberal societies such as France, deviant women tend to be treated differently than men by the judicial system, for instance by being more often prosecuted by civil courts than penal courts. And if the state seems more lenient with deviant women, isn't it because more 'caring' institutions than the prison – starting with the family – are tasked with disciplining their bodies and souls? This is precisely why militant women are such a source of fascination and repulsion for modern states and their populations: because they introduce a rupture into the politics of care, by rejecting their 'natural' assignment to family roles. Rehabilitating these women then takes the form of a reassignment to protective institutions that seem to ensure soft forms of re-socialisation but that instil other forms of violence

(Cardi, 2010). Thus, if the violent engagements of women are an invitation to decompartementalise our understanding of political activism, it is not merely by redrawing the boundaries of the personal and the political, or the 'public' and the 'private', but more originally by avoiding to consider that any institution – including the allegedly protective space of the domestic sphere – is exempt from violence (Cardi and Pruvost, 2012: 59).

More specific to the contentious lives discussed here was the difficulty of these women to turn the page of their militant past, even if they reflected differently upon it. Much like the cost of defection, the socio-biographical effects of activism depend upon the duration of this activism and its intensity (its level of risk, in particular) (McAdam, 1988), as well as upon the conditions of recruitment into a particular group, its degree of cohesion, its relation to the surrounding society and the possibilities of 'opting out' for a minimal cost (Fillieule & Bennani-Chraïbi, 2003: 123). Or to put it simply: 'the cost of activism sort of determines its value' (Fillieule, 2005: 40). In the case of women veterans of the Khalistan insurgency, the sacrifices that they made to join the movement and/or remain involved in it, their sense of duty towards their fallen comrades, their relative isolation from the rest of society throughout the uprising and the resulting intensity of their emotional attachment to the movement explain the intensity of their commitment and their difficulties to detach themselves from their past engagement. What they experienced was much more than some 'hangover identity' (Fuchs Ebaugh, 1988: 5) from their previous role. As I interviewed these women years after their return to civilian life, I was struck by their denial of having become 'exes'. On the contrary, most of them argued that the movement was merely undergoing a temporary phase of abeyance and they expressed a desire to resume their militant activities, if only they were given the opportunity. If this conviction probably amounts to one of these 'hesitating modalities of belief' talked about by Paul Veyne (1983: 67), it should not be discarded as a mere rhetorical device or, worse, as a symptom of bad faith. Since its inception, the sociology of careers, militant or otherwise, has had a predilection for 'authentic', full-fledged types (not unlike the sociology of roles, when it searches for well-rounded exes) – a tropism predicated on the over-valorisation of achievement within a certain occupational career (Poussou-Plesse, 2009: 256). Without going as far as endorsing a strictly subjective approach towards biographical bifurcations, one should seriously take into consideration these denials – that is, those refusals to endorse the identity of an ex and the desire to maintain some continuity with the militant past, however illusory this might seem. While it is probably more common to reinterpret the past as an anticipation of the present to maintain a sense of continuity in our lives (Strauss, 2008 [1959]: 148), the reconstruction of the present, in order to attune it to a more gratifying past, can also operate as a protection against the sense of self-betrayal. Such narratives may extend beyond mere acts of language to encompass a wide array of pragmatic adjustments. This is exemplified by the older and more politicised recruits of the movement for Khalistan, who began their political career as student activists and who, over the years, developed an anti-conformist attitude, a sense of self-confidence and a commitment to justice and social welfare – a durable disposition to act upon the world that amounted to an activist habitus and that informed their actions on the domestic front as much as the management of their social and political engagements. In the case of Ravinder Kaur, for instance, a deeply ingrained sense of self-confidence forged through decades of political engagement, combined with new life projects, led her to re-examine her marriage and take the highly unconventional decision to rebuild her life as a single mother. Incidentally, this critical reassessment of her marital life showed that she did acknowledge her decommissioning as a turning point in her life, which demanded some adjustments. At the same time, however, she preserved her sense of personal continuity by convincing herself that these 'new' life choices were necessary to remain true to her past engagements. Rather than as a drastic change, divorce was thus experienced as a minor concession to constancy, here.

For the most resourceful among these veterans – that is, for those who were allocated more adjustment resources along their life course – this activist habitus was re-actualised through social activism. Non-violent forms of engagement enabled them to maintain a semblance of continuity in their lives, at the cost of compromising the public image and the financial health of their educational institutions (who were often perceived as hotbeds of radicalism). This shift from militancy to a form of social activism with political undertones thus partook to a form of 'storytelling' (Polletta, 2009) that was primarily meant for personal consumption and through which these veterans of the armed struggled tried to downplay the rupture with their militant past, even as some of their actions acknowledged significant bifurcations in their lives. Such narratives were not always sufficient to provide psychological comfort to these women, however. Amandeep Kaur's political journey led her to relinquish her vendetta for the pursuit of justice, and while both quests were made personally meaningful by the same trauma, her shift to legal activism left her only more disillusioned about herself and about politics in all its forms. Other women did not even have the chance to try their luck at such a reorientation. And for those who were reclaimed by family duties and conventional gender roles, the negative impact on their self-esteem was all the greater that they had experimented, however briefly and relatively, with an intoxicating feeling of empowerment.

7

"Married Forever," Activists Forever?

What the Multi-Level and Interactionist Approaches to the Study of "Exit" Reveal about Disengagement from Radical Organizations in Contemporary Turkey

Jordi Tejel

Over the last two decades social scientists have considered state repression practiced by authoritarian regimes as the main reason for the absence of long-lasting mass mobilization in the Middle East prior to 2011. In that respect, repression of overtly political dissent came to be seen as a determining factor to explain the adoption of a human rights discourse, or civil society repertoire, by former activists (El Khawaga, 2003: 271–292; Monceau, 2007; Duboc, 2010: 61–82). However, diverse case studies prove that repression can at times have a mobilizing effect (Khawaja, 1993: 47–71; Hafez, 2003). There could be a direct relation between violence and radicalization, i.e. a higher degree of repression would provoke a higher degree of radicalization among protestors (Goodwin, 2001; Einwohner, 2003: 650–675). Finally, some scholars have suggested a "third way," thereby highlighting the need to first detect what effects of repression are submitted to close scrutiny and then observe them in relation to a given context (Opp & Roehl, 1990: 521–547).

Either approach, however, tends to focus on the macro level of analysis to observe the impact of repression on social mobilization, while neglecting a wide range of factors and dynamics belonging to the other two levels of analysis, namely the meso and micro levels. The advantage of a multi-level approach in order to study social mobilization materialized as I was conducting my history-based research project on student movements in the Middle East. In fact, a close study of the political situation of the south-eastern provinces in Turkey following the 1980 military coup d'état offers a striking paradox. While Turkey was witnessing a "cycle of demobilisation" (Tarrow, 1994) as opposed to the 1960s and 1970s (considered as the paramount of "contentious" years), observation of the Kurdish arena in Turkey suggests a different picture. Physical as well as political repression led indeed to a dramatic drop in activism between 1981 and 1984. Yet despite scarce openings in the political system or the lack of "political opportunities," from 1984 onwards, the Kurdistan Workers' Party (PKK) became the dominant dissent movement in Turkey as a whole.

Traditionally, historians, sociologists, and political scientists have chosen the political center as their unit of analysis to study the social, economic, and political transformation of nation-states – at the expense of "provinces" or the respective peripheries. In doing so, the social sciences have reproduced the asymmetric perspective advanced by the elites of the new nation-states: the "real issues" are unfolding in the capital city, whereas what is happening outside of it constitutes only a miniature image of the truly "national" issues; that is to say, those of the "center." The study of social mobilization, and particularly the student movements, in Turkey has generally followed the same approach, leaving aside the social dynamics of the "periphery" (Kabacali, 1992; Kaçmazoglu, 1995). In that regard, ethnicity (e.g. Kurdish identity) would be self-explanatory to understand the exceptionality of Eastern Turkey in the 1980s as opposed to the "center." As this chapter seeks to demonstrate, however, the observation of how the general Turkish political context, local dynamics, and individual trajectories interplayed may open new avenues to analyzing the varying effects of state repression depending on factors such as time, space, and subjectivities.

At the same time, oral accounts reveal that the PKK "success story" conceals both organizational weaknesses and a long list of defections that cannot be explained solely through the "state repression" grid of analysis; many activists devoted to the "national struggle" have been rejected by the organization itself. In that sense, my preliminary findings confirmed that "abandonment can be either voluntary or forced, depending on whether an individual makes a choice or is constrained to adopt certain behaviour" (Della Porta, 2009: 68). Yet, the *voluntariness* or *forcedness* of such a decision should be conceptualized not as a dichotomy but rather as a continuum.

More intriguingly, although the PKK has produced many ex-activists since its official establishment in 1978, individual defeat proved to be in many cases a long and complex process in which "reversibility" (the possibility to return to the role he or she has exited) was a common phenomenon. Clearly, "exit" was not only due to state coercion but also to the interplay between repression, internal organizational coercion, institutional dynamics, and other intertwined factors.

Hence, this chapter aims to shed light on the impact of state repression on activists engaged in radical movements in contemporary Turkey (1984–1991) with a special focus on the actual factors leading to defection. They should be understood as an interactive *process* requiring a *multi-level* model of disengagement, in particular at the meso level of organizations and at the micro level of biography. Drawing from the life-history method[1] and in-depth interviews with a married couple of ex-militants, the paper seeks to demonstrate that while coercion does have an effect both on social movements and on the militants individually, a closer observation of life stories suggests that other elements should also be taken into consideration to better grasp the phenomenon of "exit" in authoritarian contexts, including life-changing events, interlocked trajectories (such as activism and family), socialization, the impact of generational units and "microcohorts" on social movements (Whittier, 1997: 760–778), gender relations, and emotions. Importantly, some of these factors also serve to explain certain long-term consequences of commitment which may continue long after the decision of disengagement was made.

Admittedly, life histories of a married couple cannot pretend to have a holistic value. Yet the analysis of this case study, for several reasons, reveals interesting points that may, on the one hand, confirm some of the ideas put forward by the interactionist approach to social mobilization and, on the other hand, open new avenues for research on the biographical consequences of activism. Finally, the choice of my case study was not a random one. Within the framework of my present research project, I conducted a series of interviews with former student activists in Diyarbakir city between March and April 2013.[2] Over the course of the interviews, it appeared that although the interviewees at first described themselves as "engaged," they eventually highlighted some nuances when they admitted that there were, in fact, different *degrees* of engagement (Saunders et al., 2012: 263–280). In other words,

---

[1] The advantages of the life history method are diverse: It allows us to explore the shifting and subjective dimension of activism; the fluid character of costs: as well as retributions or gratifications of action (Leclercq & Pagis, 2011: 5–23).

[2] I interviewed twenty ex-student activists at the Faculty of Law at Dicle University (Diyarbakir) belonging to the same academic cohort (1983–1988). None belonged to the PKK.

although they did participate in some actions as members of clandestine movements in the mid-1980s, they all coincided in pointing out two students, a male and a female, of the same cohort as "really committed" or "die-hard" activists. Further, it turned out that these two students got married and after a period of high-risk activism (1985–1988) went underground, ending up in exile in Europe where they are still living. Intrigued by the first elements of a story that, to some extent, resembled a "Bonnie and Clyde" scenario, I decided to interview them, for their case study seemed to present some significant advantages.

First, since Fatma and Murat[3] appeared as "typical" activists within the Turkish political context (early commitment, prison, torture, underground experience, exile), in theory, one could expect that the biographical consequences of high-cost activism would be more important. Thus, it would allegedly be easier to observe the interaction between the different levels of analysis. Second, as a married couple, one could also expect that, on the one hand, it would also be easier at the micro-level to observe the interaction between the different spheres or sub-worlds (activism, professional and affective life), which are embedded in political life-course as well as in a marital relationship. Ultimately, it would be possible to determine what effects, if any, the participation in the Kurdish movement in the 1980s had on their subsequent lives (McAdam, 1989: 744–760; Leclercq & Pagis, 2011: 25–51). On the other hand, although they had lived and witnessed the same events to a certain extent, it would be interesting to see whether their respective gendered socialization is reflected in their individual narratives about their past, both as activists and spouses. Finally, being members of or working for different organizations (the THP-ML/TIKKO or the Communist Party of Turkey/ Marxist Leninist-Workers' and Peasants' Liberation Army of Turkey and the PKK) that nevertheless shared some characteristics (armed struggle, Marxist leaning) and came to cooperate, their case study could allow me to engage with the meso level of analysis, thereby observing two different organizational models and histories.

Overall, while militant careers and trajectories are obviously unique, drawing from my case study I seek to highlight some regularities and similarities with other "types of trajectories," show how political commitment generates or modifies dispositions to act, and offer broader explanations on the individual consequences of protest activity, as well as show the complexity of the exit process (El Khawaga, 2003: 271–292; Massicard, 2010: 1–18; Grojean, 2013: 63–88).

---

[3] The names have been changed in order to preserve their anonymity. In-depth interviews were conducted twice with both of them between September 2013 and March 2014. Additional information was requested via Skype.

A CONTEXT OF POLITICAL RADICALIZATION

In June 1968, Turkish students occupied the campuses of Ankara and Istanbul universities, shouting slogans against the presence of the US Sixth Fleet in the Mediterranean. Furthermore, as the media increased students' self-confidence in their capacity to bring about political change by alerting public opinion to the arrival of a new wave of revolutionary change, the latter became radicalized and came to view themselves as the actors in an international student movement. Yet the student revolt evolved over time: a series of bomb attacks affected Turkish campuses, while clashes between leftists and rightists, bank robberies, and even kidnappings spread between 1970 and 1971.

The state's answer conformed to the premises of the "counterinsurgency" doctrine that was popular in many Asian and Latin American countries during the 1960s and 1970s, thereby radicalizing the left-wing opposition of the youth (Bozarslan, 2004: 64–65). In 1978 alone, 820 people were killed in politically inspired violence in Turkey.[4] Yet, factional divisions and rivalries among the leftist groups became an additional factor for the escalation of political violence, "for each new factional conflict pushed the militants toward greater activism in their efforts to receive more media attention than the other groups" (Sayari, 2010: 200).

In the south-east of Turkey, the Kemalist crackdown on Kurdish revolts throughout the 1920s and 1930s brought about a "period of silence" during the following two decades. In 1959, however, one hundred Kurdish students signed a petition in favor of cultural rights, such as the right to speak Kurdish in official buildings and the right to publish in that language. Thereafter, inspired both by the resumption of the Kurdish armed struggle in Iraq in 1961 and by leftist trends in Turkey, thousands of Kurdish youngsters engaged in considerable political activism throughout the 1960s and 1970s. While Kurdish university students worked for a "renaissance" of the Kurdish language and popular culture, they also provided a new framework for mobilization to their ethnic fellows: "Eastism" (*Doguculuk*). For almost a decade, Kurdish students and intellectuals jointly organized massive meetings in south-eastern Anatolia to denounce the economic imbalance between the Eastern provinces (where the overwhelming majority of Kurds lived) and the Western parts

---

[4] NA, FCO 9/2767. British Embassy (Ankara) to Southern European Department. Ankara, January 3, 1979.

of Turkey (Gündogan, 2011: 389–416). Further, as a reaction to articles of ultra-nationalist journals as well as to hesitations of the Turkish left, Kurdish identity (*kürtçülük*) increasingly occupied a central position in Turkish debates.

However, the fierce repression from the army and Turkish elites of all Kurdish movements, as well as the violent interaction between Kurdish militants and rightist groups at universities, led the former to radicalize a new generation of student activists both in terms of demands (national independence) and means (armed struggle) by the mid-1970s. By 1974, Abdullah Öcalan, a member of the Ankara Higher Education Union (AYÖD) (an organization at least partially inspired by the Guevarist THKP-C or Turkish Popular Liberation Party-Front) together with other Kurds began to develop a separate, distinct "political-ideological" grouping, which also included some young Turkish leftists (McDowall, 1996: 418–419).

Thereafter, Öcalan was elected the leader of this group, which became known simply as the "Apocular", or followers of Apo, until the provisional name of *Ulusal Kurtulush Ordusu* (UKO, "National Liberation Army") was adopted by the group. The PKK, which was officially established in 1978, followed the same political agenda as UKO – namely, the establishment of a socialist Kurdish nation-state and the struggle against "collaborators" with "the colonizer Turkish Republic" (PKK, 1981: 35). The main ideological difference of the PKK, among other newly established groups with regard to previous organizations, was that the former considered employing political violence as the main instrument for creating political influence not only against the Turkish state but also Kurdish "challengers," namely competing Kurdish organizations and Kurdish "collaborators" (Ercan, 2010: 192).[5]

Among the latter, feudal landlords were targeted in particular in the northern hinterland of Urfa. In cities such as Siverek (40,000 inhabitants by the late 1970s) the sociopolitical power of feudal elites was quite significant in protecting and reproducing different forms of existing social inequalities. Against this backdrop, to the UKO first, and then to the PKK, the transformation of land distribution in Eastern Turkey was not a matter to be resolved through nonviolent methods; only armed struggle could accelerate the end of feudal relations. Accordingly, the UKO/PKK

---

[5] There were other political groups that pledged themselves to armed struggle as the only means to reach their political goals (independence and socialism): Rizgarî (1975), Kawa (a Maoist group, 1975), and the KUK or Kurdish National Liberators (1977).

attacked the Bucak tribe in Siverek, as well as other well-known wealthy families (van Bruinessen, 1988: 42–46).

By 1979, violence in the Siverek area was widespread. More tellingly, during the Minister of the Interior's visit in August 1979, two men were shot only a short distance from where the minister was holding his discussions.[6] The State's response was to introduce martial law in the southeast, which, according to a French survey, proved to be a complete failure.[7]

First Engagement

Fatma and Murat are two *typical* by-products of the radicalized political context in Siverek, which affected mainly youngsters in secondary school as well as at university. They constitute a glaring, albeit not "perfect" example of the emergence of a new category of young actors within the Kurdish political field: the *talebe* (students). Although the Kurdish youth emerged as an important political actor in Eastern Turkey in the 1960s, the relations between the youth and Kurdish society became *institutionalized* from the 1970s onward. As Mehmet Orhan points out, the young members of political groups targeted diverse sectors of Kurdish society, in particular villagers, in order to help construct informal networks by establishing direct relations. Like the *Shining Path* in Peru, the Kurdish *talebe*, thanks to their (supposed) cultural capital in the eyes of the local population, became both mobilized actors and agencies of socialization (Orhan, 2015). Through a rapid process of ideological radicalization, a significant number of Kurds detached themselves from schools and universities, settled both in villages and towns, and moved to political violence.

However, according to this author, the importance of *talebe* as agencies of socialization and mobilization decreased from the 1980s onward due to several interrelated reasons. On the one hand, being a student in the 1980s and 1990s provided less important social capital, as the number of Kurdish students had dramatically increased during those years. On the other hand, once mobilizations spread throughout Eastern Turkey, social categories of mobilizers became diverse. In other words, by the 1990s

[6] NA FCO 9/2883. British Embassy (Ankara) to Southern European Department. Ankara, August 29, 1979.
[7] NA FCO 9/2883. French Survey quoted by the British Embassy (Ankara) to Southern European Department. Ankara, August 24, 1979.

students were only *one* of the groups represented in the Kurdish political field. Yet Murat and Fatma do not fully fit into the "*talebe* model" for, despite their strong political commitment, they were never completely detached from their student identity. Furthermore, their early marriage added new identity layers that matter from a micro-level perspective, as we shall see in the following subsections.

In 1976, Murat got involved in politics at the age of 13 when he organized a student boycott to ask for better conditions in his school. At that time, he recalls, "there were no stoves in our class-rooms and window panes were often broken, therefore in winter we had to attend lessons dressed in pull-over and jackets." The boycott was a success and he emerged as the "leader" of a spontaneous protest action. Thereafter, different organizations (Kawa, DDKD, and TIKKO) approached him to become their representative at the secondary school. Eventually he chose TIKKO, a Maoist organization that sought to establish a socialist system within the framework of a two-state Kurdish and Turkish federal solution to the Kurdish issue, "because it was the most radical" of them.

Although he did not "understand a word from Marx and Lenin's texts," he appreciated the high level of "freedom of speech" within the organization. He rapidly took on responsibilities within the move-ment, and in 1977 he moved to Urfa to study at the School of Business, wherein he established a TIKKO cell along with his best friend. However, Urfa's schools were dominated by rightist groups; subsequently, clashes between his small group and the "fascists" soon developed. In 1978 his best friend and comrade was killed by a group of rightist students. At that very moment, a choice had to be made: "After such an event either I dropped my engagement or I went on with all the consequences the decision involved; I chose the latter option." Hence, clashes with rightist students continued, and in January 1979 he was arrested and taken into custody for twenty days and again in May of the same year. However, on this occasion the consequences became more important because Murat was transferred to Diyarbakir prison until 1982. Following her sister's path, Fatma got involved with the UKO in 1979. Although its main political goal was the establishment of a socialist Kurdish state, her immediate commitment was geared toward the Bucak family. The UKO accused the Bucaks of kidnapping women and asking families to pay ransom in return for their release. Furthermore, people in the Siverek area also had to pay extra taxes to the Bucaks. In spite of her young age (she was only 14), Fatma was responsible for propaganda matters in the main secondary school. Her linguistic skills (she speaks Turkish, Zaza, and Kurmanji) allowed her to undertake further responsibilities within the movement; thus she spread the word against the Bucaks, in particular among peasant women. At night, however, Fatma had another mission; armed with a gun, she patrolled the neighborhoods under UKO's control to prevent the Bucaks' henchmen from penetrating into their "liberated area." To sum up, between September 1979 and September 1980, Fatma was politically active 24/7. A short, albeit intense, period in which political experience seemed to determine *every* aspect of her life.

One could argue that Siverek reunited all conditions: social (poverty, feudal relations) and political (martial law, establishment of small revolutionary groups) for the politicization of youngsters, and in particular students, against both the state and its local "allies." Scholars of social movement theory would point out that students have in general a higher level of "biographical availability," defined as the "absence of personal constraints that may increase the costs and risks of movement participation" (McAdam, 1986: 70).[8] Further, because people who are more biographically available have fewer social obligations, alternative commitments, and countervailing relationships than those who are less biographically available (Snow et al., 1980: 787–801; Rochford, 1985), the costs and risks of social movement activity are likely to be lower for them. Hence, biographically available individuals should be more likely to participate in social movement activity since they have fewer constraints (Beyerlein & Hipp, 2006: 300–301).

However, in a recent article Olivier Fillieule wonders whether the cost-benefit grid of analysis may apply in the same manner to every stage in human life. In other words, do youngsters between 13 and 18 years "calculate" the cost-benefit equation as adults do? Testimonies of young activists clearly show that there was a miscalculation of their strength and capacities, as well as the risks they faced during their activist years (Fillieule, 2013). Indeed, Fatma and Murat acknowledge that nowadays they can understand neither how they managed to tell adults what to do, nor the risks they ran at that time. Although they don't regret their engagement, nowadays they admit that they would not allow their daughters to follow the same pattern. Cognitive mechanisms therefore should be taken into account while studying student activism and/or youth activism

---

[8] The costs of movement participation refer to "expenditures of time, money, and energy that are required of a person engaged in any particular form of activism, while the risks refer to the anticipated dangers – whether legal, social, physical, financial, and so forth – of engaging in a particular type of activity" (McAdam, 1986: 67).

for "they see things in ways their elders do not," in particular because "interpretative schemas of 18 to 25 years old are less encumbered by past experiences" (Johnston, 2012: 50).

To be sure, in the post-1945 era, having obtained more rights and authority, students began to act with increasing self-awareness and by the 1960s had become a more politically concerned and active group than students were in many other societies. In Turkey, the process of empowerment of the student body began already in the 1950s and grew exponentially between 1968 and 1980. As a result, one could argue that students, and youth in general, had entered into an emotional regime of risk and temporality: The actors believed that change was possible, and they hoped that through their rational violence they would be able to live in a transformed world (McDonald, 2013, 142).

All in all, these debates bring us to the ideas already formulated by Mannheim about the "impressionable years" seen as a succession of "fresh encounters" within unforeseen situations leading to the invention and quick accumulation of experiences (Fillieule, 2013). Yet, although the political context was favorable and students were in theory "available," not *all* youngsters were actually involved in revolutionary activities in Siverek. In Murat's family, for example, he was the only one out of eight siblings to be politically active. Likewise, only Fatma and one of her sisters, out of six boys and girls, were involved. As mentioned, Murat's commitment started accidentally as a result of his "eternally unsatisfied" character. In Fatma's case, however, it seems that the influence of her elder sister (member of the UKO) was combined with a strong feeling of injustice toward her own father, "eternally unemployed, who was not really interested in finding a job." As a consequence, Fatma was obliged to act as a young adult when she was only 11 years old. While her two elder sisters either got married or studied elsewhere, during her school days, Fatma had to wake up early in the morning to help her mother at the small bakery she owned before going to school.

Mockery at school about her social background and her poor command of the Turkish language was reinforced by another social marker. When Fatma was born, as with her two elder sisters, her mother asked to put a tattoo (*deq*, in Kurdish; *dövme*, in Turkish) on her left cheek. According to a popular belief among rural populations in Siverek, the tattoo was thought to protect their lives.[9] In so doing, however, she made

---

[9] Fatma's mother had lost her first two babies in their early days.

Turkish students laugh at Fatma: "I was obviously the *poor Kurdish girl* in the class whose father did not want to work." At the age of 13 she didn't really know a lot about politics, but she felt a strong feeling of shame as well as an interest in one single idea: equality rather than socialism.

In early 1979, her best friend invited her to attend a seminar organized by the DDKD. She was, however, searching for a more "radical" organization as her future "partner'.' Thus, she soon discovered the UKO and attended seminars animated by first-year university students twice a week. Although the PKK was officially formed on November 27, 1978, in the village of Fis in Diyarbakir province (White, 2000: 135), cadres in Siverek preferred the use of the UKO acronym for the sake of secrecy regarding the ongoing changes within the organization. Between 1979 and 1980, Fatma became the UKO/PKK representative of the youth section, a full-time activity that was curtailed only by the coup d'état of September 12, 1980 and its aftermath.

VIOLENCE AND ITS IMPACT

The coup of September 12, 1980 was provoked by what the military regarded as an attack on the core Kemalist values of national and territorial integrity by subversive leftist and Kurdish movements. Unlike in the previous military coups (1960 and 1971), in 1980 repression was a widespread phenomenon affecting vast sectors of Turkish society. According to some reports, "a total of 650,000 people were detained ... Over 500 people died while under detention as a result of torture; 85,000 people were placed on trial mainly in relation to thought crimes by association; 1,683,000 people were officially listed in police files as suspects ... 15,509 people were fired from their jobs for political reasons ..." (Imset, 1996: 60).

During the military coup, hundreds of PKK members and, to a lesser extent, members of the TIKKO were arrested and imprisoned in the newly built Diyarbakir Military prison No. 5, including their most high-ranking militants.[10] The brutality that took place in Diyarbakir has largely been documented in the form of personal testimonies, memoirs, and plays

---

[10] The Diyarbakir prison was built in 1980 as an E-type prison by the Ministry of Justice. Yet, after the coup, it was transferred to military administration and became a Martial Law Military Prison. The control of the prison was returned to the Ministry of Justice in 1988.

(Zeydanlioglu, 2009: 82). The list of methods of torture that were used included "severe and systematic beating, death threats, *falaka* (beating of the soles of feet), "Palestinian hangings" (hanging by the arms), electric shocks, burning with cigarettes, extraction of nails and healthy teeth, forced feeding of rotten/contaminated food or faeces, baths in prison sewers." (idem.: 83).

What's more, according to Mehdi Zana, who spent eleven years in that prison, some "torture practices [were] aimed at the Turkification of Kurdish prisoners" forcing prisoners to shout "I am so proud to be Turkish" (idem.: 85). By the same token, as speaking Kurdish was forbidden in prisons and doing so could result in severe punishment, many prisoners recall not being able to speak to their monolingual relatives (usually their mothers) during what came to be known as the "silent prison visits" (idem.: 87).

The Diyarbakir prison also saw stiff resistance by the prisoners against their treatment, some of which were successful in periodically improving their conditions and in drawing national and international attention. In 1982 there were several riots and hunger strikes, as well as cases of individual and group suicide in protests against torture. Subsequently, some of these protestors became important figures in Kurdish collective memory and in the martyrdom discourse of the PKK (Jongerden & Akkaya, 2011: 13).

Outside Diyarbakir prison, however, the 1980 coup d'état did not provoke a process of radicalization but rather of marginalization of those who had not been arrested. Between 1980 and 1984, the activist milieu in cities such as Diyarbakir had become a desert. People feared being denounced as "terrorists," and most organizations that had been active in the 1970s collapsed because their cadres had been put in jail or had left the country. Psychologically, this period is recalled as highly depressing by the activists who had been engaged prior to the coup.

Thus, following a period of an "exciting life" and having played a leading role both at school and in the city, Fatma found herself alone, plagued by a strong feeling of "emptiness" and "fragility." Placed in custody by early 1981, along with her elder sister, and released twenty days later, she realized that without the support of a group she "was nothing." In other words, Fatma went through a "vacuum experience," an experience in which "taken-for-granted anchors of self-identity are suspended, leaving exits feeling rootless and anxious" (Fuchs Ebaugh, 1988: 184). Although at that time she thought that something had to be done in the face of the political situation, she seemed to have lost her activist skills. Thus, given the lack of any prospect of renewing her dissent activism, she focused her attention on her studies; she completed the high school requirements and registered at the Faculty of Law at Dicle University of Diyarbakir in 1983.

Unlike Fatma, between 1979 and 1982, Murat did not go through a "vacuum experience" following the coup. While in prison, Murat lived a dense period of political and human socialization as he shared the cell with other political prisoners, among which were the cadres of the revolutionary organizations based in the eastern provinces of Turkey. Despite the horror he witnessed, the prison became a "popular university" where he was able to establish new networks, exchange ideas, learn from his elders' experience, and gain new activist resources that were to become very useful after his release. Furthermore, harsh conditions in Diyarbakir prison had an unintended consequence: while prior to the coup d'état, radical organizations had been fighting each other over the monopoly of the revolutionary arena, punishments and discipline measures in prison pushed the convicts to unite and establish solidarity relations.

Yet, interestingly, his release also paved the way for a period of "emptiness" since a vast majority of PKK and TIKKO members remained in jail. Like Fatma, Murat experienced a phase of frustration due to the absence of any political activity outside the prison. He therefore graduated from high school and was admitted to the Faculty of Law at Dicle University where, after some months of preliminary contacts, he animated a small leftist group made up of seven students with no real structure, but with one goal: to establish a new revolutionary organization.

In early 1984, Fatma met by chance a common friend who happened to be in contact with Murat and his comrades. She rapidly asked to join the group and took part in their clandestine gatherings. This casual encounter coincided with an important event for the region and, later on, for the whole country. On August 15, 1984, the PKK launched its military campaign against the Turkish state; several soldiers and officers were killed and wounded in the towns of Eruh and Shemdinli.[11] This unexpected action came as a relief among the small group of "revolutionary students" for two reasons. On the one hand, it was seen as the end of

---

[11] From the beginning of 1980, and thanks to its alliance with the Syrian regime, the PKK had begun to train its first groups of guerrilla fighters in Lebanon. From September 1982 onward, hundreds of militants were sent to Iraqi Kurdistan to infiltrate Turkey in small groups of three to five guerrilla fighters.

a period of silence and humiliation. On the other, being aware of the difficulties in establishing a strong armed group, they came to the conclusion that they had to join or at least cooperate with the existing one, namely the PKK. In fact, many "young boys (and some girls) welcomed this new phase of violence as a means of the re-conquest of their symbolic resources and their Kurdish identity and as the starting point of a new and violent, but nevertheless open, process of socialization" (Bozarslan, 2004: 47).

On a personal level, that encounter also proved to be a turning point in their lives as they started dating the same year. Further, in the face of social and family pressures, they decided to get married in July 1985 so that they could live together, as a couple, in a rented apartment thanks to the financial support of one of Murat's brothers. Works dealing with the notion of biographical availability suggest that marriage or the presence of children hinders social movement participation by increasing both the costs and risks associated with participation (Beyerlein and Hipp, 2006: 301). Interestingly, however, this new departure went hand in hand with the resumption of their high-risk activism and the continuation of their studies at the Faculty of Law in Diyarbakir.

However, their commitment took a differentiated direction. While Fatma became a founding member of an informal platform of solidarity with Diyarbakir's prisoners and their families along with six other activists, Murat played a training role for the PKK militants aiming to establish themselves in the city in order to spread the party's propaganda.[12] There were several reasons behind their choices.

To Fatma the prisoners' situation was central in her life because her elder sister and many friends had been in jail since 1981. Additionally, hunger strikes and collective suicides in Diyarbakir prison provoked an outcry among prisoners' families. In Fatma's words, "the fate of prisoners in Diyarbakir haunted my dreams, my thoughts; so I decided that something had to be done." Encounters with other mothers and sisters lining up in the prison's main entrance provided a favorable space for the exchange of information and, eventually, the establishment of their platform. What's more, this initiative appeared to her as feasible despite the scarcity of resources: networking, organizing marches and writing

---

[12] Having received military training in Lebanon, PKK militants were unable to successfully conduct their activities in an urban milieu; they tended to be arrested within a few days. Murat's mission was to provide them with some training on how to exchange information and establish contacts without being noticed by the police.

manifestos, and fund-raising activities in favor of their families represented a new repertoire of collective action that seemed acceptable within the political context of the mid-1980s in south-eastern Turkey where Martial Law was still in effect.[13] Finally, as a woman, Fatma could speak more easily to the mothers of prisoners as well as gather them in relatives' houses. In other words, as in 1979, Fatma's "skills" and female identity were "facilitator" elements for her political commitment within women's networks. Yet one may argue that Fatma's commitment did not significantly transform either her internally held or the externally assigned gender identity.

The quasi collapse of TIKKO in south-eastern Turkey following the 1980 coup d'état, together with Fatma's militancy for Kurdish rights, as well as encounters in Diyarbakir prison with PKK cadres, led Murat to cooperate with the PKK. As a man, unlike Fatma, he was able to move freely in the city; he met activists in cafes, houses, in the bazaar and, of course, at the university. Although he also supported Fatma in her endeavors, he did not share sensitive information about his activities with her for security reasons; they feared that if one of them were arrested, their mission would be in danger. Yet there was still another important difference in their paths. While Murat combined activism with his studies at the faculty of Law, Fatma no longer saw herself as a full-time militant; besides her studies, she also wanted to have children. Thus, between July 1987 and July 1988, Fatma held onto three identities: activist, student, and a mother of a baby, each of them belonging to a different sub-world.

In fact, despite their family projects, by 1987 Fatma and Murat worked together for a "big project." The imprisoned leaders of TIKKO and the PKK asked Fatma and Murat to prepare their escape. Thereafter, during Fatma's visits, she introduced different tools into the prison in order to dig a tunnel, which was supposed to allow about forty cadres to escape from their cells. While the PKK prisoners carved the tunnel, Fatma and Murat sought financial support for the enterprise. Given the scarcity of their economic resources, they came to the conclusion that only the "outside" PKK could help them complete this high-risk action. Therefore Murat, who was in contact with the PKK militants freshly installed in

---

[13] Between 1985 and 1988, the platform obtained significant results: (a) visiting hours were extended from 3–4 minutes to 20 minutes a week; (b) Relatives were allowed to spend one day with prisoners during religious and national holidays; (c) in 1987, Turgut Özal allowed Kurdish to be used during the visits, albeit only for those who could not speak Turkish.

town, asked the PKK for support. Faced with the lack of response from local PKK cadres, Murat decided to go to Lebanon to meet Abdullah Öcalan in person to explain the master plan to him in June 1988.

THE DISENGAGEMENT PROCESS

At one of the numerous police checkpoints spread throughout the Kurdish region, Murat and two comrades were arrested and taken into custody between June and August 1988. This short period proved to be one of a high density of events, as well as one of intense interactions between the three levels of analysis. While in custody, Murat was tortured several times. In spite of this, he did not reveal any sensitive information he knew about the PKK urban network or about his "big project." Without being charged, he was eventually released along with his comrades.

His liberation opened up a quick succession of developments that precipitated the end of his cooperation with the PKK. Following a quick exchange of information with his two inmates, Murat realized that someone from within the organization had released information about them to the police. Not without reason, experts on disengagement from radical organizations point out that betrayal is often a triggering factor for exit, a turning point in an activist's career, for militants become "bitter and acrimonious towards their former comrades" (Horgan, 2009: 113). Yet, betrayal alone can hardly account for disengagement, as it is often difficult to find out who is responsible for such an act. Therefore, loyalty to the organization may ease the first doubts.

Yet one must keep in mind that Murat was not a PKK member and, more importantly, betrayal intersected with another turning point in his life. Following Murat's arrest, Fatma decided to go underground as she feared that torture of her husband and/or his comrades in order to obtain critical information would eventually lead to her own arrest. More significantly, given Murat's activist past, she assumed that Murat would be condemned to a long prison term. Prompted by the perception of a personal threat, Fatma asked her mother to take care of her baby while she went underground. Naturally, she asked Murat's contacts to assist her. Subsequently, she hid in different Turkish cities thanks to the PKK network.

In late August, Fatma happened to meet a friend in front of a post-office who expressed condolences for the loss of her baby. Astonished, and despite the risk of being discovered, Fatma called her mother to find out what had happened to her daughter. She was informed that her baby had passed away in July due to constant high fever. They told her that the family had tried to contact her while the baby was at the hospital, but they could not reach her.

At that very moment, she felt that she had lost everything. She felt that she had lost everything – her husband, her child – and could no longer stand to remain underground. As Murat's sentencing was constantly delayed, she asked to join the PKK in the Bekaa Valley to become a guerrilla fighter. In that sense, Fatma's move did not stem from a new stage of "ideological radicalization," but from the lack of alternatives. Being on the police "black list" and having lost her closest family, the engagement within the PKK guerrilla group seemed to be, ironically enough, a *rational* choice.

Yet while waiting for the PKK's decision, she read in a national newspaper that Murat had been released. They eventually managed to meet in Ankara, where they discussed recent events including the betrayal and the loss of their daughter. Although they considered that the organization had been "*zalimi*" (cruel, without sympathy) for not informing them about their daughter's health problems, subsequently, Fatma convinced Murat of the need to ask for the PKK's assistance to prepare a new departure in their lives. Seeing her husband extremely fragile from both a psychological and physical point of view, Fatma asked the PKK to organize Murat's exit to Europe; in return, she would join the guerrilla movement. Nevertheless, while Fatma's demand was accepted, the organization refused to help Murat for, according to certain members, there were some shadows about his role within the movement.

Disappointed by the PKK response, Fatma decided to take responsibility for Murat and to try to leave the country together. Interestingly, TIKKO's reply to Murat's demand for assistance received a similar response. While the organization offered him to go to the Dersim area to join the guerrillas, TIKKO was not ready to help them leave Turkey. Being isolated from their social circle and afraid of a new arrest, Murat and Fatma went to Istanbul, where they had different small jobs to earn some money, go to Europe, and start a new life, an objective they reached in July 1989. After fifteen months they were recognized as asylum seekers in Germany.

EXILE AND THE REVERSIBILITY OF THE PROCESS

As Horgan puts it, "disengagement from radical groups or terrorist groups does not necessarily imply leaving the group, but more often than not changing roles of one kind or another" (Horgan, 2009: 151). Furthermore, the disengagement process does not exclude the possibility of returning to former roles (Saunders et al., 2012: 263–280). Glaser and Strauss (1971) suggest that roles are reversible under two conditions. The first concerns structural factors: If the rules of an organization change over time, it is possible for someone who has exited to consider returning to the organization under new conditions. The second option concerns personal factors: A person who has exited a given role may experience changes in his or her personal and social life and decide to return to the previous role.

Our case study confirms the possibility of the reversibility process for members of radical organizations too. Yet, despite the willingness of individuals to return to previous roles, structural as well as organizational factors must be taken into account for they may reveal themselves as obstacles to the renewal of political engagement. Thus, Fatma and Murat's arrival in Germany offered them a new opportunity to resume both their political activities and their family projects. Indeed, Fatma and Murat had two daughters between July 1990 and September 1991. In the meantime, Murat got in touch with his original organization, TIKKO, and traveled on a regular basis in order to strengthen the links between its different branches in Europe. As to Fatma, she approached the PKK and considered cooperating with this organization.

However, those attempts were hindered by their shifting perceptions of both organizations. To Murat, TIKKO no longer corresponded to the original movement he joined in the 1970s; "peasants and Alevis have become dominant within an organization that, in the past, had no sectarian leanings and was led mainly by intellectuals and students." Previously, "we had big debates, including disagreements, but always within a constructive framework." By 1990, however, according to Murat, new TIKKO cohorts seemed to have transformed the sociological background of the organization, which additionally became highly centralized. Against this backdrop, he felt that he had become a stranger within the "new TIKKO." Thus, although he was offered a position in the central committee, he dismissed the proposal and slowly but surely stopped attending meetings. In early 1991, he announced his complete retreat from the movement.

Fatma's first encounters with the PKK in Europe were also disappointing. The PKK seemed to have undergone a profound shift as well. As a UKO member in the late 1970s, while in Turkey, she agreed with UKO/PKK propaganda and actions. In Europe, however, while reading PKK journals, she observed that the accent of PKK outlets was not on the struggle and the movement as before, but on Öcalan's personality. Additionally, doubts emerged about the real reasons for the failure of their "big project" in Diyarbakir prison. She saw that the PKK was the strongest Kurdish organization in Europe. Therefore, one question remained: why the organization did not help them financially to free the imprisoned PKK cadres in 1987?

These thoughts coincided with the reception of a letter sent from Syria in early 1991 and signed by Memet Shener, one of the imprisoned party officials in Diyarbakir with whom Fatma and Murat had been in contact between 1985 and 1988. The letter invited Murat and Fatma to join a splinter party from the PKK: the PKK-Dirilmish (in Turkish) or PKK-Vejîn (PKK-Renaissance, in Kurdish). In effect, Memet Shener had been released and immediately joined the PKK in Syria. However, Memet Shener disagreed with the orientation of the party and, together with other cadres, he raised some criticism against Öcalan and the new leadership. What's more, he elaborated a document, which was widely distributed among the Kurdish diaspora in Europe. In this document, Shener accused Öcalan of establishing a dictatorship. Additionally, he observed that the guerrilla struggle had not brought much success; thus he wanted this "to be accorded less priority than an open political fight in mass organizations ... in order to prepare politically for the future" (White, 2000: 145).

The document authored by Shener convinced Fatma that the leadership of the PKK had never been interested in the escape they had prepared between 1987 and 1988, precisely because those cadres would have challenged the authority of the "new PKK." Moved by a sentiment of anger, she was ready to support the splinter organization and established contact with Shener's group in Europe. Yet the violent reaction of the party put an end to these first endeavors. At first, Shener was requested to engage in self-criticism before the PKK tribunals. He refused to do so; he was then accused of being a "Turkish agent" and eventually shot dead in Syria on November 1, 1991 along with two other critics (Cigerli & Le Saout, 2005: 360–361).

The killing of Memet Shener was another turning point in Fatma and Murat's political trajectories. Although Murat had already decided to abandon TIKKO prior to this event, the death of a respected leading figure resulted in a complete withdrawal from any political group. Moreover, Shener and Murat had spent three months in the same cell in 1988. Tellingly, between 1991 and 1997, Murat went through a new "vacuum experience." He focused his attention on his professional life, including training as a software developer. Subsequently, developing software programs became his obsession "day and night" and served as a psychological shelter, thereby provoking some tension between him and

Fatma, who blamed Murat for neglecting his family. Prompted by her criticism, he progressively combined his professional activity with a sort of "moral activism" as a regular contributor to several media outlets until 2010.

To Fatma, the death of Memet Shener started a long period of "hangover identity," that is the challenge of "incorporating a previous role identity into a current self-concept" (Fuchs-Ebaugh, 1988: 149). Thus she underwent a deep depression reinforced by other factors: She did not speak the local language, and she had no relatives in Germany and had to bring up her two young children alone since Murat, as a "standard Turkish male," did not cooperate in that task. In December 1991, and taking advantage of a timid opening of the Turkish political context after the elections of the same year, she decided to go back to Urfa to start a new life as a lawyer.[14] However, Murat was not allowed to enter Turkish territory, and in 1993 she went back to Germany. Despite this decision, she still kept in mind the possibility of returning to Turkey since there were no professional opportunities for her as a lawyer in Germany. In 1997, she went back to Turkey but this time her two daughters asked to return to Europe "where school teachers are nicer." Notwithstanding her professional aspirations in Turkey, she decided to settle in Europe "forever" for the sake of her family. As a consequence, the disengagement process in Fatma's case, unlike in Murat's, resulted in a lower social position.

CONCLUSION

Through the observation of the life-course activism of a married couple throughout the 1980s, we have shown the advantages of combining the three levels of analysis, macro, meso, and micro, in order to better grasp mobilization and demobilization process. Taken separately, contextual factors, organizational as well as individual dynamics, are indeed relevant to the analysis of social mobilization. Yet they are not determinant. Repression alone does not account for either exit or radicalization.

---

[14] In 1991, two political dynamics overlapped. On the one hand, the President of the Republic from 1989 until his death in 1993, Turgut Özal, proved to be a political reformer willing to resolve the Kurdish issue through administrative measures. On the other hand, the results of the legislative elections of October 1991 allowed for the formation of a "progressive" coalition including pro-Kurdish rights deputies, thereby creating expectations about a possible opening on the Kurdish issue, and in particular the end of martial law in the south-east.

Seemingly, organizational transformations do not necessarily lead to the departure of old cohorts. Finally, early socialization does not always determine later individual trajectories. Our case study suggests, on the contrary, that these three levels interplay over time and, significantly, they encompass a wide range of additional factors, such as perceptions, emotions, affective life, obligation to comply to a variety of (sometimes conflicting) norms and rules, and contingencies, which have traditionally been neglected by the structuralist approach to social mobilization.

In the same vein, the interactionist approach seems to be well suited to proposing a theoretical account of the disengagement processes for "it enables the restitution of disengagement processes diachronically, within the totality of individual life histories, and helps to contextualize individual exits synchronically at both meso/organizational and macro levels, rejecting the scholastic opposition between agency and structure" (Fillieule, 2010: 3).On the other hand, this paper confirms Horgan's (2009) viewpoint, namely that the process of disengagement from radical organizations is a long and complex one. Socialization in clandestine groups and generational effects may reinforce loyalty toward a given organization and its "revolutionary" ideals despite state coercion. In that respect, organizational transformations as well as biographical events, such as betrayal or intense personal experiences, may prove to be more relevant in leading individuals to a complete retreat from radical organizations than state repression per se, including in authoritarian contexts.

Finally, our case study suggests that further research is required in order to better analyze the impact of gender socialization within radical organizations as well. For one thing, the biographical consequences of high-risk activism do not seem to be the same for female and male activists with regard to the process of disengagement (Viterna, 2013). Research based on the notion of biographical availability suggests that marriage or the presence of children hinders social movement participation by increasing both the costs and risks associated with participation. Yet, we argue that these factors do not hamper high-risk activism *per se*; they tend to do so depending on gender relations and roles within a given organization and/or within smaller units such as a couple. By and large, however, Fatma's militant trajectory between the late 1970s and 1980s confirms feminist research central point; regardless of the actual role within a given organization, mere participation can foster emancipation (Blee, 2008). In other words, activism can play a liberating role for women in permitting them to leave the domestic universe and acquire social skills previously inaccessible to them.

8

Contextualizing the Biographical Outcomes of Provisional IRA Former Activists

A Structure-Agency Dynamic

Lorenzo Bosi

This chapter[1] shows how, in the case of the Northern Ireland conflict (1968–1998, also known as the 'troubles'), the British counter-terrorist policies and reintegration programs have produced the external factors and forces that have in part shaped the post-armed activism lives of the Provisional IRA (henceforth PIRA) volunteers. The majority of activists did not follow British reintegration programmes in the way they were designed to function, that is, by integrating disengaged Republicans into state structures and/or transform them into obedient, passive citizens of the British state. Rather the large majority of former PIRA activists formed their post-armed activism lives with their own agency and previous skills learned while in the armed group and in prison, and became involved in community activism.

By investigating the biographical outcomes of the Provisional IRA volunteers this chapter moves beyond prior research by looking at a generally untold story (Viterna, 2013). In fact, despite the literature on political violence growing massively since 9/11, it has so far been mostly silent about outcomes (Bosi & Giugni, 2012). And when it has looked at biographical outcomes of armed conflicts this was for the most done on the side of the victims (McDevitt & Williamson, 2003) or on symptoms of serious psychological trauma of former armed activists, including PTSD (Post Traumatic Stress Disorder) (Dillenburger, Fargas, & Akhonzada,

[1] For their comments on previous versions of this article, I thank Kathleen Blee, Olivier Fillieule, Abby Peterson, Enzo Nussio and Dieter Reinisch. Particularly as I did not always follow the advice I was given, any failings remain solely mine.

2008; Nussio, 2012). For useful literature on the biographical outcomes of armed activists we need to look at those sub-fields that have focused on disengagement from movement activism (Fillieule, 2005, 2010, 2015), from political violence (e.g. Bjørgo & Horgan, 2009; Horgan, 2009) and on conflict transformation (i.e. the reintegration of ex-combatants into society) (e.g. Knight & Ozerdem, 2004). These literatures, in studying the ways in which socio-political conflicts end, how armed activists exit violent conflicts, together with the post-conflict transformation of societies and institutions, provide us with valuable information on how states structure the context where post-armed activists' lives develop. This chapter locates, then, its interest at the intersection of the thematic focus on 'disengagement/transformation/outcomes', which allows us to address the following research questions: Why did the PIRA volunteers disengage from political violence? What happened to the PIRA volunteers once the Troubles came to an end? How did activism in the Provisional IRA influence the life trajectory of the actors?

The scope of this chapter is not limited to addressing a topic that has received limited attention in the literature on political violence: post-armed activism lives. Instead, in the footsteps of the interactionist approach (Becker, 1960; Berger & Luckmann, 1966; Gerth & Wright Mills, 1954; Moss-Kanter 1968), this chapter builds on the contextualization of individual trajectories at micro, meso and macro levels (multi-level analysis), with the result of fully recognizing the structure-agency dynamic shaping post-armed activism lives. In doing this it challenges the existing social movements literature on biographical outcomes (Giugni, 2004; Goldstone & McAdam, 2001; McAdam, 1989 for reviews), which has so far tended to read post-movement activists' lives as depending almost exclusively on the experience of individuals in social movements (mono-causal explanation). This chapter's ultimate goal, instead, is to promote a contextualization of biographical outcomes within individual life histories which does not challenge previous empirical results, but states how we should explain them by not forgetting to take in to account the fundamental role of the modern state in shaping activists post-movements lives.

While there is no intention in this chapter to equalize armed activism and social movement activism, it is true that despite their differences we can recognize some recurrent processes in these different types of phenomena and in how the state intervenes in the policy process in order to condition, and eventually end, their mobilization (Della Porta, 1995). In particular in looking at critical cases of armed activism we can better

show the underlying power of the modern state in shaping the life trajectory in the post-movement lives of social movement activists.

DATA COLLECTION

In this chapter I mainly draw upon twenty-five semi-structured interviews,
with former rank-and-file members of the PIRA, which I have conducted
during four field trips to Northern Ireland between 2007 and 2008. Rank
and file members are likely to provide accounts that are less ideologically
driven from the organizational agenda in comparison with those provided
from leaders. The interviews I have conducted provided a lens, in terms of
meanings and subjectivity, into how former volunteers understood themselves as Republican activists and the evolving sociological and political
context, and how these understandings oriented their post-armed activism choices.

The interview structure was made up of four sections connected with
four main periods of the activists' lives: (1) his/her life before joining the
PIRA; (2) his/her pathways to activism in the PIRA armed campaign; (3)
his/her experiences and commitment as members of the PIRA during the
struggle, with particular reference to time spent in jail; (4) his/her assessment of the struggle's efficacy and of its legacy. Such structure allows us to
examine how participation in armed activism comes to occupy a crucial
place in the lives of those involved and how its meanings change over
time. I will then reconstruct the chain of steps and changes that shaped my
respondents' lives by phases of joining, commitment, disengagement and
post-movement lives.

The interviewees were not chosen randomly, but were arranged by
staff of the Coiste na n-Iarchimi's group, who identified possible respondents from as diverse backgrounds as possible (ten out of twenty-five were
women who in the late 1960s and early 1970s joined the long-standing
women's Republican organization, Cumann na mBan) reflecting the complexity of the phenomena.[2] I had emphasized that I was interested in

---

[2] My sample of respondents is clearly biased toward the cohort of militants who are now in
their fifties and sixties. This selection bias is motivated from the fact that my research
project, back in 2007, titled 'Processes of radicalization in ethnonationalist activism:
Northern Ireland from the early 1960s to the mid-1970s' investigated why and how
individuals were joining the Republican movement in the late 1960s and early 1970s.
On younger cohorts I can only speculate on the base of previous existing scientific works,
which seem to confirm similar post-armed activists lives with those I have interviewed.

interviewing Northern Ireland armed activists who entered the PIRA between the mid-1960s and the end of 1972. By the time of the interviews, most of my respondents had served prison sentences lasting between a few months and fifteen or even twenty years. They have been released from jail throughout the 30 years of conflict, known as the "Troubles." Also those who had been released before the Good Friday Agreement (1998) had the opportunity to profit from the provisions for the reintegration of politically motivated prisoners enclosed in the GFA (Annex B, para 5). Such local community programs were financed between 1995 and 2003, for an estimated 9.2 million pounds, by the Foundation for Northern Ireland (a local NGO) and the European Special Support Programme (Rolston, 2007; Shirlow & McEvoy, 2008).

Coiste na n-Iarchimi is an umbrella organization working for the social, economic and emotional wellbeing of current and former Republican prisoners and their families (www.coiste.ie/). It also hosts a number of schemes associated with conflict transformation, social capital and community development. It is fair to say that it is politically close to the Provisional IRA/ Sinn Féin, although not all the interviewees agreed on Sinn Féin's strategy in the post-Agreement period. Despite this, at the time of the interview, none of the respondents have seen any reason in the immediate future for a return to the armed struggle strategy, which is more or less in correspondence with the large majority of former Republican volunteers. The overrepresentation in my sample of those interviewees who remained close to Sinn Féin does not affect the main argument I want to make in this chapter; however, it is fair to acknowledge that former Republican volunteers have also possibly taken four other paths as well: the path of continuing their armed struggle in dissident Republican groups such as Real IRA, Oglaigh na hEireann and Continuity IRA (Bean, 2012; Taylor & Currie, 2011); the path of joining other Republican groups, which nevertheless do not favour the return to the armed struggle in the near future; the path of not choosing to join political prisoners' groups or any political organization in their post-armed activist lives; and the path of involvement in organized crime.

THE PROVISIONAL IRA

At the end of the 1960s political contention emerged in Northern Ireland over the civil rights movement's (CRM) opposition to discrimination, a claim which the Unionist establishment and the Loyalist counter-movement resisted with harsh state repression and open violent confrontation (Bosi, 2006). This socio-political crisis in the region opened up a space, first for extreme communal violence during the summer of 1969, and then for the emergence of the Provisional IRA at the end of 1969, as a result of a split within the Irish Republican Army (IRA). From 1971 the PIRA military campaign, aiming for British withdrawal from Northern Ireland and unification with the Irish Republic, incorporated strategies such as bombings and armed attacks on security forces (from Northern Ireland and the Republic of Ireland), soldiers, commercial premises, militants from competing Republican armed groups and Loyalist paramilitaries, and civilians. The PIRA was the most violent actor in the Northern Ireland conflict (1969–1998), which also involved other Republican armed groups, Loyalist paramilitary groups, the Northern Ireland local police forces and the British Army. While the active membership of the organization never exceeded a few hundred at any one time, it is estimated that over 10,000 individuals participated in the PIRA in its almost 30 years of military campaigning.

The ending of the armed campaign started in the early 1980s and little by little progressed in the next two decades, following the decision of the PIRA leadership, through the role played by its political wing, Sinn Féin, to participate in the peace process in order to break a stalemate situation which started from the mid-1970s. This PIRA armed campaign of 'attrition', even though it could have lasted for years, was militarily and politically increasingly contained by the British counter-insurgency policies. Additionally, the armed struggle did not appear to deliver any progress to a tired and isolated northern nationalist constituency, which began to look elsewhere for a solution to its socio-economic grievances (the beginning of 'backlash'). The majority of Republican armed activists have been incorporated into the institutions through a peace process that resulted in a new negotiated settlement agreement, the Good Friday Agreement (1998) and later the St Andrews Agreement (2006), in which the PIRA decided to take part together with the other political forces present in the Northern Ireland conflict (the British and Irish states and Northern Ireland political parties). On ceasefire from 1994, the PIRA formally ended its armed campaign in July 2005 (Bosi, 2016).

The military containment by the British armed forces of the PIRA was not sufficient in ending the conflict. What complemented counter-insurgency measures were policy initiatives aimed at undermining support for the PIRA and encouraging, instead, moderate Nationalist politics within the Catholic ghetto areas. However, the increasing engagement between the British state and those communities did not eradicate the PIRA, as was the purpose of the authorities. Instead, 'it actually strengthened the Provisional movement's position within its base areas and facilitated a process of institutionalization' (Bean, 2007: 6), which made it impossible to dislodge the PIRA from its core communities. As an interviewee has noted, the IRA had in the Catholic ghettos:

> a network of welfare associations which were looking for those families of Republican activists who were in prison or who have lost their lives. The IRA had a responsibility. What happened in the 1940s and how these associations formed was that people were interned during World War II and when they were released from prison had nothing. The Republican movement was very weak. Fellows could not get a job. A non-official network took place at that stage. That's what binded the Republican family and kept us together. That type of unofficial network worked up until these days, where Republicans look after each other, but in the 1970s it started to become official as the leadership planned to keep the families within the movement. It is good because if someone gets hurt everyone gets hurt. If someone bleeds everyone bleeds.
>
> (Interviewee no. 1)

By the mid- and late 1970s the Northern Ireland leadership of the PIRA started to promote community development policies within the Catholic ghettos which could challenge British welfare (Kevlihan, 2013); however, in the early 1980s these 'community organizations and political structures that had started out as agencies of revolutionary mobilization became [with British socio-economic development policies] gatekeepers between the state and the nationalist community, as well as acting transmission belts for the Provisional movement' (Bean, 2007: 6). This was an unintended outcome of the social and economic changes produced by the British policies, but on the other hand this outcome suited British interests to use the Provisionals as partners in the peace process and interlocutors who could assure the future stability of the new negotiated settlement. So where the British state regained its power progressively within the Catholic community in the ghetto areas, such power had to be shared with the PIRA. The attempted co-optation of the broad Catholic community determined the patterns through which Republican activists became incorporated within the Northern Ireland institutions in the post-conflict era in a society dependent on service industries and the public sector to sustain employment and living standards (Bosi, 2016). In doing this, as we will see in the next section, the British state reshaped the context in which Republican politics could be conducted through voluntary and community activism for community regeneration.

MOBILIZATION AND PRISON YEARS

The twenty-five former PIRA volunteers who I have interviewed entered the armed group at a very young age, most of them even when they were teenagers. They joined following different paths, despite my respondents not mirroring "only those factors peculiar to a certain pathway or that those factors were equally relevant for each volunteer" (Bosi, 2012: 350). There were those who followed the long-term republican tradition of their families (Interviews no. 1, 6, 11, 17), those who thought that armed struggle was the only approach capable of bringing about change in Northern Ireland (Interviews no. 2, 5, 18–21), and those who did not see another "way out" and felt "obliged" to endorse an armed campaign in order to defend their own community from Loyalist violence and the authorities' repression (Interviews no. 3–4, 7–10, 12–16, 22–25) (Bosi, 2012). Those who followed the first path say they have perceived their socio-political context as open to a potentially revolutionary situation, where particular transformative events worked to confirm and support previous views and legitimize the final mobilization into armed activism. These factors made the passage to armed struggle appear as a sort of normal evolution and a goal in itself, as it offered purpose and meaning to the individuals' lives. For those who followed the second path the conversion from more conventional forms of participation to political violence was generally triggered by critical events that played a crucial role in their life histories. Finally, for the large majority of those who joined the PIRA through the third path the armed struggle was not legitimized by reference to ideology or political strategies, but rather as an everyday element in handling conflicts (Bosi, 2012; Bosi & Della Porta, 2012). However, despite these significant differences, for all of my respondents the PIRA armed campaign was the best repertoire of action capable for challenging the long-subordinate position of their own community and for creating the conditions for social transformation. A positive sense of the self and of their community was created around armed activism in the PIRA. For many individuals the armed struggle became the only meaningful environment in which to fully foster a strong sense of empowerment (Bosi, 2012; Bosi & O'Doghartaigh, 2017). The micro-mobilization into the PIRA, between 1969 and 1972, resonated with a need for action by a northern nationalist community that stemmed from a perceived, alleged or actual, sense of second-class citizenship. In its early years, much of the PIRA recruitment rested on the armed group's repertoire of action rather than on a coherent persuasive argument. For many individuals the armed struggle became the only meaningful environment in which to fully foster a strong sense of empowerment, being able, in their view, to challenge the long-subordinate position of their own community and to create the conditions for social transformations. One of my respondents describes how, despite the lack of any Republican tradition in his family and the lack of any strong political consciousness, joining the PIRA meant achieving a political voice in a society caught in conflict:

'There are many factors coming to the mind of a fourteen-, fifteen-, sixteen-year-old guy. There is no doubt about that. For some it is, "I want to be there, I want people seeing me being there." There is no doubt that that played a part. But for me the choice at the start was I could either go to school and learn about history, whether it was Irish history, ancient history, Second World War, or actually participate and make history. That wasn't so clear at the time, but it is clear now. That is why I didn't go to school. I was out watching, witnessing, and making history on the daily basis.' (Interview no. 3, quoted in Bosi, 2012: 374).

The Republican movement has been painted on different occasions from my respondents as a broad family within which they grew up and as a school of life where they have learned their value systems. Different respondents have recalled more or less similar stories. Two volunteers from Ballymurphy stated in their interviews to the author:

'The Republican movement has educated us.'

(Interview no. 14)

'For me to be involved in the Republican Movement it was an educational process, I wanted to learn more Irish history, I wanted to know more about world history, I wanted to know more about the political situation and I wanted to know more about how to fight a military campaign. To me it was an educational process that was going to lead in a very short time to a liberation.'

(Interview no.3)

Interviewer no. 3, apart from stating the educational process he went through when he has joined the PIRA, also mentioned the feeling of emergency that other respondents have referred to as well. They perceived that time locally, nationally and globally was giving them an opportunity to bring about a huge social change and they wanted to be part of this. "At the time of their involvement with the PIRA, none of my respondents in fact thought that the coming Troubles would last longer than a few years" (Bosi, 2012: 375). However, the troubles lasted for almost 30 years. During this period the main socialization of PIRA volunteers was in their local communities, conducting an armed campaign against the

British Army, or in the jail 'microcosm' (Foster, 2000: 8). My interviewees have constantly affirmed that the time spent in jail reinforced their commitment to the Republican movement:

'the prison years reinforced my militancy in the Republican movement'

(Interview no. 1)

'I went to jail for three sentences, five years each time. It made my commitment stronger and a lot of comradeship. It strengthened me and made me more determined'

(Interview no. 2)

'I have spent more than 20 years in jail, I went in and out for three times, but each time I was going out [of jail] I was then back in operation.'

(Interview no. 6)

'I spent 15 years in jail, I was arrested first in 1972–73–74, then I was arrested again in 1978, then again in 1982, then I was last arrested again 1997, I was released under the Good Friday Agreement. Going to jail for me meant absolutely nothing. It was a small sacrifice to pay within the struggle.'

(Interview no. 19)

Another respondent has suggested how different his generation was from previous generations of Republican activists:

'on previous [Republican armed] campaigns people were involved in the IRA, went to jail, then came out, and then left the campaign for the following generations. Our generation decided that this was not going to happen. We went to jail, we educated ourselves in the jails, found a strategy in the jail, come out and adopted this strategy that we found in the jails. Then we came back to jail, we continued our strategy, we came out from jail and continued our struggle. So we decided it was going to be a continuous process rather than something as it happened in the past.'

(Interview no. 19)

The experience of imprisonment was one of intense politicization within the Republican ideology and other international revolutionary struggles. As one respondent suggested: 'it was our university. The university of revolution' (Interview no. 18). In an important sense, prison confinement was a 'university of militant contention', what they called the 'University of Freedom'.[3] This is how four respondents remembered their experience in prison:

---

[3] My ten female respondents have not shown huge differences in comparison with my fifteen male respondents in their jail experience as Republican prisoners and this is confirmed from more recent literature, see: O'Keefe (forthcoming).

'I was arrested in 1973 for an armed robbery and jailed in Long Kesh. I was then staying there with a group of people that was heavily politicized. So I became politically aware very very quickly. We would have been very revolutionary socialists, international solidarity. We identified very rapidly with what was happening in Vietnam, with what was happening with the Palestinians. In the early 1970s there were many struggles going on all across the world; there were struggles in Africa, apart from the South African situation you had the military struggles in the former Portuguese colonies of Angola and Mozambique. We read [Kwame] Nkrumah in Ghana, and we read Samora Moises Machel and the stuff they did, we read Guevara extensively and other Latin American revolutionaries, we read Carlos Marighella, who was an urban guerrilla leader in Brazil, we studied the Tupamaros and Moteneros, we studied the Chinese Revolution. We also studied Irish history, particularly [James] Connolly and [Liam] Mellows, but also the educational ideas around Patrick Pearse. We read Paulo Freire, the pedagogue of the oppressed, which was a major reference book for us in the cages [behind bars]. That politicisation process took place only in prison.'

(Interview no. 7, quoted in Bosi, 2012: 365–366)

'We came out of prison very very politicized about Irish politics, about world politics as well. [In jail] we were looking at which other politics, societies, economics, administrations were working in other countries. I believe because we had the time to do that. So people came out of jail very politicized. Whenever I got arrested I was lucky enough to not been in prison for a lot of time. I was in just for a couple of months and then I got out. But I remember the day I went to jail I thought: "I am going to learn about other side, I am going to get very politicised coming out of that". It was in a way an acceptance that I was going to jail and I saw it as an opportunity: "I am going to learn all this" because these were the late 1970s'

(Interview no. 13)

'Most of the time you discuss which kind of Ireland you wanted in jail, because when you are out you have no time. Well you talk a bit about what we want or what we don't want. You don't go much in depth apart from that. Because you have no time to do that. Because you were always on the run, you were in a house and looking for another house, coming from house to house, then with friends then with sympathizers. You were trying to keep your face away. Mostly in jail we discussed about such things.'

(Interview no. 2)

'All the period in jail I went through a politicization process and we had discussions on what type of Ireland we were looking for and what type of society we needed. A lot of policies developed through discussions in jail.'

(Interview no. 19)

Rather than epitomizing a turning point in political commitment, prison was interpreted as a site of struggle and everyday resistance, where these young activists honed their individual and collective political understanding and brought these to a higher stage (Shirlow et al., 2010). While in jail they refused to comply with prison authorities and in particular resisted being treated as ordinary criminals, promoting food and clothing strikes, violent confrontations with the prison authorities, no wash protest and hunger strikes.[4] The agency they had started to experience through the armed struggle was brought as well in the prisons. The prisons became an extended site of revolutionary struggle. An interviewee who had been in jail for 20 years, and who was among the hunger strikers demanding political status for Republican prisoners (1979–1981), has stated:

During the years in jail I started to look at politics. In jail you start to question armed struggle, because you have time. You start to look for alternatives. You read about other struggles, the Vietnam, Palestine, Cuba ... I don't regret one minute in the armed struggle and in jail. My five brothers were all in jail. One brother was shot dead by the British Army. My family at the end of the day was prosecuted. I don't regret one day of what I did. I firmly believe it was right.

(Interview no. 16)

Prisons, with their physical confinement, surveillance and punishment, have often been neglected in social movements studies (see for exceptions: Goldstone & Useem, 1999; O'Hearn, 2009), as they seemed to offer little space for resources and/or opportunities to mobilize. Nevertheless, as the Northern Ireland episode shows, PIRA volunteers coped with this socio-spatial environment re-asserting their militant subjectivity by restraining and confronting the prison authorities' power. Significantly, this is how, a few years ago, Laurence McKeown, a former PIRA volunteer and today an independent scholar, recalled his experience during the hunger strike:

Locked in a cell naked over five year period has a very "levelling" effect. With no books, magazines or papers to read, no radio to listen to, no television to watch, the only thing left to you are your thoughts, ideas and opinions over that 5-year period, 1976–1981. I believe I lived through what for me was one of the most consciousness-raising periods of my life. What took place during that time was an in-depth challenge to everything I had believed in beforehand or, more correctly, everything I had taken for granted or been indoctrinated by either from Catholic Church teachings or the great and the good. The "common sense" ideas, the "natural" way of things, were now seen not to be common sense or natural at all

---

[4] In 1981 ten republican prisoners (PIRA and Irish National Liberation Army [INLA]) died on hunger strike. It is widely recognized that such protest transformed the conflict by mobilizing the entire Catholic community around the issue of political status for prisoners and was able to gain support for Sinn Fein.

but rather, social constructs and we begun to question all of it, including the central premises of Irish Republicanism ...

(McKeown 2009: 277)

Prisons are social spaces to re-assert political subjectivity, not in disjuncture from the broader political dynamics outside, since they allow militants to further reflect on their strategies and might lead them to support non-violent solutions to the conflict. Prisons provide space and time for such re-assertion, something that is lacking outside, where day-to-day issues are fundamental for the militants' and armed groups' survival. As John Morrison has suggested, in his work, 'debates within the prisons played' a fundamental role 'in the gradual dismantling of the traditional abstentionist policy, and the eventual cessation of sustained paramilitary violence' (2014: 75).

The prison was seen as another site of struggle during the conflict, a distinctive arena to the struggle on the streets of Belfast and Derry to which they were still committed (O'Hearn, 2009, forthcoming). Those years had a profound impact on the post-armed life of those I interviewed. The prison provided them the time to educate themselves (Gaelic, Irish history, World politics), as well as to develop negotiation and communications skills (MacIonnrachtaigh, 2013; McAtackney 2014; McKeown, 2001, 2009; Ryder, 2000).

'There was a huge growth in Irish language and sports and different aspects of the culture coming from the jails, especially in the late 1970s when the jail situation took a bad turn.'

(Interview no 13)

As Laurence McKeown has written "the talents and skills developed within the prisons [by prisoners] were recognised upon their release and channelled into the Republican movement and struggle' (2009: 279). What respondents recall is that the ideals of self-help and mutual aid which were paramount during their years of imprisonment became central in their post-prison activities, as we will show in the following section. The time spent in jail, not so much in the early stage of the conflict, but from the late 1970s on, has been understood from my respondents as particularly important in order to think and formulate what was needed for the next stage of their political excursion in the Republican movement (Morrison, 2014). A stage which for all was represented by a move away from political violence to an aspiration to participate with their local community to generate the conditions for conflict transformation. If they joined the Provisional IRA as the enactment of an identity, they reiterated their strong attachment to their collective identity also in their post-armed activist lives.

THE BIOGRAPHICAL OUTCOMES

Seana Walsh, a former Republican prisoner, in August 2005 read out a statement on behalf of the PIRA leadership which formally ordered the end of the armed campaign, and stated that volunteers should 'assist the development of purely political and democratic programmes through exclusively peaceful means' and that they should not 'engage in any other activities whatsoever'.[5] Within the Good Friday Agreement, reintegration programs for political prisoners had been established, including training for former prisoners, advocacy work, restorative justice projects, self-help initiatives, youth and community work, etc. (Eriksson, 2008; Mika, 2006). But my respondents, as the overall community of Republican prisoners, showed resistance to the idea that they were in need of being reintegrated within their own communities.[6] They repeatedly stated that they were not perceived as 'others' in their communities (Bosi, 2013), actually, the reverse is true in their view as a result of their past armed activism on behalf of 'their' communities:

'During the armed campaign I have never felt excluded from my own community. Vice versa I felt much more involved in it because of my militancy in the movement. At the end of the campaign people who started to know that I was involved have shown a form of respect toward me.'

(Interview no. 1)

'You couldn't have fought without the people. The people of Ballymurphy feed us, the people put us up, the people put their fucking heads down when the situation was hard. I only fought for the people, not for any fucking Gerry Adams or Martin McGuiness. I did not need to be reintegrated among my own people'.

(Interview no. 10)

'We could have not survived without our community. The community ensured the survival of the volunteers at that time. We relied for personal security on the local population'.

(Interview no. 25)

---

[5] www.youtube.com/watch?v=RCrsQRAcDqU.

[6] If they did not feel the need to be reintegrated into their communities, this is not to say that their experience in moving back to their families and friends and managing their day-to-day lives was easy; the reverse is true (Ferguson, 2014).

As a consequence of this closeness with their communities they refused to adopt the government agencies and other government sponsor organizations and chose to use the welfare groups established by the PIRA in many areas throughout Northern Ireland (Dweyer & Maruna, 2011). In doing so they say they have capitalized on their experience in jail to further passively resist reintegration programmes, and at the same time they credited their active involvement in the local communities to their experience in the PIRA. The post-armed activists all say that they have experienced high rates of participation in local community activities and of activism on behalf of Sinn Fein, including interface work, youth work, conflict transformation initiatives, community based anti-poverty and anti-racist work, truth recovery, developing sports activities, participating in alternative Irish schools, not-for-profit employment, encouraging and managing funding proposals and the like (Auld, Gormally, McEvoy, & Ritchie, 1997; McEvoy, 2008). This involvement transformed most of the lives of my interviewees while working within neighbourhood community centres, which accommodate the social needs of local residents in Catholic community areas. These centres 'while funded with public money and therefore part of the state apparatus, also function as sites for progressive resistance to the controlling institutions in the society' (Cassady, 2005: 345) since they work in parallel on behalf of the Republican movement (Knox & Monaghan, 2002). For this reason working in the neighbourhood community centres has been seen from my interviewees as a continuation of their Republicanism in another form while still feeling 'helpful' and 'determinant' for their own community (McEvoy & Shirlow, 2009). The post-armed activists' involvement in community centres fostered in them social and political dispensation. So where in the early stage such positions were taken with the awareness of British involvement, but with the willingness to use these as possible resources in their struggles, in a later phase community activism has developed as a career path allowing some of my respondents to become central figures in their own communities and progressively disengage from political violence repertoires.

When I got released from prison, the last time it was in 1994, I had a different perspective. That was difficult for me. It was a slow process. It did not happen overnight. It was a massive turning point for me. Then I got involved in the political agitation. I got involved in Sinn Fein. I was involved in street campaigns. I was then elected as Sinn Fein chancellor. I stood at the Westminster and Stormont elections but did not get elected. From 1994 until these days I have been involved in political work and agitation, trying to promote the objective of a

United Ireland, a political war instead of an armed war. I kept the same objectives and the same determination, but a different way to win.

(interview no 6)

Whether in relation to their own organizations or more generally, their work in the community in such areas as interface tension, youth and community restorative justice former PIRA volunteers gained a reputation and leadership for their commitment, dedication and reliability. Rather than representing a problem for their communities, they became a key asset contributing to community development, the strengthening of civil society and, ultimately, conflict transformation. They have been explicit that while the focus of their 'resistance' may have changed, they remain committed political activists within the broader Republican 'struggle'.

'The struggle has not yet ended, we are still fighting.'

(Interview no. 11)

'Our struggle is not over. It is not over until we achieve the Republic that you struggle for, that so many people died for, that you fought for. For us it made perfect sense and I would go out again and do it tomorrow.'

(Interview no 4)

Historically, the community centres through which they had started their 'new' activism were created by the neighbourhoods and were staffed almost exclusively by Republican militants, to compensate for the lack of services from the state in the Catholic communities. Later, as I have suggested already, the British state, as part of the counter-strategy against the PIRA, provided public funding and started to fund social welfare opportunities in deprived Catholic working class areas, which indirectly financed these same centres. If initially this was not the intent of the British state, then it shortly understood the benefit it could gain from such a dynamic, which was to de-radicalize the Republican movement through incorporation into the system. This means that the local centres, while financed with public money and therefore part of the state apparatus, also functioned as sites for progressive resistance to the controlling institutions in society. In sum, the community centres, through the work of these individuals, helped to develop a counter-hegemonic consciousness among some residents and provided a political space where Republican values could be fostered while simultaneously making available the social services funded by the state. It is the position of these community workers in their neighbourhoods that makes it possible for them to function in these seemingly contradictory roles. Representative of this development in the post-armed activists' lives is what this interviewee responded recalling in regards to her own experience:

'I learned a lot through all that. I am a community activist. I work for a festival organization, the West Belfast Festival. It is a very political festival. The birth of it was political, because our community was demonized by the British media and it was a response to that ... The legacy of what we have experienced has thought us so much that still come in what I do every day. I work also in a women centre and we have a stress clinic and I am much involved in it. All the education I have got is from my experience in the Republican movement and in jail.'

(Interview no. 12)

Significant is that almost all the respondents I have met asserted that the major legacy of the PIRA armed campaign is the pride and self-confidence that they claim to have encountered among the younger generations of their communities:

Young people now appreciate that through the conflict there were many people who have sacrificed themselves, including myself, so to give more opportunities to them. I have talked to a lot of young people, what they say to me is that they have better opportunities because "your generation X has made the sacrifice". They understand that. They have more confidence within this generation. I was growing up like this, keep your head down to the master, they do not keep down, they are free, they have a confidence of going in the job market, of going in the university. We never had those opportunities ... Now is ten years after the Good Friday Agreement, more and more young people are asking questions. I work with young people. When they hear that I was involved all the young boys get excited "how many guns did you have? Did you ever blow up people", all those questions. I guess any young boy would dream to fight a war, because it is exciting. So I talk to them "it was exciting, it had to be done, regrettably people were killed, I do not want you to that, you should not do that. We did that because we had no choice, or we thought we had no choice, which is probably what we thought at the time. I say this because we wanted something different for you" and all these changes are coming about. There is a sense of confidence and self-esteem among our young people. We go back to what I was telling you at the beginning. My father has told me when I was young "if you want to work go to America", well young people now would not go to America, they would go to New York for a week-end, but they do not feel they have to leave the country. That is a change.

(Interview no. 15)

This seems a very interesting link between the legacy of what they have done in their armed activist career and nowadays, where they are involved in instilling such self-confidence in their communities.

CONCLUSION

Empirically, this chapter has two main results. First it confirms Jocelyn Viterna's thesis (2013) that the arena in which an individual demobilizes determines his/her post-armed activist life. My interviewees, despite having been mobilized into the PIRA through different paths of mobilization (Bosi, 2012), have pursued their disengagement processes in the same arena and have shown at the time of the interview similar post-armed activist lives. But while my work confirms that there is no linearity between the different phases of activists' lives (mobilization, development, disengagement), this chapter moves a step forward, showing how the long-term impact of armed militantism was mediated by the British state's strategies of counter-insurgency and provision of social services in the case of the PIRA in Northern Ireland. With this I do not want to imply that former PIRA volunteers were puppets in the hands of the British state, but they could not avoid in the post-conflict period being influenced by the British state's counter-terrorist policies and reintegration programmes. However, the Northern Ireland case also shows that the state's power is constrained to a certain extent by those very same opponents who are able to turn force-relationships into new opportunities (O'Hearn, 2009). The very process of incorporating the Provisionals into the government of Northern Ireland illustrates the state's strength in taming its enemies, and exposes its weakness in its failure to completely defeat them, as the PIRA was capable of appropriating for itself the goods and services provided by the social service delivery system.

If the main criticism toward the social movement literature up until the turn of the millennium has been that it was over-structural in its orientation, we should point out that to date the subfield on the biographical outcomes of social movements activism, with some naivety, has not focused enough on how structures constrain activists' post-movement lives. This literature has suggested an agential argument which reads activists in their post-movement lives tending to continue to espouse political attitudes close to those they embraced during their mobilization, to show high level of socio-political commitment and to pursue different lifestyles (jobs and structure of families) in concert with their beliefs. Considering that the modern state is the most resourceful actor capable of channelling and mitigating contentious politics, in its on-going struggle to maintain order and power, through the development and enhancement of a mix of repressive and co-optation activities, surveillance practices, local policies, decentralized administrative institutions, clientelistic techniques and citizenship initiatives, we should then start to look at how the modern state in structuring the socio-political context is able to shape the life trajectory in the post-movement lives of activists. Having said that, this chapter does not argue against 'agency' explanations, and for an explanation based exclusively on 'structure'. It argues, instead, that activists' post-movement lives are shaped from social movements (agency) in combination with the capacity of modern states to shape the social and political contexts within which activists conducted their lives (structure). Only by recognizing how much structure constrains activists' lives we will be able to recognize the agency of social movements in shaping the life trajectory during the post-movement period. Which means studying 'the socialization effects of the participation to protest events' and connecting them to the 'contexts where they are developing' (Fillieule, 2013). So while the social movement experience is likely to mould the former activists' post-movement lives, it is also true that the socio-political context plays a key role here. I am not suggesting that the empirical results mainly discovered for highly committed activists within the New Left in the USA are wrong (Fendrich, 1993; Jennings, 1987; McAdam, 1988; Wilhelm, 1998), but that these results should be read by taking into account as well the role of the modern state as an actor capable of shaping the structure of the socio-political context. So, for example, it would be extremely interesting to investigate how social welfare reforms promoted in high moments of mobilization, in order to respond to social movements demands, have provided opportunities for shaping post-movement activists' lives: what I would call a clear case of the interrelated effects of the outcomes of social movements, which shifts the focus from single outcomes to processes of social change (Bosi, 2011).

If the final goal of this chapter is to suggest looking at how much social movement activists are constrained in their post-movement lives by state power, we should then be clear that such kinds of constraints are clearly much higher for former armed activists in comparison to former social movement activists. Former armed activists' biographical outcomes usually are constrained by DDR programs (demilitarization, demobilization and reintegration state strategies) that are meant to return armed activists to productive civilian lives (Humphreys & Weinstein, 2007). Those programs are meant to consolidate peace by reducing the possibilities that former armed activists re-join armed groups, continuing their campaigns of violence, or that they turn to crime since they lack economically viable skills (Soderstrom, 2013). Furthermore, the armed activist's life is transformed by two institutions, the clandestine armed group and the prison (most of the time), which have no comparison with the socialization experienced by movement activists.

This to say that there is no intention at all in this chapter to equate armed activism and social movements activism. On the other hand, it is true that despite their differences we can recognize some recurrent processes in these different types of phenomena and in how the state intervenes in the policy process in order to condition, and eventually end, their mobilization. It is time that social movement scholars started to question in their works how the state shapes the post-movement lives of activists during and after a wave of mobilization.

III

BIOGRAPHICAL TRAJECTORIES IN TIMES OF TRANSITION

Social Movement Activists into Politicians?

INTRODUCTION

Gilles Dorronsoro

The articles that follow delve into the biographies of activists who have undergone major social transformations. The first article traces the difficult transformation of the Czechoslovak dissident movement Civic Forum into a political party, which led to the break-up of a movement that as late as 1989 seemed dominant. The second concerns the path of a militant trade unionist peasant farmer, Andrzej Lepper, founder of the Self-Defense Movement during the time of Poland's transition to democracy. Driven by the crisis of the peasantry, he attempted to build on his success as a trade unionist with a career in politics that, after many twists and turns, would end in failure and his eventual suicide. Finally, the last article dealing with the Workers' Party (PT) of Brazil reveals how the high-risk engagement by the first-generation activists was transmuted into an institutionalization phase and how some activists profited from it. The methodological approach differs from article to article: a single individual's biography, a study of a limited cohort, or an observation of grassroots activists. However, all these texts evince the interwoven effects that high-intensity engagement and structural societal transformations have on activists' biographies. We thus satisfy ourselves that activist biographies make excellent analyzers of macrosocial elements such as autonomy in the political arena, forms of repression.

Characteristic of the original engagements is their "holistic" nature at start, both because they engage individuals totally by dint of their intensity (and sometimes of risks incurred) and because the political in the narrow sense of the word is trumped by the cause, with revolutionary projects and moral considerations playing a pivotal role. These articles confirm the relationship between intensity of commitment and transformation of dispositions, which brings up three observations all pointing to a nonfunctional and nonintegrated conception of the habitus. For one, traumatic experiences in authoritarian contexts, as much as engagement per se, play a key role in transforming dispositions to act. For another, the effects of activism persist all the more, the more the activists are inserted in networks that activate these dispositions. Lastly, Lepper's extraordinary reinvention of himself as a professional politician prompts us to explore the effect of delayed socializations permitted by a – perceived as well as objective – transformation of social rules.

These three accounts are stamped with unfulfillment: The apparent victory of a cause brings with it the movement's institutionalization, a normalization that marks the end of the heroic period and entails various types of at least partial retreats of the activists. This letdown, far from being mainly a psychological and individual problem, relates to structural transformations, foremost among them the autonomization of politics. Indeed, democratic consolidation entails an unequivocal entry into the political arena through the professionalization of cadres and apparatus. Multivalent engagements – in Lula's case, straddling politics and trade unionism, the PT moreover federating diverse movements (leftists, students, linked to the Catholic church), or assembling a coalition of individuals on a moral foundation for the dissidents of the Civic Forum – mutate into an activism that is more narrowly oriented toward supporting a political party. The case of Lepper, whose post-1989 activism never was of a high-risk nature, is part of the same dynamic. In a consolidation phase of the new political system, the union-party hybrid character of the initial movement progressively cedes to a more clear-cut entry into politics.

How does the conversion of activist resources take place in these transformed contexts? Two hypotheses emerge from the analyses put forward here. On the one hand, while some decidedly activist skills become obsolete in the new political systems, the social and cultural capital associated with activism remains relevant outside the political arena. On the other hand, the party has a central place in the handling and redeployment of resources. The key challenge of the transition is nothing less than that of holding the party together. Here, activists with large amounts of capital can balk at the party's discipline, while disengagement is more likely in the case of less well-endowed activists.

In the first instance, Hadjiisky notes that repression under the Communist regime facilitated keeping activists with very different profiles together in one organization, while democratization requires a stronger internal discipline. Hence, the generation owning the strongest cultural capital in the Civic Forum will be the one most reluctant to accept its constraints. Indeed, the moral engagement of the first-generation dissidents (besides being born of an adaptation to the repression post-1968) has elitist connotations that, for example, explain the refusal to remunerate activists, even if symbolically. The Civic Forum's new generation, more radical and not as rich in cultural capital, will be more apt to convert its activist capital in the political field. In the second article, Camille Goirand shows how the party makes possible the conversion of activist resources in the new political system. The roles taken on in the PT's institutionalization phase functionally mirror the dispositions acquired beforehand in the movement. Engagement makes possible a social upgrade (educational capital, specialized work in the movement, political professionalization). Beyond activists who became professional politicians, conversions took place in the associative field, in law and in education. Finally, the career of Lepper, the Polish activist trade union man, offers an interesting counterpoint. His capital from trade union recognition was converted politically in a charismatic, authoritarian mode without the activist solidarity found in the PT or Civic Forum. Despite this dimension not being the complete explanation – his success after all was not impossible – his isolation helps us comprehend his difficulty in building a political organization, the only means for perpetuating his role.

We will close with a question about inverse transitions, i.e., a descent into authoritarianism, such as that which took place after the 1980 coup in Turkey, accompanied by loss of autonomy in politics and the weakening of opposition parties (see Tejel in Part II of this book). Activist trajectories are brutally interrupted and activist skills converted to other, frequently associative, activities, but also to economic ones. Here also, the activists are profoundly affected in the long-term, including when they are impelled to abandon political activism.

9

When Prophecy Succeeds

The Political Failure of Dissidents in the New Czech Democracy

Magdaléna Hadjiisky[1]

INTRODUCTION

Groups resisting the Soviet system in Central and Eastern Europe have been gathered since the 1970s under the term "dissidence." They have often been presented as laboratories of democracy. These resisters hoped that their activities could create a space of freedom within the interstices of the Soviet system, a "Parallel Polis"[2] preparing the advent of the "civil society" to come.[3]

Thirty years after the political regime change, the influence of these dissidents on the current political system appears very modest in the Czech Republic, which is the focus of this chapter. The rise of playwright Václav Havel to the presidency of Czechoslovakia in December 1989 seemed to indicate continuity with the dissident period. But his presidency was dominated by a charismatic form of leadership, and did not ignite the collective political engagement of former dissidents. Furthermore, the ideas developed by Havel and the other dissidents during the Soviet period – reclaiming the autonomy of citizens, freeing them from institutional and partisan shackles – appear not to have had a notable impact

[1] This chapter received support from the Excellence Initiative of the University of Strasbourg, funded by the French government's Future Investments program. It has been translated by Jean-Yves Bart.
[2] *Parallel Polis* is the title of a 1978 essay by Catholic dissident Václav Benda, published in Prague in *samizdat* form [clandestinely].
[3] I wish to thank editors Erik Neveu and Olivier Fillieule for their constructive and thoughtful input and for the creative dynamic they breathed into the "Activists Forever" project. Thanks also go to Gildas Renou for his indispensably informed advice.

on contemporary Czech political life, except for the occasional reminders of hopes left unfulfilled.

Many scholars have studied the structural and contextual causes of the quick political marginalization of the former dissidents in the Czech lands. Remaining faithful to an interpretation of the period in terms of "democratic transition," Claus Offe evidenced the confrontation of temporalities of a threefold transformation – political, economic, and national (Offe, 1991). Because of the "dilemma of simultaneity," the premium on "economic transition" facilitated the rise of "professionals" of politics to the detriment of dissidents, who presented themselves as enlightened amateurs. Others have explored the specific dynamics that enabled newcomers often from the world of Soviet business to appear in the eyes of voters as *manažers* capable of quickly turning Czechoslovakia (and subsequently the Czech Republic) into a "normal" democracy and avoiding uncertain democratic experiments (terms between quotation marks are those used by the actors at the time) (Hadjiisky, 2001; Hanley et al., 2008).

This chapter focuses on the role played by former dissidents in this trend. The period that began in 1989 has been characterized by a political and ideological fluidity that requires – even more than in more routine periods – denaturalizing the usual categories of political analysis – "activists," "professionals," "parties" ... The relative political failure of the former dissidents cannot be explained in purely institutional terms (of fit to the "function") or teleological ones (of fit to the "necessity" of the times).

More broadly, the Czech case provides an opportunity to study the introduction of former resisters into political activity in a post-authoritarian period. In light of their political commitment against the ousted regime, they were a credible political alternative at the time of the regime change. To what extent could this fit to the regime change context translate into institutionalized political engagement? Indeed, routine active engagement in politics does not require the same type of commitment as resistance to a political and social system. Do former resisters participate in the (now democratic) dominant system, leave their mark on it, or again enter the resistance (even in a different way)?

Complementing the studies that contextualize their intervention in the post-1989 political space, a sociobiographical analysis looking closely at the former dissidents themselves appears necessary to understand the nature of their democratic investment and in some cases their own lack of fit to the new representative system. Beyond the discourses in favor of citizens' autonomy, what type of democratic leadership have they put into practice? To what extent and in which ways did the dissident experience prepare (or fail to prepare) its participants for political engagement in a pluralistic electoral system?

This study relies on two types of data. First of all, a set of archives, documents, published biographies, and personal interviews were used to re-enact the diverse contextual dynamics of the periods studied (from the 1970s to the 2000s). Second, I put together a database of about 130[4] brief biographies of the participants in the Coordination Centre of the Civic Forum (KCOF), using diverse sources checked for consistency (interviews, *Who is Who*, newspapers, academic studies, etc.). Roughly two-thirds of individuals in this corpus more or less openly participated in the activities of 1970s and 1980s dissidence.[5] The KCOF was the deliberative body of the main movement initiated by dissidents in 1989, the Civic Forum, which played a decisive political role in the first phase of Czechoslovakian democratization (1989–1992). In the early 1990s, leaders of the Civic Forum as well as ministers and many deputies in the Federal Parliament and the Czech National Council were picked among the members of KCOF.[6]

Biographies systematically replace individual data within their historical and social environment in order to account for the succession of life phases and for periodicities of activism.[7] This contextualization diachronic perspective is essential because most KCOF members have experienced several periods of public engagement of varying natures and intensities. What is at stake here is giving back to what James Jasper calls "the biographical dimension of protest" its primordial place (Jasper, 1997: 215–216). Activism is not only a choice made to pursue specific ends; it has origins and effects that relate to the remainder of the individual's existence, and the overlap between private life and public engagement is the rule rather than the exception.

---

[4] The list of these individuals can be consulted in Hadjiisky, 2004, chapter 4.

[5] The non-dissident members of KCOF, which will not be addressed further here, are for the most part "professionals" (in the Civic Forum terminology), i.e. specialists of various disciplines that have unlike the dissidents not ceased to work in the so-called official structures of their specialist area. The dissidents who founded the Forum had encouraged their presence for social representativeness purposes.

[6] Between half and two-thirds of KCOF participants held elective or political-administrative office after 1989.

[7] Political activism is a process, not the result of predispositions determined once and for all at a given moment in life (Fillieule, 2001: 201–202).

Having characterized the type of proximity created by the dissident experience among its members, we will understand why, after *resisting* together (1), the former dissidents did not *govern* together after 1989 (2), even though they share a democratic elitism that leads them to favor moral leadership over electoral leadership (3).

THE EMERGENCE OF A COMMUNITY
OF INSUBORDINATION

Upon reading the biographies, one is first struck by the diversity of political backgrounds among the members of the KCOF dissidents group. Some are from the contingent of former reform communists of 1968 who lost their place in the party and their job after 1969[8]; others belonged to various strands of the opposition to the Communist regime, from the former prisoners of the 1950s who were freed in the mid-1960s to non-communist intellectuals and representatives of parallel churches.

The unity of this group is therefore not to be found in a shared initial political identity. Can it be found in the social backgrounds of the main members of the dissidence? Because they played a prominent role during the Prague Spring, many representatives of the sixties intelligentsia were outcasts in the so-called "normalization" regime.[9] Among the forty-one members of the main collective of Czech dissidents (the Charter 77) of our corpus, only four did not pursue higher education (the youngest among them). Academics and researchers at the Academy of Sciences constitute the main contingent of the former KCOF dissidents, followed by artists, journalists, employees, and technicians.

The forms of activism valued among Czech dissidents, emphasizing "personal qualities," self-reliance, intellectual or artistic production, classically reflect those favored in the educated social categories with a strong cultural potential. The socioprofessional backgrounds of the dissidents have undoubtedly influenced their conception of political activism, but to what extent and in function of which context? As underlined in the

---

[8] The KCOF comprises nineteen former members of the Czechoslovakian Communist Party, all former reform communists that participated in the Prague Spring and were excluded from the Party after the implementation of "normalization" in 1969.

[9] The term "normalization" refers to the period that followed the military intervention of the Warsaw Pact armies in August 1968, led by Gustav Husák and "supported" by the Soviet armies stationed in Czechoslovakia, marked by the return of a firm rule over Czechoslovakian society.

introduction of this book, political commitment has to be analyzed as a process. Biographical study allows us to refine this macro-biographical hypothesis and to nuance the relationships of causality it implies by putting the contextual dimension back in the analysis.[10]

Two main biographical elements, marking two decisive shifts, stand out among these backgrounds: participation in the Prague Spring and the repression of the "normalization" regime.

A (Trans)Formative Disappointment: The Aftermath of the Prague Spring

Active engagement in the cultural then political liberalization of 1966–1968 is the first common feature of these trajectories. The testimonies of Civic Forum leaders who participated in the Prague Spring indicate that they had placed hopes in the Communist Party's "renewal" and in the "awakening" of the 1960s society.[11] The disappointment they felt when the Prague Spring was crushed militarily (with the intervention of the Warsaw Pact armies on August 21, 1968) and then politically (with the "normalization" process) in 1968–1969 was all the more devastating.

Two examples, one well known and the other less so, provide illustrations of this. Born in 1936 to a family of big industrial landowners, Václav Havel experienced downward social mobility in the 1950s, which came with a ban on pursuing higher education. However, like others, he benefited from the progressive liberalization of the regime in the 1960s. Hired in 1965 on the editorial board of the non-dogmatic journal *Tvář*, he was elected in 1968 president of a newly created group within the Writers' Union, the "Circle of Independent Writers" (Havel, 1989). In that capacity, he took part in all the debates and public stances of the Writers' Union. Although it was an "official" body (or precisely because it could assert that it was part of the system), the Writers' Union one was one of the main venues for protesting the cultural and political dogmatism of the Czechoslovakian Communist Party.

---

[10] Indeed, sociographical analysis cannot replace the analysis of trajectories to solve "the problem of the influence of practical contexts of action on the operationality of incorporated dispositions." (Agrikoliansky, 2001, 30).

[11] There is a wealth of fascinating literature on that period. Some books are written by historical witnesses (Jiři Pelikan, Antonín Liehm, Pavel Tigrid, Karel Bartošek ...). For scholarly analysis, see for instance: Fejtö, Rupnik, 1999; Kusin, 2002; Pierre Grémion, 1984; Williams, 1997.

In an interview, Havel recounted the period that followed the invasion of August 21, 1968 as an intense experience of solidarity among citizens betrayed by the leaders in whom they had placed their trust: "*Of all the things I have seen and experienced, the confraternal solidarity of the population that characterized those days* [of civil resistance to the invasion of Warsaw Pact troops] *impressed me the most ... Our leaders were making concessions left and right, in the hope of saving some of the gains of the "Prague Spring". But in fact they were only sawing off the branch they were sitting on. ... The death of Jan Palach* [a student who set himself on fire on 16 January 1969], *which would have been inexplicable at another time, was perfectly understood by all of society, because it was a virtually symbolic expression of the collective state of mind.*" (Havel, 1989)

Born in 1949 in Plzeň, Daniel Kroupa was nineteen in 1968 and had just begun studying philosophy at the Charles University in Prague. He remembers 1968 as "*this immense hope that the space of freedom in our country would expand, something truly breathtaking*" (Kroupa, 1996: 9). After the invasion, he was in awe of the "*incredible solidarity among the people*" and took part in the student strikes of November 1968 against the plenum of the Central Committee. He was subsequently disappointed by the reform communists, who spoke out mostly "*to quiet the opinion.*" He considers 1970 and 1971 as the "*worst experience of [his] life.*" At the time, "*writers, actors, singers, reform communists popped up on the television screen one after the other to let the opinion know that they had been wrong in 1968, that we had benefited from a 'fraternal aid'* [from the USSR] *and that now they understood. ...People started to break*" (Kroupa, 1996: 9–10). Kroupa remembers that "*most people of [his] generation then reacted with utter disgust, they turned towards alternative culture, which wanted nothing to do with that goody-goody adult world*" (Kroupa, 1996: 10). Kroupa did not go down that path, preferring to study philosophy, which he says progressively led him to converting to Catholicism.

A Shared Social Segmentation

The experience of sudden downward social mobility for political reasons is another shared feature in these trajectories. As a consequence of their participation in the Prague Spring, the KCOF members who belonged to these age groups faced the repression of the "normalization" regime. The former reform communists left the party or were expelled from the party during the massive purge of 1969–1970.[12] The non-communists who were engaged in 1968 saw the academic and professional doors that had opened in the previous years slam shut.

Fifty-eight KCOF members (out of eighty-seven whose biographies feature all the relevant information) had to abandon their studies, change their area of specialization, or most frequently leave their job after 1968. This proportion is even higher if we stick to the generation of those who experienced the Prague Spring as adults.[13] The now emblematic figure of the window cleaner or heating engineer intellectual-dissident, popularized by Václav Havel and narrativized by Ivan Klíma (both signatory to the Charter and future KCOF members), came out of the personal experiences of the two authors but also of that of many of their companions.

The goal of the repressive arsenal that had been set up was among other things to cut off protesters from their original professional socialization. This policy was tellingly enough named "operation isolation" by State Security. Charter signatories were accused by the regime propaganda of being "henchmen of the West" and "spies paid by capitalist countries." It was difficult to get in touch with non-dissidents, either because they posed a threat to the dissidents or because of the incomprehension and fear that dissidents inspired among many of their fellow citizens.

Thus the former KCOF dissidents experienced, at least once in their life, ideological discrimination that hindered their opportunities of personal and social development. Communist and non-communists, politically active individuals and members of cultural spheres with no previous political experience, atheists and believers all faced the same segregation at the time, which would then have an impact.

The Charter 77: Collective Logics

Less than ten years after the Prague Spring was crushed, the Charter 77 was formed. First made up of a list of signatories to a petition that

---

[12] As of January 1968, the Communist Party comprised 1.7 million members. 150,000 left after the intervention. 1.5 million were submitted to checks: nearly 22 percent did not find their card and 28 percent did not renew their membership. The purges at the top levels of state and of the party were extensive. The trials began in 1970 and went on without interruption until 1989 (Mares, 1995: 344–345).

[13] Forty-four out of fifty-nine KCOF members born between 1910 and 1949 lost their job after August 1968.

defended human and citizens' rights in reference to the CSCE's Helsinki Accords, Charter 77 then operated a discussion forum and a venue of coordination between various opposition groups whose rise it contributed to facilitating.

The idea of bringing together an ideologically varied collective around the reference to human rights was common to all the groups that made up the Charter: the former reform communists (around Zdeněk Mlynář and Jiří Hájek), groups inspired by philosophical and religious doctrines (around Jiří Němec and Ladislav Hejdánek), and non-communist artists (around Havel). This convergence was the product of a specific strategic and ideological context, which characterized the period that followed the failure of the Prague Spring.

For the former reform communists, participating in a nonideological, apartisan initiative that embraced the notion of human rights and its legacy of Western philosophy had required a significant shift. The precedent of the swift dismantling of the opposition groups that appeared in the early 1970s like Petr Uhl's Revolutionary Socialist Party by the political police, who were able to track down the entire party hierarchy, likely played a role in their rallying. Their adhesion to the apartisan agenda was thus partly dictated by strategic motivations. It is, however, important to note that compliance with law, the accountability of the governing toward the governed, and the primacy of the human factor had found a place in the discursive output of the Prague Spring (Grémion, 1984: 20–28, 49). This context had lent a new impact to the philosophical conceptions of Jan Patočka. Born in 1907 and dead after being subjected to police interrogation in 1977, the philosopher was a major influence on the intellectual development of Charter 77. Although he wasn't a Marxist, he had influenced communist philosopher Karel Kosík and the development of a humanist Marxism through his work on Husserl (Skilling, 1981: 21; Tücker, 2000: 102–103). Members of groups – particularly Trotskyists – who embraced the self-managed legacy of the Prague Spring and the resistance of workers' councils to the Warsaw Pact invasion, identified with the anti-bureaucratic ideal defended by Patočka and Havel. This is an indirect effect of the evolution of some political groups of the Czechoslovakian left in their activist experiences and thinking.

Patočka was also an inspiration for Václav Havel, who drew on his philosophy of the phenomenological subject to shape his conception of activism. He conceived the citizen primarily as a moral individual, not engaged in a quest of collective fusion, let alone a member of a social class.[14] In the system Havel called "post-totalitarian" (the post-Stalin regime), which he analyzed as a bureaucratic hierarchy founded on lies and things left unsaid, the individual is described as imprisoned in a fabric of social pressures and moral compromises that offer him no way out except "withdrawal" to the private sphere and disinterest in public engagement.[15] In order to engage in resistance, the individual should therefore assert his status of "responsible citizen." This philosophical inspiration should be replaced within the context of the disillusionment that prevailed after the failure of the Prague Spring, which had triggered an important intellectual and political shift for Havel. In 1978, he elaborated on this in "The Power of the Powerless": "*In 1968, I felt that our problem could be solved by forming an opposition party that would compete publicly for power with the Communist Party. I have long since come to realize, however, that it is just not that simple and that no opposition party in and of itself, just as no new electoral laws in and of themselves, could make society proof against some new form of violence*" (Havel, 1978).

In terms of substance, making a philosophical and moral argument allowed the collective to situate its action on a different terrain than that of the authorities in place, which constituted a fundamental break from the Prague Spring periods and the attempts at reforming Communism.[16] Founded on the inalienable autonomy of the people in the face of political power, the Charter's critique was potentially more radical than previous ones. Chartists felt that the philosophical and moral nature of their message was one of the conditions of possibility of what they saw as their main strength: the convergence of former communists and anti-communists around the idea that the human factor must prevail over the political factor.

Alternatives to the moral and existential conception of resistance to Soviet rule existed within the Charter. They were defended by (among

---

[14] Phenomenology is a philosophy centered on individual consciousness. Revolution is primarily existential and happens primarily at the individual's level; its ultimate goal, especially in Heidegger's work, is to achieve the authenticity of Being. On the construction of Havel's thought and how it relates to Patočka's philosophy: Hadjiisky, 2007; Mayer, 2004: 141–142, 145.

[15] These themes are addressed in all of Havel's philosophical and political essays.

[16] According to Pierre Grémion, therein lies the Charter's main historical novelty (Grémion, 1984: 134).

others[17]) the historian Jaroslav Šabata and the philosopher and mathe-matician Václav Benda;[18] the two intellectuals (even if coming from different political circles) argued that they should think as "politicians" or "resisters." Debates on forms of action could, however, not have much of an outcome in practice considering the harsh repression dissidents faced.

In addition to these political and intellectual transformations, more intimate factors should be pointed out. The shared experience of segrega-tion made the sociability that had developed in small groups based on interpersonal trust indispensable to the dissidents. Despite their eagerness to have a public existence, these dissident groups constituted segmented groupings in the sense of Anthony Oberschall.[19]

Reflecting the repression that it faced, the opposition of the 1970s and 1980s interfered in all aspects of individual, professional, and family life. Due to the repression, activities that were once considered as professional or leisure were now often "politicized." An example of this is the politi-cization of the fans of alternative rock band *Plastic People of the Universe* after its members were jailed in 1975, and their participation in the foundation of Charter 77. The late 1970s–early 1980s period was marked by a surge in "parallel" activities: the musical and artistic underground thrived (Bolton, 2012), literary and scientific *samizdat* were dissemin-ated,[20] clandestine religious meetings and "apartment seminars" on research and teaching were organized.

For former artists and academics, the Charter represented to some extent an opportunity to win back their professional identity and fight

---

[17] Françoise Mayer points out rightly the different standpoint defended by Emanuel Man-dler (the future founder of the small party "Democratic initiative"), who considered that the antipolitical strategy of the Charter was useless because it was inefficient (Mayer, 2004: 142–143). See *Cas Demokraticke Iniciativy 1969–1989, sbornik dokumentu,* 1993, Praha, Maxdorf, and especially the introduction by Milan Otahal.

[18] The discussions that had begun in the summer of 1977 with the circulation among Chartists of a text signed by an "initiative group," entitled *What should we do with the Charter?*, were an example of this. Reportedly penned by Petr Uhl and Jaroslav Šabata, the document called for more integration between spokespersons and signatories. Václav Benda, on the other hand, promoted a more active conception of the Charter and co-organized meetings between dissidents at the Czechoslovakia–Poland border and intended to extend this co-operation to other countries (Skilling, 1981: 35).

[19] A social structure is said to be "segmented" when the relations between a group and other social groups, particularly the dominant group, are nonexistent, difficult or one-sided (e.g. exploitation) (Oberschall, 1973: 119–120).

[20] Literally meaning "self-published," a *samizdat* is a clandestine publication distributed to trusted individuals.

the isolation and idleness that the regime had forced on them. Dissidents teamed up by professional group, and controversies were sparked among them that resembled fights between competing schools. A striking example of this can be found in the community of historians, in which two groups exchanged arguments via *samizdats* on the role of Germany in Czech identity (Bazin, 2002: chapter 2).

Despite their socioprofessional affinities, it could not be expected or evident that these actors would share the same forms of engagement. One of the processes that brought dissidents of the 1970s together is the external constraint of the regime surveillance and repression, applied indistinctly to these diverse individuals. A collective dynamic was allowed to emerge thanks to the moral generalization of discourses and forms of action and the unanticipated development of shared frameworks under the combined effects of reaction to the crushing of the Prague Spring, Husák's repression and the communalization of dissidence. This context was conducive to the rise of a form of activism that was *not* presented as competing with political authorities and was built on the basis of rationales drawn from outside the political field and the field of social protest. In particular, Chartists had received no common political training and had not developed a program involving concrete political proposals (unlike the National Council of the Resistance in France). In effect, dissident communities created a counter-culture rather than a counter-power.

What became of it after 1989? Does this case study confirm the hypothesis, put forward in the introduction of this book, that if activism can generate profound and widespread socialization effects on individuals by transforming the sense of identity and politicizing the resulting social identification, this is especially true in situations where activism is repressed or criminalized (Introduction)?

FROM RESISTANCE TO GOVERNMENT: SPLITS AMONG DISSIDENTS

After the mass demonstration organized by Prague students on November 17, 1989, dissident groups met with their supporters in the small Cinoherni theater to create a movement, the Civic Forum (Občanske Fórum, OF). Bringing together the majority of dissident circles as well as non-dissidents, the OF's mission was to support mobilized students and call for large-scale protest against the Soviet regime. Alongside student groups, the OF, whose main spokesperson was Václav Havel, played throughout the period of the demonstrations a key role in the spread of mobilization and the generalization of its framing (Suk, 2003: chapters 1, 2). The OF also represented these forces in the "round table" negotiations with the Communist authorities. Local Forum cells were formed in the country's main cities, and soon thereafter in the smaller municipalities.[21]

The OF became one of the central actors of the move toward representative democracy in Czechoslovakia. Havel was elected President of the Federation in December 1989. The movement ran in the legislative elections of June 1990 and won, with 53 percent of votes in the Czech lands. The political forces from the fallen regime struggled to win back some legitimacy, while the new political parties and the former "historical" parties that were recreated in 1989 (like the Social Democrat party) failed to secure representation in Parliament as they did not reach the threshold of five percent of votes. The OF *movement* appeared at the time to be the only political force liable to embody the renewal of politics.

Suffering from major internal splits, the OF was unable to benefit from this dominant position to refine and implement a reform agenda. Despite the consistency of the OF's discourse, the movement was torn apart by debates that first began in dissident circles.

Internal movements started emerging in the Civic Forum in December 1989 on the initiative of former Charter co-signatories. They lay claim to the status of "member" political parties of the Civic Forum. These movements were the Christian-Democratic party (KDS), founded by Václav Benda, and the Civic Democratic Alliance (ODA), created by Daniel Kroupa and Pavel Bratinka. These seemingly harmless events turned out to have major long-term impacts: after the OF's electoral victory, the OF representatives who had ties with ODA created a split within the parliamentary group by founding (in September 1990) the Inter-Parliamentary Club of the Democratic Right-Wing. The rival group, the Liberal Club, was founded on December 13, 1990 by Jiří Dienstbier, Dagmar Burešová, and Pavel Rychetský, all former members of the Charter. These two parliamentary groups foreshadowed the split of the Civic Forum in March 1990 when three different political actors emerged: ODA and the ODS (Civic Democratic Party), which both had right-wing allegiances, and the Civic Movement, which described itself as a "liberal"

---

[21] It is difficult to assess the extent of the OF's grassroots membership because these local offices were staffed by volunteers and did not require formal adhesion. A sociological study conducted at the time suggests that the Civic Forum had a remarkable presence at the local level, including in small municipalities (Hermanová et al., 1992).

group defending the legacy of the Forum's civic politics (the KDS had already left the OF before the June 1990 elections).

Ultimately, the shared experience of dissidence during the previous period did *not* result in lasting political solidarity after 1989. In an apparent (and only apparent) paradox, the restrictive and repressive turn of the system turned out to be more conducive to bringing people with distinct trajectories together than the open, pluralistic political system. The internal diversity of the dissidence was a source of strength during the resistance as it symbolized the wide spectrum of the opposition to the power in place. Internal solidarity was partly cemented by this common opponent and by the identity stigma it placed on them. This diversity became more visible and caused more conflicts after the political regime change. Disagreement (on forms of de-communization, on federation, reconciliation with Germany, etc.) were no longer aired in small circulation *samizdats*, and became roots for concrete political alternatives. Differences in ideological allegiance, which during the period of resistance to the Communist regime had been understated considering the necessity of sticking together, became increasingly significant when choices had to be made in a pluralistic political scene in the making.

Collectives Marked by the Former Dissident Communities

Far from being indeterminate or only relating to immediate strategic stakes, the post-1989 debates actualized preexisting divides among Czech dissidents. These divides had faded into the background within the context of resistance to the Soviet regime, but the democratization period brought them back into the limelight. The analysis of the biographic itineraries and positions of former dissidents before and after 1989 allows us to distinguish between two groups of former dissidents, which to a large extent overlap with the protagonists of the aforementioned debates,[22] and that we call the "wise rebels" and the "converted conservatives."

The "Wise Rebels": The Charter as a Legacy

Formed by close friends of Patočka and Havel in the late 1970s, a first group was actively invested in the functioning of Charter 77 (taking up

---

[22] For reasons of concision and consistency, I leave aside the case of the dissidents who took advantage of the wider set of opportunities available to them after the regime change and were not politically active after 1989.

the role of spokesperson, drafting *samizdats* on the Charter, etc.), which it considered as the driving force of a new form of activism. Those I call the "*wise rebels*" responded to the disillusionment of the post-1968 period by pursuing the quest of a new discourse on politics. They owe their "wisdom" to their philosophical moderation and their "rebellion" to the radical individual autonomy they supported as well as the openly stated experimental and creative dimension of their action.

After November 1989, the "wise rebels" thought that the future of democracy lay in the emphasis on direct citizen participation: They wanted the OF to pave the way for a new form of organization of political life, without necessarily committing themselves to it. Influenced by the anti-party stance of Charter 77, they praised the virtues of debate and tolerance toward different opinions. Their brand of activism emphasized the exemplarity of their conduct and their uncompromising argumentation.

In November and December 1989, the movement's representatives were actively involved in the anti-regime mobilization but did not target governmental power positions. They intended to act as a vigilant counter-power, and sought to influence democratization without governing. The analysis of these weeks of mobilization in effect shows that these former dissidents' rise to power was the result of a crisis dynamic, not of a deliberate strategy (Suk, 2003: chapter 1).

After the OF's split, most wise rebels became active in the political movement that most openly took on the OF's legacy: the Civic Movement (*Občanské hnutí*, OH), which became the Free Democrats in 1993. In order to facilitate a peaceful transition and a reflexive stance of shared responsibility on the Communist past, they continually opposed the criminalization of the Communist Party and the purging laws voted by the Chamber of Representatives (as exemplified by President Havel's opposition to the Lustration Act). Michal Kopeček showed that the electoral strategy of OH and the Free Democrats was deeply influenced (and ultimately hindered) by two characteristics relating to the experiences of their founders as dissidents. On the one hand, the OH pursued a democratic consensus and avoided the use of aggressive electoral rhetoric. On the other, the Free Democrats never attempted to position themselves on the center-left, to avoid any potential associations with Communism (Kopeček, 2011).

This first group of "wise rebels" was joined in the 1970s by an originally different group, whose post-1989 choices confirm the turning point that the experience of Charter 77 represented for them. They were former members of the revolutionary (non-Communist) left or former

Communist Party members who had grown more distant from Leninism than the other reform communists and who were also generally younger. For many of these former *"political combatants,"* their post-1989 allegiance was to their Chartist companions rather than to their pre-1977 political roots.

Petr UHL, a political combatant

Petr Uhl's journey illustrates the trajectory of those individuals I call the *"political combatants."* After mechanical engineering studies (1963), Uhl worked as a technical manager, and then in the 1970s and 1980s as a simple worker as a result of sanctions. He was an activist known in Socialist and self-management groups, a student during the Prague Spring, and took part in the student resistance against occupation in 1968–1969. Eager to mobilize public opposition to Husák's regime, he was a driving force in the Revolutionary Socialist Party, before his imprisonment in 1969. After his release in 1973, he was one of the founders of Charter 77 and the editor-in-chief of the periodical *Information on the Charter* (1978–1990), which earned him a second jail sentence, from 1979 to 1984. He became active in the Committee for the Defense of the Unjustly Prosecuted (VONS) in 1978, in Polish-Czech Solidarity until 1987, in the *Helsinki Committee until* 1988, and in the (Trotskyist) Fourth International until 1984.

In 1989, Petr Uhl did not resume the partisan strategy that had been interrupted by political repression in 1972. On the contrary, he became active in the OF (he sat on the organization's restricted board from December 1989 to February 1990). Admittedly, he remained faithful to his political sensibility by creating a movement (not a party) within OF, the Left-Wing Alternative, but he neither joined the Communist Party, which had become the Communist Party of Bohemia and Moravia, nor the Social Democratic Party. When the OF split, he participated in the Civic Movement (OH). Alongside his political activities, Uhl worked as a journalist and defended minorities and human rights. He was close to President Havel, who in February 1990 appointed him Director-General of Czech television (a position he held for two years). He was a regular contributor to the Socialist-leaning daily paper *Právo*. Known for his active support of the Roma community, he also led the government's Human Rights Committee (1998–2001).

Subsequently, he grew closer to the Social Democrats, but did not really work actively with them. On the other hand, he became a member of the Green Party when the latter opened up to individuals outside of partisan structures in 2002. He left in 2007 to protest the Greens' participation in the ODS government.

The "Converted Conservatives": An Ideological Revelation

Among those who remained publically active after 1989, a second group of signatories to the Charter defended a different type of engagement, more frontal and politicized – anti-Communist activists from Christian circles who I call the *"converted conservatives."* They responded to the disappointment of the failure of the Prague Spring not by looking for something new (like the "wise rebels" did) but by borrowing from existing philosophical and political theories, especially from the West. The reference to "conservatism" reflects a mix of British philosophical and political (Tory) conservatism (Roger Scruton held clandestine seminars in Prague and Brno in the 1980s – see Day, 1999) and Austrian-American liberal inspiration (Hayek's *Road to Serfdom*). They saw the positions of the "wise rebels" as utopian experiments, far from the political and social "realities" "evidenced" by Western examples.

Unlike other Chartist groups, they valued ideological radicalism. They embraced conservatism as an anti-conformist outlook in the context of "real socialism." This radicalism attests to a process of complete disengagement from a strategy consisted in reforming socialism, which showed its limitations in 1968 but remained dominant in many intellectual circles.

Daniel Kroupa, a converted conservative

An example of these converted conservatives is **Daniel Kroupa**. After August 1968, Kroupa was forced to abandon his studies in philosophy for reasons of political non-conformity. He attended the clandestine classes held by Jan Patočka between 1969 and 1976. In the immediate post-1968 aftermath, Kroupa converted to Catholicism (he got married in church in 1972); he saw no other salvation than religious and political conversion. From 1972 to 1990, he had a variety of jobs as a manual worker. He signed the Charter in early 1977. Alone or with others, he founded several apartment seminars. In the second half of the 1980s, one of those seminars addressed questions of "political philosophy," adopting a "very clear-cut conservative point of view." His biography, entitled *Freedom and Order*, describes a process of deliberate unlearning of the Marxist way of thinking that "deeply penetrated [everyone's] unconscious" (Kroupa, 1996: 16). He cited his 1973 encounter with Pavel Bratinka as a decisive step in that direction. Bratinka was studying Anglophone literature and was very attracted by the US neo-conservatives.

Within the Civic Forum, Kroupa and Bratinka founded the ODA; the former was its president from 1998 to 2001. In the political realm, the ODA's program defended a legal guarantee of the maximum degree of individual liberties; in the economic realm it supported a liberal market-based system. Kroupa was continually elected from 1990 to 2004, first in the Chamber of Deputies and then in the Senate. He left the ODA due to disagreements with the party line in 2003. He unsuccessfully ran in the 2004 European election as an independent candidate on the Christian-Democratic ticket and failed again in 2014 as a candidate of the Group of European Independent-Democratic Candidates. Kroupa also teaches philosophy at university level.

While Havel presented the Forum as a driving force of civic renewal, these actors saw it as a temporary protective arena enabling the emergence of the "real" political parties set to engage in political competition. By asserting their status as "party" leaders, the founders of ODA, KDS, and *Demockratická Iniciativa* sought to present themselves as the guardians of a liberal democracy freed from the shackles of State socialism.[23]

While the Charter was on principle founded on cooperation with the former reform communists, the leaders of ODA and KDS became in 1990 the most tireless advocates of the criminalization of the former system and its leaders. The debates in which they fought President Havel and OH on the Lustration Act[24] were so heated that participants came to see their disagreements as irrevocable. The relation to the old system was also a bone of contention between former dissidents in 1995, at the time of the creation of the Office for the Documentation and the Investigation of the Crimes of Communism, whose first director was Václav Benda (the KDS founder).[25]

A number of former dissidents of the 1980s were attracted by the positions of the "converted conservatives" for reasons in which the sociobiographical dimension appears to play an important part. They relate to a generational divide within the dissidence, between KCOF members born before 1945, who therefore experienced the events of 1968 as adults, and those born after 1945 and only lived through the period of "normalization" of the Communist regime. There were no former communists within the ranks of the younger KCOF members, which set them apart from their elders.

[23] See for instance Kroupa's interview "Nová totalita či ne ?" (A new totalitarian regime, or not?) *Fórum* 25/1990.
[24] Voted on in 1990, this law introduced checks on political antecedents for candidates to some top-level civil service positions.
[25] On the "impossible dissident memory": Mayer, 2004: 158–165.

There was also a significant social aspect to this divide; not so much in terms of background as of professional opportunities offered by the historical period in which these people looked for their first job. The older members were generally able to complete their studies and start working at least during the liberalization of the 1960s. Their younger counterparts often had to give up on that entirely.

While they generally identified with the Charter founders morally and intellectually, the younger members pursued more direct means of political intervention during the Soviet period. They were active in groups considered to be more aggressive than the Charter, such as the Movement for Civic Freedom (HOS), which promoted a strictly political agenda demanding the introduction of pluralistic democracy and the liberalization of private property. They also got involved in smaller thematic groups with more concrete goals. They could be musical or cultural (*Jazz Section*, founded in 1969 and banned in 1984: Jana Petrová, Tomáš Drabek), have Christian, pacifist leanings (the *Independent Peace Association,* created in April 1988: Hana Marvanová), or have ecological objectives.

Their engagement was frequently characterized by an anti-Communist discourse and a wholesale rejection of the system.

I call some of these young people the *"hotheads"* of dissidence. They squared off with police more often than the others, especially as they systematically took part in meetings and demonstrations. They referred to Jan Palach and Pavel Wonka and valued a radical brand of anti-conformism.

A "Hothead" of contestation

Jan Ruml, born in 1953, the son of a well-known Communist journalist in the preceding period, founded in 1989 the samizdat paper *Sport*, in which he adopted a line of head-on opposition to the system in place. Having been barred from university, he worked as a driver, a lumberjack, a bookseller, a hospital worker, etc. He took part in all of the dissidents' fights: A Charter member since the beginning, in 1978 he signed letters protesting police repression that were sent to the Interior Ministry; he participated in VONS in 1979 and was arrested and jailed for a year in 1981. He was an active member of HOS. Due to his activism he had an irregular life trajectory and hesitated for a long time before he started a family (he ended up marrying in December 1994). In 1989, he joined the OF before being appointed federal Interior Vice-Minister by President Havel in April 1990. After the OF's split, he joined ODS and was elected in parliament in 1992 and 1996.

After 1989, this generation was more drawn toward the traditional partisan path, which was new to them. Some of the young KCOF members did follow the Charter founders within the Civic Forum and then OH (Sasa Vondra) or ODA and KDS (Marek Benda). Yet, others pursued different paths by exiting the political sphere altogether or joining the ODS. This was the case of five of them, whereas among the older members, no dissident and KCOF member directly joined the ODS.[26]

The historical reality is of course more nuanced and diverse than is suggested by these categories, elaborated to highlight contrasts. They are ideal types aimed at putting into perspective the positioning of former dissidents after 1989. Some dissident groups have tilted back and forth between two types, like the dissident circles of religious obedience, whose representatives could be wise rebels or converted conservatives. Furthermore, some key protagonists of the post-1989 period, like Zdeňek Jičinský and Pavel Rychetský, partly resist this categorization.[27]

Participation in *the* dissidence is not, however, the discriminating factor accounting for the political choices of former dissidents after 1989. The term "dissidence" can act as an obstacle to understanding the phenomenon, due to the unity entailed by the use of the singular and the range of "mythologies" associated with the word in public space.[28] The unity of Charter 77 was a source of strength during the resistance period. But it was the concrete micro-communities, the dissident "micro-cohorts" (in the sense of Nancy Whittier, 1997, 2013) that made up a space of politicization in practice. One of the key factors in the development of these micro-cohorts appears to be what I call "politicizing ruptures." Even though they could already be participants in the public debate and in collective action, the dissidents experienced an event related to the political context that had a transformative effect on them (repression, the loss of their job, a religious conversion ...). Encounters and affinities actualized during such "politicizing ruptures" had the biggest impact on their trajectories of political activism.

---

[26] Those among the older KCOF members who joined ODS did so after KDS was merged into ODS in 1996.

[27] An example of this can be found in lawyer and former Communist Party representative during the Prague Spring Zdeňek Jičinský. While he was in favor of traditional political parties and saw himself as a "realpolitician," Jičinský remained close to the wise rebels throughout the 1989–1992 period. His past as a Communist Party member indeed made interaction with the converted conservatives difficult. He eventually joined the Social Democratic Party in 1992, after considering membership in OH for a brief while.

[28] This criticism was first voiced by former resisters themselves and later elaborated upon, for example, by Jonathan Bolton (2012).

FROM COMMUNITARIAN SOCIABILITY TO OPEN
ACTIVISM: DEMOCRATIC ELITISM

Unlike in other Central European countries (Poland aside), the popular mobilization of 1989 in the Czech lands gave rise to a countrywide movement whose influence would last beyond the demonstrations. Yet, at the turn of 1990, an underlying but crucial cleavage began undermining the OF, progressively creating a gap between the founders, who were from or close to the dissidence's ranks, and the other members of the movement. My investigations in the Czech Republic show that the relationships between the OF in Prague and many of the local branches were marred by growing mutual incomprehension. It particularly evidences the consequences of the founders' lasting reluctance to lead a mass political organization on the movement's grassroots support (Hadjiisky, 2004, 2005).

This distance played an important role in the popularity met by the project and personality of economist Václav Klaus within the movement. Klaus, who was neither a Communist Party member nor a participant in dissident circles, had joined KCOF in its early days. He had, however, quickly distanced himself from the former dissidents to devote his time to his functions as Federal Minister of Economy. Václav Klaus's popularity in the local Forums was highlighted by the election of the movement's president by the Assembly of October 13, 1990. Even though his competitor (the young philosopher Martin Palouš) was openly supported by President Havel, Klaus registered a sweeping victory, earning 70 percent of the delegates' votes. His program included the movement's transformation into a strongly structured political party, the polar opposite of the Forum's anti-bureaucratic and participative roots.

Following the OF's split, the succeeding organization, the OH, won only 4.4 percent of the vote – failing to enter the Parliament. The new party created in March 1991 by Klaus with the majority of local OF offices, the Civic Democratic Party (ODS), came out victorious with 33.9 percent of votes. It would remain the main party of the Czech conservative right for ten years. The dissidents who founded the OF experienced Klaus's political success as a personal failure. They were his most adamant critics in the following years, sometimes more radical than the Social Democrats.[29]

---

[29] The publicist Jiří Pehe, a friend of Havel, was one of the most assiduous detractors of Klaus's politics; on the political scene Jiří Dienstbier and Petr Pithart, not to mention Havel himself during his presidential terms, were very vocal. Havel discussed his painful experience of working with Prime Minister Klaus in a book of interviews whose title

Due to the central role played by the issue of parties in the Czech democratization, some scholars have argued that the "anti-partisanism" of the former dissidents was the main cause of their political marginalization after 1989. These include the Czech sociologists and political scientists Dvořáková and Kunc (1996: 55–56), as well as the historian Michal Kopeček (2011), who rightly emphasized the disadvantage caused by this hostility toward parties in the context of the quick partisanization of Czech political life after 1992. It was not, however, a distinguishing characteristic of the former Czech dissidents. Due to their opposition to the hierarchical system of the Leninist Party, movements of resistance to the Soviet regime had in common their support for social self-organization and citizens' autonomy against hierarchical and impersonal forms of political and administrative domination (Bugajski & Pollack, 1989).

Although they are right in pointing out its relevance, the aforementioned scholars do not always give us insights into what lies behind this "anti-partisanism" precisely. Some questions remain open: Which part do self-legitimation strategies play in it? What about forms of "reluctance" unrelated to self-presentation strategies?

Two facets of the same phenomenon, both related to the experience of dissidence, will allow us to specify the groups under study: the irreducible premium on individual autonomy on the one hand, and the elitist practice of collective activism on the other.

A Premium on Individual Autonomy

The emphasis on individual autonomy vis-à-vis the "party line" appears as a lasting characteristic of the former dissidents on the Czech political scene. Even within the framework of a democratic party, having a majority group impose a position was considered at odds with an individual, autonomous practice of activism.

This prominence of personal conviction is unsurprising in movements such as OH, which after 1989 defended an anti-bureaucratic stance. But the partisan indiscipline of the former dissidents also manifested itself in the 1990s in the ODS, which was a much more conventionally hierarchical party. Aside from a few exceptions, the few former dissidents who joined that party kept asserting their difference until the split.

reflects the distance between Havel the level-headed thinker and Klaus, who was always in a rush: *"Keep it short, would you?"* (*"Prosím, stručně,"* 2006, Praha, Gallery).

Autonomy vis-à-vis the party: let's come back to Jan Ruml

During the winter of 1997–1978, Jan Ruml led one of the most serious internal revolts in ODS history. In the context of a damning scandal of the party's funding, Ruml, followed by Hana Marvanová,[30] publically demanded Klaus's resignation and then launched a minority platform within the ODS. Disavowed at the party's special Congress, he seceded and teamed up with several ODS leaders to form Freedom Union (January 1998), which won over 8 percent of votes in the legislative elections of June 1998. He was elected senator in November 1998. A year later, however, he stepped down as Freedom Union president, justifying his resignation by claiming that he saw himself as partly responsible for the country's state of political standstill.[31] He also mentioned being shaken by the 'Thank you, now leave' demonstrations that took place on the tenth anniversary of the revolution, in which protestors called the politicians in power since the regime change to "draw conclusions from the country's economic and moral crisis." During the crisis that rocked Czech national television in December 2000 surrounding the issue of the independence of public media, Ruml supported the strikers against the ODS's attempt at a political takeover. Ruml moved away from the Freedom Union when the latter participated in the coalition governments alongside the Social Democrats. He joined the Green Party in March 2010. He took part in the happening organized for the launch of the Green Party section in the second district of Prague, with many prominent personalities in attendance including former President Václav Havel (who claimed that "the Greens are the only alternative to the major political parties") and representatives from the arts world (like the writer and former Charter member Ivan Klíma).[32] After a long experience of activism in the ODS, Ruml eventually adopted a critical stance toward the dominant partisan order in Czech politics.

Regardless of their obedience, it is worth noting that many of the former KCOF dissidents decided to run in the senatorial rather than the legislative elections. The first past the post voting system of the senatorial elections was thought in those circles to allow for more independence of thought and individual political exposure (whereas members of the lower

---

[30] While I do not go into the details of her case in this chapter, Hana Marvanová's trajectory is also significant and resembles Jan Ruml's.

[31] After the Freedom Union turned down an alliance with the Social Democrats who had won a relative electoral majority, the latter concluded a nonaggression alliance with the ODS.

[32] Novinky.cz, March 16, 2010, consulted on April 16, 2015.

chamber were elected through a proportional representation system). Some used it to attempt a political comeback after their electoral misfortunes of the mid-1990s. This was the case of Petr Pithart, Jan Sokol, and Dagmar Burešová, all former unsuccessful candidates of the Free Democrats movement (ex-Civic Movement), who, when the latter disappeared, accepted the offer of the Christian Democratic Popular Party to run as independents in the 1996 senatorial race (successfully in Pithart's case). Others also ran for independents with support from a party: the Greens (Šabatová and Uhl, in 2008) or directly as party members (Žantovský, Kroupa, Ruml, Rychetský). Yet others attempted, in vain, to run as completely independent candidates, like Rudolf Battěk (1996), Jaroslav Šabata (1996), and John Bok (2000).

A Democracy without Tribunes?

The anti-partisanism evidenced by the trajectories of former dissidents goes beyond the emphasis on individual autonomy over a majority collective line. Classically, the properties of party leaders are associated with control over the party organization, i.e. on power relations between high- and mid-level permanent executives ("the apparatus"). The case of the former dissidents requires further analysis and special attention to the mobilization-inducing properties of party leaders in *electoral* democracies, such as the art of local activism (with grassroots party members and sympathizers) and the mastery of the electoral tribune (media marketing, speeches in public gatherings, etc.).

They may have often remained undisciplined members, but many former dissidents ended up joining a party. Arguably, the fundamental reluctance of a number of them did not lay in a wholesale rejection of parties as such, but rather in the impossibility of acting as electoralist leaders, of engaging in the search or consolidation of local supports, grassroots activists, and sympathizers.

Even those among the former dissidents who were convinced that the "party" form needed to regain clout after 1989 did not seek to gather a solid base of sympathizers. Despite their support to the partisanization of politics, the ODA and KDS remained largely nonhierarchical and had little local presence. Freely borrowing from Maurice Duverger's categorization, their leaders referred for some time to the "cadre party" model, emphasizing the intellectual prestige of party heads, and to the US caucuses. "*Unlike the ODS, Kroupa explained in an interview, the ODA is an electoral party, which means it doesn't seek to have a massive member base. The ODA's internal structures have to reflect the voters' interests, not those of party secretaries."*[33]

This would have the most historically significant consequences within the OF. The movement's leaders behaved as "anti-populist" political leaders: they avoided direct relationships with grassroots activists and rejected all forms of political demagoguery.

A notable episode in the OF's history illustrates this point. Before he became Prime Minister of the Czech Republic, the former Chartist Petr Pithart was one of the movement's leaders. At the time, grassroots members pushed for the acceleration of the "de-communization" policy. Local OF offices complained that they were insufficiently represented in decisions concerning national politics. The movement's spokesmen – including Pithart – perceived those demands as worrying evidence of a "partisan" and "revolutionary" spirit. Pithart then gave a televised speech that would be remembered by the movement's activists for a long time. He denounced the "zealous" initiatives taken by "profiteers" and "flip-floppers."[34] By choosing to speak out publically on television on an internal conflict, Pithart behaved as a public official concerned with avoiding being confused with the activities led in his name, and not as a party leader.

The OF's founders did not intend to develop a strategy to support the citizen engagement that they called for over the long-term (Hadjiisky, 2005). They adamantly refused to have recourse to or even consider material or symbolic forms of recognition of activism (which was entirely based on volunteering).[35] Reflecting on the period of the first free elections five years later, Petr Pithart noted: "we hadn't understood that it was important to reward the activists, in one way or another, for their voluntary (unpaid) participation, all over the country, in the electoral victory of the Civic Forum. None of us even thought to tell them: 'Bravo, this victory belongs to you!' Maybe this was an error, but we thought it

---

[33] D. Kroupa, interview with V. Mlynář, *Respekt*, 16, 1992, p.9.

[34] Speech by Petr Pithart, OF spokesman, in the news broadcast of Czechoslovakian Television, January 19, 1990.

[35] This relates to Weber's definition of "professional politicians" (distinguished from "occasional" ones), "primary interest in political activity, that is, in sharing in political power," who makes the party an *"organization of interested parties,"* "create a following through open recruitment, offer themselves or their protégés as candidates for election, raise funds, and sally forth in search of votes" (Weber, 2004: 58). (Also Gaxie, 1977: 124).

was more urgent to contribute directly, by our action in the government, to the construction of the basis of the democratic system."[36]

This way of dealing with grassroots activists obviously reflected views inspired by the Charter, in which the call for solidarity took on the form of a promise of individual emancipation. In "The meaning of Charter 77," Havel stressed that citizen participation must remain selfless, as any expectation of a reward poses a risk that the individual will not be moved solely by his inner conviction. Participation in collective action aimed at the common good of the Polis was valuable in itself, and alone justified the cost of participation – high as it may be.

This philosophically informed take on activism, experienced in the specific context of dissident communities, faced a changed reality after 1989. The absence of a mechanism for rekindling activism, building member loyalty in the fallow periods, meant that the OF had to continue to operate under the "communalist"[37] system that had prevailed in the close-knit dissident groups. Yet, as it expanded its recruitment, the OF quickly came to be composed of a majority of "uninitiated" members, who were not familiar with the functioning and debates of the dissidence. In their eyes, the dissidents' distant form of leadership contradicted the call for citizen engagement that lay at the core of the OF's political agenda. Unlike the leaders of Poland's *Solidarnosc*, the OF's future founders were active in the resistance for a long time without having led a large organization in which interpersonal sociability is not enough to unite members. In the case of *Solidarnosc*, the trade union background, the shared setting of the factories and shipyards and forms of action (strikes, occupations) facilitated the rise of orators and tribunes at the head of the movement. The closed context of the "normalized" Czechoslovakia saw, on the other hand, the emergence of mentors of small communities.[38]

The former dissidents' attempts to meet citizens in their image came up against a strong incomprehension among the movement's grassroots

---

[36] Interview of the author with Petr Pithart on March 27, 1995.

[37] The "social relationship" that Max Weber calls "communalization" is essentially "based on the subjective feeling of the parties, whether affectual or traditional, that they belong together" (Weber, 1978).

[38] The Czech case is an opportunity to revisit Mancur Olson's hypothesis on the importance of the size of a group of volunteers on forms of activism. According to Olson, the existence of small groups may make up for the "tendency towards suboptimality" of collective action (Gaxie, 1977: 138; Olson, 1974: 33). Although it was in principle open to all, the Charter remained a small group: In the late 1970s, it had 1065 signatories; in 1986, 1200 individuals had signed the Charter.

members, characterized by the social segmentation that was typical of pre-1989 dissidents. In his stimulating analysis of the end of the Soviet system in the Czech lands, the sociologist Ivo Možny (2009) showed the extent to which the dissidents could be perceived as fundamentally different in the everyday functioning of "real socialism." Within the clientelistic Soviet system, their "family" was perceived as too remote from usual concerns to be expected to be shown solidarity. Here the temporal dimension plays an important role. The speed of the regime change and of the accession of former dissidents to prominent positions did not allow (or make indispensable) a process of mutual learning between the former dissidents and the "uninitiated." Unlike what happened in Brazil, Czechoslovakia did not experience a period of liberalization of the authoritarian regime, which would have been conducive to the de-segmentation of the opposing groups in relation to the rest of society.

Most dissidents developed during the resistance a habitus of "elitist democrats," which later proved to be a disadvantage for political engagement in a system based on electoral competition. Regardless of their post-1989 political allegiances, the former dissidents shared an elitist democratic form of activism that gives each individual the right (and duty) to choose and act in his own name. This habitus led them to place a premium on individual autonomy and intellectual and moral leadership, to the detriment of the ability to attract and coordinate a group of sympathizers.[39] Thus the former dissidents picked political movements that did not have a grassroots base or followers, that were based on the free participation of citizens instead of building member loyalty. They were also – often successfully – active in the nonprofit sector and in civil society human rights groups.[40]

CONCLUSION

Two series of conclusions can be drawn from this case study. First of all, the study confirms the importance of personal exposure to political events (see Introduction). More precisely, the share of what I call a "politicizing rupture" can have a powerful effect in terms of personal trajectories and

---

[39] For an analysis of the political consequences of the Human rights discourse, which talks to individuals and not to groups: Vašiček, 1994.

[40] There are many examples of this to be found in various circles of dissidents. We can for instance mention Anna Šabatová and Petr Uhl, but also Pavel Bratinka and Jan Sokol, or the *Fórum 2000* international conferences launched by Havel in 1997. Such investments reflected the dissidents' beliefs as much as possible, and were therefore often made in the fields of human rights, alternative lifestyles, and opening up to the West.

political activism. The case study shows the importance of studying the personal conditions of this rupture (period of the life-cycle, impacts on the life-course, etc.): in our case, the way the individuals have (or haven't) "lived" the Prague Spring and its failure is a crucial variable differentiating the types of political commitments (and more specifically the relationship to the Communist past of the country and to the partisan activism) of the micro-cohorts we have named the "wise rebel," the "converted conservatives" and their respective sub-groups, the "political combatants," and the "hotheads of dissidence." This study shows, secondly, that, beyond these differences in political self-definitions (and self-esteem), the former dissidents share the same kind of individual, autonomous practice of activism inherited from their resistance to a repression that tried to endanger their moral integrity. The long-term effect of the type of resistance experienced together (even if in different cohorts) explains why none of them could act after 1989 as electoralist leaders and engage in the search of grassroots activists and left the practice of electoral democracy to others. This resistance did not create an ideological collective, or even an "activist" one (in the sense of shared collective project), but rather a group of resisters based on self-construction as an autonomous individual defending his legitimacy to intervene in the public sphere. Trajectories indicate these individuals' shared disposition to assert their singularity compared to the dominant social norm. They share the same reluctance to submit to organizational discipline and to conform to a pre-established role. Despite relatively contrasted trajectories after 1989, the former dissidents remained "prophets."[41]

The lasting inclination of resisters to Soviet rule toward insubordination instead of party discipline reveals the misunderstanding at the heart of the narrative that makes the 1989 *revoluce* the founding event of the new Czech democracy. Liberal democracy is based on procedures of submission to collective principles and strategies of investment in partisan and state careers that are sometimes closer to the old political order than to the wide-eyed ideals on the reign of citizens' self-determination that support many prophecies that enabled resistance to authoritarian regimes.

---

[41] For Max Weber, "The personal call is the decisive element distinguishing the prophet from the priest ... the prophet's claim is based on personal revelation and charisma. It is no accident that almost no prophets have emerged from the priestly class." (1978)

10

From Grassroots Activism to the Cabinet. Round-Trip

The Puzzling Political Career of a Peasant Leader in Post-Communist Poland

Cédric Pellen

On 5 August 2011, Andrzej Lepper was found hanged in his office in downtown Warsaw. A former Polish Deputy Prime Minister, the 57-year-old was the co-founder and long-standing president of the 'Self-Defense movement' (Samoobrona), which combined into a single entity two legally distinct organisations, one an agricultural trade union and the other a political party. Lepper's death put a brutal end to one of the most striking political trajectories in post-communist Poland. A private farmer who used to manage a State Agricultural Farm (Państwowe Gospodarstwo Rolne, PGR) before regime change, Andrzej Lepper entered into activism and first became famous in the early 1990s, during the first post-communist wave of farmers' protests (Foryś & Gorlach, 2002: 53). He then tried to exploit politically his increasingly well-known profile and took part in every national election from 1993 on. After several failed attempts, he finally managed to get elected, leading his movement to an unexpected electoral success in the 2001 parliamentary elections. Samoobrona then gathered more than 10 per cent of the votes and established itself as the third largest political force in the country. Building on this success, Lepper swiftly became one of the most influential Polish politicians. Between 2001 and 2007, he was successively appointed Deputy-Marshal of the lower chamber of Parliament (the Sejm), Minister of Agriculture and Deputy Prime Minister. Meanwhile, he did not stay long at the political pinnacle. During the 2007 elections, Samoobrona was swept out of Parliament and Lepper lost all his elected positions. Thereafter, he failed to regain them and appeared increasingly isolated in the months before his death.

Through a study of Lepper's political trajectory in post-communist Poland, this chapter aims to discuss the processes underlying activist commitment and political professionalisation in a context of democratisation. More broadly, it aims at contributing to the most recent developments in the trajectory of social movements and activists during democratic transitions (Klandermans & Van Stralen, 2015). How is it that a farmer who was barely involved in politics under communist rule became a bustling activist after regime change? How did he get involved in the creation of new organisations? What have been the effects of accession to resources that allow him to 'live off' politics in his life-course? Conversely, what have been the consequences of the loss of such resources?

Two main sets of explanations have commonly been put forward to account for Lepper's puzzling political trajectory. The first insists on Lepper's uncommon personality traits: depending on opinions, either his clear-sightedness or his craziness, his persistence or his stubbornness, his charisma or his authoritarian nature (e.g. Piskorski, 2004; Kącki, 2013). The second focuses on the role of external factors, notably the harsh economic and political crisis experienced by Poland in the years following regime change. From that perspective, Lepper's and Samoobrona's successes are interpreted as symptoms of growing resentment among the population towards the ruling elite in those challenging times (e.g. Krok-Paszkowska, 2003; Szawiel, 2004). Conversely, their marginalisation after the 2007 elections is regarded as an encouraging sign towards political and economic stabilisation of Poland.

In contrast with the two above-mentioned dominant explanations, I will favour in this chapter a processual approach aimed at integrating and connecting in the analysis both personal and contextual factors. Using the sociological concept of career (Barley, 1989), I will pay specific attention to the contextual and intersubjective dimensions of successive changes in Lepper's situation over a period of 20 years, from its initial involvement to his suicide. As Fillieule notes, using the concept of career to study activism enables one 'to think activism as a process and therefore to combine in the analysis the questions of predispositions to activism, the shift to action, differentiated and variable forms of engagement over time, the multiplicity of engagements throughout the life cycle, and the retraction or extension of commitments' (Fillieule, 2001: 201).

The article is organised into six parts, each of them dealing with a specific 'sequence' of Lepper's political career. While the two first parts focus on the dynamics of Lepper's entry into activism (1) and the gradual intensification of his involvement in the early 1990s (2), the third deals with the forced slowdown of his activism in the mid-decade (3). The fourth part addresses the conditions of Lepper's comeback to high-intensity activism during the 1998–1999 wave of farmers' protests (4). The two last parts deal with the deep changes in Lepper's personal and professional lives following his first election to Parliament in 2001 (5) and the brutal loss of all his political mandates six years later (6).

At the empirical level, the analysis offered in this chapter is based on personal research on Samoobrona conducted between 2004 and 2010 (Pellen, 2010). First, I have conducted more than twenty semi-structured interviews with Polish politicians and Samoobrona's leaders (including Andrzej Lepper). Second, I have analysed hundreds of archival documents from various sources, including Samoobrona's website, Lepper's personal publications, the Polish Parliamentary archives and the archives of Political Parties gathered by the Polish Institute of Political Studies. Third, in order to obtain further information on Lepper's activities and how they were publicised, I have scrutinised and analysed the content of different newspapers over the period 1990–2011, notably the daily newspaper Gazeta Wyborcza, the weekly newsmagazine Polityka and two agricultural magazines: Zielony Sztandar and Chłopska Droga.

SEQUENCE 1: AN UNLIKELY ENTRY INTO ACTIVISM

Andrzej Lepper was born and raised in the village of Stowięcino, in the region of Słupsk, north-western Poland. The tenth child of a modest rural family, he enjoyed clear upward social mobility during the communist period. After having graduated from an agricultural technical school in 1974, at the age of 20, he was quickly promoted to manager of a small PGR. Meanwhile, in 1980, he made use of new arrangements in the agricultural laws to leave the public agricultural sector. With his newly wedded wife, he bought 22.5 hectares of arable land in the Darłowo district, 50 kilometres from Słupsk. As a young mid-manager of a PGR, Lepper fits perfectly the profile of those Marie-Claude Maurel identifies as having been the more inclined to take advantage of the conversion possi-bilities offered by the Gierek administration to engage in the creation of a private farm (Maurel, 1994: 139). Throughout the whole 1980s, Lepper continued to take advantage of successive agricultural reforms to buy new land and expand his farm, either by renting or buying on credit.

At the time of regime change, Andrzej Lepper had become a prominent landowner. Nevertheless, his profile also differed widely from that of the early post-communist period elite. A worker in the commonly stigmatised agricultural sector (Zalewski, 2006a: 148), he had spent all his life in the same rural region and had never been actively involved in politics. Although he had been a member of regime-sponsored organisations in his early twenties, which was then the norm when occupying a managerial position in the public sector, he had left them all as soon as he had stepped out of his job in a PGR. A declared Catholic entrepreneur, he had not participated either in the massive opposition movement Solidarity (Ost, 1990; Potel, 2006) and there is no evidence showing that he ever took part in any protest against the communist regime. Given that most studies of political recruitment in post-communist Poland emphasise the import-ance of political experience and networks, high educational level and prestigious professional status (Wasilewski & Wnuk-Lipinski, 1995; Heurtaux, 2004), one can safely say that, in the early 1990s, it seemed very improbable that Andrzej Lepper would ever begin a career in polit-ics. Even less that he was then in his late 30s and had three young children.

When asked why he had belatedly entered activism, Andrzej Lepper invariably mentioned the deterioration of economic conditions following regime change. Having faced poverty for the first time in his adult life, he had "become aware of the inaptitude of ruling politicians". Therefore, he had 'no choice but personally taking a step into politics' to make things improve (Lepper, 1993, 1999). Meanwhile, individual motives are not sufficient to account for someone's entry into activism (Snow, Zurcher, & Ekland-Olson, 1980). In Lepper's case, at least two other more contextual factors have also to be taken into account.

First, the specific salience of agricultural over-indebtedness in Lepper's neighbourhood. This specificity of Darłowo's agrarian structure favoured the emergence of a shared sense of grievance among the relatively numer-ous over-extended farmers of the region and the gradual strengthening of social ties between them (McAdam & Paulsen, 1993). Eventually, some of them, including Lepper, agreed to establish in July 1991 a 'District Committee of Agricultural Self-Defense' (Gminny Komitet Samoobrony Rolnictwa: GKSR) aimed at publicising agricultural over-indebtedness and pushing bankers to reschedule loans. For these purposes, GKSR initiated several local demonstrations and even registered a local electoral committee of three candidates, among them Lepper, for the October 1991 parliamentary elections.

Second, the political context also played a key role in Lepper's early activism. In Poland, the October 1991 parliamentary elections, the first entirely competitive held in the country since the interwar period, were an important step in the ongoing process of 'democratisation' characterised by high uncertainty (Dobry, 2000; Schedler, 2001). More than one hundred electoral committees, standing for very different conceptions of what the post-communist political system should be, ran for election (Jasiewicz, 1992). The competition was particularly intense among those claiming to defend specifically the interests of the still large rural population. In the early 1990s, two agrarian political alliances were indeed fiercely competing both in the realm of institutional politics and in that of social movements: a 'post-solidarity agrarian alliance', composed of the trade union Rural Solidarity and the Polish People's Party – Solidarity (PSL– "S"), and a 'post-communist agrarian alliance', composed of the trade union Agricultural Circles and the Polish People's Party (PSL) (Zalewski, 2006b). The vivid opposition between those two alliances decisively favoured Lepper's activism.

On the one hand, the late attempt of the post-Solidarity agrarian alliance to extend its electoral support base by taking hold of the issue of agricultural over-indebtedness it had previously ignored provided GKSR's members an unexpected opportunity to give a national dimension to their activities. Three weeks before the elections, Rural Solidarity initiated a protest encampment in support of overextended farmers in Warsaw, just in front of the Polish Parliament, and invited a dozen delegates from local protest committees to join it, among whom were members of GKSR and Lepper. The initially tiny action would eventually last more than one month and receive massive media coverage. Lepper did not leave the encampment until it was removed in mid-November and thus experienced for the first time a long-lasting and high-intensity participation in a protest action.

On the other hand, the effort of the post-communist agrarian alliance to contest the leadership of Rural Solidarity on the movement also proved to be decisive in the intensification of Lepper's activism. Few days after the beginning of the protest encampment in Warsaw, tensions started to emerge between its participants, as some non-affiliate protesters began to accuse Rural Solidarity of electoralism. By mid-October those maverick protesters, among them Lepper, decided to proclaim their full autonomy within the encampment. Taking the opportunity to undermine Rural Solidarity's influence, the leaders of Agricultural Circles actively supported the construction of the National Committee of Agricultural Self-Defense (Krajowy Komitet Samoobrony Rolnictwa: KKSR), which was then established.

Although it had no legal existence and gathered only a dozen protesters, KKSR managed to impose itself as a key actor of the protest encampment, especially after it initiated a ten-day hunger strike. Eventually, it succeeded in getting invited by the new government to the negotiation table set to solve the conflict in November 1991.

For Andrzej Lepper, the summer of 1991 was the time of the discovery of activism. That first experience would prove to be a mixed one. It provided him the opportunity to be confronted with new situations totally out of his ordinary farmer life, such as organising protest actions, registering for an election, giving press conferences, hunger striking or being involved in top-level negotiations. Meanwhile, the results of this activism rapidly proved to be rather disappointing. First, without any surprise, GKSR's local electoral committee did not succeed (by far) in obtaining any mandate in the parliamentary elections. Second, and foremost, most of the measures foreseen by the November 1991 agreement were forsaken even before they had been implemented. As the main agricultural organisations and the new government were rapidly losing interest on the issue they had developed in an electoral context, Lepper's activism seemed to have been in vain in the last weeks of 1991.

SEQUENCE 2: A GRADUAL INTENSIFICATION AND PROFESSIONALISATION OF ACTIVISM

In the summer of 1993, Andrzej Lepper was not an anonymous farmer anymore. The president of a national agricultural trade union, he had become a well-known public figure with the reputation of being a radical opponent to the government. Three key moments can be identified in the concomitant processes of intensification and professionalisation of Lepper's activism between the end of 1991 and the summer of 1993.

The first is the creation of the Agricultural Trade Union Self-Defence (ZZR Samoobrona) in January 1992. During the November 1991 negotiation, the government had agreed to treat KKSR as a legitimate representative of protesting farmers alongside the two officially representative agricultural unions Rural Solidarity and the Agricultural Circles. However, the still informal protest group lost that status as soon as the negotiation ended. Some of its founders then decided to turn it into an official trade union. Because of his activism during the autumn 1991 protest encampment, his lack of political record, and his political inexperience that indeed appeared a clear asset for a movement claiming to be apolitical, Andrzej Lepper was selected as the first president.

Ryszard Kozik, Lech Marek, Andrzej Lepper, Zbigniew Okorski, Paweł Skórski and Roman Wycech. Those are the names of the founders of the ZZR Samoobrona according to the trade union's publication Rolnik Rzeczypospolitej dating from April 1992. The six of them are middle-aged men who work in agriculture. Unlike the vast majority of Polish farmers of the early 1990s, they all owned relatively large farms (more than 10 hectares) and graduated from high school. Three of them, including Andrzej Lepper, had been working in a PGR during communist times, while the others had an extra-agricultural occupation back then (e.g. Ryszard Kozik was an electrician) and only acquired their farm after regime change. With the notable exception of Lepper, most of the founders of the ZZR Samoobrona have also in common that they had already been actively involved in trade unionism in the 1980s, mostly within the Solidarity movement.

The second key moment that shaped Lepper's entry into professional activism took place in April 1992. In order to force the government to recognise it as a legitimate social partner, ZZR Samoobrona's leaders decided to make what can be regarded as a last chance attempt. Building on the presence in Warsaw of most of the few active members of the new trade union on the occasion of its first congress, they launched a protest action right in the centre of the capital city. On 9 April, around one hundred activists, among them Lepper, occupied the building of the Ministry of Agriculture. That action rapidly obtained massive media attention and eventually enabled ZZR Samoobrona to take advantage of the vivid institutional conflicts of that time (Baylis, 1996) to gain official recognition. Unexpectedly, President Wałęsa indeed accepted most of the protesters' demands, which had previously been firmly rejected by the government, notably their representation in official agricultural advisory bodies.

Finally, the third key moment is the wave of protests that led to the fall of the Suchocka cabinet in May 1993. Following the April 1992 action, the leaders of ZZR Samoobrona strove to strengthen its new acquired position as the third officially representative agricultural trade union. On the one hand, in order to expand its potential support base beyond over-extended farmers, its stances and demands were gradually extended to new issues such as rural unemployment or guaranteed agricultural prices. On the other hand, it was quickly reengaged in the realm of protest actions. From the formation of a new Cabinet by Hanna Suchocka in July 1992 to its fall in May 1993, it initiated no less than twenty road blockades and official building occupations across the country

(Foryś & Gorlach, 2002). While spectacular, those two forms of protests had the advantage of requiring neither complex logistics nor a lot of participants. Initially, ZZR Samoobrona was the only national agricultural trade union to take to the streets against the new government. Yet, from December 1992 on, it was joined by most other unions in what would become the biggest wave of protests in post-communist Poland (Ekiert & Kubik, 1999; Osa, 1998). As one of its first and main active participants, ZZR Samoobrona was among the main beneficiaries of the anti-Suchocka protest movement (Pellen, 2010: 158). Building on the extension of its stance, its reputation of activism and its growing visibility in the media, it managed to recruit thousands of members and to spread its structures across the country, following a process which is not without similarities with that identified by Gitlin in his study of the Students for a Democratic Society (Gitlin, 1980).

The spectacular growth of ZZR Samoobrona hugely impacted on Andrzej Lepper's life. His activities as a unionist gradually took precedence over his work as a farmer. Seating regularly in representative agricultural bodies in Warsaw, he was personally involved in almost every protest action set up by his union during that period and was thus spending most of his time far away from his farm:

> At that time, I was really struggling to organise my time between the farm and the protest actions. My son was not old enough to manage the farm, so my wife had to do it with the help of neighbours. Hopefully, the farm was no more than 42 hectares large at that time [NA: since 1991, Lepper had sold or leased nearly 80 hectares of lands to pay his loans]. So it was not that big for the region and she could manage it. Yet, it was very complicated . . .
>
> Interview, with Andrzej Lepper, Warsaw, 25 June 2008

Besides this, thanks to the spectacular growth in its membership, ZZR Samoobrona could accumulate enough money to take over the expenses of and even pay a small salary to some of its national leaders. Andrzej Lepper could thus begin making a living out of his activities as a unionist. Also, from July 1992 to May 1993, Lepper gave hundreds of interviews and became something of a symbol of the peasants' discontent in the media. In reference to the Romanian Mineriada, the protests initiated by farmers were even nicknamed Lepperiada by some journalists. Lastly, as the anti-Suchocka protest movement was growing, Andrzej Lepper started behaving more and more as a politician. In total contradiction with the initial claim of political neutrality of the trade union, he was making it clearer every day that he was intending to build on its fame to enter electoral politics. The unexpected dissolution of Parliament in May 1993 provided him a golden opportunity to take the plunge. Lepper announced without delay the creation of an election committee based on the trade union and named, with all due modesty, Samoobrona of Lepper (Samoobrona Leppera). Less than two years after his first entry into activism, Lepper had made a clear career change. Having put aside his family life and his work as a farmer to become a professional unionist, he was now expecting to be elected Member of Parliament and enter professional politics.

SEQUENCE 3: A JOURNEY INTO POLITICAL WILDERNESS

On 19 September 1993, the committee Samoobrona-Leppera won only 2.78 per cent of the total votes cast, and thus failed to reach the election threshold of 5 per cent. The day after, most journalists agreed to present the committee as one of the main losers of the early parliamentary election. That interpretation also rapidly spread within ZZR Samoobrona and fuelled the first open challenge to Lepper's leadership. As the leading actor in the politicisation of the trade union, he was accused by several influential members of its board of being responsible for the electoral failure. Lepper opted to play hardball against those internal opponents and proclaimed their exclusion from the trade union. In the following months, he would not hesitate to initiate new rounds of internal 'purges' each time his authority was challenged. That brutal way of dealing with contestation enabled Lepper to strengthen his control over ZZR Samoobrona. Nevertheless, it also contributed to a dramatic weakening of the trade union. In a context of economic growth, of relative stabilisation of the political situation and of rarefaction of protest actions, the trade union indeed proved unable to secure the collective resources it had accumulated (Pellen, 2010: 219). Its weaknesses were put in full light during the 1997 parliamentary elections. The electoral committee initiated by the trade union then proved unable to register candidate lists in more than sixteen constituencies (out of fifty-two) and obtained only 0.08 per cent of the total votes cast. Following the elections, most commentators agreed that ZZR Samoobrona was dead and that Andrzej Lepper would join Stanisław Tymiński on the list of politicians who had totally vanished after having experienced popularity for a short period of time.[1]

---

[1] A Canadian businessman of Polish origin, Tymiński ran as an independent candidate in the 1990 presidential elections. He unexpectedly gathered 23.1 per cent of the vote and placed second behind Lech Wałęsa, but ahead of the prime minister Mazowiecki. In the second round, Tymiński lost to Wałęsa and never managed to experience success anew in the following years.

Despite these gloomy predictions, Andrzej Lepper did not put an end to his career as an activist. Three complementary hypotheses may explain his somehow paradoxical sustained activism. The first one is that his intense commitment to ZZR Samoobrona since its creation made it harder for him to consider quitting activism (Fillieule, 2010). The second one is that it was even more difficult for him to put an end to his commitment, given that he had once enjoyed the exhilarating and memorable experiences of public celebrity and political influence. Finally, the third hypothesis is that, given that ZZR Samoobrona was still officially a representative agricultural trade union in spite of the almost total disintegration of its structures, Lepper could continue to sit in agricultural advisory bodies, even though his influence in them was reduced to almost zero.

Nevertheless, Lepper was forced to dramatically refine his activist engagement following 1997 elections. For the first time in years, his farm was his sole source of income and he could not afford anymore to be a unionist on a full-time basis. He had no choice but to favour punctual and discreet forms of activism, mostly at the local level. With the support of a handful of faithful fellows, he henceforth dedicated most of his activities as a unionist to organising small local meetings aimed at promoting the trade union and recruiting new members:

[After the 1997 elections], some persons were thinking that it was the end of Samoobrona, that Samoobrona could never ever recover from such a defeat, that it was the end of Lepper. But at that moment, we decided with a small group of members that we should continue our activism across the country despite the difficulties ... There was very few activists left ... only the most dedicated to the cause. We had no offices, almost no means. It was really special. I had to say to those who wanted to invite me to come [e.g. to a public meeting] that they would have to pay for everything. They had to pay for my transportation, my accommodation .... People were contributing to pay the fuel, I was sleeping in private homes ... Following the 1997 electoral failure, it was really really hard to rebuild the movement.

Interview with Andrzej Lepper, Warsaw, 25 June 2008

SEQUENCE 4: A SPECTACULAR COME-BACK TO
HIGH-INTENSITY PROFESSIONAL ACTIVISM

On 10 July 1998, around 15,000 farmers marched in Warsaw to express their opposition to the Buzek government's agricultural policy. That demonstration marked the beginning of a year-long wave of farmers' protests across the country (Foryś, 2008). Besides a significant fall in farmers' income and the new government's non-interventionist economic approach, the political marginalisation of all the major agricultural organisations also played a decisive role in the resurgence of farmers' protests after years of relative calmness (Pellen, 2009). If not as dramatically as ZZR Samoobrona, Rural Solidarity, the Agricultural Circles and the PSL had indeed all come out very weakened from the 1997 election. Consequently, for the first time since regime change, none of them was represented in the government. Eventually, such a marginalisation favoured a hitherto unseen collaboration between agricultural organisations. Because of their common persistent inability to influence the government's agricultural policy, they eventually agreed in the early summer of 1998 to temporarily overcome their rivalry and collaborate "to ensure a decent representation of farmers' professional and social interests" (as stated in an agreement signed by their presidents on 24 June 1998).

With only a handful of active members in few regions, ZZR Samoobrona was then by far the weakest of all the agricultural organisations involved in the nascent protest movement. Yet, it rapidly managed to become its main beneficiary. First of all, the common front offered the union the opportunity to get involved in visible protest actions it would not have been able to organise by itself. Second, building on journalists' prejudice against farmers as being prone to brutality, the few remaining activists of ZZR Samoobrona managed to attract media coverage much wider than their real influence by 'playing their part' during protest actions (Pellen, 2009). Andrzej Lepper himself was systematically behaving as a caricature of a revolutionary peasant leader during demonstrations, going as far as calling on peasants to overthrow the government while provocatively brandishing a scythe in front of police forces. Such a strategy had ambivalent effects on the union. On the one hand, Samoobrona's excesses were a source of growing tensions with the other agricultural unions and gradually weakened its position within the common front. On the other hand, they enabled it to take advantage of journalists' prejudices, governmental intransigence and other protesting groups' hesitancy to gain the reputation of being the most resolute and determined in opposing the government. Building on that reputation, ZZR Samoobrona managed to recruit numerous new members and to swiftly redevelop its structures across the country. On 5 May 1999 – a few days before the signing of an agreement with the government that would put an end to the almost one-year-long protest movement – Lepper's union showed how strong it had become again by gathering in Warsaw more than 2,000 delegates from all around Poland at the occasion of its national congress.

At a more personal level, Lepper also came out considerably strengthened from the protest movement. Thanks to the unions' common front, he
was able to resume his activities as a unionist on an almost full-time basis
and to obtain for the first time an electoral mandate. In October 1998, he
was indeed elected regional councillor in his home region of West Pomer-
ania on a coalition ticket led by the agrarian party PSL. Furthermore,
thanks to his 'performances' during protest actions, he gradually managed again to focus media attention, becoming a true media star by early
1999. Finally, he also managed to reinforce his control over the organisation, through a very centralised process of re-organisation; all the more
that he was its only public figure and one of its last still-active founding
members. Lepper was triumphantly re-elected at the head of the organisation at the May 1999 Congress and would not face any challenge to his
leadership for several years. Thus, in spite of the past fiascos, his decision
to re-politicise the trade union by creating a Siamese twin party named
Self-Defense of the Polish Republic (Samoobrona RP)[2] and by standing as
a candidate in the 2000 presidential election was not subject to much
internal debate. Similarly, although Lepper failed by far to achieve his
initial stated goal and gathered only 3.5 per cent of the votes, nobody
within the union dared to question his post-electoral interpretation of that
result as 'very promising'. Finally, and likewise, Lepper's risky decision to
re-engage Samoobrona in parliamentary elections on the occasion of the
2001 poll did not cause any major internal controversy and was almost
unanimously approved internally.

SEQUENCE 5: REACHING THE APEX OF THE STATE

Prior to the 2001 parliamentary elections, Samoobrona's electoral committee could rely on the collective resources which had been gathered
by the trade union during the 1998–1999 farmers' protest to lead an
active campaign. While core activists of the trade union were put to work
to collect funds and canvass, its officials were systematically propelled to
leading positions on the constituency candidate lists. Lepper himself got
very actively involved in every aspect of the campaign and spent his whole

---

[2] Strictly speaking, the party *Samoobrona* RP was taking over the party *Przymierze Samoobrona*, which had been registered by ZZR *Samoobrona*'s founders in June 1992 and had
been totally forsaken since.

summer routing across the country to participate to Samoobrona's local rallies and meetings:

Back then, our main idea was that local grassroots campaigning was the best way to convince voters. Our bad result at the 1997 elections indeed made us understand ... that we should be on the field as much as possible during electoral campaigns. We did so for the first time during the 2000 presidential elections. It worked pretty well as I ranked 4th or 5th [he ranked 5th]. So we decided to continue to develop the local structures of the movement all around the country and to be very active at the local level the following year, in view of the Parliamentary elections.

Interview with Andrzej Lepper, Warsaw, 25 June 2008

In a context of economic crisis and profound recomposition of the party system, especially within its right-wing spectrum (Szczerbiak, 2004), Samoobrona's electoral committee performed much better than anticipated by pollsters and its own leaders. With 10.2 per cent of the total votes, it ranked third nationally and obtained fifty-three seats in the Sejm (out of 460) and two in the Senate (out of 100). Lepper himself was elected deputy in his home constituency. A unionist activist for a decade and a regional counsellor for three years, he had at last succeeded in entering the realm of institutional politics at the national level.

Becoming a parliamentary force gave Samoobrona access to new means of action and influence, but also new means of funding. On the one hand, almost all the managerial staff members were now receiving a comfortable salary as parliamentarians. They could even hire assistants on their allowances. They who used to be, in the large majority, volunteer unionists were brutally turned into salaried politicians. On the other hand, through Samoobrona RP, the movement was now eligible for public party subsidies. Between 2002 and 2007, it received a large, and growing, amount of subsidies, between 1 and 3 million euros annually. That massive influx of public money led to a spectacular increase in its budget and enabled it to hire permanent staff and purchase new offices in the very centre of Warsaw. That spectacular transformation had of course a strong impact on Andrzej Lepper, the unquestioned leader of all its three components (the trade union, the political party and the parliamentary group). Although he had de facto already been a professional politician for several years, Lepper was now a prominent deputy who was in charge of a flourishing organisation, with thousands of members, more than fifty elected officials and dozens of staff. His new schedule was packed with parliamentary meetings, staff briefings and interviews, which forced him to spend most of his time in Warsaw. He took a flat in the capital city, just one floor above the movement's new offices, and henceforth only occasionally visited his family and farm.

However, the euphoria of electoral success did not last long. The integration of Samoobrona's new parliamentarians into the realm of institutional politics indeed proved to be particularly difficult. In addition to their affiliation to a movement commonly labelled as radical agrarian, their lack of political experience and their low education level were all very atypical attributes amongst Polish parliamentarians. In the first months of the Sejm's 4th term (2001–2005), they were regularly mocked as incompetent, uncouth and even undemocratic fools by journalists and politicians from other parties. Andrzej Lepper was by far the main target of those harsh critics. It must be said that he had not renounced the coarse language, the vocal denunciations of elites and the participation in spectacular protest actions on which he had built his fame. Such behaviour resulted in a deepening of Samoobrona's political marginalisation and, eventually, in its weakening. As the stigma related to being a member of Samoobrona kept on increasing, the ability of the movement to ensure the allegiance of its parliamentarians was indeed crumbling.[3] From January 2002 to August 2003, no less than twenty of its fifty-three deputies splintered to join other less ostracised parliamentary groups. By mid-2003, defections had been so massive that it had begun seriously undermining, not only its position in Parliament, but also its structures in several regions.

In order to deal with that sticky situation, Lepper and his closest collaborators eventually decided to conform Samoobrona to what they then perceived as the dominant rules of institutional politics. First, in order to break down its reputation of radicalism, the use of extra-institutional protest actions by the trade union was put on standby. Second, in order to mitigate its agricultural profile and close the huge gap in social characteristics between its elected officials and those from other parties, dozens of lawyers, businessmen or academics were invited to join the movement and propelled into leading positions in both its organisation and candidate lists. Finally, Samoobrona's public stances were deeply reshaped. A bright new electoral program was drafted, with a profusion of statistics and references aiming at demonstrating its

---

[3] The processes of social stigmatisation, institutional marginalisation and gradual internal weakening of *Samoobrona*'s parliamentary group during the early *Sejm* 4th term present numerous similarities with those experienced by the *Poujadist* parliamentary group in France's 4th Republic (Collovald, 1989).

credibility. Moreover, with the help of media advisors, Andrzej Lepper dramatically transformed his appearance and behaviour to appear as a respectable statesman. Besides getting a very neat new haircut, he began wearing perfectly tailored suits and endeavouring to moderate his language, notably by limiting slangs and insults.

Prima facie, the profound reshaping of Samoobrona appeared to be a complete success. It enabled it to stem defections and political marginalisation, without affecting its electoral performance. With 11.41 per cent and 15.11 per cent of the votes, Samoobrona and Lepper even obtained their best results ever during 2005 parliamentary and presidential elections. With fifty-six deputies in the Sejm 5th term, most of them being highly educated men who had recently joined the party, Samoobrona was emerging once again as the third biggest force in Parliament. Thanks to its strong institutional representation and political conformation, Lepper's movement rapidly appeared as a key actor in the formation of a new majority.

A deeply renewed parliamentary group

In the run-up-up to the 2005 elections, Andrzej Lepper's stated goal was to turn Samoobrona into a respectable party of government. The desire to change the movement's image reflected in a deep change in the way its candidates to Parliament were selected. Whereas in 2001 most of them had been chosen directly by local branches of the trade union, the selection process was much more centralised in 2005. The list of recommended candidates was established directly by Lepper and a handful of advisors without any participation from the local level. According to Mateusz Piskorski, then one of Lepper's closest collaborators, the idea was to make sure the new parliamentary group would be more diverse and more 'professionalised' than the previous one: 'Our political strategy in 2005 was to try to enlarge Samoobrona's electorate. That's why we went looking for candidates who were coming from different social groups so we could show to a maximum number of voters that they could be well represented by our party, even though they were not farmers or inhabitants of the countryside. The second important element was our wish to fix the problems of lack of professionalism and expertise we had experienced during the previous term. Being more professional was an obligation for us after four years in Parliament and that's why our candidates lists had a completely different face in 2005 than in 2001' (Interview, Warsaw, 25 June 2008). Such a strategy of candidate selection led to the promotion of many newcomers in the party at the expense of long time activists. Out of the 833 candidates recommended by Samoobrona in 2005, only 97 already ran for the party in 2001.

Eventually, the renewal rate of Samoobrona's parliamentary group was very impressive following the 2005 elections. Only seventeen of the fifty-one Samoobrona members who had been elected to the Sejm 4th term in 2001 got re-elected. Unsurprisingly, given the way they were selected, the fifty-six representatives from Lepper's party in the Sejm 5th term also had a very different profile than their predecessors. On the one hand, they were in average much more educated. Fifty-seven per cent of them held a higher education qualification, whereas there were less than 19 per cent in that situation in 2001. On the other hand, their professional background was much less likely to be in agriculture. Only 36 per cent were working in the agricultural sector prior to their election (versus 66 per cent in 2001) and 60 per cent of them belonged to upper socio-professional groups (versus only 15 per cent in 2001). In sum, even though they remain slightly less educated and experienced politically than their colleagues from other political parties, the profile of Samoobrona's deputies in the Sejm was much closer to the parliamentary average in 2005 than it was four years earlier.

After months of negotiations, Samoobrona eventually joined, in May 2006, a coalition government led by the Kaczyński brothers' party Law and Justice (PiS). Samoobrona obtained three seats in the new Cabinet and Lepper was appointed Minister of Agriculture and Vice-Prime Minister. Fifteen years after his entry into activism, the former agricultural technician had risen to be one of the most powerful statesmen in the country. The leader of a major political movement with hundreds of elected officials at every levels of government, he was at the head of one of the most important Polish administrations. However, his situation and that of his movement were much more fragile than it seemed. Both were in fact giants with feet of clay.

SEQUENCE 6: A TRAGIC END TO AN UNSTOPPABLE POLITICAL CAREER

The Kaczyński coalition government collapsed in July 2007 after months of internal struggles. Early parliamentary elections were called for October. They proved to be a disaster for Samoobrona, which gathered only 1.5 per cent of the vote and lost all its seats in Parliament. Two main explanations have commonly been provided to account for Lepper's movement's spectacular fall: its incapacity to adapt to the constraints of governmental politics and the ability of PiS to siphon off traditional voters from its former coalition partners (Gwiazda, 2008; Markowski, 2008). Yet, two other internal factors also played a decisive role (Pellen, 2010: 567). First, the anaemia of Samoobrona's grassroot structures. The profound reshaping of the movement after 2003 indeed had the unforeseen consequence of causing the gradual departure of almost all its grassroots activists, mostly because of the growing apathy of a trade union most of them had joined during 1998–1999 protests, the movement's moderating political stances and their systematic marginalisation to the benefit of 'high-profile' newcomers. Second, on the eve of the 2007 elections, Samoobrona was also marked by sharp tensions between its leaders. In the late 1990s, Andrzej Lepper had succeeded in imposing his almost total leadership. Yet, his authority was gradually undermined after 2003 and the profound reshaping of the movement. The highly educated and wealthy new members that then joined the movement indeed proved to be much less faithful to Lepper than its 'historical' activists and did not hesitate to openly contest him as soon as his popularity began fading in opinion polls.

Following the 2007 elections, Samoobrona was looking in very bad shape. First, its already weakened membership base was seriously eroded by further wave of defections. As the weeks passed, Lepper was appearing increasingly isolated at the head of a movement with crumbling structures. Second, Samoobrona was facing bankruptcy. Having lost all its seats in Parliament, it was deprived of most of its public subsidies and thus faced great difficulties in repaying the loans it had taken out to finance its past electoral campaigns. Lepper found himself in a very delicate personal economic situation as he had made several of those loans in his private name. And to make matters even worse, third, a handful of senior officials of the movement, among them Lepper, were faced with criminal charges, mostly for corruption and sexual harassment within the party (Krzyżanowska, 2010).

In spite of these very serious difficulties, Andrzej Lepper always publicly ruled out putting an end to his political career. Even though he had lost all his elected positions and had no official charges for the first time since 1998, he kept on expressing his certainty that the movement he had been leading for more than 15 years would very soon be back at the top. He argued that Samoobrona was entering a new phase of 'regeneration', during which, just like it had in the late 1990s, it would redevelop its structures and support base through participating in extra-institutional protest actions. Thus, in addition to the length of his commitment to activism and his recent experience as a prominent professional politician, the fact that Lepper had already managed to perform an unexpected political comeback in the past proved to be decisive in his refusal to consider leaving politics after the 2007 elections:

> I think that what people appreciate the most in politics is action. For me, success or failure is never final in politics. [A politician] is not a star that would shine high in the sky one day and crash abruptly as a meteorite the day after. If you don't believe in that, then it is pointless to try to come back. I rather think that the dominant principle in politics is that of the sine wave: once you are at the top, once all the way down, then back at the top again ... I must confess that sometimes it crossed my mind to stop politics and become a simple farmer again. But I have committed myself to Samoobrona for too long. I just cannot abandon everything like that and tell myself that this time it is truly over. I am convinced that we will rise again from ashes and that Samoobrona will return to Parliament in the future.
>
> Interview with Andrzej Lepper, Warsaw, 25 June 2008

Yet, Samoobrona never succeeded in redeveloping its membership base, nor in reorganising significant protest actions, nor in regaining electoral success. Samoobrona's inability to perform a second political comeback can be explained by two main factors. First, the clear preference expressed by of all the other unions for institutional forms of farmers' representation over protest actions since the EU accession of Poland in 2004. Thus, unlike what had happened in the late 1990s, ZZR Samoobrona could not count anymore on their support to initiate a protest movement that would help it compensate for its lack of mobilisation capability and media visibility. Second, after 2007, the Polish party system was increasingly dominated by two rival parties, Kaczyński brothers' PiS and Donald Tusk's Civic Platform. In that context, it was much more complex than ten years earlier for other parties to make ground in the electorate and meet the electoral threshold (Szczerbiak, 2008). Besides those contextual factors, it must also be underlined that Andrzej Lepper did not behave in the same way following the 1997 and the 2007 elections. Whereas he had resumed his work as a farmer and returned to grassroots unionism in the late 1990s, he, who had been in the meantime Vice-Prime Minister, never moved back to his farm (and family) in Darłowo and did not stop acting like a prominent statesman after 2007. Rather than touring the countryside to promote Samoobrona and mobilise new members, he spent most of his time in Warsaw between the movement's headquarters, where he was working on its 'regeneration' with the last handful of faithful companions, and TV studios, where he was tirelessly expressing his confidence that he would come back to power in the near future. He did so until he was found hanged in August 2011.

Lepper's sudden death led to much speculation (Frye, 2011). While conspiracy theories are still flourishing, the prosecutor's report clearly concluded suicide and pointed out Lepper's depressive mood. It was indeed disclosed that, besides his already publicly known financial and judicial troubles, he was dealing with serious issues with his family, from whom he had been living apart for years. In addition to those elements, the fact that he decided to take his own life a few months after having performed poorly in the 2010 presidential election (with only 1.28 per cent of votes) and a few weeks before new parliamentary elections which were shaping up to be a disaster for Samoobrona is probably not totally accidental. One can indeed argue that, after years of high-intensity activism that had led him to the apex of the state, suicide was a method for an increasingly isolated and weakened man to put an end to his political career his own way, before being forced to do so by circumstances.

CONCLUSION

The activist and political career of Andrzej Lepper this chapter studies in detail is a particular case on several counts. Lepper's trajectory from farming to the summit of national politics through unionism indeed appears as an exception in a post-communist Polish society characterised by gradual political demobilisation of rural populations and elitism in the selection of politicians. Additionally, even though the emergence of outsiders claiming to shake the political establishment has become something of a habit in Polish contemporary politics – Janusz Palikot, Janusz Korwin-Mikke and Paweł Kukiz being the most recent examples – none of them had either an agricultural background or rich experience of activism in protest movements, and none has managed so far to obtain good results over several elections and enter the government, like Lepper and Samoobrona did in the early 2000s. Nevertheless, in spite of this somewhat atypical nature, at least two general lessons can be drawn from Lepper's trajectory.

The first lesson has to do with activist engagement in times of democratisation. While the vast literature on transition from authoritarian to democratic rule has long tended to focus on the sole elites (Bermeo, 1997: 305), the decisive pro-democratic role played by social movement organisations in the collapse of socialist regimes in Central and Eastern Europe has led scholars to reassess the importance of these actors on processes of regime change. It notably stimulated original research on the peculiar logics and dynamics of activism in times of transition, which have recently been supplemented by new studies on the so-called Arab Spring (e.g. Bennani-Chraïbi & Fillieule, 2012; Della Porta, 2014). Meanwhile, although studies dealing with the processes of joining activism, continuance commitment and politicisation in a revolutionary context are now numerous, those addressing these issues in the immediate post-authoritarian period are much rarer. The specialised literature indeed remains dominated by the thesis of a rapid demobilisation of civil society in the aftermath of authoritarian breakdown, which would notably be characterised by re-institutionalisation of politics and citizens' retreat into the private sphere (Howard, 2003). Our analysis of Andrzej Lepper's trajectory prompts us to qualify such a general statement. Recent works have usefully stressed the diversity of trajectory that movements can in practice take in a context of transition (Klandermans & Van Stralen, 2015), pointing out that the immediate post-authoritarian period can also, in certain cases, be conducive to activism. The high uncertainty that characterises the new political configuration still in the process of definition can indeed offer opportunities for activists to pursue their activities but also for previously non-activist actors, like Lepper, to mobilise around new issues, to initiate protest actions, or to create new social or political organisations. That was particularly the case in post-communist Poland, where the registration of an association, a trade union or a political party were very easy and collective protests remained intense until the mid-1990s (Ekiert & Kubik, 1999). What the study of Lepper's activist career also shows us is that the way the rules of the new post-authoritarian political configuration are defined deeply influences the possibilities and shape of activism. For instance, in Poland, the fact that the border between the realm of institutional politics and that of social movements remained loose and permeable for several years after regime change proved to be favourable to multi-positional activism. Unlike most other post-communist countries, it was indeed considered normal for social activists to contest elections and to hold an elected mandate until the late 1990s. This element most certainly played a decisive role in Lepper's decision to combine unionist and political activism after 1993. Conversely, the gradual compartmentalisation of institutional politics and separation between parties and trade unions in the early 2000s (Heurtaux, 2005: 479) made it harder and harder for him to continue behaving as an agricultural unionist once he had become a deputy, and a fortiori, a minister.

The second lesson that can be drawn from Lepper's trajectory has to do with the effects of long-lasting, high-level activism on individual habitus (Bourdieu, 1979). On the one hand, Lepper's case reminds us that initial dispositions and socialisation have an enduring and resilient influence on activist career. Lepper's past managerial and entrepreneurial experiences thus played a key role on his ability and manner to handle Samoobrona, to set up protest actions and electoral campaigns but also, more broadly, to conceive his activism in the long run through crises and successes. Besides, his agricultural background, lack of political experience prior to regime change and modes of entry into activism through protest were also prominent in the shaping and nurturing of his lasting public image as a hot-tempered and determined self-made political outsider. While this image enabled him to stand out in the particularly intense post-communist Poland political competition, it also exposed him to harsh criticism and stigmatisation during his whole political career, even after he had reached top institutional positions. On the other hand, Lepper's trajectory also illustrates the transformative effects of durable engagement on individual biographies. Over the years, as he became a professional activist and subsequently a full-time politician, Lepper dramatically grew apart from his former professional and personal environments. So much so that, by the mid-2000s, he had almost nothing left in common with the anonymous Pomeranian farmer he once had been. He who had experienced fame, electoral success and prestigious political positions was now a high self-esteemed full-time politician with the displayed ambition to reach the highest ranks of the political hierarchy. In parallel, his entourage had also dramatically changed. While he still loved to describe himself as an ordinary rural family man, he was in fact barely seeing his wife, children and fellow farmers anymore and was spending most of his time with his ambitious and highly educated new collaborators in Warsaw. Meanwhile, Samoobrona's electoral failure in 2007 painfully proved to him that his gradual transformation from a farmer into a statesman had been at very high cost. His physical and cognitive breakaway from his initial environment indeed made it impossible for him to consider returning to his past life and leaving a Varsovian political elite which had never fully accepted him. Social isolation from family and friends had been unexpected secondary effects of his twenty-year-long sustained activism at the head of Samoobrona.

Red T-Shirt or Executive Suit

About Some Biographical Consequences of Contentious Engagement in the Workers' Party in Recife, Brazil

Camille Goirand

When Luís Ignacio da Silva Lula was elected a President of Brazil in October 2002, the national and international media underlined repetitively how his biography was remarkable, if not exceptional. Before becoming a metal-worker and a union leader, Lula grew up in a very humble family in the rural Northeast who followed the migration wave to the Southeast when he was a child. This itinerary, that led Lula from the deprived interior of Northeastern Brazil in 1952 to the presidential palace in 2002, after passing through the metal plants of São Paulo's industrial suburbs, invites us to look beyond the individual and beyond the event of his access to the presidency in October 2002. For many reasons, Lula's victory in 2002 is a fruit of the transform-ations of the party that supported it, the Workers' Party (PT), whose most prominent leaders became members of the federal government in 2003. In the wake of Lula, many activists' itineraries also followed paths that drove them through the changes in the position of their party, from contention to government, but also through larger changes regarding the political environ-ment. All those processes are part of larger issues, such as the consolidation of Brazilian democracy and profound changes in the Brazilian political system. They are also linked to a continent-wide transformation process of the left since the regime changes (Garibay, 2005; Combes, 2011).

In the case of the PT, gaining a large legislative representation and assuming executive power was linked to deep redefinitions of the meaning of political action for rank-and-file activists. For some, it had biographical impacts as it brought changes either in their professional careers or in their commitment in the party. For those who had experienced the political repression of the authoritarian period and had taken part in the foundation of the party in 1980, the most meaningful transformations of the 2000s were linked not only to their relations to the political institutions, but also to the meaning they gave to their own commitment and to the identity of a party that came from contentious social movements and now had taken office.

Box 11.1 Research methods: contextualized biographies

This chapter is based on ethnographic observations of PT activists in Recife, Northeastern Brazil, that were conducted between 2003 and 2010, as well as on semi-direct interviews (three waves of ten to fifteen interviews each) with long-term party members who engaged before the period of the democratic transition of the mid-1980s and shared a life-long commitment as rank-and-file. However, individuals with various positions at the time of the interview have been selected, from disengaged activists to recently elected PT state deputies. The latter were selected for interviews when they had a long-term trajectory of social movement activism before being elected.

Here, we only mobilize a limited number of biographies that we consider among the most meaningful in order to understand the long-term impact of activism (Auyero, 2003). Those few biographies, associated to a case study of the PT in Recife (local archives, a survey made during internal party elections in 2009, and the observation of electoral mobilization on various occasions) enable us to address larger issues such as the transformations of the Brazilian party system after the democratic transition as well as the logics of the relationships between social movements and political parties.

In this chapter, I first present a brief discussion of the approaches that may be adopted to analyze the interaction between changes in the party organization and activist trajectories, and I show to what extent activist biographies may shed light on party institutionalization processes. Then, I turn to the case study and explore the interactions between the changes of the PT's organization in Recife, and the trajectories of its long-term activists. Finally, I will resume the discussion about the biographical impacts of long-term activism and about some difficulties in identifying them.

PARTY ACTIVISTS CAUGHT IN AN INSTITUTIONALIZATION PROCESS

Party Institutionalization: A Multifaceted Process

The notion of institutionalization may be understood according to various approaches that are linked to a narrower or larger definition of an "institution" (Hall & Taylor, 1997): in the first type of approaches, institutionalizing means entering existing formal institutions and accepting their main rules (Piven & Cloward, 1979), whereas with a more open meaning, it refers to the process of being socialized to the norms, values, and practices shared by a group, and taking part in their reshaping or change. The forms of an institution are designed by "the sedimentation of prescriptions, practices, knowledge and beliefs" that modify the rules through which the institution emerges (Lagroye & Offerlé, 2010: 331). Instead of thinking of institutions as having effects on actors, this approach analyzes the uses of "institutional roles as the products of a dialectic game between objective institutional prescriptions and actors' interiorized dispositions" (Freymond, 2010: 48).

Following this perspective, our analysis doesn't focus on organizational logics or on the strategic rationality of the party, but on how people engage in a party, how they model the rules of the organization, or how they internalize its legitimate practices; and how those logics are reassessed when the party's position within the party system changes. When activists gain access to institutional positions, such as authority status or public jobs, not only do they control new material and symbolic resources, but they also hold new roles. In those new positions, individuals learn how to perform their institutional roles, but their behavior is also shaped by their prior socialization, for example by their long-term experience of activist mobilization, and by their long-term participation in the social movement. To examine those processes, I have recourse to the observation of activists' behavior and interaction with others, as well as to interviews focusing on the way activists portray their party and their life trajectories. Therefore, I analyze jointly how the PT became part of the party system *and* how this process interacted with the sedimentation of a "group style" (Eliasoph & Lichterman, 2003). The latter was shaped by the memory of past commitments, by the intensity of electoral mobilizations, and by the representation of the party and its members as coming from a long-term combative activism.

Observation of the PT in Recife has been based on the analytical distinction between three different aspects of the process of institutionalization. First, the gradual moderation of the PT's revolutionary discourse is a symptom of a change in public action preferences among party leaders. Second, while the PT won majorities, its local and national leaders professionalized and, as a consequence, their relationship with social movements was transformed. Third, since the end of the 1990s, the transformation of the former extremely committed activism into a more distant and often disenchanted participation was combined with a widening distance, within the party, between a professional elite and rank-and-file activists, on the one hand, and with a change in the activist *ethos* and party identity, on the other. A considerable part of the research on Latin American social movements analyzes their institutionalization as a failure, pointing at the adoption of electoral strategies and alliances with traditional political parties (Goirand, 2010). This approach is based on a tendency among social movement observers to assume that they act within extra-institutional arenas by nature, and that they risk demobilizing when they act in other spheres (Piven & Cloward, 1979; Tarrow, 1994). Thus, institutionalization is understood as an explanation for the decline in the intensity of mobilizations. However, in the case of democratic constructions, individual participation in social movements and political parties are not alternatives but may be complementary activities, and, to a larger extent, electoral and contentious politics are not automatically opposed. In the cases when an opposition party wins local or national elections, like the PT during the 1990s, its members still circulate within the social movement spaces and continue interacting with their actors. It is only progressively that they adjust their behaviors, discourses, strategies, and aims to their new positions (Goldstone, 2003).

Until now, research on the Brazilian PT have followed institutional and national lines and have been rarely based on ethnographical methods and sociological perspectives (Meneguello, 1989; Keck, 1991; Amaral, 2010; Hunter, 2010; Ribeiro, 2010). On the contrary, our approach, inspired by interactionist sociology (Gerth & Wright-Mills, 1954; Becker, 1963), focuses on the local level and the life course of rank-and-file party activists. It is also inspired by various research works that have renewed the study of political parties since the end of the 1980s in France, and more precisely by Bernard Pudal's proposals for the study of the French Communist Party in 1989. Pudal meant to "de-construct the collective actor in order to re-construct historical and social processes by which individual actors, in their diversity, aggregate, exclude one another, institutionalize" (Pudal, 1989: 14). Aiming at observing the transformations of a party organization through the life stories of its members and through their interactions, this paper makes an attempt at de-constructing it further. To that end, it observes the local differentiations of the party organization, as well as the social interactions that link its members at the base, within but also outside the party, in its social *milieu*. Thus, it is through the analysis of activist trajectories at the intermediate and low levels of the PT hierarchy that we observe the process of institutionalization.

Observing individual itineraries of engagement may highlight the ways the Party took root at the local level, how its organization transformed and how it institutionalized. Those life paths, be they unique, paradigmatic, or recurrent, offer a glimpse of individual actors *within* the organization during its transformation, from various points of view: the alterations in the meaning given to the collective, the reshaping of party members' identities, the changes in the practices of activism or the ways long-term activists tolerate or disapprove of changes when they are related to a dramatic growth in the number of party members, to the moderation of electoral platforms, to the alliances with right-wing parties or to the growing distance from local party leadership, now in office. Thus, the transformations of a party and its social space may be perceived, first, through the changes in the ways individual trajectories are rooted in the social movement space in which the party is included; second, through commitment itineraries that diverge, wander, accelerate, stop, are reshaped, or are redefined while the organization changes.

In Recife, activist itineraries were profoundly reoriented by the sudden changes in the position of their organization in the local party system. After being a minority for 30 years, the PT won the municipal election in Recife in 2001 and gained access to local executive power for the first time; a victory that meant not only changes in the political position of the party but also in the professional and social places occupied by its leaders. This new position transformed activists' identities and the way they looked at the PT. At the same time, it meant that its leaders had to learn how to be professional politicians and to behave as such. It also implied redefining the relationship between the party and the social movement organizations from which its members had originally come, and to which most of them still belonged.

The PT: From Contention to Institutionalization

There were more than 30 years between the creation of the PT in February 1980 and its first presidential victory in October 2002, during which the party changed drastically. After 15 years of authoritarian rule, the amnesty law in August 1979 and the return to multipartism in December 1979 took place in the context of a protest cycle initiated by the metalworkers trade unions in May 1978. In 1980, the PT gathered together various branches of the radical left. With its union component – clearly the strongest – the PT also included left-wing figures back from exile, contentious student groups, especially from the National Union of

Student (UNE), human rights movements, various armed struggle organizations that had fought against the military regime after 1968, movements linked to the progressive Catholic church, and various popular "base" movements.

During its first years, the PT had limited electoral successes, hardly going beyond the state of São Paulo, as in Porto Alegre in 1988. The following decade was that of a gradual electoral consolidation for the PT. The number of its deputies increased progressively during the 1990s, while its presidential candidate, Luis Ignácio da Silva, who was defeated in 1989, 1994, and 1998 finally won in 2002 and again in 2006. Those electoral victories are deeply linked to the transformations of the PT, a complex process that presents multiple facets (Goirand, 2014). First, it "entered" the political institutions via the administration of several state capitals and via the conquest of legislative mandates. For party leaders, becoming a majority implied learning how to practice power and absorbing dominant norms of behavior of the Brazilian political field; even if they tried to change those rules from within (Fleischer, 2004). Until the beginning of the 1990s, the PT had a strategy of opposing the construction of the New Republic and it proved very selective when it allied with other parties, generally limiting alliances to small left-wing parties such as the Brazilian Socialist Party (PSB) and the Communist Party of Brazil (PCdoB). In contrast, since the end of the 1990s, alliances between the PT and small right-wing parties became common practice, especially since 2002 when the PT and the Liberal Party (PL) joined in the same presidential ticket, Lula-José Alencar. This strategy created public controversy and was regarded as a serious betrayal by numerous PT militants.

From 1980 until 2002, the votes in favor of the PT's candidates kept increasing, at all levels of government, but with persistent geographical disparities (Samuels, 2004). During the 1990s, the increase was particularly clear at the federal level. In the Chamber of Deputies, it moved up from seventh position in 1990 to first in 2002, moving to third position in the Senate at the same time (Kinzo, 2004). For municipal elections, the PT regularly won a growing number of cities in all regions. In November 2000, it won 29 cities of more than 200,000 inhabitants, with 6 state capitals, including São Paulo and Recife. In the country as a whole, the PT tripled the number of city executives it won in 2000 compared to 1996. By 2002, the PT had not only won the federal Presidency but it had also turned into a central actor at Congress, with 91 deputies out of 513 in the Chamber of Deputies in 2002. Between 2002 and 2010, the PT candidates in the presidential election won with very high scores, always over 45 percent of the vote in the first ballot, and 55 percent in the second.[1] In 2002, PT's electoral forces expanded to the whole national territory, and by 2006 it had consolidated in the Northeast. This switch, from the Southeast in its first years to the Northeast in the 2000s, was already obvious in 2002 and was confirmed in 2006 and 2010. As Hunter and Power put it, in terms of region and class, the 2006 election showed an obvious divide between "two Brazils," with a switch in the social distribution of the vote between 1989 and 2006 (Hunter & Power, 2007: 7).

A second facet of the PT's institutionalization was the consolidation of the party organization. In 1991, a new charter was adopted, which recognized the existence of internal "tendencies," thus prohibiting the "organizations" that had founded the party from following their own strategies, defining their own rules, publishing their own journals, or handling their own financial resources. With this reform, the local and national directions attempted to unify the organization and manage its ramifications more tightly. In 1994, the national direction chose to replace the traditional "cells" (Davis, 1997) by groups defined either by the geographical "zone" where they lived or according to their social "sectors."[2] After 1994, as a consequence of this reform, each "zonal" group gathered more members than "cells" did in the past, which meant a loosening of the social ties that used to cement the party at its basis. For anonymous rank-and-file members, those organizational changes also meant a growing distance from the party leadership. Those changes led to a reform of the party's internal representation system in 2001, with the introduction of "direct" primaries for the selection of party directions, which brought about an acute electoral competition between leaders, both at the national and local levels, turning the competition between tendencies into an individual issue, especially for those who aimed at being invested as candidates in the following elections in order to stabilize their professional positions.

In a third aspect, the PT's institutionalization meant a double transformation, of its image among the public, and of its political platform and discourse. During its first years, the image of the PT was that of a contentious party, formed by radical democrats, an *avant-garde* of the working class. By the mid-1990s, the PT needed a new identity; that of a party with a skilled and honest leadership, able to administrate the big cities of

---

[1] Source: Electoral Superior Court, www.tse.gov.br.
[2] In Portuguese: *núcleos*, *zonais*, and *setoriais*.

the country. Thus, in the course of the 1990s, the issue of participative democracy took on considerable prominence in the PT's discourses, while revolutionary connotations gradually lost ground and were replaced by "good governance" references for public action. Now aiming at reforming democracy through popular participation, the PT was acting within the frame of the existing representative system, and it recognized the legitimacy of its values and norms, only proposing to change its practices.

By the 2000s, the references to "the PT's way of governing – *O modo petista de governar*" had become a label, an instrument for showing the specific features of PT municipal administrations and for keeping their "differences" in mind (Genro, 1999). PT leaders still referred to "change," but now contemplated it within the institutions. As a hypothesis, we suggest that "participative politics" were not a mere legitimating resource after the party had abandoned references to Marxism and revolution; nor was it only a useful instrument for bypassing municipal assemblies, in which the PT was usually a minority. Participative politics also got along with, or even counterbalanced, the political professionalization of PT leaders and the institutionalization of the party as a whole. For the PT's local leaderships, attached to their identities as activists coming from the popular movements, appealing to the "people" and asking "inhabitants" to participate was a means of bringing politics and citizens closer, of giving proof of their true will to change politics, and of showing that, after all, they had not changed that much.

Although the PT continued to show itself as a "different" party during the 1990s (Keck, 1991), it gradually adopted classical electoral strategies and adjusted to the institutional game. As a consequence, professional opportunities opened for a relatively high number of militants, in the close social circle of each party representative. The reforms of the party organization interacted with upward social mobilities for some of its members.

THE SINUOUS PATHS TO INSTITUTIONALIZATION –
THE PT AND ITS ACTIVISTS IN RECIFE

In Recife, activists' itineraries were profoundly reoriented by the sudden repositioning of their organization within the local party system, after their party won the municipal election for the first time. This victory changed not only the political position of the party but also the professional and social position of its leaders. The identities of activists and the way they viewed the PT changed. At the same time, the party's leaders had to learn how to be professional politicians and to behave as such.

This meant redefining the relationship between the party and the social movement organizations from which its members had originally come, and to which most of them still belonged. For our case study in Recife, our observations of the PT have been based on an analytical distinction between different aspects of the institutionalization process. First, while the PT won majorities, its local and national leaders professionalized and, as a consequence, their relationship with social movements was transformed. Second, this process combined with an increasing distance within the party between the professional elite and its rank-and-file activists, on the one hand, and with a change in the activist *ethos* and party identity, on the other.

Box 11.2 PT members' social positions: climbing the social ladder

Although published research on PT members' social positions since the 1980s is very scarce, a few general characteristics may be drawn. According to a survey applied during the first PT national congress in 1991, Rodriguês stated that "the PT is fundamentally a party of the educated segments of the wage-earning middle classes, with a high proportion of civil servants and workers' leaders" (Rodriguês, 1997: 306), and with a high education level (71 percent at university level, 18 percent at secondary level and only 11 percent at primary level). However, their main characteristic is a generalized tendency of climbing the social ladder. Rocha showed that at the end of the 1990s most PT members "descended from families with low education resources" and were "coming from the lower levels of the social ladder" but showed "a clear tendency of social ascension in relation to their origins." Coming mostly from popular classes, PT members formed two groups with distinct social positions that were represented in almost similar proportions: higher socioprofessional classes (white collars, intellectual professions, artists), on the one hand, the least qualified professions (domestic servants, informal sector workers, industry workers), on the other hand (Rocha, 2007: 74–85).

In a study on the participation of local section delegates in the PT's national congresses since 1990, Amaral confirms this social mobility tendency but he also draws other changes. If delegates have had a stable, high education level since the 1990s with an average of 60 percent at university level, the PT's congress participants went through a pronounced ageing process, as the proportion of delegates of more than 41 years old grew from 32 percent in 1997 to 64.8 percent in 2007. The ratio of delegates who are members of a social movement organization has been stable since 1990 (around 70 percent) but they increasingly professionalize in the political sector, from 40 percent in 1990 to 59 percent in 2007 (Amaral, 2010: 90–99).

For a closer period, a lack of published research on those issues prevents us from bringing this information up to date. Actually, this is a clear symptom of some shortcomings of most of the English-written party research about the social processes and interactions that take shape within those organizations (Amaral & Power, 2016).

To analyze the social components of the PT's institutionalization, three types of life paths have been distinguished, underlining some biographical impacts of commitment as well as the various ways in which individual careers may interact with organizational change. All those itineraries of long-term activism share an early commitment during the youth, an extended period without leadership positions in the party, as well as a long-lasting insertion into local social movement networks. For their analysis, the following information has been taken into account: social position during childhood, types of social environment and groups within which initial political socialization occurred, types of activities through which the first engagement occurred, and the types of activist groups in which people got involved (catholic social action, working class union-ism, students movement, neighborhood movement, etc.), circumstances of the first entry into the party, successive professional and political position occupied during the last 30 years, occupation at the moment of the interview, and position regarding the party at that moment (membership, distance, exit). According to the recurrence of those characteristics, three types of paths have been defined: upward social mobility associated to professionalization out of the political field, political professionalization in the backstage of politics, and professionalization in the local political field. The recurrences in those itineraries shed a light on some of the logics of interactions between individual trajectories and the institutionalization of the party.

Upward Social Mobility

First, some of the long-term rank-and-file members of the PT have followed an upward trajectory since the 1980s. Engagement, in some cases, paralleled the decision to go back to school or complement their education. Several factors may account for it. Within militant groups, political information circulated and there were many opportunities to debate about political issues and interact with authorities. Joining the party helped to reinforce their skills, and motivated them to study or learn new behavioral norms.[3] The life paths that we observed in Recife confirm that for the most strongly committed individuals, opportunities opened up for further education and jobs appeared that gave them social resources to use in the political and professional fields. For example, their organizations sometimes paid for travel from the countryside to the state capital. Or, through jobs they sometimes got in the contentious space, they acquired new professional skills as well as financial conditions for further education. In some cases, they were even given scholarships. More generally, even for the majority who didn't benefit from these direct returns, the insertion into a group of activists initiated a process of acculturation that helped construct new social dispositions.

Currently a journalist, Paula works as a communication coordinator in a solidarity association in the center of Recife. Of very humble origins, she first engaged when she was a young teenager, living in the city of Catende, in the southern part of the State of Pernambuco. As a member of the youth group of the local church, she had contacts with the Catholic social movements and with local PT activists, a party she joined in 1986. At the age of 24, in 1988, she moved to Recife, where she got a job at the documentation center of the Diocese of Olinda and drew a salary from ACR (*Ação Cristão Rural*), a Catholic militant organization. This center was located in the heart of Recife, in a building that hosted several other organizations linked to the Church of the Poor that were active in various sectors such as human rights or housing. According to Paula, her new job in Recife opened new militant, professional, and personal horizons for her. While working in a social movement organization, she acquired new skills, such as writing papers, conducting interviews, and coordinating a group. In 1994, she joined the Catholic University of Pernambuco (UNICAP) in order to study journalism and was granted a fee-exemption by the Diocese. After graduating in 1997, she worked in communication for the Bank Workers' Union of Pernambuco, one of the biggest local branches of the CUT (*Central única dos trabalhadores*). In 2003, she was recruited by an association devoted to rural development. During these years, Paula was a member of the PT and participated in the activities of her local group (*núcleo*), among whose members she met her husband. In her life path, engagement created job opportunities, which in turn gave

---

[3] In the case of the Federal District in Brasilia, Daniella Rocha compared the professions of rank-and-file PT members to those of their parents. According to her survey, most members came from the lower levels of the social pyramid and showed an obvious tendency to upward social mobility (Rocha, 2007: 74–78).

her the chance to resume her university education. At the same time, she dedicated her professional activities to militant action and worked into her forties for social movement organizations. However, at the time of the interview, she was becoming more distant from the social movement field, as her job was less connected with her former mobilizations, as she now kept away from the church, and she expressed doubts about her membership in the PT.

Paula's itinerary is comparable with that of other activists interviewed in Recife. Coming from very humble rural families, they had their first contacts with contentious politics through the local progressive Catholic church, or through local workers' unions. Social interactions in the contentious field led them to resume their schooling or gave them access to professionalizing jobs. In several cases, militants chose to study at university and practiced as qualified professionals in the same sector in which they had participated as activists. At the time of the interviews, they were high or middle-level professionals, such as lawyers, university teachers, journalists, or NGO coordinators. Thus, for rank-and-file activists, commitment brought various types of indirect returns such as acculturation, political skills, access to education, and qualifications.

Political Professionalization in the Backstage

A second path is that of low-level, unelected professionals who work in the political entourage of the PT's leaders. In Pernambuco, the PT had no deputy in the 1980s and it never had more than five federal deputies and five state deputies during the 1990s and 2000s. Although those seats weren't many, winning them made it possible for each deputy to recruit staff, mainly to help with the administration of their legislative mandates (Ribeiro, 2009). Generally chosen among PT members close to each representative and among his long-term fellow comrades, this staff worked on the large variety of jobs necessary in the political backstage, from cabinet heads to office helps. Thus, a new category of PT members emerged in the direct entourage of its elected representatives. For them, the party's social *milieu* not only was a space in which they could mobilize, but also enabled them to make a living and find a professional space in which a career was now possible. Generally, those unelected collaborators managed to get a paid job in the political field because of the professional skills associated to an activist *know-how*, which they had acquired over a long period of mobilization. In interviews, they spoke of their work with a mixture of political conviction and professional logic.

There are various ways in which they may be recruited, but most of the time two paths may be distinguished.

First, a lot of office assistants or cabinet collaborators have personal links with the party leader, such as neighborhood relationships, family links, or early intimacy as grass roots militants. This is the case for Maria, who was the coordinator for Pernambuco of the staff of the Federal Deputy Fernando Ferro, at the time of the interview. She had her first contact with politics at the end of the 1980s when she was a sociology student at UNICAP, the Catholic University of Pernambuco. Although she was interested in politics, she chose to keep her distance from student mobilizations because, as she confesses, she felt reluctant to join any political party as she was afraid of feeling "imprisoned" if she did. She was first politically mobilized in 1986 when she took part in Miguel Arrães' campaign for Governor, as he was heading a left-wing coalition. In 1990 Fernando Ferro, whom she knew because they were neighbors and members of the same neighborhood association, hired her as a cabinet collaborator. Maria joined his staff as a communication professional, without having any previous party involvement. According to Maria, her only motivation was professional and it was only after some time that she decided to become a formal member of the party, in 1994 – in order to "defend our positions" in the local organization, as she explains. In Maria's trajectory toward a job as a collaborator of a local PT leader, there was no prerequisite beyond being a left-wing sympathizer. Having no previous long-term involvement with activist networks, Maria became a political professional by activating the personal links she had with her boss as a neighbor, and because she had specialized skills to offer.

Following another type of path, some skilled collaborators are chosen according to their technical knowledge of a particularly sensitive issue, along with their acquaintances in the social movements of their professional sector. For Victor, who grew up in a very humble family in the rural interior of the state of Pernambuco, education and activist engagement went together. He first encountered politics in 1980, when he was only 16 years old, through Padre Gusmão, a Catholic priest of the liberation theology, when he took part in the activities of the local church's youth group and got in touch with activists who were beginning to organize a local PT branch. In 1983, he left Palmares for Recife in order to study at the ITER (*Instituto de Teologia do Recife*), a Catholic seminar owned by the Diocese of Olinda, well known for its defense of progressive Catholic positions. During his formation as a seminarist,

Victor would study during the week and mobilize with the Rural Pastoral in support of sugar cane workers at the weekends, in the southern part of Pernambuco. In 1986, after he decided to quit his religious vocation, Victor chose to study law in order to "get educated in the area of human rights." For this he received a grant from a Catholic social movement organization, the CPT (*Comissão Pastoral da Terra*), which also hired him as a lawyer working in support of rural communities in the sugar cane regions of Pernambuco, Alagoas, Paraiba, and Rio Grande do Norte. After he graduated in law, in 1988, Victor made use of his specialized professional skills and his know-how as a long-term activist. The combination of those two types of resources enabled him to work for various PT representatives after 1988. From 1993 to 1996, he was a legal advisor specializing in land issues for Jorge Leite, one of the PT's *vereadores* (members of the town council) in Recife. Afterward, he began to work for Humberto Costa and was still collaborating with this federal deputy at the time of the interview. Victor's engagement in the PT is connected to upward social mobility. In his life path, socialization into the social movement field opened up education and job opportunities, thus changing what it meant to be a member of the PT.

In two out of three of these careers, the access to administrative and political jobs within the party *milieu* and in the staff of its elected leaders was a result of double membership in both the PT and in a social movement organization at the same time. This double membership makes the individual familiar with the political issues of a specific sector and with its social networks – two resources that are strategic in a deputy's cabinet. It is this close articulation between party or associative engagement and professional activities that turns activism into a career, a career that was transferred into the field of professional politics when the PT won its first legislative seats in Pernambuco (Fillieule, 2001; Louault, 2006).

Learning to Be a Professional Politician

The third category is composed of a small number of elected professional politicians who won legislative mandates during the 1990s. Their entry into the institutions had several consequences and social meanings: growing political legitimacy, the need to learn how to manage their new positions, and clear and rapid social mobility. According to André Marenco dos Santos, PT local leaders have long-term itineraries of political professionalization that depend more on militant than personal resources

(Santos, 2001). Most PT representatives in Pernambuco professionalized in the political sphere following a lengthy contentious engagement. Their entry into the professional political field was anchored in activist networks that had been formed previously in the social movement space, now an electoral basis. At first, they learned about political action from two positions – the party and the contentious space – but their main engagement took place originally in their professional sector, mostly in unions.

This is the case of Roberto Leandro, a state deputy who won a seat for the first time in 2002. Roberto Leandro first engaged as a student in the public administration department of Pernambuco's Federal University. He was elected a President of the Student Council (*"diretório acadé-mico"*) in 1977, and at the same time was also a member of the clandestine PCR (*Partido comunista revolucionario*). In 1979, he represented his university in the first national congress held for the re-founding of the UNE (*União nacional dos estudantes*) in Salvador. After being hired as a bank worker in 1979 for Bandepe (Pernambuco's state bank), he became a member of the bank workers' union of Pernambuco. During the 1980s, Roberto Leandro acted as a union leader as well as a party activist, first as a member of the PCB (*Partido comunista brasileiro*) then as a member of the PT. In 1991, he was elected a president of the bank workers' union of Pernambuco, a powerful organization affiliated to the CUT (*Central Única dos Trabalhadores*). He experienced his first legislative campaign as a candidate in 1994 and it took no less than two more attempts before he was elected in 2002. In this itinerary, the entry into the political sphere is directly continuous with union activism in the professional sphere, a space where this deputy mobilized support for political action and electoral campaigning.

Some common points may be identified with the path followed by Isaltino Nascimento, another state deputy in Pernambuco. Like Roberto Leandro, Isaltino Nascimento followed the path of an activist for a long time before becoming a professional politician. A president of the social security workers' union of Pernambuco for 14 years (since 1985), as well as a president of his neighborhood association in Casa Amarela, he was also a rank-and-file member of the PT and had no responsibilities during this period. Thus, his main resource was his links with various activist networks. This is why the PT's majority tendency urged him to be a candidate. Because he was asked by the PT's dominating tendency, Isaltino Nascimento agreed to be a candidate, in spite of his having little experience of party games and although he had very limited education.

After the PT launched his campaign, he was first elected to the Municipal Chamber of Recife in 2000, and to the state Legislative Assembly two years later. In an interview, he recalled straighforwardly how intense it had been for him to discover politics in parliament, the rituals of assembly life and the expected behavior of professional politicians: "I was shocked, because my trajectory was that of a union activist." In the assembly, he had to learn "the parliament ballet, all this dramatization, this construction," he had "to become more mature." He recalled that his entry into professional politics affected his social position, and also required him to learn how to behave according to rules that were specific to the professional group he was now part of. For this former employee and unionist, learning to be a politician meant discovering how to control "the behavior of the language," how "to be cautious when criticizing," how to listen, how to talk pleasantly with his adversaries, and how to negotiate in the corridors: "in Parliament, you have to chat individually, in person; you have to construct." He remembers "learning with the elders, conversing with the elders, even with those on the right" who taught him indirectly how to behave in the parliament space.

The professionalization of those two deputies in the political field was directly continuous with their former commitment as union leaders, when they acquired political skills and resources that they were able to mobilize afterward for political action. The process of incorporating the informal rules of parliamentary life is part of the PT's institutionalization, as its representatives adopted the norms and practices of professional politics and learned to comply with the routines of these institutions. As a consequence, the PT was increasingly populated by individuals whose professional career and social ascent depended on their position in the party organization. For a large number of local PT leaders, this upward mobility was based on resources that emerged through party work; resources such as political skills, activist know-how, social networks, and the resources of increasing power and incomes. In return, this process interacted not only with the obvious changes in the organization's position in the party system but also with its identity and with the everyday behavior of activists.

FACING PARTY CHANGE: LOYALTIES AND DISENCHANTMENTS

In the 2000s, the way rank-and-file PT members looked at their party emphasized changes in various aspects such as the growing gap between party leaders and base members, the electoralist turn, or the weakening of the contentious spirit. Most of them, blaming the PT nowadays, remembered past struggles with an evident disapproval of their fading, also showing an unconfessed feeling of nostalgia. Today's professionalized party is opposed, in their memories, to the PT of the 1980s, "a leftwing party, able to protest," as one of the interviewees puts it. However, activists' assessments of the fading of struggles are not homogeneous. They vary according to the path they followed until today and according to their current position, in relation to their party, but also to the political field in a larger way; a position that affects both the evaluation of current strategies and the components of their memory. In this regard, views on party change are rather coherent with the types of trajectories that have been analyzed here, with a distinction between professional politicians, their collaborators, loyal rank-and-file party members, and disengaged activists.

In a general manner, PT mandate holders and the members of their staff tend to describe their contentious past as a component of today's identities, both of individual activists and of the party itself. For them, the point is never to denounce the decrease of struggles. They rather remember them as learning episodes, and as the steps toward today's skillful and professionalized practices. "It is a learning process," as Roberto Leandro puts it. This view of past struggles is mainly that of individuals whose trajectories went from contention to the practice of power, which generally meant that they professionalized in the political field while experiencing upward social mobility. Instead of showing nostalgia about past contentious practices, they value institutionalized political action, the capacity to negotiate and to search for compromise, like Isaltino in the previous quotations where he presents today's behaviors as the results of a "construction."

On the contrary, long-term, base activists tend to dispraise present behaviors and to oppose them to a heroic past made of real struggles. Among our interviewees, those who remained loyal and those who decided to quit share a deep disapproval of today's party practices and reject the growing distance between the rank-and-file and party leaders within the organization. Activists who express regrets about the fading of struggles are those who engaged at the moment of the formation of the PT, who never became professional politicians, but are still present in the party social space, for example through their professional activities; as in the case of Paula. Today, as one of the interviewees put it, for individual party leaders "what is dominating is the perspective of getting a power

share." Here, a former period of genuine struggles in the opposition is
compared to the current position of the party at the head of public
administrations. It is now described as a machine, conceived for winning
elections and as one that got rid of the troublesome weight of "socialism."
In the PT depicted here, individual strategies and personal political careers
prevail: "it is not a struggle strategy anymore, it is not socialism anymore.
It is a competition for power, for electors, for government. Now, what
dominates is: 'my space, my power, my seat, my salary' . . .," as Daniel, a
long-term rank-and-file activist, puts it. The PT lost its identity as a left-
wing party, because it now acts "within the system" and "nobody debates
on the issue of socialism anymore." According to Daniel, reading the
Capital was replaced by debates on city budgets: "now, the issue is:
participative budget and all those affirmative politics. But it takes the
fighting spirit away."

The rank-and-file militants we interviewed oppose the collective
memory of past mobilizations and the current position of their party,
with intense questioning about the changes in the meaning of commitment and about the redefinitions of the PT's identity. For those who
have been socialized to politics in a period of opposition and contention,
remembering past struggles is a way of legitimating present action, a way
of cementing the group through its memory, and of keeping the contentious component of its identity alive. During the 2000s, the PT and the
social movement organizations that had accompanied its struggles since
the 1980s gradually broke up. Since 2003, some unions, associations, and
political figures on the left of the PT have clearly expressed their discordance with the politics of Lula's government in Brasilia, as well as with the
PT's new discourse, which some consider as a renunciation or a betrayal.[4]
Alongside with public critics, PT has faced disenchantments, individual
disengagement, and silent exits. It had the effect of limiting the intensity
and frequency of activists' circulations and, thus, it reduced the party's
local space. Historical PT militants still like to activate the old identity tale
of the party, which is now reinforced with other tales, that refer to the
participative administration of cities, to "the PT's way of governing," to
competence, efficiency and good governance, or to social policies for the
deprived. While the party organization was consolidating, the identity
tales produced by its members diversified (Hastings, 2001). Today, the

---

[4] See, for example, the *Letter to President Lula* (*Carta ao Presidente Lula*) published in the
media by a collective of famous left-wing figures on May 1, 2004. Then available on the
website of the Landless Rural Workers' Movement, www.mst.org.br.

memory of the heroic contentious past of a "different" party[5] obviously contradicts the disparaging look at the "normal" organization that has taken shape since the 2000s. The disillusioned words of long-term activists express the feeling that their party turned similar to others and that, with the loss of transparency and probity, it also lost its exceptional characteristics. For people that mobilized during years of uncompromising opposition, institutionalization and the practice of local and national power mean much more than an *aggiornamento* or a mere "adaptation" to reality (Hunter, 2010). It implies a redefinition of political engagement, in its social meanings.

CONCLUSION

The case of PT activists in Recife leads us to revisit some of the questioning proposed by Doug McAdam on the biographical impacts of long-term engagement. The biographies selected here confirm that "the consequences of this process may be life-long or at least long-term" and have a "strong enduring impact" (McAdam, 1989: 758, 753). However confirmed, this impact may vary. When, in Recife, PT militants had a tendency of climbing the social ladder – a tendency that was supported by their commitment – Freedom Summer's activists seem more unstable in their social, professional, and private lives than those who didn't participate. As in the cases analyzed by McAdam, high-risk commitment in Recife brought radical re-socialization processes, which in turn consolidated commitment, for example when professional careers took place within the social movement space. However, in Recife, if the access to jobs was largely defined by activism, there is no evidence that the professional lives of PT activists were less stable than those of uncommitted people of the same social background. On the contrary, some biographies show that activism may have brought opportunities for skill acquisition as well as access to qualified or highly qualified jobs, thus leading to employment situations that were much more stable than in the original social background of those activists.

In this book, Pagis' research confirms that the more intensely people engage, the more chances they have to remain activists in the following years. Trajectories within the PT show additional elements. In those cases,

---

[5] For an example, see the website of Perseu Abramo's Foundation, the PT's cultural foundation in São-Paulo, www.fpa.org.br.

intense engagement was not only long lasting but was also linked to upward social mobility. However, after 30 years, it is only those who professionalized in the political sphere that continued to be active in the PT. Others were either disengaged or had converted the skills they had acquired through activism into other kinds of activities, in various professional sectors such as development NGOs, education, or law. How long may the impacts of engagement be observed? What is the probable duration of its resonances in the lives of activists? This notion, which is proposed by Olivier and Tamayo in their chapter, suggests that, even if biographical impacts of engagement may be strong, they diminish with time; thus after 30 years, it may be uncertain to seize them distinctly, especially because other unidentified factors may have also decisive impacts on peoples' biographies. In the case of PT activists, biographical impacts of commitment may not have been caused only by initial risks (McAdam, 1988) but also by the confluence of the transformations of the party organization and of the political environment, on the one side, and of individual life courses, on the other side – which is related to endless debates on the respective weight of structural factors and agency, indeed. For this reason, in activists' biographies, long-term impacts of high-risk events, which would coincide with the entry in the contentious space, are hardly identifiable. Rather, various processes intertwine, in different life spheres: social logics (mobility), private logics (marriage, children), professional logics (education, skill acquisition, changes in positions), and logics specific to the political sphere (professionalization, disengagement).

So, what were the consequences of engagement for rank-and-file PT activists in Northeastern Brazil? In the long run, their biographies are composed of the sedimentation of identities as well as of sinuous social position changes, with ruptures and bifurcations. As biographies are not linear, today's observable behaviors, positions, or identities can't be explained with absolute certainty by yesterdays' commitment, by the risks people took, by the paths they followed at that time. But, for sure, identities and memories, either in their political or in their private side, include imprints of the committed past. In the narration of those moments, most interviewees remember not only defending a noble cause and taking risks but also getting out of their social background of origin, discovering other social and political horizons, constructing identities, as well as learning skills and behaviors within activist circles. Those ruptures launched long-term processes and opened paths that make engagement and party socialization decisive – but without linearity – for understanding their positions decades after.

Field research in Recife showed that the institutionalization of the PT was composed of the mixture of gradual transformations of political positions of the party, of its members' social identities, of the skills of its leaders, of their individual interests and professional careers. The insertion of the PT in existing institutions interacted with individual trajectories, and both produced changes at different levels such as the party system, the orientation given to public policies at the national and local level, the social roots of the party, its image within the electorate but also among its members, or the way collective action is organized within the party. It was translated into a reconfiguration of activist practices as well as into a bifurcation of activist trajectories, that split between distance and professionalization, between exit and loyalty. Since the beginning of the 2000s, being a member of the PT has turned out to be less demanding, since activists are more distanced and intermittent than they used to be, because they often express doubts, and act at the side of professionalized party leaderships. Between militant fatigue and questionings, on the one hand, and the career expectations of the loyalists, on the other hand, the transformations of the PT have various facets.

Analyzing long-term impacts of engagement also gives some clues about institutionalization processes. For a contentious movement, institutionalizing is not an "adaptation" or a mere change in strategies (Hunter, 2010), nor does it simply mean shifting from the social movement space to institutional action (Goldstone, 2003), or renouncing, even if disenchanted activists regret the fading of past struggles. Activist trajectories show that this process involves a long but transitory period during which the social movement space intertwines with the spaces of the party and of local public administrations, but also a period during which a progressive distance slowly appears. As time passes by, this distance deepens, following the changes in the political and social positions of activists, the learning of new behaviors and strategies by those who entered the political field, and also the progressive redefinitions of their preferences in relation to public action.

The focus on militant itineraries shows that, in representative democracies, the frontiers between party politics and contentious politics may be either fluid and blurred or clear and distinct, according to the political environment and its transformations, and according to the changes in the position of the organizations. Jack Goldstone showed the "complementarity of protest and conventional political action" and argued that when social movements chose institutional strategies, "their repertoire of collective action did not shift from protest to politics; rather, it expanded to include both" (Goldstone, 2003: 7). The case of the Brazilian PT tends to confirm this analysis. However, the focus on individual trajectories at the local level enables us to go beyond this approach. First, it shows that those complementarities are not only strategic but also depend on the way a party is rooted in its local society. If complementarity and alliances between organizations exist at the macro-level, they rest on specific micro-level configurations, when individuals have multiple memberships and circulate between different spaces, as the itineraries analyzed here tend to show. Second, the case of the PT also shows that if party networks are intertwined with other social networks (associations, public administrations) this configuration may be unstable and reversible. After a few years in office, party networks may detach from social movement networks.

In the case of the PT, when the party was created, activists circulated mostly within the social movement space and they were located in opposition to the regime without any ambiguity, first as illegal groups then as a minority. With the institutionalization process, the contentious space and the power sphere straddled for many years, and the party activist networks penetrated public administrations at all levels. Those networks included actors of very different status and nature: representatives, unionists, members of neighborhood associations, social workers, municipal, state and federal agents, etc. (Tatagiba & Dagnino, 2010) Today, more often than not, those actors occupy multiple and unstable locations; they circulate and change status. However, activist biographies show that straddling positions may be temporary and specific to the process of institutionalization. At the leadership level, nowadays, the link between the party and social movement organizations has turned rather instrumental, strategic, and electoral. If this relationship may exist as a negotiated alliance between former comrades, it may often be used as a basis for informal political exchanges between local PT leaders in office and deprived electors; and they also take the shape of conflicts between contentious groups and governmental authorities. This opposition between an institutionalized party and social movement groups is reflected in the growing distance between, on the one side, professionalized party leaders who now act within institutional frames and, on the other side, most rank-and-file party members who are still mutipositioned activists.

Addendum

Life History as a Tool for Sociological Inquiry

Olivier Fillieule

We are safe in saying that personal life-records, as complete as possible, constitute the perfect type of sociological material, and that if social science has to use other materials at all it is only because of the practical difficulty of obtaining at the moment a sufficient number of such records to cover the totality of sociological problems.

Thomas and Znaniecki, 1918–1920: 6.

Life history interviews are popular in sociological analysis. There are a number of methods for analyzing biographies, corresponding to the range of social sciences. These include linguistic, historical, psychoanalytic, psycho-cognitive, etc. approaches. In sociology, biography as material established its pedigree with *The Polish Peasant in Europe and America* by Thomas and Znaniecki (1918–1920), *The Hobo* (Anderson, 1923), *The Children of Sanchez* by Oscar Lewis (1961) and, of course, the work of culturalist anthropologists in the wake of the pioneering research of Franz Boas.

In the interactionist sociology of the Second Chicago School, one of the foundational texts is Howard Becker's preface to *The Jack Roller* by Clifford Shaw (1966), in which he proposes a systematic reflection on the role of life history in contemporary sociology: "To understand why someone behaves as he does you must understand how it looked to him, what he thought he had to contend with, what alternatives he saw open to him; you can only understand the effects of opportunity structures, delinquent subcultures, social norms, and other commonly invoked explanations of behavior by seeing them from the actor's point of view." (Becker, 1966: V–VI).

After a prolonged period of slumber, it was in the 1980s that life history returned to the scene, notably with the Association Internationale de Sociologie's creation in 1984 of the research committee *Biography and Society*, at the initiative of Daniel Bertaux (1984).

From our structural interactionist perspective, the components of which are detailed in the Introduction to this book, the collection of biographical data in itself is not sufficient to understand how individual life course or collective paths (family lineages, groups, and cohorts) are related not to individual psychological traits, but to sociohistorical processes, including values and beliefs, as well as to socially identifiable standards and rules, and how, conversely, these processes may be understood from the analysis of their expressions at the individual level of life course. More precisely, the singularity of biographical material rests on three elements.

First, far from opposing so-called objective "social facts" and supposedly subjective "social significance" (what Max Weber calls *subjective meaning*), interactionist approaches endeavor to consider them together. In other words, life history is based on a particular epistemology which considers that "neither the life of an individual nor the history of a society can be understood without understanding both" (Wright Mills, 1959: 3): The social existence of individuals is seen as a process and the history of societies and that of individuals are treated as interdependent (Elias, 1991). Then, life history obliges us to reason, while always taking into account the unfolding of observed processes. These include the temporality of life span, contexts, and scenes of interaction. "The dimension of temporality is certainly the first principle of intelligibility" of a biography (Coninck & Godard, 1989:24). Finally, biographical material compels us to explore the multiplicity of configurations in which individuals are successively or simultaneously stakeholders, that is, the multiplicity of life spheres (including work, family, social activities, activism, etc.) which, as we have shown in the Introduction, are interdependent.

The sociological literature offers a magnificent, although incomplete, example of the added value of life history, that of *Mozart: The Sociology of a Genius* by Elias (2010). He constructed a sociological analysis of Mozart's biography in first studying the configuration of royal courts at the time and, on another level, the process of transformation of artists from the position of servants to that of independent creators, in a new art market, a process related to the *Civilisation Process* that he had also studied (1969–1982). In addition, he showed, especially based on Mozart's correspondence, how the artist is caught in a conflict of norms, which takes account of his twofold social revolt (against his subordinate status as a domestic, and within the family, against his father), leading him to break with protectors and his father to make himself an independent artist. In this work, Mozart's biography is considered by Elias to present an ideal perspective from which to observe a particular situation, allowing for a clear view of social constraints weighing on the musician during his life; an understanding of the way in which he comported himself with respect to these constraints (sometimes accepting them, sometimes refusing them); and the development of a theoretical model of the configuration of an individual's social existence. As the sociologist Bernard Lahire stresses, from a perspective inspired by this Elasian thought, "Understanding one case, is understanding how the social world is reflected in it and absorbed, little by little. ... To understand how the social world is embodied in one individual, one must have knowledge of the social on the whole and be familiar with the structural components of his or her family, academic, emotional, professional, religious life and so on and so forth" (Lahire, 2010: 71).

Staying with European sociologists, other research strongly suggests how the combination of a subtle mapping of institutions, fields, and cultures, combined with a deep-investigation of one's individual resources, background and, trajectories may be illuminating. Anna Boschetti's work on *"Sartre et les Temps Modernes"* (1985) faces the challenge of making sense of Jean-Paul Sartre's extraordinary status as the embodiment of The French Intellectual, deconstructing his myth. Far from being just a biography or monograph, this research gives keys to understand the disappearance of the character of the French Intellectual, to highlight from an individual case the structural changes in the fields of cultural production. Sartre could have been a living myth and symbolic authority, as he was able to combine resources in the political space, as a philosopher respected by his peers but also as a major novelist and playwright. Such multi-positioning would be unreachable, even for a "genius," in a world in which the social spaces of politics, art, and academia are from now on much more autonomous and disconnected. Even if it supplies more a sketch than a fully developed analysis, Bourdieu's unachieved *Manet* (2013) also weaves the microscopic exploration of individual dispositions and the meso and macro social dimensions of structural changes. Manet reaches consecration while the painters' activities are deeply changed by the move from the closed structures of schools, *academies*, and *salons* exhibitions – that Bourdieu compares to the disciplinary organization of the church in Weber's sociology of religion – to the more open and competitive dimension of a field, itself connected to an expanding art market. But if Manet is a "revolutionary" in art, he is not the passive agent or mirror of structural changes. His specific dispositions, linked to his socialization, explain his production; his paintings are produced by *"an habitus working in a field."* He is typical of a cleaved habitus: Coming from a wealthy family, he has however embodied many habits of a "Bohemian." Like Flaubert in literature, he is rich enough to make the risky choice of searching success by challenging the established authorities of the ruling *"pompier"* school. He re-visits the most classical patterns of pictures (nude paintings, the *"déjeuner sur l'herbe"*) in heretic style.

As with any social science material, a life history contains difficulties and raises questions about epistemology and methodology, giving rise to a vast literature. Without proposing here a review, which could easily become a massive undertaking since the methods of collection and treatment may vary from one author to another and from one sociological tradition to another,[1] we will simply discuss the obstacles faced by our structuralist and interactionist perspective, more precisely, in the context of a sociology of activism.

The sociology of activism from an interactionist perspective is quite demanding. It is the difficulty in meeting them that constitutes the initial obstacle to its satisfactory achievement. An optimal career analysis would involve observing, from adolescence (indeed childhood), all the stages that lead activists to become interested in political action, to become committed and then, if applicable, to defect, but also to reestablish how this political trajectory unfolds in different dimensions of social life that could affect activism – thus, in parallel, to reestablish the dynamic of professional, friendship, family, romantic, sexual, etc. trajectories over a shorter or longer period (potentially: a life ...). As relations of sociability give meaning to experiences and play an essential role in the construction of individual and collective identities, one must also reestablish the dynamic of these social environments and not only through retrospective interviews. This is why observation *in situ* of relations of sociability within organizations or collectives would be necessary to understand how they contribute to the perennial attachment of activists. Merely

---

[1] The sociological analysis of biographies can be constructed starting with a single case, with a small sample of interviews, with a larger sample of retrospective interviews, with a panel of questionnaires or with repeated interviews (panel studies). Each of these approaches has advantages, biases, and limitations.

setting out the possibility of such a program reveals how largely unrealistic it is. The research protocol to be deployed is hard to imagine: certainly, if there were infinite financial resources, one could have a research team dedicated exclusively to continuous observation and the conducting of repeated interviews with a panel of activists, while examining their entire social lives. Yet such a perspective today seems out of the question. In most cases, research must bear on a bygone past. This necessarily means working with retrospective interviews, reconstructions *a posteriori* of experiences, all while endeavoring through various methods of historical analysis to reconstitute local contexts in which the activists were present, including the organizational stage, step by step.

By definition, all knowledge of the past is "a result of only partial reconstruction" (Langlois & Seignobos, 1993 [1898]: 65) and this also applies to oral sources. However, should one conclude that they are, thus, useless and misleading? We do not believe so. Indeed, life history interviews allow for the collection of three broad categories of data, each of which poses specific questions: *event history*, their dates, their duration, and the manner in which they occurred; the measure of where individuals were in this at a particular moment of their life journeys (which brings us back to the accumulation of experiences, for example, the number of children, the years of study or professional experience); and, finally, individuals' subjective evaluation of their life experience. As Florence Descamps writes, "all historians and all oral archivists agree, oral testimony cannot precisely re-establish a chronology or reliably date an event ... On the other hand, oral sources are capable of proposing a diachrony, that is a succession of events as they are experienced over time ..." (Descamps, 2001: 507). Of course, this does not amount to a denial of the phenomena of forgetting and of lying but allows us to stress the validity and reliability of this type of source *nonetheless*.

This is even more the case in that, from the interactionist perspective, the identification of turning points in a life journey cannot be merely a search for historical truth but is rather an attempt to reconstitute a sequential and incremental subjective and objective logic. Turning points do not always correspond to precise moments and may, depending on the temporalities, reach into different spheres of life. In this sense, if the analysis of a career does not allow for the reconstruction *a posteriori* of the perception of the activist experience by its actors, at least it offers the possibility of grasping another dimension, imperceptible at the time: the more long-term *incentives* and the inflexions whose meaning is not immediately apparent but which produce lasting effects. To take only one example, the biographical impact of activism is impossible to measure immediately since it only occurs over the long term. As Abbott (2009, 2011) suggested, certain concepts are narrative in as much as they can only be operationalized *a posteriori*. The succession of career phases and certain effects of activist practice can only, for example, be observed much after the operative event has occurred. Finally, it is only at the end of the *a posteriori* biography that one can evaluate their effects.

If we return to subjective evaluations and their usefulness for the contemporary sociologist or historian, there is always a risk in retrospectively assigning meaning to a series of events selected by the person being questioned. "Each person's account of his life," writes Anselm Strauss, "as he writes or thinks about it, is a symbolic ordering of events. The sense that you make of your own life rests upon what concepts, what interpretations, you bring to bear upon the multitudinous and disorderly crowd of past acts. If your interpretations are convincing to yourself, if you trust your terminology, then there is some kind of continuous meaning assigned to your life as a whole." (Strauss, 1959: 145) And because this is a sure sign of "the palpitating flesh of life" (Passeron, 1980: 5), the life story has an unequalled power of suggestion and fascination. It seems obvious, it appears immediately intelligible, at the risk of abandoning any other critical interrogation on the pertinence of the story and its exemplary nature. A number of scholars (e.g. Schwartz & Sudman, 1994) have shown how subjective evaluations are dependent on the manner in which individuals perceive change or permanence. More precisely, Denis Peschanski (1992) suggested how the process of reconstruction operates through successive strata, filtering, and elimination and reconstructs individual and collective memory, pointing out phenomena such as *extrapolation* (which leads to generalizing about an individual experience), subjective *hierarchization* of facts as a function of experience and of the present situation, and finally, *teleologism*, that is the reconstruction of facts and behavior as a function of what the actor has seen or become later, producing anachronisms and false determinisms. To these limitations, we may also add, with Descamps (2001), the *address effect* (the testimony is provoked and therefore is also a product of the interaction with the interviewer), *recognition effect* (the witness wants his or her role to be recognized), and the *transmission effect*.

However, there are ways to improve the quality of the least reliable data, which this book's authors utilize: on one hand, drawing upon contemporary data on past events (which all the authors do) and, on the other, collective biography (which Pagis and Corrigall-Brown employ). We will end with these two tracks of career analysis.

The first point comes back to the distinction introduced by Bertaux and Kohli (1984) between *life story* and *life history*, which means that in retrospective interviews one may correlate data collected elsewhere, in line with the seminal work of James in his classic *Varieties of Religious Experience* (1902) or of Thomas and Znaniecki (1918–1920/1998). It is in light of a profound knowledge of economic, social, and activist configurations of their respective terrains that the authors of this volume select (amongst the groups investigated) and analyze the biographical material presented.

The second point comes back to the pitfalls of the singular narrative, that is, the illusion of a complete history grasped through a single life history, which Bourdieu (1986) called the biographical illusion. Thus, it is vital to systematically note once again the singularity of trajectories observed qualitatively in a larger mapping of possible itineraries. The famous metaphor of the metro plan, inspired to Bourdieu (1986) by that of Schumpeter's bus, is a good illustration of this: Before being able to describe individual passengers' trajectories, one must have a clear picture of the network structure, of its lines and possible connections. One must think structures and interactions. The objective is not to accumulate single cases, studied intensively, but to construct from them a structural array of possible itineraries, and to measure the frequency of paths taken by these social voyagers who are political activists. On a very different issue, Muriel Darmon (2009) suggests the analytical power of these combined approaches when she studies young anorexic women, mapping the different stages of an "anorexic career," showing how each new stage opens a new space of possible, the need for new strategies to manage friends, parents, and physicians. But, going beyond Becker's analysis of career, and borrowing then from Bourdieu, she questions the unequal probabilities of experiencing anorexia depending on one's social background. She suggests that paying attention to social differences reveals profiles (female, families with cultural capital, ambitions of over-achievement at school) generating a higher disposition to the anorexic experience and very different resources in the ability to manage a lasting commitment in food rejection.

Thus, a career analysis could be based on a strategy of qualitative investigation, through exploring in depth a certain number of significant cases, even, *in fine*, in only presenting one or two considered exemplary in the written restitution of the research, or based on a quantitative approach to resituate each case in the context of possible journeys (which prosopographic analyses or sequential analyses *via* optimal matching allow), or by combining them, employing a quali/quanti approach. This later strategy was recently applied successfully in the framework of a research project on the personal consequences of activism for French '68ers (Fillieule & Sommier, 2018; Fillieule et al., 2018).

The studies presented in this volume, whichever approach they take, all hinge on narratives in the context of which they also refer to the characteristics of the people interviewed, thus allowing us to see, beyond the singularity of individual journeys, some patterns. Furthermore, the very confrontation of such different undertakings as those analyzed here allows us to come closer to an overall understanding of the activist phenomenon, with its differences and similarities. As Becker (1966) stressed, with regards to monographs by the Chicago School, it is the mosaic of cases studied and the placing of them in perspective that allows for the comprehension of multiple facets of a phenomenon, in his case of deviance and, for us, the logic of activism.

References

Abbott, A. 1999. *Department and Discipline: Chicago Sociology at One Hundred*. Chicago: Chicago University Press.

—— 2009. "À propos du concept de Turning Point". In *Bifurcations, Les sciences sociales face aux ruptures et à l'événement*, edited by Grossetti, M., Bessin, M. and Bidart, C. Paris: La Découverte.

—— 2011. "Time matters. Traduction de l'épilogue par Claire Lemercier et Carine Ollivier". *Terrains & Travaux* 19(2): 183–203.

Adam, A. 1969. "Chronique sociale et culturelle". *Annuaire de l'Afrique du Nord* (8): 472–484.

—— 1971. "Chronique sociale et culturelle. Maroc 1970". *Annuaire de l'Afrique du Nord* (10): 366–379.

—— 1976. "Chronique sociale et culturelle Maroc". *Annuaire de l'Afrique du Nord* (15): 579–589.

Adam, A. and Granai, G. 1962. "Chronique sociale et culturelle Algérie, Maroc & Tunisie", *Annuaire de l'Afrique du Nord* (1): 516–526.

Agrikoliansky, É. 2001. "Carrières militantes et vocation à la morale : les militants de la LDH dans les années 1980". *Revue française de science politique* 51 (1): 27–46.

Alison, M. H. 2009. *Women and Political Violence: Female Combatants in Ethno-National Conflict*. Milton Park: Routledge.

Amaral, O. 2010. As transformações na organização interna do partido dos trabalhadores entre 1995 e 1989. PhD, University of Campinas.

Amaral, O. and Power, T. 2016. "The PT at 35: Revisiting Scholarly Interpretations of the Brazilian Worker's Party". *Journal of Latin American Studies* 48: 147–171.

Andersen, E. A. and Jennings, M. K. 2010. "Exploring Multi-Issue Activism". *Political Science and Politics* 43: 62–67.

Anderson, N. 1923. *The Hobo: The Sociology of the Homeless Man*. Chicago: The University of Chicago Press.

Andrews, M. 1991. *Lifetimes of Commitment: Aging, Politics, Psychology*. Cambridge: Cambridge University Press.

Artières, P. and Zancarini-Fournel, M. 2008. *68 Une histoire collective (1962–1981)*. Paris: La Découverte.

Audier, S. 2008. *La pensée anti-'68*. Paris: La découverte.

Audrain, X. 2004. "Devenir baay-fall pour être soi: le religieux comme vecteur d'émancipation individuelle au Sénégal". *Politique africaine* 94: 149–165.

Auld, J., Gormally, B., McEvoy, K. and Ritchie, M. 1997. *Designing a System of Restorative Justice in Northern Ireland*. Belfast: The Authors.

Auyero, J. 2003. *Contentious Lives: Two Argentine Women, Two Protests, and the Quest for Recognition*. Durham, NC: Duke University Press.

Banaznak, L. A. 2010. *The Women's Movement Inside and Outside the State*. Cambridge: Cambridge University Press.

Bargel, L. 2009. "Socialisation Politique". In *Dictionnaire des mouvements sociaux*, edited by Fillieule, O., Mathieu, L. and Péchu, C. Paris: Les Presses de Sciences-Po, 510–517.

Barley, S. R. 1989. "Careers, Identities, and Institutions: The Legacy of the Chicago School of Sociology". In *Handbook of Career Theory*, edited by Michael, A. B., Hall, D. T. and Lawrence, B. S. Cambridge: Cambridge University Press, 41–65.

Baylis, T. A. 1996. "Presidents versus Prime Ministers: Shaping Executive Authority in Eastern Europe". *World Politics* 48(3): 297–323.

Bazin, A. 2002. Les relations tchéco-allemandes depuis 1989. De la réconciliation bilatérale à l'intégration européenne. PhD Political Science, Institut d'Etudes Politiques, Paris.

Bean, K. 2007. *The New Politics of Sinn Fein*. Liverpool: Liverpool University Press.

2012. "'New Dissidents Are but Old Provisionals Writ Large'? The Dynamics of Dissident Republicanism in the New Northern Treland". *The Political Quaterly* 83: 210–218.

Bechir, A. M. 2009. *S'engager en régime autoritaire: gauchistes et islamistes dans la Tunisie indépendante*. PhD Aix-Marseille III.

Becker, H. 1960 "Notes on the Concept of Commitment". *American Journal of Sociology* 66 (1): 32–40.

1963.*Outsiders, Studies in the Sociology of Deviance*. New York: The Free Press.

1966. *A Delinquent Boy's Own Story*, foreword to Shaw, C. The Jack Roller. Chicago: Chicago University Press.

1970. "The Relevance of Life Histories". In *Sociological Methods: A Source Book*, edited by Denzin, N. K. Chicago: Aldine, 419–428.

Beckett, M., Weinstein M., Goldman N. and Yu-Hsuan, L. 2000. "Do Health Interview Surveys Yield Reliable Data on Chronic Illness among Older Respondents?" *American Journal of Epidemiology* 151L: 315–323.

Beckwith, K. 2016. "All Is Not Lost: The 1984–1985 British Miner's Strike and Mobilization after Defeat". In *The Consequences of Social Movements*, edited by Bosi, L., Giugni, M. and Uba, K. Cambridge: Cambridge University Press, 41–65.

Bennani-Chraïbi, M. 2003. "Parcours, cercles et médiations à Casablanca". In *Résistances et protestations dans les sociétés musulmanes*, edited by Bennani-Chraïbi, M. and Fillieule, O. Paris: Presses de Science Po.

2013. "L'espace partisan marocain: un microcosme polarisé?" *Revue française de science politique* 63(6): 1163–1192.

Bennani-Chraibi, M. and Fillieule, O. (eds.). 2003. *Résistances et protestations dans les sociétés musulmanes*. Paris: Presses de Sciences Po.

2012. "Towards a Sociology of Revolutionary Situations: Reflections on the Arab Uprisings". *Revue Française de Science Politique English* 62(5–6): 767–796.

Bennani-Chraïbi, M. and Jeghllaly, M. 2012. "La dynamique protestataire du Mouvement du 20 février à Casablanca". *Revue française de science politique* 62(5–6): 867–894.

Bennett, M. 1981. *The Survival of a Counterculture; Ideological Work and Everyday Life among Rural Communards*. Berkeley: University of California Press.

Berger, P. L. and Luckmann, T. 1966. *The Social Construction of Reality: A Treatise in the Sociology of Knowledge*. New York: Anchor Books.

Bermeo, N. 1997. "Myths of Moderation: Confrontation and Conflict during Democratic Transitions". *Comparative Politics* 29(3): 305–322.

Bertaux, D. (ed.). 1981. *Biography and Society: The Life History Approach in the Social Sciences*. London: Sage.

Bertaux, D. and Kohli, M. 1984. "The Life Story Approach: A Continental View". *Annual Review of Sociology* 10: 215–237.

Bessière, C. 2004. "Les 'arrangements de famille': équité et transmission d'une exploitation familiale viticole". *Sociétés contemporaines* 4(56): 69–89.

Beyerlein, K. and Hipp, J. R. 2006. "A Two-Stage Model for a Two-Stage Process: How Biographical Availability Matters for Social Movement Mobilization". *Mobilization* 11(3): 299–320.

Bjørgo, T. and Horgan, J. (eds.). 2009. *Leaving Terrorism Behind: Individual and Collective Disengagement*. London and New York: Routledge.

Blee, K. M. 2008. *Women of the Klan: Racism and Gender in the 1920s, with a New Preface*. San Francisco: University of California Press.

Bolos, S. 1999. *La constitución de actores sociales y la política*. Mexico: Plaza y Valdés.

Boltanski, L. and Chiapello, E. 1999. *Le Nouvel Esprit du Capitalisme*. Paris: Gallimard. English Trans. 2018. The New Spirit of Capitalism, London: Pluto.

Bolton, J. 2012. *Worlds of Dissent: Charter 77, The Plastic People of the Universe, and Czech Culture under Communism*. Cambridge, MA: Harvard University Press.

Boschetti, A. 1985. *Sartre et Les temps modernes : Une entreprise intellectuelle*. Paris: Minuit.

Bosi, L. 2006. "The Dynamic of Social Movement Development: Northern Ireland's Civil Rights Movement in the 1960s". *Mobilization* 11 (1): 81–100.

2011. "Movimenti e cambiamento sociale: l'interrelazione delle conseguenze". *Società degli Individui* 42 (3): 69–78.

2012. "Explaining Pathways to armed Activism in the Provisional IRA, 1969–1972". *Social Science History* 36 (3): 347–390.

2013. "Safe Territories and Political Violence: The Persistence and Disengagement of Violent Political Organizations". *Nationalism and Ethnic Politics* 19 (1): 80–101.

2016. "Incorporation and Democratization: The Long Term Process of Institutionalization of the Northern Ireland Civil Rights Movement". In *The Consequences of Social Movements: People, Policies and Institutions*, edited by Bosi L., Giugni M., and Uba K. Cambridge: Cambridge University Press.

Bosi, L. and Della Porta, D. 2012. "Micro-Mobilization Into Armed Groups: The Ideological, Instrumental and Solidaristic Paths". *Qualitative Sociology* 35: 361–383.

2015. "Patterns of Disengagement from Political Armed Activism: A Comparative Historical Sociology Analysis of Italy and Northern Ireland". In *Researching Terrorism, Peace and Conflict Studies: Interaction, Synthesis and Opposition*, edited by Tellidis, I. and Toros, H. Abingdon: Routledge, 81–99.

Bosi, L. and Giugni, M. 2012. "Political Violence Outcomes: A Contentious Politics Approach". *Mobilization* 18(1): 85–98.

Bosi, L. and O'Dochartaigh, N. 2017. "Armed Activism as the Enactment of a Collective Identity: The Case of the Provisional IRA 1969–1972". *Social Movement Studies* 17(1): 35–47.

Bosi, L. and Uba, K. 2009. "Introduction: The Outcomes of Social Movements". *Mobilization* 14(4): 409–415.

Bosi, L., Demetriou, C., and Malthaner, S. 2014. *Dynamics of Political Violence: A Process-Oriented Perspective on Radicalization and the Escalation of Political Conflict*. Farnham: Ashgate.

Bosi, L., Giugni, M., and Uba, K. (eds.). 2016. *The Consequences of Social Movements*. Cambridge: Cambridge University Press.

Bouissef Rekab, D. 1989. *À l'ombre de Lalla Chafia*. Casablanca: Tarik Editions.

Bourdieu, P. 1978. "Classement, déclassement, reclassement". *Actes de la Recherche en Sciences Sociales* 24: 2–22.

1979. *La Distinction*. Paris: Minuit.

1980. *Le Sens pratique*. Paris: Minuit.

1981. "La représentation politique: éléments pour une théorie du champ politique". *Actes de la Recherche en Sciences Sociales*, 1981 (36–37): 3–24.

1986. "L'illusion biographique". *Actes de la recherche en sciences sociales* 62 (1): 66–73.

2013. *Manet, Une révolution symbolique*. Paris: Seuil.

2015. *Sociologie générale*. Volume 1. Paris: Seuil.

Bourdieu, P. and Passeron, J.-C. 1964. *Les Héritiers*. Paris: Minuit.

Bozarslan, H. 2004. *Violence in the Middle East: From Political Struggle to Self-Sacrifice*. Princeton, NJ: Markus Wiener Publishers.

Bozon, M. 1987. "Histoire et sociologie d'un bien symbolique, le prénom". *Population* 1: 83–98.

Braungart, M. M. and Braungart, R. G. 1991. "The Effects of the 1960s Political Generation on Former Left- and Right-Wing Youth Activist Leaders". *Social Problems* 38 (3): 297–315.

Brockett, C. 2005. *Political Movements and Violence in Central America*. New York: Cambridge University Press.

Brubaker, R. and Cooper, F. 2000. "Beyond 'Identity'". *Theory and Society* 29 (1): 1–47.

Bugajski, J. and Pollack, M. 1989. *East European Fault Lines: Dissent, Opposition and Social Activism*. San Francisco and London: Boulder, Westview Press.

Burgat, F. 1988. *L'islamisme au Maghreb*. Paris: Payot, La voix du Sud.

Camau, M. and Massardier, G. 2009. *Démocracies et Autoritarismes: fragmentation et hybridation des régimes*. Paris: Karthala.

Camou, A. 2001. *Los desafíos de la gobernabilidad*. Mexico: FLACSO, IIS-UNAM and Fondo de Cultura Económica.

Cardi, C. 2010. "Les mauvaises mères entre prison, justice et travail social". In *Reproduire le genre*, edited by Dorlin E. and Fassin E. Paris: Centre Georges Pompidou.

Cardi, C. and Pruvost, G. 2012. "Penser la violence des femmes: enjeux politiques et épistémologiques". In *Penser la violence des femmes*, edited by Cardi, C. and Pruvost, G. Paris: La Découverte: 13–64.

Carnac, R. 2014. "L'Église catholique contre 'la théorie du genre' : Construction d'un objet polémique dans le débat public français contemporain". *Synergies Italie* 10: 125–143.

Carothers, T. 2004. *Critical Mission: Essays on Democracy Promotion*. Washington, DC: Carnegie, Endowment for International Peace.

Cassady, K. 2005. "Organic Intellectuals and the Committed Community: Irish Republicanism and Sinn Féin in the North". *Irish Political Studies* 20 (3): 341–356.

Catusse, M. 2002. "Le charme discret de la société civile: Ressorts politiques de la formation d'un groupe dans le Maroc 'ajusté'". *Revue internationale de politique compare* 2: 297–318.

2008. *Le temps des entrepreneurs. Politique et transformations du capitalisme au Maroc*. Paris: Maisonneuve et Larose.

Catusse, M. and Vairel, F. 2010. "Le Maroc de Mohammed VI: mobilisations et action publique". *Politique africaine* 120: 5–23.

Cefaï, D., Carrel, M., Talpin, J., Eliasoph, N., and Lichterman, P. 2012. "Ethnographies de la participation". *Participations* 4: 7–48.

Chabanet, D. and Guigni, M. 2010. "Les conséquences des mouvements sociaux". In *Penser les mouvements sociaux. Conflits sociaux et contestations dans les sociétés contemporaines*, edited by Fillieule, O., Agrikoliansky E., and Sommier, I.. Paris: La Découverte.

Chambergeat, P. 1965. "Bilan de l'expérience parlementaire marocaine". *Annuaire de l'Afrique du Nord* IV: 101–116.

Champy, F., Israël, L. 2009. "Professions et engagement public". *Sociétés contemporaines* 1(73): 7–19.

Chauvel, L. 2002. *Le Destin des générations. Structure sociale et cohortes en France au XXe siècle*. Paris: PUF.

Cheynis, E., 2013. "Les reconversions dans l'associatif de militants politiques marocains. Ruptures, continuités et fidélité à soi". *Politix* 2 (102):147–173.

2008. *L'espace des transformations de l'action associative au Maroc. Réforme de l'action publique, investissements militants et légitimation internationale.* PhD Social Sciences, University Paris I- Panthéon-Sorbonne, 2008.

Cigerli, S. and Le Saout, D. 2005. *Öcalan et le PKK: Les mutations de la question kurde.* Paris: Maisonneuve & Larose.

Collovald, A. 1989. "Les poujadistes, ou l'échec en politique". *Revue d'histoire moderne et contemporaine* 36 (1): 113–165.

Collovald, A. and Neveu, E. 2001. "Le néo-polar: du gauchisme politique au gauchisme littéraire". *Sociétés et Représentations* 11: 77–93.

Combes, H. 2011. *Faire parti. Trajectoires de gauche au Mexique.* Paris: Karthala.

2012. "Tomar partido: sociología de los asistentes y militantes en los cierres de campaña". In *Apropiación Política del Espacio Público. Miradas Etnográficas de los Cierres de las Campañas Electorales del 2006*, edited by Tamayo, S. and López-Saavedra, N. Mexico: IFE and UAM, 201–232.

Combes, H. and Fillieule, O. 2011. "Repression and Protest Structural Models and Strategic Interactions". *Revue française de science politique (English)* 61 (6): 1–24.

Coninck, F. de and Godard, F. 1989. "Introduction". In *Biographie et cycles de vie*, edited by Coninck F. de &and Godard F. *Enquête* (5). EHESS/CNRS/Université de Nice, 1–5.

Cormier, P. 2016. *Les conséquences biographiques de l'engagement en contexte répressif. Militer au sein la gauche radicale en Turquie: 1974.* PhD in Political Science, University of Lausanne and Institute for Political Studies, Bordeaux.

Corrigall-Brown, C. 2011. *Patterns of Protest: Trajectories of Participation in Social Movements.* Stanford, CA: Stanford University Press.

2012. "From the Balconies to the Barricades, and Back? Trajectories of Participation in Contentious Politics". *Journal of Civil Society* 8 (1): 17–38.

Coser, L., 1974. *Greedy Institutions: Patterns of Undivided Commitment.* New York: The Free Press.

Cress, D. M., Miller J. and McPherson, T. R. 1997. "Competition and Commitment in Voluntary Memberships: The Paradox of Persistence and Participation". *Sociological Perspectives* 40 (1): 61–79.

Crouch, C. 2004. *Post-Democracy.* Polity: London.

Crozier, M., Huntington, S., and Watanuki, J. 1975. *The Crisis of Democracy.* New York: NYU Press.

Da, B. 1999. *The Velvet Philosophers.* London: The Claridge Press.

Dalton, R. J. 2008. *The Good Citizen: How a Younger Generation Is Reshaping American Politics.* Washington, DC: CQ Press.

Dalton, R. J., Van Sickle, A., and Weldon, S. 2010. "The Individual-Institutional Nexus of Protest Behaviour." *British Journal of Political Science* 40 (1): 51–73.

Dammame, D., Gobille, B., Matonti, F., and Pudal, B. 2008. *Mai-Juin '68.* Paris: Editions de l'atelier.

Darmon, M. 2009. "The Fifth Element: Social Class and the Sociology of Anorexia". *Sociology* 43 (4): 717–733.

Dauvin, P. and Siméant, J. 2002. *Le travail humanitaire. Les acteurs des ONG, du siège au terrain.* Paris: Presses de Sciences Po.

Davis, D. E. 1997. "New Social Movements, Old Party Structures: Discursive and Organizational Transformations in Mexican and Brazilian Party Politics". In *Politics, Social Change and Economic Restructuring in Latin America*, edited by Smith, W. C. and Korzeniewicz, R. B. Boulder, CO: Lynne Rienner, 151–187.

Della Porta, D. 1995. *Social Movements, Political Violence and the State: A Comparative Analysis of Italy and Germany.* New York: Cambridge University Press.

2009. "Leaving Underground Organizations: A Sociological Analysis of the Italian Case". In *Leaving Terrorism Behind: Individual and Collective Disengagement*, edited by Björgo, T. and Horgan, J. London: Routledge, 67–87.

(ed.). 2014. *Mobilizing for Democracy. Comparing 1989 and 2011.* Oxford: Oxford Universiy Press.

DeMartni, J. R. 1983. "Social Movement Participation: Political Socialization, Generation Consciousness, and Lasting Effects". *Youth and Society* 15: 195–223.

Demerath, III. N. J., Marwell, G., and Aiken, M. T. 1971. *Dynamics of Idealism.* San Francisco: Jossey-Bass Inc Publishers.

Descamps, F. 2001. *L'historien, l'archiviste et le magnétophone. De la constitution de la source orale à son exploitation.* Paris: Comité pour l'histoire économique et financière-Ministère de l'Économie, des Finances et de l'Industrie.

Dillenburger, K., Montserrat, F., and Rym A. 2008. "Long Term Effects of Political Violence: Narrative Inquiry across a 20-Year Period". *Qualitative Health Research* 18 (10): 1312–1322.

Dobry, M. 2000. "Les voies incertaines de la transitologie: choix stratégiques, séquences historiques, bifurcations et processus de path dependence". *Revue française de science politique* 50 (4–5): 585–614.

2009 (1984). *Sociologie des crises politiques.* Paris: Presses de la FNSP.

Dormoy-Rajramanan, C., Gobille, B., and Neveu, E. 2018. *Mai 68 par celles et ceux qui l'ont vécu.* Paris: Editions de l'Atelier.

Downton, J. Jr. and Wehr, P. 1997. *The Persistent Activist: How Peace Commitment Develops and Survives.* Boulder, CO: Westview Press.

Dressen, M. 2000. *De l'amphi à l'établi. Les étudiants maoïstes à l'usine (1967–1989).* Paris: Belin.

Duboc, M. 2010. "Egyptian Leftist Intellectuals' Activism from the Margins. Overcoming the Mobilization/Demobilization Dichotomy". In *Social Movements, Mobilization, and Contestation in the Middle East and North Africa*, edited by Beinin, J. and Vairel, F. Stanford, CA: Stanford University Press, 61–79.

Durkheim, E. 1974 (1902). *L'éducation Morale.* Paris: PUF.

Dvorakova, V. and Kunc, J. 1996. "Zrod ceskeho stranickeho system". In *Krystalizace struktury politickych stran v Ceske republice po roce 1989*, edited by Dvorakova, V. and Gerloch, A. Prague: Ceska Spolecnost pro Politicke Vedy.

Dwyer, C. and Shadd, M. 2011. "The Role of Self-Help Efforts in the Reintegration of 'Politically Motivated' Former Prisoners: Implications from the Northern Irish Experience". *Crime, Law and Social Change* 55: 293–309.

Einwohner, R. L. 2003. "Opportunity, Honor, and Action in the Warsaw Ghetto Uprising of 1943". *American Journal of Sociology* 109 (3): 650–675.

Einwohner, R., Hollander, K., and Olson, T. 2000. "Engendering Social Movements, Cultural Images and Movement dynamics". *Gender and Society* 124 (5): 679–699.

Eisenstein, H. 1996. *Inside Agitators*. Philadelphia, PA: Temple University Press.

Ekiert, G. and Kubik, J. 1999. *Rebellious Civil Society: Popular Protest and Democratic Consolidation in Poland, 1989–1993*. Ann Arbor, MI: University of Michigan Press.

El Ayadi, M. 2004. "Entre l'Islam et l'islamisme, la religion dans l'école publique marocaine". *Revue internationale d'Education de Sèvres* 36: 111–121.

El Ayadi, M., Rachik, H., and Tozy, M. 2013. *L'Islam au quotidien. Enquête sur les valeurs et les pratiques religieuses eu Maroc*. Casablanca: Éditions la Croisée des Chemins.

El Khawaga, D. 2003. "La génération seventies en Egypte. La société civile comme répertoire d'action alternative". In *Résistance et protestations dans les sociétés musulmanes*, edited by Bennani-Chraïbi, M. and Fillieule, O. Paris: Sciences Po, 271–292.

Elias, N.1969. *The Civilizing Process: Vol.I, The History of Manners*. Oxford: Blackwell.

1982. *The Civilizing Process: Vol.II, State Formation and Civilization*. Oxford: Blackwell.

1984. *What Is Sociology?* New-York: Columbia University.

1991. *The Society of Individuals*. Oxford: Blackwell.

2010. *Mozart, and Other Essays on Courtly Culture*. Dublin: UCD Press.

Eliasoph, N. and Lichterman, P. 2003. "Culture in Interaction". *American Journal of Sociology* 108 (4): 735–794.

Ercan, H. 2010. *Dynamics of Mobilization and Radicalization of the Kurdish Movement in the 1970s in Turkey*, nonpublished thesis, Koç University.

Eriksson, A. 2008. "Challenging Cultures of Violence through Community Restorative Justice in Northern Ireland". *Sociology of Crime, Law and Deviance* 11: 231–260.

Falquet, J. 2003. "Division sexuelle du travail révolutionnaire: réflexions à partir de la participation des femmes salvadoriennes à la lutte armée (1981–1992)". *Cahiers d'Amérique Latine* 40: 109–128.

Fejtö, F. and Rupnik, J. eds. 1999. *Le printemps tchécoslovaque 1968*. Brussels: Editions Complexe.

Fendrich, J. and Lovoy, K. 1988. "Back to the Future: Adult Political Behavior of Former Student Activists". *American Sociological Review* 53:780–794.

Fendrich, J. M. 1977. "Keeping the Faith or Pursuing the Good Life: A Study of the Consequences of Participation in the Civil Rights Movement". *American Sociological Review* 42: 144–157.

1993. *Ideal Citizens: The Legacy of the Civil Rights Movement*. Albany: State University of New York Press.

Ferguson, J. 2013. "Declarations of Dependence: Labour, Personhood, and Welfare in Southern Africa". *Journal of the Royal Anthropological Institute* 19: 223–242.

Ferguson, N. 2014. "Northern Irish Ex-Prisoners: The Impact of Imprisonment on Prisoners and the Peace Process in Northern Ireland". In *Prisons, Terrorism and Extremism: Critical issues in Management, Radicalisation and Reform*, edited by Silke, A. New York: Routledge, 270–283.

Ferry, L. and Renaud, A. 1985. *La pensée '68. Essai sur l'anti-humanisme contemporain*. Paris: Gallimard.

Fillieule, O. 1997. *Stratégies de la rue*. Paris: Presses de Sciences Po.

2001. "Propositions pour une analyse processuelle de l'engagement individuel". *Revue française de science politique* 51 (1–2): 199–215.

2005. "Temps biographique, temps social et variabilités des retributions". In *Le désengagement militant*, edited by Fillieule, O. Paris: Belin, 17–47.

(ed). 2005. *Le désengagement militant*, Paris: Belin.

2009. "Conséquences biographiques de l'engagement". In *Dictionnaire des mouvements sociaux*, edited by Fillieule, O. et al. Paris: Presses de Sciences Po.

2010. "Some Elements of an Interactionist Approach to Political Disengagement." *Social Movement Studies* 9 (1): 1–15.

2013a "Political Socialization and Social Movements". In *The Wiley-Blackwell Encyclopedia of Social and Political Movements*, edited by Snow, D. A., Della Porta, D., Klandermans, B., and McAdam, D. Oxford: Blackwell, 968–974.

2013b. "Some thoughts on student circles in demobilization dynamics". *European Journal of Turkish Studies* (17) [Online].

2015. "Disengagement from Radical Organizations: A Process and Multi Level Model of Analysis". In *Movements in Times of Transition*, edited by Klandermans, B. and van Stralen, C. Philadelphia, PA: Temple University Press, 34–63.

2016. "Demobilization and Disengagement in a Life Course Perspective". In *Oxford Handbook of Social Movements*, edited by Della Porta, D. and Diani, M. Oxford: Oxford University Press.

Fillieule, O. and Bennani-Chraïbi, M. 2005. "Exit, Voice, Loyalty et bien d'autres choses encore…". In *Résistances et protestations dans les societés musulmanes*, edited by Fillieule, O. and Bennani- Chraïbi, M. Paris: Presses de Sciences Po, 43–126.

Fillieule, O. and Mayer, N. 2001. "Introduction : Dossier 'Devenirs militants'". *Revue française de science politique* 51 (1–2):19–25.

Fillieule, O. and Sommier, I. (eds.). 2018. *Marseille, années 68*. Paris: Presses de Sciences Po.

Fillieule, O., Agrikoliansky, E., and Sommier, I. 2010. *Penser les mouvements sociaux*. Paris: La Découverte.

Fillieule, O., Béroud, S., Masclet, C., Sommier, I., and Collectif Sombrero. 2018. *Changer le monde, changer sa vie. Enquête sur les militantes et les militants des années 68 en France*. Arles: Actes-Sud.

Flacks, R. 1988. *Making History: The American Left and the American Mind*. Columbia, NY: Columbia University Press.

Fleischer, D. 2004. "Reforma política en Brasil: una historia sin fin". *America Latina Hoy* 37: 81–99.

Flesher-Fominaya, C. 2010. "Collective Identity in Social Movements: Central Concepts and Debates". *Sociology Compass* 4 (6): 393–404.

Fligstein, N. and McAdam, D. 2012. *A Theory of Fields*. Oxford: Oxford University Press.

Foryś, G. 2008. *Dynamika sporu: protesty rolników w III Rzeczpospolitej*. Warsaw: WN Scholar.

Foryś, G. and Krzysztof, G. 2002. "The Dynamics of Polish Peasants Protests under Post-Communism". *Eastern European Countryside* 8: 47–65.

Foster, P. 2000. "Inside Story of the Maze, a Jail like No Other". *The Daily Telegraph* July, 28.

Foucault, M. 1976. *La volonté de savoir*. Paris: Gallimard.

Frampton, M. 2011. *Legion of Rearguard: Dissident Irish Republicanism*. Dublin: Irish Academic Press.

Freymond, N. 2010. "La 'redécouverte' des institutions par les sociologies". In *Sociologie de l'institution*, edited by Lagroye, J. and Offerlé, M. Paris: Belin, 33–53.

Frye, B. 2011. "A Death With Several Causes, and Uses". *Transitions Online* 8–9: 1–2. Accessed February 23, 2015. http://eastofcenter.tol.org/2011/08/a-death-with-several-causes-and-uses/.

Fuchs-Ebaugh, Helen R. 1988. *Becoming an Ex: The Process of Role Exit*. Chicago: Chicago University Press.

Gamson, W. 1985. *The Strategy of Social protest*. Belmont, CA: Wadsworth Publishing.

1998. "Social Movements and Cultural Change". In *From Contention to Democracy*, edited by Giugni, M., McAdam, D., and Tilly, C. Boston: Rowman and Littlefield, 57–77.

Garibay, D. 2005. "De la lutte armée à la lutte électorale, itinéraires divergents d'une trajectoire insolite". *Revue internationale de politique comparée* 12 (3): 283–297.

Gaxie, D. 1977. "Economie des partis et rétributions du militantisme". *Revue française de science politique* 27 (1): 123–154.

2005. "Rétributions du militantisme et paradoxes de l'action collective". Swiss Political Science Review 11 (1): 157–188.

Gayer, L. 2012. "Liberation and Containment: The Ambivalent Empowerment of Sikh Female Fighters". *Pôle Sud* 36: 49–65.

2013. "'Love-Marriage-Sex' in the People's Liberation Army of Nepal: The Libidinal Economy of a Greedy Institution". In *Revolution in Nepal: An Anthropological and Historical Approach to the People's War*, edited by Lecomte-Tilouine, M. Delhi: Oxford University Press, 333–366.

Geertz, C. 1974. "'From the Native's Point of View'": On the Nature of Anthropological Understanding". *Bulletin of the American Academy of Arts and Sciences* 28 (1): 26–45.

Geisser, V., Karam, K., and Vairel, F. 2006. "Espaces du politique : Mobilisations et protestations". In *La politique dans le monde arabe*, edited by Picard, E. Paris: Armand Colin, 193–213.

Genro, T. et al. 1999. *Governo e Cidadania: Balanço e reflexões sobre o modo petista de governar*. São Paulo: Fundação Perseu Abramo.

Gerth, H. and Mills, C. W. 1954. *Character and Social Structure: The Psychology of Social Institutions*. London: Routledge & Kegan Paul.

Gitlin, T. 1987. *The 60s: Years of Hope, Days of rage*. New York: Bantam.

Giugni, M. 1980. *The Whole World Is Watching: Mass Media in the Making & Unmaking of the New Left*. Berkeley: University of California Press.

1998. "Was it Worth the Effort ? The Outcomes and Consequences of Social Movements". *Annual Review of Sociology* 24: 371–393.

2004. "Personal and Biographical Consequences". In *The Blackwell Companion to Social Movements MA*, edited by Snow, D. A., Soule, S. A., and Kriesi, H. Malden, MA: Blackwell Publishing, 412–432.

2008. "Political, Biographical and Cultural Consequences of Social Movements". *Sociology Compass* 2 (5): 1582–1600.

2013."Biographical Consequences of Activism". In *The Wiley-Blackwell Encyclopedia of Social and Political Movements*, edited by Snow, D., Della Porta, D., Klandermans, B., and McAdam, D. Oxford: Blackwell, 138–144.

Glaser, B. G. and Strauss, A. L. 1971. *Status Passage*. Chicago: Aldine.

Goffman, E. 1961. *Asylums: Essays on the Social Situation of Mental Patients and Other Inmates*. Piscataway, NJ: Aldine transaction.

1991 (1963). *Stigma: Notes on the Management of Spoiled Identity*. New York: Simon and Schuster.

Goirand, C. 2010. "Penser les mouvements sociaux d'Amérique latine: Les approches des mobilisations depuis les années 1970". *Revue française de science politique* 60 (3): 445–466.

2014. "The Worker's Party, from Contention to Public Action: A Case of Institutionalization". *Journal of Politics in Latin America* 6 (3): 95–127.

Goldstone, J. (ed). 2003. *States, Parties and Social Movements*. Cambridge: Cambridge University Press.

Goldstone, J. and McAdam, D. 2001. "Contention in Demographic and Life-Course Context". In *Silence and Voice in the Study of Contentious Politics*, edited by Aminzade, R., Goldstone, J., McAdam, D., Perry, E., Sewell Jr., W.H., Tarrow, S. and Tilly, C. Cambridge and New York: Cambridge University Press, 195–221.

Goldstone, J. and Useem, B. 1999. "Prison Riots and Microrevolutions: An Extension of State-Centered Theories of Revolution". *American Journal of Sociology* 104 (4): 985–1029.

Goodwin, J. 2001. *No Other Way Out: States and Revolutionary Movements, 1945–1991*. Cambridge: Cambridge University Press.

Goodwin, J. and Jasper, J. M. 1999. "Caught in a Winding, Snarling Vine: The Structural Bias of Political Process Theory". *Sociological Forum* 14 (1): 27–54.

2003. "What Do Movement Participants Think and Feel?". In *The Social Movements Reader: Cases and Concepts*, edited by Goodwin, J. and Jasper, J. M. Malden, MA: Blackwell Publishing, 131–133.

2004. *Rethinking Social Movements: Structure, Meaning and Emotions*. Lanham, MD: Rowman and Littlefield.

Goodwin, J., Jasper, J. M., and Polleta, F. 2007. "Emotional Dimensions of Social Movements". In *The Blackwell Companion to Social Movements*, edited by

Snow, D. A., Soule, S. A., and Kriesi, H. Malden, MA: Blackwell Publishing, 413–432.

Gordon, C. 1991. "Governmental Rationality: An Introduction". In *The Foucault Effect: Studies in Governmentality*, edited by Burchell, G., Gordon, C., and Miller, P. Hampstead: Harvester, 1–52.

Gottraux, P. 1997. *Socialisme et Barbarie : Un engagement politique et intellectuel dans la France de l'après guerre*. Lausanne: Payot.

Grémion, P. 1984. *Paris-Prague : La gauche face au renouveau et à la régression tchécoslovaques*. Paris: Julliard.

Grojean, O. 2013. "Comment gérer une crise politique interne? Façonnage organisationnel du militantisme, maintien de l'engagement et trajectoires de défection". *Politix* 102: 63–87.

Gruel, L. 2004. *La rébellion de '68 : Une relecture sociologique*. Rennes: Presses Universitaires de Rennes.

Gunder Frank, A. and Fuentes, M. 1995. "El estudios de los ciclos en los movimientos sociales". *Sociológica* 10 (28): 37–60.

Gündogan, A. Z. 2011. "Space, State-Making and Contentious Kurdish Politics in the East of Turkey: The Case of Eastern Meetings, 1967". *Journal of Balkan and Near Eastern Studies* 13 (4): 389–416.

Gurin, P. and Epps, E. 1975. *Black Consciousness, Identity and Achievement*. New York: Wiley.

Gwiazda, A. 2008. "The Parliamentary Election in Poland, October 2007". *Electoral Studies* 27 (4): 760–764.

Hadjiisky, M. 2001. "The Failure of Participatory Democracy in the Czech Republic". *West European Politics* 24 (3): 43–64.

2004. *De la mobilisation citoyenne à la démocratie de partis. Participation et délégation politiques dans la nouvelle démocratie tchèque (1989–1996)*. PhD, Political Science, Institut d'Etudes Politiques, Paris.

2005. "Des leaders 'sans parti' : Engagement résistant et désengagement dirigeant: les anciens dissidents en République tchèque". In *Les frontières du politique*, edited by Arnaud, L. and Guionnet, C. Rennes: PUR.

2007. "La culture 'civique' en Pays tchèques : Généalogie d'une référence politique". In *Cultures et pratiques participatives : Perspectives comparatives*, edited by Neveu, C. Paris: L'Harmattan, 331–351.

Hafez, M. M. 2003. *Why Muslims Rebel: Repression and Resistance in the Islamic World*. London: Lynne Rienner.

Hall, P. A. and Taylor, R. C. R. 1997. "La science politique et les trois néo-institutionnalismes". *Revue française de science politique* 47 (3): 469–496.

Hamon, H. and Rotman, P. 1987, 1988. *Génération*. Paris: Seuil.

Hanley, S., Szczerbiak, A., Haughton, T., and Fowler, B. 2008. "Sticking Together: Explaining Comparative Centre – Right Party Success in Post-Communist Central and Eastern Europe". *Party Politics* 14 (4): 407–434.

Hastings, M. 2001. "Partis et administration du sens". In *Les partis politiques, quelles perspectives ?* edited by Andolfatto, D., Greffet, F., and Olivier, L. Paris: L'Harmattan, 21–36.

Havel, V. 1989. *Dalkovy vyslech. Rozhovor s Karlem Hvizd'alou* [Remote Questionning. Interview with Karel Hvizd'ala]. Prague: Melantrich.

Havryshko, M. 2016. "Illegitimate Sexual Practices in the OUN Underground and UPA in Western Ukraine in the 1940s and 1950s". *The Journal of Power Institutions in Post-Soviet Societies* 17 [https://pipss.revues.org/4214].

Hay, C. 2004. *Why We Hate Politics*. London: Polity.

Heaney, M. and Rojas, F. 2007. "Partisans, Non-partisans, and the Antiwar Movement in the United States". *American Politics Research* 35 (4): 431–464.

Hélardot, V. 2010. "Vouloir ce qui arrive? Les bifurcations biographiques entre logiques structurelles et choix individuels". In *Bifurcations : Les sciences sociales face aux ruptures et à l'événement*, edited by Bessin, M., Bidart, C., and Grossetti, M. Paris: La Découverte: 160–175.

Hercus, C. 1999. "Identity, Emotions and Feminist Collective Action". *Gender and Society* 13 (1): 34–55.

Hermanova, E., Illner, M., and Vajdova, Z. 1992. "Politicke jaro 1990 na venkove a v malem meste" [Political Spring 1990 in countryside and small cities]. *Sociologicky casopis/Sociological Review* 28 (3): 369–385.

Heurtaux, J. 2004. "Démocratie populaire versus Démocratie élitaire: les inégalités politiques et leurs justifications en Pologne". *La Nouvelle Alternative* 62 (19): 39–50.

— 2005. *Une partisanisation controversée. Codification de la compétition politique et construction de la Démocratie en Pologne (1989–2001)*. PhD Political Science, University Lille 2.

Hirsch, E. L. 1990. "Sacrifice for the Cause: Group Processes, Recruitment, and Commitment in a Student Social Movement." *American Sociological Review* 55: 243–254.

— 2003. "Generating Commitment among Students". In *The Social Movements Reader: Cases and Concepts*, edited by Goodwin, J. and Jasper, J. M. Malden, MA: Blackwell Publishing, 94–102.

Hivert, J., 2013. "Se désengager du mouvement du '20 février': le cas des étudiants du supérieur de la coordination de Rabat". *European Journal of Turkish Studies* 17: 1–24.

Horgan, J. 2009. *Walking Away from Terrorism: Accounts of Disengagement from Radical and Extremist Movements*. New York: Routledge.

Howard, M. M. 2003. *The Weakness of Civil Society in Post-Communist Europe*. Cambridge: Cambridge University Press.

Humphreys, M. and Weinstein, J.M. 2007. "Demobilization and Reintegration". *Journal of Conflict Resolution* 51 (4): 531–567.

Hunter, W. 2010. *The Transformation of the Workers' Party in Brazil, 1989–2009*. Cambridge: Cambridge University Press.

Hunter, W. and Power, T. 2007. "Rewarding Lula: The Brazilian Election of 2006". *Latin American Politics and Society* 49 (1): 1–30.

Imset, I. G. 1996. "The PKK Terrorist or Freedom Fighters?". *The International Journal of Kurdish Studies* 10 (1/2): 45–100.

Inglehart, R. 2008. "Changing Values in Post-Industrial Societies". In *The Social Movements Reader: Cases and Concepts*, edited by Goodwin, J. and Jasper, J. M. Malden, MA: Blackwell Publishing.

Jaffrelot, C. 2000. Habermas (Jürgen). Après l'État-nation. Une nouvelle constellation politique. Paris: *Critique Internationale*, Presses de sciences po: 74–75.

James, W. 1902. *The Varieties of Religious Experience: A Study in Human Nature* [Online: https://csrs.nd.edu/assets/59930/williams_1902.pdf].

Jasiewicz, K. 1992. "From Solidarity to Fragmentation". *Journal of Democracy* 3 (2): 55–69.

Jasper, J. 1997. *The Art of Moral Protest. Culture, Biography and Creativity in Social Movements.* Chicago: Chicago University Press.

2006. *Getting Your Way: Strategic Dilemnas in the Real World.* Chicago: The University of Chicago Press.

2008 (2003). "The Emotions of Protest". In *The Social Movements Reader: Cases and Concepts*, edited by Goodwin, J. and Jasper, J. M. Malden, MA: Blackwell Publishing: 153–162.

Jasper J. and Duyvendack, J. W. (eds.). 2015. *Players and Arena: The Interactive Dynamics of Protest.* Amsterdam: Amsterdam University Press.

Jennings, M. K. 1981. *Generations and Politics.* Princeton, NJ: Princeton University Press.

1987. "Residues of a Movement: The Aging of the American Protest Generation". *American Political Science Review* 81 (2): 367–382.

2002. "Generation Units and the Student Protest Movement in the United States: An Intra and Intergenerational Analysis". *Political Psychology* 23: 303–324.

2004. *Youth-Parent Socialization Panel Study, 1965–1997: Youth Wave IV, 1997.* Ann Arbor: University of Michigan.

Jennings, M. K. and Niemi, R. G. 1968. "The Transmission of Political Values from Parent to Child". *American Political Science Review* 62 (1): 169–184.

Jennings, M. K. and Stoker, L. 2004. "Social Trust and Civic Engagement across Time and Generations". *Acta Politica* 39 (4): 342–379.

Johnston, H. 2012. "Age Cohorts, Cognition and Collective Violence". In *Violent Protest, Contentious Politics, and the Neoliberal State*, edited by Seferiades, S. and Johnston, H. Farnham: Ashgate: 39–54.

Johsua, F. 2016. *Anticapitalistes.* Paris: La Découverte.

Jongerden, J. and Akkaya, A. H. 2011. "Born from the Left. The Making of the PKK". In *Nationalisms and Politics and the Kurdish Issue*, edited by Casier, M. and Jongerden, J. London: Routledge: 123–162.

Juhem, P. 2009. "Effets de Génération". In *Dictionnaire des mouvements sociaux*, edited by Fillieule, O., Mathieu, L., and Péchu, C. Paris: Presses de Sciences-Po, 188–197.

Kabacali, A. 1992. *Türkiye'de Gençlik Hareketli.* Istanbul: Altin.

Kącki, M. 2013. *Lepperiada.* Warsaw: Wydawnictwo Czarne.

Kaçmazoglu, B. 1995. *Türkiye'de Siyasal Fikir Hareketleri.* Istanbul: Birey.

Kampwirth, K. 2002. *Women and Guerilla Movements: Nicaragua, El Salvador, Chiapas, Cuba.* University Park: University of Pennsylvania Press.

Kapferer, B. 2015. "Introduction: In the Event: Toward an Anthropology of Generic Moments." In *In the Event: Toward an Anthropology of Generic Moments*, edited by Meinert, L. and Kapferer, B. New York, London: Berghahn.

Katzenstein, M. F. 1998. "Stepsisters: Feminist Movement Activism in Different Institutional Spaces". In *The Social Movement Society: Contentious Politics for a New Century*, editedy by Meyer, D. S. and Tarrow, S. Lanham: Rowman and Littlefield: 195–216.

Kaur, S. 2004. *Bikhra Painda (Punjabi) (The Scattered Road)*. Amritsar: Azad Khalsa Prakhashan.

Keck, M. E. 1991. *A lógica da diferença. O Partido dos Trabalhadores na construção da democracia brasileira*, São Paulo: Atica.

Keniston, K. 1968. *Young Radicals*. New York: Harcourt, Brace and World.

Kevlihan, R. 2013. *Aid, Insurgencies and Conflict Transformation, When Greed is Good*. New York: Routledge.

Khawaja, M. 1993. "Repression and Popular Collective Action: Evidence from the West Bank". *Sociological Forum* 8 (1): 47–71.

Killian, L. M. 1973. "Social Movements: A Review of the Field". In *Social Movements: A Reader and a Source Book*, edited by Evans, R. R. Chicago: Rand McNally.

Kinzo, M. D. 2004. "Partidos, eleições e democracia no Brasil pós-1985". *Revista Brasileira de Ciencias Sociais* 19 (54): 23–40.

Kitschelt, H. 1986. "Political Opportunity Structure and Political Protest: Anti-Nuclear Movements in Four Democracies". *British Journal of Political Science*: 57–85.

1993. "Social Movements, Political Parties and Democratic Theory". *ANNALS AAPSS* 528: 13–29.

Klandermans, B. 1997. *The Social Psychology of Protest*. Oxford: Blackwell.

2003. "Disengaging from Movements". In *The Social Movements Reader: Cases and Concepts*, edited by Goodwin, J. and Jasper, J. M. Malden, MA: Blackwell Publishing, 116–127.

Klandermans, B. and Van Stralen, C. 2015. *Movements in Times of Democratic Transition*. Philadelphia, PA: Temple University Press.

Klatch, R. E. 1999. *A Generation Divided: The New Left, the New Right, and the 1960s*. Berkeley: University of California Press.

Klawiter, M. 2008. *The Biopolitics of Breast Cancer*. Minnesota: University of Minnesota Press.

Knight, M. and Ozerdem, A. 2004. "Guns, Camps and Cash: Disarmament, Demobilization and Reinsertion of Former Combatants in Transitions from War to Peace". *Journal of Peace Research* 41: 449–516.

Konx, C. and Monaghan, R. 2002. *Informal Justice in Divided Societies: Northern Ireland and South Africa*. Basingstoke: Palgrave Macmillan.

Kopecek, M. 2011. "Disent jako minulost, liberalismus jako projekt: Obcanske hnuti-Svobodni demokrate v ceske polistopadove politice" [Dissidence as a Past, Liberalism as a Project: The Civic Movement-Free Democrats in Post-November Politics]. In Gjuricova, A., Kopecek, M., Roubal, P., Suk, J., and Zahradnicek, T. *Rozdeleni minulosti* [Division of the Past]. Prague: KVH: 61–106.

Kriesi, H. 1993. *Political Mobilization and Social Change: The Dutch Case in Comparative Perspective*, Brookfield, VT: Avebury.

Krok-Paszkowska, A. 2003. "Samoobrona: The Polish Self-Defence Movement". In *Uncivil Society? Contentious Politics in Post- Communist Europe*, edited by Mudde, C. and Kopecky, P. London: Routledge, 114–133.

Kroupa, D. 1996. *Svoboda a rad [Liberty and Order]*. Prague: Éós.

Krzyżanowska, N. 2010. "Denying the Right to Speak in Public: Sexist and Homophobic Discourses in Post-1989 Poland." In *The Post-Communist Condition: Public and Private Discourses of Transformation*, edited by Galasińska, A. and Galasiński, D. Amsterdam: John Benjamins Publishing Company, 105–130.

Kumar, P., Dagar, R., and Neerja. 1999. *Victims of Militancy*. Chandigarh: Institute of Development and Communication.

Kusin, V. 2002 (1971). *The Intellectual Origins of the Prague Spring: The Development of Reformist Ideas in Czechoslovakia*. Cambridge: Cambridge University Press.

La Garza, E., Ejea T., and Macias, L. 1986. *El otro movimiento estudiantil*. Mexico: Contemporáneos.

Laâbi, A. 2001. *Les rêves sont têtus. Écrits politiques*. Casablanca: EDDIF et Paris-Méditerranée.

Laclau, E. 2003 (2000). "Identidad y Hegemonía: el rol de la universalidad en la construcción de lógicas políticas". In *Contingencia, Hegemonía, Universalidad. Diálogos Contemporáneos en la Izquierda*, edited by Butler, J., Laclau, E., and Zizek, S. Buenos Aires: Fondo de Cultura Económica: 49–94.

Lacroix, B. 1981. *L'utopie communautaire*. Paris: PUF.

Lagroye, J. and Offerlé, M. (eds.). 2010. *Sociologie de l'institution*. Paris: Belin.

Lahire, B. 2010. *Franz Kafka. Éléments pour une théorie de la création littéraire*. Paris: La Découverte.

2007. *L'homme pluriel: les ressorts de l'action*. Paris: Hachette Littératures.

Langlois, C.-V. and Seignobos, C. (1898). *Introduction aux études historiques, Livre II, Opérations analytiques*. Lyon: ENS.

Lanzona,V. A. 2009. *Amazons of the Huk Rebellion: Gender, Sex, and Revolution in the Philippines*. Madison: The University of Wisconsin Press.

Latté, S. 2015. "Le choix des larmes. La commémoration comme mode de protestation". *Politix* 110: 7–34.

Leclercq, C. and Pagis, J. 2011. "Les incidences biographiques de l'engagement. Socialisations militantes et mobilité sociale. Introduction". *Sociétés contemporaines* 4 (84): 5–23.

Lee, A.-R. 1997. "Exploration of the Sources of Student Activism: The Case of South Korea". *International Journal of Public Opinion Research* 9: 48–65.

Lepper, A. 1993. *Samoobrona. Dlaczego? Przed czym*. Warsaw: Kamea.

1999. *Niepokorny*. Warsaw: Kamea.

Lewis, O. 1961. *The Children of Sanchez: Autobiography of a Mexican Family*. New York: Random House.

Lindberg, S. 2009; *Democratization by Elections. A New Mode of transition?* Baltimore, MD: Johns Hopkins University Press.

Lindendberg, D. 1975. *Le Marxisme Introuvable*. Paris: Calmann-Lévy.

Lipsitz, G. 1988. *A life in Struggle: Ivory Perry and the Culture of Opposition*. Philadelphia, PA: Temple University Press.

Louault, F. 2006. "Coups et coûts d'un échec électoral : La défaite du Parti des Travailleurs à Porto Alegre (octobre 2004)". *Lusotopie* 13 (2): 73–90.

Loveman, M. 1998. "High Risk Collective Action: Defending Human Rights in Chile, Uruguay, and Argentina". *American Journal of Sociology* 104 (2): 477–525.

Lucardie, P. 2000. "Prophets, Purifiers and Prolocutors. Towards a Theory on the Emergence of New Parties". *Party Politics* 6 (2): 175–185.

Luck, S. and Dechezelles, S. 2011. *Voix de la rue ou voie des urnes? Mouvements sociaux et partis politiques*. Rennes: PUR.

Luker, K. 2003. "World Views of Pro- and Anti-Abortion Activists". In *The Social Movements Reader. Cases and Concepts*, edited by Goodwin, J. and Jasper, J. M. Malden, MA: Blackwell Publishing, 134–146.

MacIonnrachtaigh, F. 2013. *Language, Resistance and Revival: Republican Prisoners and the Irish Language in The North of Ireland*. London: Pluto Press.

Mannheim, K. 1952 (1928). *The Problem of Generations in Essays on the Sociology of Knowledge*. London: Routledge and Kegan, 276–332.

Marès, A. 1995. *Histoire des Pays tchèques et slovaques*. Paris: Hatier.

Markowski, R. 2008. "The 2007 Polish Parliamentary Election: Some Structuring, Still a Lot of Chaos". *West European Politics* 31 (5): 1055–1068.

Markus, G. B. 1986. "Stability and Change in Political Attitudes: Observed, Recalled, and 'Explained'". *Political Behavior* 8: 21–44.

Martínez Cruz, J., Quintanilla, J., Hernández, A., and Melchor, J. 2002. *Desde abajo. La izquierda y los movimientos sociales en Morelos*. Mexico: Convergencia Socialista.

Marwell, G. A. and Demerath, J. 1987. "The Persistence of Political Attitudes among 1960's Civil Rights Activists". *Public Opinion Quarterly* 51: 359–375.

Masclet, C. 2015. "Le féminisme en héritage? Enfants de militantes de la deuxième vague". *Politix* 1 (109): 45–68.

2016. "Examining the Intergenerational Outcomes of Social Movements: The Case of Feminist Activists and Their Children". In *The Consequences of Social Movements*, edited by Bosi, L., Giugni, M., and Uba, K. Cambridge: Cambridge University Press, 106–129.

Massicard, E. 2010. "Répression et changement des formes de militantisme: carrières de remobilisation à gauche après 1980 en Turquie". *Sociétés politiques compares* 28: 1–18.

Mastropaolo, A. 2012. *Is Democracy a Lost Cause? Paradoxes of an Imperfect Invention*. Colchester: ECPR Press.

Mauger, G. 1994. "Gauchisme, Contre Culture et Néo-Libéralisme: Pour une histoire de la génération de mai '68". In *L'Identité Politique*, CURAPP. Paris: PUF, 206–226.

2006. *L'émeute de novembre 2005 : Une révolte proto-politique*. Bellecombes en Bauges: Editions du Croquant.

Maurel, M.-C. 1994. "La naissance des nouveaux acteurs sociaux sur la scène locale". *Revue d'Etudes Comparatives Est-Ouest* 4: 131–145.

Mayer, F. 2004. *Les Tchèques et leur communisme: Mémoire et identités politiques*. Paris: Editions de l'Ecole des Hautes Etudes en Sciences Sociales.

McAdam, D. 1986. "Recruitment to High-Risk Activism: The Case of Freedom Summer". *The American Journal of Sociology* 92 (1): 64–90.

——— 1988. *Freedom Summer*. Oxford: Oxford University Press.

——— 1989. "The Biographical Consequences of Activism". *American Sociological Review* 54 (5): 744–760.

——— 1999. "The Biographical Impact of Activism". In *How Social Movements Matter: Theoretical and Comparative Studies on the Consequences of Social Movements*, edited by Giugni, M., McAdam, D., and Tilly, C. Minneapolis: University of Minnesota Press: 119–146.

McAdam, D. and Paulsen, R. 1993. "Specifying the Relationship between Social Ties and Activism". *American Journal of Sociology* 99 (3): 640–667.

McAdam, D. and Schaffer Boudet, H. 2012. *Putting Social Movements in Their Place*. Cambridge: Cambridge University Press.

McAdam, D., Tarrow, S., and Tilly, C. 2003 (2001). *Dynamics of Contention*. Cambridge: Cambridge University Press.

——— 2008. "Measuring Mechanisms of Contention". *Qualitative Sociology* 31: 307–332.

McAtackney, L. 2014. *An Archaeology of the Troubles: The Dark Heritage of Long Kesh/Maze Prison*. Oxford: Oxford University Press.

McCarthy, J.-D. and Zald, M. 1977. "Resource Mobilization and Social Movements: A Partial Theory". *American Journal of Sociology* 38: 1212–1241.

McDewitt, J. and Williamson, J. 2003. "Hate Crimes Directed at Gay, lesbian, Bisexual and Transgendered Victims". in *International Handbook of Violence Research*, edited by Heitmeyer, W. and Horgan, J. New York: Springer, 810–815.

McDonald, K. 2013. "Grammars of Violence, Modes of Embodiment and Frontiers of the Subject". In *War and Body. Militarisation, Practice and Experience*, edited by McSorley, K. London: Routledge, 138–150.

McDowall, D. 1996. *A Modern History of the Kurds*. London: I.B. Tauris.

McEvoy, K. and Shirlow, P. 2009. "Re-Imagining DDR. Ex-Combatants, Leadership and Moral Agency in Conflict Transformation". *Theoretical Criminology* 13 (1): 31–59.

McKeown, L. 2001. *Out of Time: Irish Republican Prisoners, Long Kesh, 1972–2000*. Belfast: Beyond the Pale.

——— 2009. "Casualties of War" or "Agents of Change" Irish Republican Prisoners, Maze/Long Kesh Prison, 1972–200". In *Political Ideology in Ireland: From the Enlightenment to the Present*, edited by Coquelin, O., Galliou, P., and Robin, T., Newcastle-Upon-Tyne: Cambridge Scholars Publications, 274–283.

McPherson, J. M., Popielarz, P., and Drobnic, S. 1992. "Social Networks and Organizational Dynamics". *American Sociological Review* 57 (2): 153–170.

Memmi, D. 1996. "Les déplacés. Travail sur soi et ascension sociale: la promotion littéraire de Jules Romain". *Genèses* 24 sept.: 57–80.

Meneguello, R. 1989. *PT, a Formação de um Partido, 1979–1982*. São Paulo: Paz e Terra.

Meyer, D. S. and Whittier, N. 2004. "Social Movement Spillover". *Social Problems* 41 (2): 277–298.

Mika, H. 2006. *Community Based Restorative Justice in Northern Ireland: An Evaluation*. Belfast Institute of Criminology and Criminal Justice: Queens University of Belfast.

Monceau, N. 2007. *Générations démocrates. Les élites turques et le pouvoir.* Paris: Dalloz.

Morris, A. D. and Staggenborg, S. 2007. "Leadership in Social Movements". In *The Blackwell Companion to Social Movements*, edited by Snow, D. A., Soule, S. A., and Kriesi, H. Malden, MA: Blackwell Publishing, 171–196.

Morrison, J. 2014. "A Time to Think, a Time to Talk: Irish Republicanism Prisoners in the Northern Irish Peace Process". In *Prisons, Terrorism and Extremism. Critical Issues in Management, Radicalisation and Reform*, edited by Silke, A. New York: Routledge, 75–87.

Moss-Kanter, R. 1968. "Commitment and Social Organization: A Study of Commitment Mechanisms in Utopian Communities". *American Sociological Review* 33 (4): 499–517.

1972. "Commitment and Community". *Communes and Utopias in Sociological Perspective.* Cambridge, MA: Harvard Universtiy Press.

Mouride, A. 2001. *On affame bien les rats.* Casablanca: Tarik Éditions.

Mozny, I. 2009 (1991). *Proc tak snadno ? Nektere rodinne duvody sametove revoluce.* [Why so easy? Some family reasons of the Velvet Revolution]. Prague: SLON.

Muel-Dreyfus, F. 1983. *Le métier d'éducateur.* Paris: Minuit.

Muller, E. N. and Jukam, T. O. 1977. "The Meaning of Political Support". *American Political Science Review* 71: 1561–1595.

Nepstad, S. E. and Smith, C. 1999. "Rethinking Recruitment to High-Risk/Cost Activism: The Case of Nicaragua Exchange". *Mobilization* 4 (1): 25–40.

Neveu, E. 2008. "Trajectoires de soixante-huitards ordinaires". In *Mai-Juin 68*, edited by Damamme, D., Gobille, B., Matonti, F., and Pudal, B. Paris: Editions de l'Atelier, 306–318.

2014. "Memory Battles over Mai '68: Interpretative Struggles as Cultural Re-Play of Social Movements". In *Conceptualizing Culture in Social Movement Research*, edited by Baumgarten, B., Daphi, P., and Ullrich, P. London: Palgrave/Macmillan, 275–299.

2015. "French Literature and the Construction and Transformations of May '68's Memory". In *From Multitudes to Crowds. Collective Action and the Media*, edited by Torres, C. and Mateus, S. Bern: Peter Lang, 89–110.

Neveu, E. and Quéré, L. 1996. "Le temps de l'événement. Présentation". *Réseaux* 14 (75): 7–21.

Nussio, E, 2012. "Emotional Legacies of War among Former Colombian Paramilitaries". *Peace and Conflict Journal of Peace and Psychology* 18 (4): 369–383.

O'Donnel, G., Schmitter, P., and Whitehead, L. 1986. *Transitions from Authoritarian Rule.* Baltimore, MD: Johns Hopkins University Press.

O'Hearn, D. 2017. "Movements Inside and Outside of Prison: The H-Block Protest". In *The Troubles: Northern Ireland and Theories of Social Movements*, edited by Bosi, L. and DeFazio, G. Amsterdam: Amsterdam University Press.

2009. "Repression and Solidarity Cultures of Resistance: Irish Political Prisoners on Protest". *American Journal of Sociology* 115 (2): 491–526.

O'Keefe, T. 2017. "'Mother Ireland, Get off Our Backs': Republican Feminist Resistance in the North of Ireland". In *The Troubles: Northern Ireland and Theories of Social Movements*, edited by Bosi, L. and DeFazio, G. Amsterdam: Amsterdam University Press.

Oberschall, A. 1973. *Social Conflicts and Social Movements*. Englewood Cliffs, NJ: Prentice-Hall.

Offe, C. 1991. "Capitalism by Democratic Design?' Democratic Theory Facing the Triple Transition in East Central Europe". *Social Research* 58 (4): 865–881.

Olivier-Téllez, G., Tamayo-Flores-Alatorre, S., and Voegtli, M. 2013. "La démobilisation étudiante au Mexique: le double visage de la répression (juillet-décembre 1968)". *European Journal of Turkish Studies* [Online], 17, accessed March 13, 2013 http://ejts.revues.org/4819.

Olivier, G. 2007. *Educación superior privada en México. Veinte años de expansión: 1982–2002*. Mexico: Universidad Pedagógica Nacional. Colección Más Textos, No. 29.

Olson, M. 1974. *The Logic of Collective Action. Public Good and the Theory of Groups*. Cambridge MA: Harvard University Press.

Opp, K.-D. and Roehl, W. 1990. "Repression, Micromobilization, and Political Protest". *Social Forces* 69 (2): 521–547.

Orhan, M. 2015. *Political Violence and Kurds in Turkey: Fragmentations, Mobilizations, Participations and Repertoires*. New York: Routledge.

Osa, M. 1998. "Contention and Democracy: Labor Protest in Poland, 1989–1993". *Communist and Postcommunist Studies* 31 (1): 29–42.

Ost, D. 1990. *Solidarity and the Politics of Anti-Politics: Opposition and Reform in Poland since 1968*. Philadelphia, PA: Temple University Press.

Pacewicz, J. 2015. "Playing the Neoliberal Game: Why Community Leaders Left Party Politics to Partisan Activists". *American Journal of Sociology* 121 (3): 826–881.

Pagis, J. 2009. "Repenser la formation de générations politiques sous l'angle du genre: Le cas de 'Mai–Juin 68.'" *CLIO Histoire Femmes et Sociétés* 29 (May): 97–118.

2010. The politicization of religious commitments. Reassessing the determinants of participation in May '68, Revue française de science politique/English, vol. 60 (1): 61–89.

2014. *Mai 68. Un pavé dans leur histoire*. Paris: Presses de Sciences Po.

2018. *May'68: Shaping Political Generations*. Amsterdam: Amsterdam University Press.

Parkinson, S. E. 2013. "Organizing Rebellion: Rethinking High-Risk Mobilization and Social Networks in War". *American Political Science Review* 107 (3): 418–432.

Passerini, L. 1996. *Autoritratto Di Gruppo*. Milan: Giunti.

Passeron, J.-C. 1980. "Biographies, flux, itinéraires, trajectoires". *Revue française de sociologie* 31 (1): 3–22.

Pellen, C. 2009. "Les manifestations paysannes polonaises de 1998–1999. Politisation, médiatisation et personnalisation d'une mobilisation contestataire". *Politix* 86: 167–188.

———. 2010. *Sociologie d'un groupement politique illégitime. Le mouvement Samoobrona (Autodéfense) en Pologne (1991–2010)*. Ph D Political Science, Institut d'Etudes Politiques Bordeaux.

Percheron, A. 1974. *L'univers politique des enfants*. Paris: Armand Colin.

Percheron, A. and Jennings, M. K. 1981. "Political Continuities in French Families: A New Perspective on an Old Controversy". *Comparative Politics* 13: 421–436.

Persell, C. H. 1990. "Becoming a Member of Society through Socialization". In *Understanding, Society: An introduction to Sociology*. 3rd. edn, edited by Persell, C. H. New York: Harper & Row Publishers Inc., 98–107.

Peschansky, D. 1992. "Les enjeux du témoignage. Effets pervers". In *La bouche de la Vérité ? La recherche historique et les sources orales*, edited by Voldman, D. Paris: CNRS, Les Cahiers de l'IHTP, 21.

Piskorski, M. 2004. "Samoobrona Rzeczypospolitej Polskiej". In *Polskie partie i ugrupowanie parlamentarne*, edited by Kowalczyk, K. and Sielski, J. Torun: Wydawnictwo Adam Marszałek: 197–226.

Piven, F. F. and Cloward, R. A. 1979. *Poor People's Movements: Why They Succeed, How They Fail*. New York: Vintage Books.

PKK Program. 1981. September, N.A.

Pollak, M. 1982. "La régulation technologique: le difficile mariage entre le droit et la technologie". *Revue française de science politique* 2: 165–185.

Polletta, F. 1998a. "Contending Stories: Narrative in Social Movements." *Qualitative Sociology* 21 (4): 419 –446.

———. 1998b. "'It Was like a Fever ...' Narrative and Identity in Social Protest". *Social Problems* 45 (2): 137–59.

———. 2009. "Storytelling in Social Movements". In *Culture, Social Movements, and Protest*, edited by Johnston, H. Farnham: Ashgate: 33–53.

Polletta, F. and Jasper, J. 2001. "Collective Identity and Social Movements". *Annual Review of Sociology* 27: 283–305.

Porhel, V. 2008. *Ouvriers bretons: Conflits d'usines, conflits identitaires en Bretagne dans les années 19'68*. Rennes: PUR.

Potel, J.-Y. 2006. *Scènes de grèves en Pologne*. Paris: Noir sur blanc.

Poussou-Plesse, M. 2009 "Le turning point sous le regard du point final. Retour sur un usage canonique de la notion de carrière en sociologie". In *Bifurcations : Les sciences sociales face aux ruptures et à l'événement*, edited by Grossetti. M, Bessin, M, and Bidart, C. Paris: La Découverte: 254–270.

Przeworski, A. 1996. "II. La democracia como resultado contingente de conflictos". In *Constitucionalismo y democracia. Estudio introductorio de Alejandro Herrera*, editey by Elster, J. and Slagstad, R. Mexico: Colegio Nacional de Ciencias Políticas y Administración Pública A.C. and Fondo de Cultura Económica, 89–110.

Pudal, B. 1989. *Prendre parti. Pour une sociologie historique du PCF*. Paris: Presses de la FNSP.

Pushkarna, V. 1998a. "Terrorists' Children". *The Week*, 19 April.

  1998b. "Interview: Jasmeet Kaur, Widow of a Terrorist". *The Week*, 19 April.

Quintanilla, J. 2014. *Y tú apareces por mi ventana. Doña Naty, lo que nos dejó.* Cuernavaca: Edición independiente.

Ray, R. 1998. "Women's Movements and Political Fields: A Comparison of Two Indian Cities". *Social Problems* 45 (1): 21–36.

Ribeiro, P. F. 2009. "O PT, o Estado e a sociedade (1980–2005)". In *O Partido dos Trabalhadores e a Política Brasileira (1980–2006). Uma história revisitada,* edited by Angelo de, V. A. and Villa, M. A. São Paolo: Edufscar, 183–217.

  2010. *Dos sindicatos ao governo. A organização nacional do PT de 1980 a 2005.* São Paolo: Edufscar.

Rioux, J.-P. 2008. "L'évènement-mémoire. Quarante ans de commemorations". *Le Débat* (149).

Roberts, B. 1995. *The Making of Citizens.* London: Arnold.

Robnett, B. 1996. "Afro-American Women in the Civil Tights Movement, 1954–1965: Gender, Leadership and Micromobilization". *American Journal of Sociology* 101 (6): 1661–1693.

Rocha, D. 2007. *Le parti des travailleurs à l'épreuve du pouvoir. Le PT dans le district fédéral au Brésil (1980–2000).* PhD dissertation. Paris: EHESS.

Rochford, E. B. 1985. *Hare Krishma in America.* New Jersey: Rutgers University Press.

Rodriguês, L. M. 1997. "PT, a New Actor in Brazilian Politics". In *Political Culture, Social Movements and Democratic Transitions in South America in the Twentieth Century,* edited by Devoto, F. J. and de Tella, T. Milan: Fondazione Giangiacomo Feltrinelli, 293–316.

Rokkan, S. 2008. *Citizens, Elections, Parties: Approaches to the Comparative Study of the Processes of Development.* Colchester: ECPR Press.

Rolston, B. 2007. "Demobilization and Reintegration of Ex-Combatants: The Irish Case in International Perspective". *Social & Legal Studies* 16 (2): 259–280.

Rosanvallon, P. and Viveret, P. 1977. *Pour une Nouvelle Culture Politique.* Paris: Seuil-Intervention.

Ross, K. 2004. *May' '68 and Its Afterlives.* Chicago: Chicago University Press.

Roth, S. 2007. "Biographical Consequences of Social Movements". In *Blackwell Encyclopedia of Sociology,* edited by Ritzer, G. Malden, MA: Blackwell Pub., 4451–4453.

Rupp, L. and Taylor, V. 1986, "The Women's Movement since 1960: Structure, Strategies, and New Directions". In *American Choices: Social Dilemmas and Public Policy Since 1960,* edited by Bremmer, R. H., Reichard, G. W., and Hopkins, R. J. Columbus: Ohio State University Press, 75–104.

  1987, *Survival in the Doldrums.* New York/Oxford: Oxford University Press.

Ryder, C. 2000. *Inside the Maze: The Inside Story of the Northern Ireland Prison Service.* London: Methuen.

Salles, J.-P. 2005. *La Ligue Communiste Révolutionnaire (1968–1981) Instrument du grand soir ou lieu d'apprentissage ?* Rennes: PUR.

Samuels, D. 2004. "From Socialism to Social Democracy ? Party Organization and the Transformation of the Worker's Party in Brazil". *Comparative Political Studies* 37 (9): 999–1024.

Sandhu, A. 2009. *Jat Sikh Women: Social Transformation: Changing Status and Life Style*. Delhi: Unistar Books.

Santos dos, A. M. 2001. "Sedimentação de lealdades partidárias no Brasil: tendências e descompassos". *Revista Brasileira de Ciências Sociais* 16 (45): 69–83.

Sapiro, V. 1989. "The Women's Movement and the Creation of Gender Consciousness." In *Political Socialization for Democracy*, edited by Ichilov, O. New York: Teachers College Press, 266–280.

Saunders, C., Grasso, M., Olcese, C., Rainsford, E., and Rootes, C. 2012. "Explaining Differential Protest Participation: Novices, Returners, Repeaters, and Stalwarts". *Mobilization* 17 (3): 263–280.

Sayari, S. 2010. "Political Violence and Terrorism in Turkey, 1976–80: A Retrospective Analysis". *Terrorism and Political Violence* 22 (2): 198–215.

Schacter, D. L. 1996. *Searching for Memory: The Brain, the Mind, and the Past*. New York: Basic Books.

Schalk, P. 1997. "Resistance and Martyrdom in the Process of State Formation of Tamililam". In *Martyrdom and Political Resistance: Essays from Asia and Europe*, edited by Pettigrew, J. Amsterdam: Amsterdam University Press.

Schedler, A. 2001. "Taking Uncertainty Seriously: The Blurred Boundaries of Democratic Transition and Consolidation". *Democratization* 8 (4): 1–22.

Schwartz, M. 2010. "Interactions between Social Movements and US Political Parties". *Party Politics* 16 (5): 587–607.

Schwartz N. and Seymour, S. 1994. *Autobiographical Memory and the Validity of Retrospective Reports*. New York: Springer Verlag.

Scott, J. and Alwin, D. 1998. "Retrospective versus Prospective Measurement of Life Histories in Longitudinal Research." In *Methods of Life Course Research: Qualitative and Quantitative Approaches*, edited by Elder, G. and Ziele, J. Thousand Oaks, CA: Sage, 98–127.

Sears, D. and McConahay, J. B. 1973. *The Politics of Violence: The New Urban Blacks and the Watts Riot*. Boston: Houghton-Mifflin.

Serret, E. 2001. *El género y lo simbólico: La constitución imaginaria de la identidad femenina*. Mexico: UAM Azcapotzalco.

Sewell, W. H. 1996. "Historical Events as Transformations of Structures: Inventing Revolution at the Bastille". *Theory and Society* 25: 841–881.

Shahnazarian, N. 2016. "A Good Soldier and a Good Mother: New Conditions and New Roles in the Nagorno-Karabakh War". *The Journal of Power Institutions in Post-Soviet Societies* 17 [https://pipss.revues.org/4241].

Sherkat, D. and Blocker, J. 1994. "The Political Development of Sixties' Activists: Identifying the Influence of Class, Gender and Socialisation on Protest Participation". *Social Forces* 72 (3): 821–842.

Sherkat, D. E. and Blocker, J. T. 1997. "Explaining the Political and Personal Consequences of Protest". *Social Forces* 75: 1049–1076.

Shirlow, P. and McEvoy, K. 2008. *Beyond the Wire: Former Prisoners and Conflict Transformation in Northern Ireland*. London. Pluto.

Shirlow, P. Tonge, J., McAueley, J., and McGlym, C. 2010. *Abandoning Historical Conflict? Former Political Prisoners and Reconciliation in Northern Ireland*. Manchester: Manchester University Press.

Sigel, R. (ed). 1989. *Political Learning in Adulthood*. Chicago: University of Chicago Press.

Skilling, G. 1981. *Charter 77 and Human Rights in Czechoslovakia*. London: Allen and Unwin.

Skockpol, T. 1988. "An 'Uppity Generation' and the Revitalization of Macroscopic Sociology: Reflections at Mid-Career by a Woman from the Sixties". *Theory and Society* 17: 627–643.

Smaoui, S. and Wazif, M. 2013. "Étendard de lutte ou pavillon de complaisance ? S'engager sous la bannière du "mouvement du 20 février" à Casablanca". In *Devenir révolutionnaires. Au cœur des révoltes arabes*, edited by Allal, A. and Pierret, T. Paris: Armand Colin: 55–85.

Snow, D. 2001. "Analyse de cadres et mouvements sociaux". In *Les Formes de l'action Collective. Mobilisations dans des Arénes Publiques*, edited by Cefaï, D. and Trom, D. Paris: Editions de l'École des Hautes Études en Sciences Sociales, 27–49.

Snow, D. A., Zurcher, L. A., and Ekland-Olson, S. 1980. "Social Networks and Social Movements: A Microstructural Approach to Differential Recruitment". *American Sociological Review* 45 (5): 787–801.

Soderstrom, J. 2013. "The Political Consequences of Reintegration Programmes in Current Peace-Building: A Framework for Analysis". *Conflict, Security and Development* 13 (1): 87–116.

Sommier, I. 1994. "Mai '68: Sous les pavés d'une plage officielle". *Sociétés Contemporaines* 20 (1): 63–82.

1998. *La violence politique et son deuil*. Rennes: PUR.

2008. "Les gauchismes". In *Mai-Juin 68*, edited by Damamme, D., Gobille, B., Matonti, F., and Pudal, B. Paris: Ed. de l'Atelier. Paris: 306–318.

2010. *La violence révolutionnaire*. Paris: Presses de SciencesPo.

Soulet, M.-H. 2010. "Changer de vie, devenir autre: essai de formalisation des processus engages". In *Bifurcations. Les sciences sociales face aux ruptures et à l'événement*, edited by Bessin, M., Bidart, C., and Grossetto, M. Paris: La Découverte: 273–288.

Spanou, C. 2000 (1991). *Fonctionnaires et militants*. Paris: L'Harmattan.

Steinhoff, P. and Zwerman, G. 2008. "Introduction to the Special Issue on Political Violence". *Qualitative Sociology* 31 (3): 213–220.

Strauss, A. L. 2008 (1959). *Mirrors and Masks: The Search for Identity*. New Brunswick, NJ: Transaction Publishers.

Suk, J. 2003 (2009). *Labyrintem revoluce. Akteri, zapletky a krizovatky jedne politicke krize (od listopadu 1989 do cervna 1990)* [The Labyrinth of the Revolutioon. Actors, Storylines and Crossroads of a Political Crisis (from November 1989 until June 1990)]. Prague: Prostor.

Szawiel, T. 2004. "Kryzys demokracji a poparcie systemu politycznego w Polsce". In *Populizm a demokracja*, edited by Markowski, R. Warsaw: ISP-PAN: 145–171.

Szczerbiak, A. 2004. "The Polish Centre-Right's (Last ?) Best Hope: The Rise and Fall of Solidarity Electoral Action". *Journal of Communist Studies and Transition Politics* 20 (3): 55–79.

2008. "The Birth of a Bipolar Party System or a Referendum on a Polarizing Government? The October 2007 Polish Parliamentary Election". *Journal of Communist Studies and Transition Politics* 24 (3): 415–443.

Tackett, T. 2006. *Becoming a Revolutionary: The Deputies of the French National Assembly and the Emergence of a Revolutionary Culture*. Philadelphia: Pennsylvania State University Press.

2015. *The Coming of Terror in the French Revolution*. Cambridge, MA: The Belknap Press.

Tamayo, S. 1999. *Los veinte octubres mexicanos. Ciudadanías e identidades colectivas*. Mexico: Universidad Autónoma Metropolitana, Azcapotzalco.

Tarrow, S. 1989. *Democracy and Disorder: Protest and Politics in Italy 1965–1975*. Oxford: Clarendon Press.

1994. *Power in Movement Social Movements, Collective Action and Politics*. Cambridge: Cambridge University Press.

Tatagiba, L. and Dagnino, E. 2010. "Mouvements sociaux et participation institutionnelle: répertoires d'action collective et dynamiques culturelles dans la difficile construction de la démocratie brésilienne". *Revue internationale de politique comparée* 17 (2): 167–185.

Taylor, M. and Currie, P. 2011. *Dissident Irish Republicanism*. London: Bloomsbury.

Taylor, V. 1989. "Social Movement Continuity: The Women's Movement in Abeyance". *American Sociological Review* 54 (5): 761–775.

2010. "Culture, Identity and Emotions: Studying Social Movements as if People Really matter". *Mobilization* 15 (2): 113–134.

Thomas, W. I. and Znaniecki, F. 1918–1920. *The Polish Peasant*. Boston: Richard G. Badger, The Gorham Press. (http://chla.library.cornell.edu/c/chla/browse/title/3074959.html)

Tilly, C. 1986. *The Contentious French*. Cambridge, MA: Harvard University Press.

2008. *Contentious Performances*. Cambridge: Cambridge University Press.

Tilly, C. and Tarrow, S. 2006. *Contentious Politics*. New York: Paradigm Publishers.

Tissot, S., Gaubert, C., and Lechien M.-H. 2005. *Reconversions militantes*. Limoges: PULIM.

Torfason, M. T. and Ingram, P. 2010. "The Global Rise of Democracy: A Network Account". *American Sociological Review* 75: 355–377.

Tücker, A. 2000. *The Philosophy and Politics of Czech Dissidence from Patocka to Havel*. Pittsburgh, PA: University of Pittsburgh Press.

Uysal, A. 2009. "Importation du mouvement 68 en Turquie. Circulation des idées et des pratiques". *Storicamente* 5 (16) [Online].

Vairel, F. 2005. *Espace protestataire et autoritarisme*. PhD Political Science, University Aix-Marseille III.

2008. "L'opposition en situation autoritaire: statut et modes d'action". In *Autoritarismes démocratiques et démocraties autoritaires au XXIe siècle*, edited by Dabène, O. et al. Paris: La Découverte, 228–231.

2009. "La liste nationale, un quota électoral pour quoi faire?" In *Terrains de campagne au Maroc. Les élections législatives de 2007*, edited by Zaki, L. Paris: Karthala, 135–157.

2012. "Qu'avez-vous fait de vos vingt ans ? Militantismes marocains du 23-mars (1965) au 20 février (2011)". *L'Année du Maghreb* VIII: 219–223.

2014. *La révolution désamorcée? Politique et mouvements sociaux au Maroc.* Paris: Presses de Sciences Po.

Vaissié, C. 1999. *Pour votre liberté et pour la nôtre. Le combat des dissidents de Russie.* Paris: Robert Laffont.

Valocchi, S. 2013. "Activism as a Career, Calling, and Way of Life". *Journal of Contemporary Ethnography* 42 (2): 169–200.

Van Bruinessen, M. 1988. "Between Guerrilla War and Political Murder: The Workers' Party of Kurdistan". *MERIP* 153: 40–46.

Van Dyke, N., McAdam, D., and Wilhelm, B. 2000. "Gendered Outcomes: Gender Differences in the Biographical Consequences of Activism". *Mobilization* 5: 161–177.

Vasicek, Z.1994. "Lidska prava a ukradene dejiny" [Human Rights and Stolen History]. In *Dve desetileti pred listopadem 89* [Two decades before November 89], edited by Mandler, E. Prague: Maxdorf, 87–92.

Vaughan, D. 1986. *Uncoupling: Turning Points in Intimate Relationships.* Oxford: Oxford University Press.

Veyne, P. 1983. *Les Grecs ont-ils cru à leurs mythes ?* Paris: Seuil.

Vigna, X. 2007. *L'insubordination ouvrière dans les années '68. Essai d'histoire politique des usines.* Rennes: PUR.

Vigna, X. and Zancarini-Fournel, M. 2009. "Les rencontres improbables dans 'les années 68'". *Vingtième siècle*, n° 101: 163–177.

Vila, P. 1997. "Hacia una reconsideración de la antropología visual como metodología de la investigación social". *Estudios sobre las culturas contemporáneas* 3 (6): 125–161.

Viterna, J. 2013. *Women in War: The Micro-Processes of Mobilization in El Salvador.* Oxford: Oxford University Press.

Wasilewski, J. and Wnuk-Lipinski, E. 1995. "Poland: Winding Road from the Communist to the post-Solidarity Elite". *Theory and Society* 24: 669–696.

Weber, M. 1978. *Economy and Society: An Outline of Interpretive Sociology.* Berkeley: University of California Press.

2004. "Politics as a Vocation". In *The Vocation Lectures*, edited by Owen, D. and Strong, T. B. Indianapolis, IN/Cambridge: Hackett Publishing.

Whalen, J. and Flacks, R. 1989. *Beyond the Barricades: The Sixties Generation Grows Up.* Philadelphia, PA: Temple University Press.

White, P. J. 2000. *Primitive Rebels or Revolutionary Modernizers? The Kurdish National Movement in Turkey.* London: Zed Books.

Whittier, N. 1995. *Feminist Generations: The Persistence of the Radical Women's Movement.* Philadelphia, PA: Temple University Press.

1997. "Political Generations, Micro-Cohorts, and the Transformation of Social Movements". *American Sociological Review* 62 (5): 760–778.

2013. "Generational and Cohort Analysis". In *The Wiley-Blackwell Encyclopedia of Social and Political Movements*, edited by Snow, D. A., della Porta, D., Klandermans, B., and McAdam, D. Oxford: Blackwell.

Wilhelm, B. 1998. "Changes in Cohabitation across Cohorts: The Influence of Political Activism". *Social Forces* 77: 289–310.

Williams, K. 1997. *The Prague Spring and Its Aftermath: Czechoslovak Politics, 1968–1970*. Cambridge: Cambridge University Press.

Wouters, C. 2007. *Informalization: Manners and Emotions since 1890*. London: Sage.

Wright-Mills, W. 1959. *The Sociological Imagination*. New York: Oxford University Press.

Yang, G. 2000. "The Liminal Effects of Social Movements: Red Guards and the Transformation of Identity". *Sociological Forum* 15 (3): 379–406.

Young, L. 1996. "Women's Movements and Political Parties: A Canadian-American Comparison". *Party Politics* 2: 229–250.

Zalewski, F. 2006a. "Démobilisation et politisation de la paysannerie en Pologne depuis 1989". *Critique internationale* 31: 145–159.

2006b. *Paysannerie et politique en Pologne: trajectoire du Parti paysan polonais du communisme à l'après communisme. 1945–2005*. Paris: Michel Houdiard Éditeur.

Zeitlin, M. 1967. *Revolutionary Politics and the Cuban Working Class*. Princeton, NJ: Princeton University Press.

Zeydanlioglu, W. 2009. "Torture and Turkification in the Diyarbakir Military Prison". In *Rights, Citizenship and Torture: Perspectives on Evil, Law and the State*, edited by Zeydanlioglu, W. and Parry, J. T. Oxford: Inter-Disciplinary Press: 73–92.

Zwerman, G. and Steinhoff, P. 2005 "When Activists Ask for Trouble: State-Dissident Interactions and the New Left Cycle of Resistance in the United-States and Japan". In *Repression and Mobilization (Social Movements, Protest & Contention)*, edited by Davenport, C., Johnston, H., and Mueller, C., Minneapolis: University of Minnesota Press: 85–107.

Index

68ers, 18, 32, 63, 65, 81, 86, 94, 103, 301

Abbott, A, 10, 299
abeyance, 3, 85, 89, 96, 178
Adam, A, 137
age, 5, 7–8, 10–11, 14, 22–23, 44, 71, 90,
    114–116, 136, 164, 208, 280, 282
agency, 19, 22, 201–203, 212, 218, 291
Agrikoliansky, E, 36, 84, 228
Aiken, M. T, 62
Akhonzada, R, 202
Akkaya, A, H, 192
alternation, 14–15
Alwin, D, 50
Amaral, O, 275, 280–281
Andersen, E. A, 45
Anderson, N, 294
Andrews, M, 19, 62
anti-institutional, 32, 34, 63, 83, 94, 104,
    106
armed struggle, 27–28, 159–160, 165–167,
    174, 182, 184–185, 205–206, 208,
    212, 277
Artières, P, 86
association, 18, 21, 99, 123, 129, 141, 144,
    153, 174–175, 191, 270, 282, 284, 286
attitudinal affinity, 114, 116–118
Audier, S, 93
Audrain, X, 162
Auld, J, 215
authoritarian, 20, 34, 135–137, 140, 150,
    183, 201, 223, 252, 269, 272, 276
    regimes, 4, 20, 23, 181, 222
Auyero, J, 24, 160, 169, 273

Banaznak, L, 17
Bargel, L, 109
Barley, S. R, 252
Baylis, T, A, 257
Bazin, A, 234
Bean, K, 205, 207
Béchir-Ayari, M, 4
Beckett, M, 50
Beckwith, K, 15
Bennani-Chraïbi, M, 20, 28–29, 79, 136,
    155, 178, 270
Bennet, M, 15
Berger, P. L, 15, 203
Bermeo, N, 269
Bertaux, D, 295, 300
Bessière, C, 155
Beyerlein, K, 189, 194
bifurcative resources, 160, 173, 177
biographical affinity, 130
biographical analysis, 24, 40, 110, 221,
    273, 294
Biographical analysis, 228
biographical availability, 12, 38, 56,
    112, 116, 124, 141–142, 189, 194,
    201
biographical illusion, 50, 64, 300
Biographical Resonance, 109–112, 114,
    120–121, 123–124, 128–129
biographical time, 163, 176
Bjørgo, T, 203
Blee, K, 6, 201–202
Blocker, J, 5, 132
Blumer, H, 13
Boas, F, 294

Bolos, S, 20
Boltanski, L, 96
Bolton, J, 233, 242
Boschetti, A, 296
Bosi, L, 4, 17, 28–29, 133, 202, 206–209, 211, 214, 218–219
Bouissef Rekab, D., 148
Bourdieu, P, 16, 19, 32, 79, 84, 91, 93–94, 102, 105, 124–125, 271, 296, 300
Bozarslan, H, 185, 194
Bozon, M, 152
Braungart, L and R, 45, 95
Brockett, C, 28
Broqua, C, 10
Brubaker, R, 137
Bugajski, J, 244
Burgat, F, 135

Camau, M, 4
Camou, A, 109
capital, 30, 32, 34, 77, 94, 103, 124–125, 128, 140–141, 143–144, 160, 175, 187, 205, 222, 300
Cardi, C, 177
care, 74, 91, 98, 105, 159, 177
Career, 2, 11, 13, 18–19, 24, 28, 33, 35, 44, 85, 96, 106, 109, 116, 132, 136, 151, 159, 177, 183, 196, 203, 217, 270, 273, 275, 292
career (concept of), 13, 21, 28, 35, 76, 91, 252, 297–298, 300
Carnac, R, 34
Carothers, T, 4
Carrel, M, 31
Cassady, K, 215
Catholic, 43, 53, 72, 91, 93, 206–207, 212, 215–216, 222, 282–284
Catusse, M, 145
Cefaï, D, 31
Chabanet, D, 84, 109
Chambergeat, P, 138
Champy, F, 25, 146
charisma, 250
Chauvel, L, 99
Cheynis, E, 136, 150
Chiapello, E, 96
children, 24, 47–48, 56, 60, 63–64, 80, 91, 101, 119, 132, 135–138, 146, 151–157, 166, 168, 173–175, 194–195, 200–201, 254, 271, 291, 298
Cigerli, S, 199

civil rights, 5, 124, 131, 205
Cloward, R, 274–275
collective behaviour, 2
Collovald, A, 102, 264
Combes, H, 20, 27, 111, 124, 272
community activism, 111, 202, 207, 215
community of practice, 16
Coninck, F de, 295
conversion/reconversion, 12, 14–15, 18, 25, 29, 76–77, 79–80, 82, 135, 145, 148–150, 152, 208, 222, 253
Cooper, F, 137
co-optation, 33, 207, 218
Cormier, P, 20–21, 29
Corrigall-Brown, C, 16, 27, 45–47, 136, 300
Coser, L, 15, 92
costs, 34, 133, 146–147, 149, 183, 189, 194, 201
counter terrorist policies, 17
critical events, 208
Crouch, C, 10
Crozier, M, 18
cultural good will, 94
Currie, P, 205

Dagnino, E, 293
Dalton, R, 45
Dammame, D, 86, 94
Darmon, M, 300
Dauvin, P, 146
Davis, D. E, 278
Dechezelles, S, 9
Della Porta, D, 2, 27–28, 182, 203, 208, 270
DeMartini, J. R, 62
Demerath, N. J, 5, 62
Demetriou, C, 28
demobilization, 111, 121, 133, 139–141, 181, 200, 219, 269–270
democratic transition, 109, 273
demonstrations, 31, 47, 65, 68, 81, 98, 155–156, 234, 254, 260–261
Descamps, F, 298–299
diaspora/diasporisation, 114, 123, 127, 166, 168, 177, 199
Dillenburger, K, 202
disenchantment, 287, 289
disengagement, 12–13, 19, 38, 50, 83, 85, 133, 135–136, 141, 143, 183–184,

196–197, 200–201, 203–204, 218, 222, 289, 291
dispositions, 3, 7–8, 15–17, 19, 25, 31–32, 34, 63, 70, 76, 78, 80, 82, 84, 88, 91, 94, 102, 106, 124, 154–155, 157, 160, 184, 222–223, 270, 274, 282, 296
dissident, 143, 205, 221, 224
Dobry, M, 255
Downton, J, 42
Dressen, M, 86
Duboc, M, 181
Durkheim, E, 91
Duverger, M, 9, 246
Duyvendak, J, W, 3, 10
Dvořáková, V, 244
Dweyer, C, 215
dynamic destabilization, 62, 66, 83

Einwohner, R, 120, 181
Eisenstein, H, 17
Ejea, T, 20
Ekiert, G, 258, 270
Ekland-Olson, S, 254
El Ayadi, M, 153
El Khawaga, D, 181, 184
elections, 1, 81, 105–106, 123–124, 126, 128, 141, 173, 200, 215, 251–252, 254–256, 259–260, 262, 265–270, 273, 275, 277–278, 289
electoral politics, 23, 33, 55, 258
Elias, N, 1, 15, 85, 295
Eliasoph, N, 31, 274
emotions, 3, 22, 24, 27, 30, 34, 92, 111–112, 114, 116–119, 122, 127, 130, 133, 178, 183, 190, 201, 205, 296
entrepreneurs, 15, 17, 97, 101
Epps, E, 5
Ercan, H, 186
Eriksson, A, 214
établis, 78, 95
exit, 19, 79, 83, 133, 182, 184, 196, 198, 200, 203, 281, 289, 292

Falquet, J, 159
Fargas, M, 202
farmer, 90, 117, 221, 251–252, 256, 258–259, 268, 271
Fejtö, F, 228

feminism/feminist, 6, 17, 68, 76, 90, 98, 110, 114–116, 121, 124–126, 144, 171, 201
Fendrich, J, 5, 44, 62, 64, 76, 79, 95, 132, 219
Ferguson, J, 162
Ferguson, N, 213–214
Ferry, L, 93
field, 3, 10, 13, 16, 36, 63, 65, 81, 84, 100, 105, 124, 149–150, 166, 204, 223, 263, 281, 283, 285, 297
Fillieule, O, 2–4, 8, 10, 12, 16, 22, 26, 28, 63, 79, 84–85, 98, 146, 163, 178, 189–190, 202–203, 219, 224, 226, 252, 260, 270, 285, 301
Flacks, R, 5, 24–25, 38, 40, 44, 62, 85
Fleischer, D, 277
Flesher Fominaya, C, 15
Fligstein, N, 3
formative years, 8
Foryś, G, 251, 258, 260
Foster, P, 210
Foucault, M, 18, 93
Frampton, M, 205
free rider, 38
Freedom summer, 2, 5, 64, 85, 95, 131, 290
Freymond, N, 274
frustration, 2, 25, 27, 193
Frye, B, 269
Fuchs Ebaugh, H, 12, 178, 192, 200
Fuentes, M, 109

Gamson, W, 84
Garibay, D, 272
Gaubert, C, 103
Gaxie, D, 30
Gaxie, D, 247–248
Gayer, L, 25, 29, 132, 159
Geertz, C, 137
Geisser, V, 138
gender, 6, 23, 25, 27, 72, 105, 110, 114, 118–121, 123, 126, 132–133, 154–155, 160, 162, 165, 170–171, 175–177, 180, 183–184, 195, 201
generation, 4–5, 8, 19, 22–24, 29, 32, 36–37, 41, 62–63, 83, 88–89, 95, 99, 103, 115, 135–139, 146, 158, 186, 210, 217
Genro, T, 279

Gerth, H, 15–16, 203, 275
Giddens, A, 19
Gitlin, T, 95, 258
Giugni, M, 4, 42, 44, 63, 84, 109, 112, 136, 202–203
Glaser, B, 198
Gobille, B, 86, 94
Godard, F, 295
Goffman, E, 15, 154
Goirand, C, 31, 33, 223, 275, 277
Goldstone, R, 4, 9, 136, 203, 212, 275, 292
Goodwin, J, 2, 110, 118, 120, 125, 181
Gordon, C, 18
Gorlach, K, 251, 258
Gottraux, P, 85
governmentality, 18
grassroots, 10–11, 221, 235, 243, 246–251, 263, 267–268
greedy institutions, 15, 92
Grémion, P, 228, 231–232
Grojean, O, 184
group style, 274
Gruel, L, 86
guerrilla, 115, 121, 163, 177, 193, 197, 199, 211
Gunder Frank, A, 109
Gündogan, A. Z, 186
Gurin, P, 5
Gwiazda, A, 267

habitus, 16, 18, 22–24, 32, 84, 89, 91–92, 94–96, 99–100, 103, 106, 155, 163, 179, 222, 249, 270, 297
Hadjiisky, M, 31, 106, 223–226, 232, 243, 247
Hafez, M, 181
Hall, P, 274
Hamon, H, 88
hangover identity, 178, 200
Hanley, S, 225
Hastings, M, 289
Havel, V, 31, 228–229, 232, 245
Havryshko, M, 159
Hay, C, 10
Heaney, M, 11
hedonism, 92, 105
Hélardot, V, 177
Hercus, C, 119
Hermanová, E, 235
Hernández, A, 120

Heurtaux, J, 254, 270
high-risk activism, 2, 27, 38, 42, 96, 131–133, 136, 160, 163, 184, 194–195, 201, 221–222, 290–291
Hipp, J. R, 194
Hirsch, E, L, 45, 126
Hivert, J, 26, 29, 34, 132, 155
Hollander, 120
Horgan, J, 14, 16, 159, 196–197, 201, 203
Howard, M, M, 270, 294
Hughes, E, 13
human rights, 116, 123, 129–130, 141–143, 154, 175, 181, 249, 277, 282, 285
Humphreys, M, 219
hunger strike, 172, 212
Hunter, H, 275, 278, 290, 292
Huntington, S, 18

identity (collective and individual), 6–7, 16, 26–27, 29, 31, 35, 64, 80–81, 97–98, 113, 116, 120, 123, 125–126, 132, 136, 141, 143, 150, 172, 175, 182, 192, 194, 214, 276, 278–279, 287, 297
ideology, 5, 16, 27, 40, 42–43, 45–47, 51, 54, 124, 130, 171, 208, 210
Illner, M, 235
illusio, 95
impressionable years model, 8
Imset, G, 191
incentive, 11, 15, 21, 30–31, 106, 183, 298
informalization, 89, 105
Inglehart, R, 109
Ingram, 4
institutional politics, 34–35, 55, 255, 263–264, 270
institutionalization, 30, 70, 130, 207, 221–223, 270, 273–276, 278–279, 281, 287, 290, 292–293
intellectuals, 74, 93, 127, 185, 198
organic, 128
interactional field, 10
interactionism, 10, 12, 14–15, 85, 91, 183, 201, 203, 275, 294–295, 297–298
intergenerational transmission, 29, 137, 146, 152–153, 155–157
islamism, 135, 137, 143
isolation, 130, 141, 148, 178, 223, 271
Israël, L, 25, 146

Jaffrelot, C, 4
James, W, 300

Jasiewicz, K, 255
Jasper, J, 1–3, 6, 24, 30, 97, 110, 118, 120, 125, 226
Jeghllaly, M, 155
Jennings, M, K, 5, 7–8, 45, 47, 50, 56, 63, 71, 157, 219
Johnston, H, 190
Johsua, F, 25, 85
Jongerden, J, 192
Juhem, P, 109
Jukam, T, O, 45

Kabacali, A, 182
Kącki, M, 252
Kaçmazoglu, B, 182
Kampwirth, K, 159, 171
Kapferer, B, 14
Karam, K, 138
Katzenstein, M, F, 17
Kaur, S, 159–160, 162
Keck, M, 275, 279
Keniston, K, 14
Kevlihan, B, 207
Khawaja, M, 181
Killian, L, 14
Kinzo, M, 277
Kitschelt, H, 4, 84
Klandermans, B, 12, 123, 127, 252, 270
Klatch, R, 42, 44
Klawiter, M, 6
Knight, M, 203
know-how (Activist), 12, 16, 24–25, 30, 34, 90, 96, 143, 150, 154, 283, 285, 287. *See also* skills
Knox, C, 215
Kopeček, M, 237, 244
Kriesi, H, 35
Krok-Paszkowska, A, 252
Kroupa, D, 229, 235
Krzyżanowska, N, 267
Kubik, J, 258, 270
Kumar, P, 176
Kunc, J, 244
Kusin, V, 228

La Garza, E, 20
Laâbi, A, 139
Laclau, E, 125
Lacroix, B, 83
Lagroye, J, 274
Lahire, B, 153, 296

Langlois, C, V, 298
Lanzona, V, 159
Latté, S, 14
Le Goff, J, 176
Le Saout, D, 199
leader/leadership, 9, 11–12, 31, 33, 36, 39, 45, 49, 75, 87–88, 93–94, 97, 99–100, 103, 112, 114–116, 118–125, 128–130, 139–140, 143–144, 147, 155, 164, 169, 172, 186, 188, 195, 204, 211, 224, 253, 255, 257–258, 261, 263, 266, 272, 274, 276–280, 283–285, 287–288, 292–293
Lechien, M-H, 103
Leclercq, C, 25, 151, 183
Lee, A, R, 45
leftism, 44, 70, 72–73, 76, 86, 123
Lewis, O, 294
libidinal economy, 22, 30
libido, 15, 94, 105
Lichterman, P, 31, 274
life history, 65, 76, 80, 108, 110, 114, 183, 201, 203, 208, 294–295
Life sphere
    affective, 5, 8, 24, 48, 73, 151, 184, 201, 291, 295
    professional, 6, 11, 24–27, 39, 44, 52, 63, 73, 77, 79, 95–96, 99, 103, 137, 142, 144, 146, 149, 151, 169, 173, 176, 178, 215, 221, 241, 291, 295
life story, 19, 22, 39–40, 64, 90, 96, 111, 160, 163, 183, 275, 299–300
life-course, 3, 5, 7, 12, 14, 16, 24, 43, 46, 48–51, 54–55, 111, 120, 131–133, 160, 163, 166, 179, 200, 250, 275–276, 281–282
life-cycle, 14, 30, 39–40, 250
lifelong openness model, 7
liminality, 22
Lindberg, 4
Lindendberg, D, 93
Lipsitz, G, 111, 128
longitudinal studies, 2, 7, 12
Louault, F, 285
Loveman, M, 136
Lovoy, J, 5, 64, 95
Lucardie, P, 11
Luck, S, 9
Luckmann, T, 15, 203
Luker, K, 111

Macías, L, 20
MacIonnrachtaigh, F, 213
Malthaner, S, 28
Mannheim, K, 8, 62, 83, 92, 136, 138, 190
Maoist, 67, 74–75, 87, 92–93, 100, 103,
    121, 139, 143, 186, 188
Marès, A, 230
Markowski, R, 267
Markus, G, B, 50
Martínez, C, J, 120
Maruna, S, 215
Marwell, G, 5, 62
Masclet, C, 29, 137, 152
Massardier, G, 4
Massicard, E, 184
Mastropaolo, A., 10
Matonti, F, 86
Mauger, G, 26, 93
Maurel, M, C, 253
May 68, 12, 18, 20, 25–26, 62, 64–65,
    71–72, 76–77, 79, 85, 87, 92, 103
Mayer, F, 232–233, 240
McAdam, D, 2, 4–6, 12, 14, 25, 38, 44, 62,
    64–65, 76, 85, 95, 106, 109, 112,
    116–117, 120, 131–133, 136, 142,
    146, 178, 184, 203, 219, 254, 290–291
McAtackney, L, 213
McCarthy, J, 97
McConahay, J, B,'s, 5
McDevitt, J, 202
McDonald, K, 190
McDowall, D, 186
McEvoy, K, 203, 205
McKeown, L, 213
McPherson, J, M, 12
Mead, G, H, 13
Melchor, J, 120
Memmi, D, 151
memory, 29, 50, 64, 85, 88, 103, 105, 110,
    152, 168, 172, 192, 274, 288–289, 299
Meneguello, R, 275
Meyer, D, S, 17
micro-cohort, 3, 28, 242, 250
microsociological, 2, 13
Mika, H, 214
milieu, 26, 75, 96, 152, 192, 194, 275, 283,
    285
Miller McPherson, J, 142
Monaghan, R, 215
Monceau, N, 181
moral career, 5, 15

moral dilemma, 31, 35
Morris, A, 116, 121
Morrison, J, 213
Moss-Kanter, R, 12, 15, 203
motives, 14, 19, 254
Mouride, A, 141
Možny, I, 249
Muel-Dreyfus, F, 80, 102
Muller, E, N, 45
multi-level approaches, 18

narratives, 64, 138, 160, 179, 184, 301
Nepstad, S,E, 136
network (activist), 12, 19–20, 84
network (sociability), 12, 16, 27, 96, 101,
    110, 196, 207, 300
Neveu, E, 14, 17, 25–26, 31–32, 83–85,
    102, 224
new social movements, 12, 34, 36, 41, 98
Niemi, R, R, 5, 7, 157
nominal activism, 27, 52
Nussio, E, 202–203

O'Doghartaigh, N, 208
O'Donnel, 4
O'Hearn, D, 212–213, 218
O'Keefe, T, 210
Oberschall, A, 233
Offe, C, 225
Offerlé, M, 274
Olivier-Télez, G, 24, 32, 108–109, 291
Olson, M, 38, 120, 248
Opp, K, D, 181
organizational modeling, 7–8, 11, 14–16,
    21, 184
Orhan, M, 187
Osa, M, 258
Ost, D, 254
outcomes (of movements), 4, 11, 16, 21, 84,
    103, 106, 136, 202, 219
Ozerdem, A, 203

Pacewicz, J, 10
Pagis, J, 14, 25–26, 29, 32, 37, 63, 71, 76,
    137, 151–153, 184, 290, 300
parenthood, 7, 29, 51, 63, 71, 73, 79,
    91–92, 133, 137–138, 142, 151–156,
    158, 164, 169, 174, 282, 300
Parkinson, S, E, 136
party politics, 10, 28, 33–34, 36, 99, 145,
    173

party-movements relationships, 4, 9–10, 21,
29–30, 32–35, 130, 138, 155, 270,
275, 292
Passerini, L, 3
Passeron, J-C, 93, 299
Paulsen, R, 254
Pellen, C, 31, 253, 258–259, 261, 267
Percheron, Y, 71, 152
Persell, C, H, 109
persistence model, 7
personal development, 37, 116
Peschanski, D, 299
Peterson, A, 202
Piskorski, M, 252
Piven, F, 274–275
political crisis, 65, 72, 115, 206, 252
political events, 8, 14, 19
political field, 11, 31, 106, 144, 187–188,
223, 277, 281, 283, 286–288, 292
political opportunities, 17, 34, 124, 182
political participation, 4, 9, 122, 226, 237
political professionalization, 223, 225, 252,
279, 281, 283, 285
political socialization, 4, 6, 8, 62, 66, 70–71,
153, 156–157, 281
politicians, 10, 29, 31–32, 145, 168, 173,
221, 223, 251, 253–254, 259,
263–264, 269, 276, 279, 285, 287–288
politicization, 63, 70, 72, 83, 121–122, 148,
150, 160, 189, 210–211, 259, 270
Pollack, M, 18, 244
Polletta, F, 3, 6, 118, 120, 125, 179
Porhel, V, 86
Potel, J-Y, 254
Poussou-Plesse, M, 178
Power, T, 278, 281
prison, 12, 22, 29, 95, 97, 133, 135–136,
139–145, 148–149, 157–158, 165,
167–168, 172–173, 177, 184, 188,
191–196, 199, 202, 204–205,
207–208, 210–213, 215, 219
processual, 2, 6, 8, 12–13, 16, 19, 22–23,
63, 85, 126, 252, 295
prosopography, 24, 300–301
Pruvost, G, 177
Przeworski, A, 109
Pudal, B, 74, 86, 275
Pushkarna, V, 159, 174–175

Quéré, L, 14
Quintanilla, J, 114, 120

Rachik, H, 153
radicalization, 20–21, 28, 111, 114, 127,
130, 181, 185, 187, 192, 197, 200,
204
Raka Ray, R, 9
rational choice, 2, 4, 22, 197
recruitment, 2, 10, 14, 20, 29–30, 81,
102, 111, 114, 117, 120–121,
125, 130, 169, 171, 178, 208,
254
refus de parvenir, 89, 104
Reinisch, D, 202
relative deprivation, 25
Renault, R, 93
Renou, G, 224
repertoire, 10, 15, 28, 33, 64, 98, 138, 181,
195, 208, 215, 233, 292
repression, 12, 20–21, 23, 27–29, 95,
108, 115, 117, 121, 132–133,
135–136, 138–141, 148–149, 153,
157, 163, 174, 181–183, 186, 191,
201, 205, 208, 221, 223, 233–234,
250, 272
resistance, 28, 83, 129–130, 144, 162, 192,
211, 214–216
resonance, 32, 108–111, 114, 117, 120,
123, 126, 129, 291
revolution, 20–21, 28, 31, 40, 70, 76, 79,
86, 92–93, 101, 116–117, 120,
123–124, 127–128, 130, 133, 140,
144, 148, 156, 185, 189–190, 193,
201, 207–208, 210, 212, 222, 261,
270, 274, 279
Ribeiro, P, F, 275, 283
Rioux, J-P, 85
risks, 5, 22, 95, 117, 142, 189, 194, 201,
221, 291
Roberts, B, 109
Robnett, B, 122
Rocha, D, 280, 282
Rochford, E, B, 189
Rodrigues, L, M, 280
Roehl, W, 181
Rojas, F, 11
Rokkan, S, 9
role, 7, 12, 15, 24, 38–39, 120, 142, 178,
197, 200, 216, 274
role (sociology of), 38–39, 89,
145, 166, 173, 176, 178, 182,
200–201
Rolston, B, 205

Rosanvallon, P, 97
Ross, K, 86
Roth, R, 71
Rotman, P, 88
Rotolo, T, 142
Rupnik, J, 228
Rupp, L, 24, 84
Ryder, C, 213

sacrifice, 94, 112, 133, 142, 210, 217
Sahlins, M, 19
Sainclivier, J, 86
Salles, J-P, 102
Samizdat, 233, 236
Samuels, D, 277
Sandhu, A, 161
Santos, A, M, 286
Sapiro, V, 6–7
Saunders, C, 183, 198
Sayari, S, 185
Schacter, D, 50
Schaffer-Boudet, H, 3
Schalk, P, 165
Schedler, A, 255
Schwartz, M, 9, 35
Schwartz, N, 299
Scott, J, 50
Sears, D, 5
Seignobos, C, 298
sequential analysis, 301
Serret, E, 110
Sewell, W, 14
sexualities, 32, 74, 119, 159, 161, 176–177, 267, 297
Shahnazarian, N, 159
Shaw, C, 294
Sherkat, D, 5, 132
Shirlow, P, 205, 211, 215
Shirlow, P, 215
Sigel, R, 6–7
Siméant, J, 146
sixties generation, 20, 23, 39–40, 64
Skilling, G, 231, 233
skills (Activist), 6, 11, 17, 28, 30, 32–33, 79, 82, 84, 89, 91, 94, 96–99, 106, 117, 136–137, 142, 144–145, 148–150, 156, 174, 188, 193, 195, 201–202, 213, 219, 222–223, 281–284, 287, 291. *See also* know-how
Skocpol, T, 8
Smaoui, S, 155

Smith, C, 136
Snow, D, 124, 189, 254
social change, 17, 26, 43, 84, 86, 89, 92, 97, 99–100, 103–104, 110, 112, 116, 122, 129, 133, 209, 219
social mobility, 25–26, 31–33, 35, 75, 81–82, 94, 99, 104, 136, 145–147, 149–151, 155, 253, 279–281, 285, 287–288, 291
social networks, 16, 26, 80, 111, 120, 136, 150, 164, 285, 287, 293
social work, 39, 41, 52, 54, 57, 101–103, 164, 167, 173, 293
socialization, 3, 6–8, 14–16, 19, 21, 24, 29, 79, 91, 93, 109, 111, 116, 125, 132, 136–137, 152–153, 157, 177, 183–184, 187, 193–194, 201, 209, 219, 270, 274, 285, 290–291
socialization, 234
Soderstrom, J, 219
Sommier, I, 29, 76, 84–86, 301
Soulet, M,-H, 160
Spanou, C, 18, 102
Staggenborg, S, 116, 121
Steinhoff, P, 28
stigma, 32, 34, 90, 153–154, 157, 176, 236, 254, 264
Stoker, L, 50
Strauss, A, 13, 179, 198, 299
students, 20, 36, 45, 64, 70, 72, 74–75, 77, 81, 86–88, 92, 95, 108, 115–117, 120, 122–123, 131, 138, 184–185, 187–191, 193, 198, 222, 281
Sudman, S, 299
Suk, J, 235, 237
Szawiel, T, 252
Szczerbiak, A, 263, 268

Tackett, T, 14, 62
Talpin, J, 31
Tamayo, S, 20, 24, 32, 108–109, 115, 291
Tarrow, S, 2, 28, 65, 84, 109, 113, 181, 275
Tatagiba, L, 293
Taylor, M, 205
Taylor, R, C.R, 274
Taylor, V, 3, 84–85, 116
Tejel, J, 25, 29, 133, 223
temporality, 190, 295
terrorism, 21, 27–28
thick description, 13
Thomas, W, I, 294, 300

Tilly, C, 2, 65, 84, 109, 113, 120
Tissot, S, 25, 102
Torfason, M, T, 4
torture, 12, 22, 27, 29, 139–142, 152, 157, 166, 168, 184, 191–192, 196
total institutions, 15
Tozy, M, 153
Trade Union, 9, 21, 33, 36, 52, 67, 73, 75, 77–78, 81–82, 86–87, 89–91, 94, 96–97, 111, 113, 115, 118, 120–122, 124–126, 128–129, 138, 150, 152, 222–223, 251, 255–257, 259, 262, 264–265, 267, 270, 272, 276, 283, 286, 289
Trotskyist, 67, 71, 85, 87, 98, 102, 116, 120–122, 124, 139, 143
Tücker, A, 231
Turner, R, 22
turning point, 27, 95–96, 120, 160, 163, 173, 176, 179, 194, 196, 199, 211, 298

Uba, C, 4
Useem, B, 212
utopias, 83, 127
Uysal, A, 20

Vairel, F, 21, 26, 29, 34, 132, 135–136, 138, 144, 155
Vaissié, 32
Vajdová, Z, 235
Valocchi, S, 35, 62
Van Bruinessen, M, 187
Van Dyke, N, 5, 63
Van Sickle, A, 45
Van Stralen, C, 252, 270
Vaughan, S, 12
Veyne, P, 178
Vigna, X, 26, 75, 86

Vila, P, 110
violence (political), 23, 27–28, 112, 129, 132, 137, 172, 177, 181, 185–187, 190, 194, 202–203, 206, 208, 213, 215, 219
Viterna, J, 4, 159, 201–202, 217
Viveret, P., 97
vocation of heterodoxy, 94
Voegtli, M, 108

Wasilewski, J, 254
Watanuki, J, 18
Wazif, M, 155
Weber, M, 247, 250, 295–296
Wehr, P, 42
Weinstein, J, M, 219
Weldon, S, 45
Whalen, J, 5, 25, 40, 44, 62, 85
White, P, J, 191, 199
Whittier, N, 3, 6, 17, 28, 64, 86, 183, 242
Wilhelm, B, 63, 219
Williams, K, 228
Williamson, J, 202
Wnuk-Lipinski, E, 254
Wouters, C, 89
Wright-Mills, C, 1, 15, 203, 275, 295

Yang, G, 22
Young, L, 10

Zald, M, N, 97
Zalewski, F, 254–255
Zancarini-Fournel, M, 26, 86
Zeitlin, M, 8
Zeydanlioglu, W, 192
Znaniecki, F, 294, 300
Zurcher, L, A, 254
Zwerman, G, 28

CPSIA information can be obtained
at www.ICGtesting.com
Printed in the USA
BVHW042023050422
633465BV00009B/75